EU LAW AND INTEGRATION

This book contains a collection of articles on different aspects of EU law written by one of Europe's most distinguished jurists during the past twenty years, some of which appear here for the first time in English. The book includes a Foreword by Judge Koen Lenaerts, Vice-President of the European Court of Justice.

The book is divided into five parts, covering EU constitutional law, the EU's judicial architecture, access to justice, European competition law and various other aspects of substantive EU law. In the field of EU constitutional law, the central text discusses the existence of implied material limits to the revision of the Treaties. The author argues that the powers of the Member States to amend the Treaties is limited by the existence of a hard core of principles of EU Treaty law, which cannot be revised without changing the 'constitutional' identity of the Union, leading to the conclusion that Member States can no longer be considered as the 'absolute masters of the Treaties'. Four articles relating to the EU's judicial system constitute the cornerstone of the collection. Drawing on his own experiences, the author examines the problems and challenges facing the setting up of a new EU court and explores different lines of reform of the EU judicial system.

EU Law and Integration

Twenty Years of Judicial Application of EU Law

José Luís da Cruz Vilaça

•HART•
PUBLISHING

OXFORD AND PORTLAND, OREGON
2016

Published in the United Kingdom by Hart Publishing Ltd
16C Worcester Place, Oxford, OX1 2JW
Telephone: +44 (0)1865 517530
Fax: +44 (0)1865 510710
E-mail: mail@hartpub.co.uk
Website: http://www.hartpub.co.uk

Published in North America (US and Canada) by
Hart Publishing
c/o International Specialized Book Services
920 NE 58th Avenue, Suite 300
Portland, OR 97213-3786
USA
Tel: +1 503 287 3093 or toll-free: (1) 800 944 6190
Fax: +1 503 280 8832
E-mail: orders@isbs.com
Website: http://www.isbs.com

First published in hardback 2014
Paperback edition, 2016

Hart Publishing is an imprint of Bloomsbury Publishing plc.

British Library Cataloguing in Publication Data
Data Available

ISBN: HB: 978-1-84946-508-3
PB: 978-1-50990-988-9

Typeset by Compuscript Ltd, Shannon
Printed and bound in Great Britain by
Lightning Source UK Ltd

Foreword

When Professor José Luís da Cruz Vilaça asked me to write this foreword, I was delighted to accept. Aside from our mutual friendship, which stretches back for over two decades, I have witnessed his qualities, both professional and personal, at first hand, in his role as Founding President of the Court of First Instance of the European Communities, today the General Court of the European Union, in the period from 1989 until 1995. As a tribute to his contribution to the European Union's judiciary during that period, I still think of him as 'our Founding President'.

His role as President of the Court of First Instance followed a period as Advocate General at the Court of Justice (1986–1988), to which he returned on 6th October 2012, this time as judge.

In honour of his return to the Kirchberg Plateau, this book contains a collection of articles written by José Luis da Cruz Vilaça. This collection is of great academic interest in that it presents an overview of European Union law that, despite covering a period that goes back more than twenty years, has lost none of its relevance. Moreover, the author's academic approach is enriched by his practical experience both as a practitioner at the bar and as a member of the Court of Justice and the Court of First Instance, as it then was. From a thematic perspective, this collection has the quality of great diversity. It is divided into five parts covering EU constitutional law, the EU judicial architecture, individuals' access to justice, European competition law and various other aspects of substantive EU law under the heading 'Studies on EU Law and Economic Integration'.

First, the collection of chapters relating to EU constitutional law opens with a chapter entitled 'Constitutional Law and Community Law: the Case of Portugal' concerning the relationship between Community law and national legal orders, specifically that of Portugal. It provides a compelling account of the development of Portuguese national law, both by means of constitutional amendments and decisions of the courts themselves, leading to the gradual acceptance by the Portuguese courts of the primacy of Community law and of their own duty to cooperate with the European Court of Justice through the preliminary ruling mechanism. In the following chapter 'Are there Substantive Limits to the Amendment of the Treaties?' (*Cahiers de droit européen*, 1993), the author argues that Member States cannot invoke principles drawn from public international law in order to circumvent the formal and procedural requirements for amending the Treaties. In the same way, their power to amend the Treaties is limited by the existence of a 'hard core' of EU Treaty law. That hard core includes the prohibition on any reversal of measures creating the internal market, the principle of conferred powers and strict adherence to the procedure for amendment of the Treaties. It is true that the limits on amendment of the Treaties are implicit and difficult to determine, in the absence of any objective criteria making it possible to define those limits with any certainty. However, given that the founding Treaties create not only obligations for Member States but also rights for individuals, 'the Treaty is not, and neither could it be, wholly at the disposal of the Member States, no more so than the rights enshrined in their [national] constitutions'. In this chapter, the author thus shares with us his vision of EU law, emphasising the 'constitutional' character of the Treaties as well as the 'autonomy' that the EU legal order has acquired. In the third and final chapter in Part I, entitled 'Reflections on Judicial Review of the Constitutionality of EU Legislation', which first appeared in the collection of essays 'Vers une nouvelle architecture de l'Union européenne' (*Bruylant*, 2004), José Luis da Cruz Vilaça examines the role of the Court of Justice as a 'Constitutional Court' of the EU, underlining the Court's contribution to the process whereby the Treaties are gradually mutating into a true constitution. He also describes the positive impact that the creation of the Court of First Instance has had in improving the judicial protection of litigants.

Second, four chapters relating to the EU judicial architecture (4 to 7) constitute Part II that forms the cornerstone of the collection. Indeed, in light of the different functions he has occupied, José Luis da Cruz Vilaça has given a great deal of thought to the judicial architecture of the EU, the possible reforms that might be made to that structure and their consequences; these four pieces of work are the fruit of those reflections. His contribution entitled 'The Setting Up of a New Community Court—the First Year of the Court of First Instance', initially published in French in 'L'Europe et le droit: Mélanges en hommage à Jean Boulouis' (*Dalloz*, 1991), is of particular historical value, describing the problems faced by that Court at its inception, from the perspective of its then President. As the author explains, one of the first tasks of the Court of First Instance was to prepare its draft Rules of Procedure. Those provisions of the Court of Justice's Rules of Procedure that could be applied *mutatis mutandis* were adopted wholesale whilst those that were incompatible, either with the composition and structure of the Court of First Instance or with the type of case and the nature of the task of judicial review that had been conferred on it, were not included. The same was true where the experience of applying the Rules of Procedure of the Court of Justice had revealed certain flaws or discrepancies. The author underlines that the establishment of a double degree of jurisdiction improves the judicial protection of individuals.

Regarding the various reforms proposed to modify the judicial architecture of the EU to the treatment of an increasing number of cases, whilst José Luis da Cruz Vilaça is certainly in favour of specific incremental changes, he rejects any radical reforms that might compromise the balance of the EU's judicial system. In that context, mention must be made of the final chapter in Part II, entitled 'The Court System of the European Communities' (*La Conférence intergouvernementale sur l'Union européenne: répondre aux défis du XXIe siècle*, 1996), where the author considers that the roles of the Court of Justice and the General Court may be approximated, respectively, to those of a constitutional court and of an administrative court. Any reform of the court system of the EU should be directed towards preserving the balance of that system and the coherence of the case law. Thus, in order to improve the Court of First Instance's productivity, the author proposes pragmatic reforms, such as an increase in the number of judges, the specialisation of chambers (but not of judges), the appointment of assistant *rapporteurs*, the appointment of a small number of Advocates General, and the treatment of cases by a single judge. On the other hand, he is firmly opposed to the creation of a constitutional court alongside the Court of Justice, since the latter already fulfils the functions of a constitutional court. Moreover, any such reform is undesirable because it springs from a belief—an erroneous one, in the author's view—that the Court of Justice is excessively 'activist' in its attitude.

José Luis da Cruz Vilaça has, third, examined in detail the judicial protection of individuals. Part III on this theme contains three chapters (8 to 10). Whereas the first two relate to the protection of individuals under EU law, the third examines the application of Article 6 of the ECHR to disputes involving civil servants. Firstly, in his contribution to the collection of chapters 'Scritti in Onore di Giuseppe Federico Mancini' (*Giuffrè*, 1998), 'Interim Measures in Judicial Proceedings as an Instrument of Protection for Individuals in European Community Law', he explains that the interim measures procedure is a tool serving the judicial protection of individuals, given that this procedure makes it possible to 'achieve a rapid ruling within a time frame that is compatible with the need for the effective administration of justice'. By sharing his experiences as President of the Court of First Instance, in whom, by virtue of the Rules of Procedure, jurisdiction to rule on requests for interim measures is vested, the author describes the legal framework of the interim measures procedure as well as the conditions of admissibility and for the substantive grant of interim measures. That analysis is supplemented by a whole range of examples taken from the Court of First Instance's case law. Next, José Luis da Cruz Vilaça studied the concept of 'direct concern' in the context of actions for annulment brought against decisions addressed to a Member State in the area of EU funding. In his contribution to the 'Mélanges en l'honneur de Philippe Manin, L'Union européenne: Union de droit, Union des droits' (*Ed A Pédone*, 2010), bearing the title 'Effective Judicial Protection with Regard to Community Funds—May One be Directly Concerned by a Decision Addressed to a Member State?', he makes the case that individuals should be considered as being directly concerned, within the meaning of Article 263 TFEU, when an EU regulation or a contested Commission decision expressly impose on the Member State addressee an obligation to pass on to those individuals the financial consequences of that regulation or decision. The same is true where the Member State addressee has a margin of assessment that it does not exercise. A more restrictive interpretation of that concept would, according to the author, go against the principle of effective judicial protection, in particular when the Member State in question has a system of administrative law that is opposed to granting rights of action against purely implementing measures on the basis that the act being executed could have been challenged before the competent court. Finally, in this Part, in his analysis of Article 6 of the ECHR contained in 'Mélanges en hommage à Georges Vandersanden: Promenade au sein du droit européen' (*Bruylant*, 2008), José Luis da Cruz Vilaça analyses, with approval, the case law of the European Court of Human Rights to the effect that there is a presumption of applicability in favour of Article 6 of the ECHR to any dispute between a civil servant and a Contracting State.

Fourth, regarding competition law, José Luis da Cruz Vilaça published three articles in the prestigious *European State Aid Law Quarterly* (2005, 2006, 2009). In that respect, I would like to draw attention, in particular, to the excellent analysis undertaken by the author in chapter 12 concerning the concept of 'selectivity', both geographical and material, notably in the light of the 'Azores' case law. Part IV closes with a contribution that provides a highly detailed and technical analysis of a specific but vitally important question, the permitted duration of non-compete obligations in full-function joint ventures.

Fifth, and lastly, the collection contains three chapters (15 to 17), concerning a range of subjects under the heading 'Studies on EU Law and Economic Integration' which illustrate the interest that José Luis da Cruz Vilaça has taken in the study of EU law in the round, and even in subjects extending beyond the borders of the EU, as evidenced by his insightful work on the Andean Community (*European Foreign Affairs Review*, 1998). Moreover, we may refer to his contribution in the collection of essays *Services and Free Movement in EU Law* (Oxford University Press, 2003) in which the author explains, with particular emphasis on the "neck" came, the complexity of situations in which national measures relating to advertising may impinge upon both the free movement of goods and the free movement of services. In this section, mention must, finally, be made of his article published in the *European Public Law Review* (2004), which is already a 'classic' of European legal literature, analysing the precautionary principle, particularly through a detailed study of the 'Pfizer' judgment.

In conclusion, I warmly recommend this collection to readers who are looking for a work that covers a wide range of rich and varied ideas in the field of EU law.

Koen Lenaerts
Vice-President of the Court of Justice of the European Union
Former Judge at the Court of First Instance of the European Communities
(1989–2003)

Acknowledgements

This collection of my published writings from the past twenty years, some of which were originally written in a language other than English, owes much to many people.

Several of the texts published here were either written in collaboration with another author or benefited from the assistance of younger colleagues, in terms either of the research that they carried out for me or of the work that they did in helping to produce the text of the article in the language of original publication. On the one hand, my co-authors thus share, to the extent of their respective contributions, the authorship of this book. On the other hand, the cooperation of those who assisted me in the preparation of the articles is acknowledged, as appropriate, at the beginning of the relevant text.

I am also grateful to the original publishers of the articles included in this book for making possible the re-use of the published materials, some of them after translation into English. The content of each article is essentially the same as in the original version but I have taken this opportunity to make marginal amendments or refinements to certain passages.

Turning to the book itself, I am particularly indebted to my friend and colleague Koen Lenaerts, Vice-President of the Court of Justice of the European Union and founding member, together with me and our ten other former colleagues, of the Court of First Instance of the European Communities, as it then was, for the elegant and overly generous Foreword that he kindly wrote as an introduction to this book.

My special gratitude also goes to Mathew Radley, legal secretary in Judge Lenaerts' chambers, for the invaluable contribution he made in revising the English versions of those articles that had originally been published in French. Any inaccuracies that may remain are mine alone.

Two other colleagues, Judge Allan Rosas and former Advocate General Miguel Poiares Maduro kindly encouraged me to undertake this project, for which I thank them also.

In addition, I am grateful to my younger colleagues and '*stagiaires*', who assisted me in preparing the English versions of some of the published materials. Thanks are thus due to Maria João Melícias, Carla Farinhas, Sara Sousa, Marie Lauzanne, Stijn Lamberigts, Stephanie Lodola and Luísa Lourenço, as well as to my assistants Anna Bella Marinho and Marina Artigas for their work in diligently re-typing some of the older texts that were not available in electronic form.

I sincerely thank Hart Publishing, and more particularly Richard Hart, for agreeing to publish the book, thereby giving it the support of his prestigious publishing house. I am also grateful to Rachel Turner for her unfailing attention to detail and for her patience when I significantly overran the deadlines that we had agreed.

Finally, I should like to pay tribute to my friends and, above all, to my family, in particular my wife and children, in recognition of all the time, attention and even physical presence that I was unable to devote to them over a period of many months. As a token of my gratitude, I dedicate this book to Marie-Charlotte and to my children.

José Luís da Cruz Vilaça
Luxembourg, February 2014

Table of Contents

Part I

EU Constitutional Law

1

Constitutional Law and Community Law: The Case of Portugal[*]

I. THE UNDERLYING PRINCIPLES

SINCE THE BEGINNING of the 1960s, the Court of Justice of the European Communities has been called upon to answer questions concerning the relationship between Community law and national legal orders, through the mechanism of references for a preliminary ruling provided for in Article 177 of the EEC Treaty.

Those questions have given the Court the opportunity, in landmark decisions, to set out the main principles that should govern those relations.

In *Van Gend & Loos*,[1] whose importance stems above all from the establishment of the principle of direct effect of certain rules of the Treaty,[2] the Court held that

> the Community constitutes a new legal order of international law for the benefit of which the states have limited their sovereignty rights, albeit within limited fields, and the subjects of which comprise not only the Member States but also their nationals.

This statement was reiterated and developed in *Costa v ENEL*,[3] where the Court stressed that

> [b]y contrast with ordinary international treaties, the EEC Treaty has created its own legal system which, on the entry into force of the Treaty, became an integral part of the legal systems of the Member States and which their courts are bound to apply.

Together with another famous judgment in *Simmenthal*,[4] *Costa v ENEL* deduced from this key concept of the Community legal order all the consequences concerning the recognition of the supremacy of Community law provisions over national law provisions that conflict with it, irrespective of whether the latter are prior or subsequent to the former.

[*] First published as 'Droit constitutionnel et droit communautaire. Le cas portugais' (1991) 2 *Rivista di Diritto Europeo* 301–10.

[1] Case 26/62 *Van Gend & Loos v Netherlands Inland Revenue Administration* [1963] ECR-1.

[2] In that case, Article 12 of the EEC Treaty.

[3] Case 6/64 *Flaminio Costa v ENEL* [1964] ECR-585.

[4] Case 106/77 *Amministrazione delle Finanze dello Stato v Simmenthal SpA* [1978] ECR-629.

The Court has made clear that the incorporation into the legal system of each Member State of provisions of Community law, adopted on the basis of a transfer of competences and which must be applied in an uniform manner throughout the territory of the Community, has prohibited the application by Member States of any unilateral measure which is incompatible with the legal order accepted by them when they signed the Treaties.

As stated in *Simmenthal*,

> any recognition that national legislative measures which encroach upon the field within which the Community exercises its legislatives power or which are otherwise incompatible with the provisions of Community law had any legal effect would amount to a corresponding denial of the effectiveness of obligations undertaken unconditionally and irrevocably by Member States pursuant to the Treaty and would thus imperil the very foundations of the Community.[5]

From the outset, the Court of Justice gave these principles a broad scope, regardless of whether the national provisions involved were of a constitutional nature.

It specified on several occasions how such principles should apply to the relations between Community law and the constitutional law of the Member States. Reference must be made, in this regard, to the *Storck*,[6] *Nold*,[7] *Internationale Handelgesellchaft*[8] and *San Michele*[9] cases, as well as to the *Simmenthal* judgment.

Some national Courts, especially those responsible for reviewing the constitutionality of laws have, not surprisingly, been reluctant to accept the authority of the EC judiciary. Such was the case of the Italian *Corte Costituzionale*, the German *Bundesverfassungsgericht* and the French *Conseil Constitutionnel*.

The reservations expressed in that regard mainly concerned the 'compatibility' or the 'structural congruence' of the two legal systems, but also the protection due to fundamental rights as protected in national constitutions and respect for the principle of national sovereignty.

The attitude of the abovementioned constitutional courts has, nevertheless, subsequently evolved.

Indeed, even in those cases where constitutional courts appeared less willing to abandon what they considered to be their exclusive prerogative to review compliance of all internally applicable legislation with national constitutions, the tendency over the years has clearly been in favour of the recognition of the specific characteristics of the Community legal order.

[5] ibid, para 18.

[6] Case 1/58 *Friedrich Stork & Cie v High Authority of the European Coal and Steel Community* [1959] ECR-17.

[7] Joined Cases 36, 37, 38–59 and 40–59 *Präsident Ruhrkolen-Verkaufsgesellschaft mbH, Geitling Ruhrkohlen-Verkaufsgesellschaft mbH, Mausegatt Ruhrkohlen-Verkaufsgesellschaft mbH and I Nold KG v High Authority of the European Coal and Steel Community* [1960] ECR-423.

[8] Case 11/70 *Internationale Handelsgesellschaft mbH v Einfuhr- und Vorratsstelle für Getreide und Futtermittel* [1970] ECR-1125.

[9] Case 9/65 *Acciaierie San Michele SpA (in liquidation) v High Authority* [1965] ECR-27.

This has been accompanied by the progressive affirmation of the Community as an entity empowered with the prerogatives of statehood and by the gradual establishment of Community law as an autonomous and complete legal order constituting the bedrock of European integration.

Whilst national and Community law courts have continued to exercise their competences within their respective legal orders, the cooperation sought by the authors of the Treaties between the courts of those different legal orders has developed and been placed on an ever firmer foundation, both sides cooperating with the common aim of ensuring that the law is observed in the interpretation and application of the Treaties.[10]

The purpose of this chapter is to provide an overview of how the question of the relationship between Community law and the national Constitution is regarded by one of the most recent Member States to join the Community: Portugal.

II. THE CONSTITUTIONAL CONTEXT IN PORTUGAL

Since 1976 it has been Article 8 of the Constitution of the Portuguese Republic that governs the relationships between national and international law. According to paragraph 1 of that provision, '[t]he rules and principles of general or common international law shall form an integral part of Portuguese law'. Article 8(1) establishes a system of 'automatic reception', under which no further formalities need to be satisfied.

International conventional law is also automatically received into the internal legal order by Article 8(2), according to which '[t]he rules set out in duly ratified or adopted international agreements shall take full effect in [Portuguese] internal law'. However, that is only true once such conventions have been officially published in the Official Journal (*Diário da República*) and for as long as they are internationally binding on the Portuguese State.

In their 1976 version, the constitutional rules governing the relations between national law and international law were limited to the aforementioned provisions. In particular, the Constitution contained no provisions on the hierarchy of sources.

Academic writers also hesitated about the correct interpretation to be given to those provisions.

[10] On the relations between Community law and national law, see among the most recent studies, M Darmon, 'Juridictions constitutionnelles et droit communautaire' (1988) *Revue triestrielle de Droit européen* 271–51; G Isaac, *Droit communautaire général*, 2nd edn (Paris, 1989) 171–82; JV Louis, *L'ordre juridique communautaire* 4th edn (Luxembourg, OPOCE, 1989); J Rideau, 'Constitution et droit international dans les Etats membres des Communautés européennes' (1990) *Revue française de Droit constitutionnel* 2–3.

Jorge Miranda[11] was of the opinion that the Constitution established a 'monist' system recognising the supremacy of international law. A Gonçalves Pereira[12] saw instead in the Constitution a 'moderate monism', which did not necessarily render invalid a national law that was contrary to an applicable international law provision.[13]

Gomes Canotilho and Vital Moreira,[14] for their part, relied on the principle of equivalence between public international law and national law, inherent to the system of automatic reception, to claim that although the Portuguese Constitution enjoys supremacy with respect to international law, whether conventional or not, the latter revokes, or at least suspends the application of, pre-existing conflicting 'infra-constitutional' rules. However, given the absence in the Portuguese Constitution of any explicit rule conferring 'supra-legislative' value on international law, those authors hesitated as to the treatment to be given to any internal measure conflicting with rules of international law which were anterior to them and applicable in the domestic legal order.

By contrast, J Mota Campos[15] expressed a clear preference for interpreting Article 8 of the Constitution as laying down a principle of supremacy of international law over infra-constitutional law.[16]

The situation did not significantly change with the first constitutional amendment in 1982 (Constitutional law No 1/82, of 30 September 1982).

In fact, as regards the point under consideration, the amendment confined itself to adding a third paragraph to Article 8, according to which 'rules issued by the competent bodies of international organisations to which Portugal belongs shall come directly into force in Portuguese internal law, on condition that this is expressly laid down in the respective constituent treaties'.

Not surprisingly then, academic opinion in Portugal continued to be split as to the hierarchical relationship between national and international law under the Portuguese Constitution.

By way of illustration, one can cite an article by A Barbosa de Melo[17] as compared with the 1984 edition of the *Constituição Anotada* by Canotilho and Moreira.[18] Indeed, the former, taking into consideration the constitutional principle

[11] Jorge Miranda, *A Constituição de 1976: formação, estrutura, princípios fundamentais* (Lisboa, 1978) 302.

[12] A Gonçalves Pereira, 'O Direito Internacional na Constituição de 1976' in J Miranda (ed), *Estudos sobre a Constituição* 1 (Lisboa, Petrony, 1977) 40.

[13] However, at the cost of engaging the international liability of the State and, in the author's view, depending on the attitude of the body in charge of reviewing the constitutionality, which should decide whether domestic law was formally unconstitutional or not. ibid, 40.

[14] G Canotilho and V Moreira, *Constituição da República Portuguesa Anotada* (Coimbra, 1978) 44–45.

[15] J Mota Campos, *A Ordem Constitucional Portuguesa e o Direito Comunitário* (Braga, 1981) 175.

[16] But not over constitutional law.

[17] A Barbosa de Melo, 'A preferência de lei posterior em conflito com normas convencionais recebidas na ordem interna ao abrigo do n.º 2 do art. 8.º da Constituição da República (a propósito do art. 4.º do Decreto-Lei n.º 262/83, de 16 de Junho)' (1984) IV *Colectânea de jurisprudência* 21.

[18] G Canotilho and V Moreira (n 14) 92–93.

that the courts are subject to the law (Article 208, in fine, of the Constitution) as well as the principle of national independence, argued in favour of the validity in the national legal order of internal measures that contravene prior international agreements.[19]

Mota Campos,[20] for his part, reaffirmed the approach he had adopted, prior to the constitutional amendment, in favour of the supremacy of international law.

In a judgment of 12 October 1988, the Constitutional Court (*Tribunal Constitucional*) put an end to the controversy by interpreting Article 8(2) of the Constitution as meaning that provisions in international agreements take precedence over infra-constitutional law, whether previous or subsequent.[21]

Whereas the relationship between conventional international law and *ordinary* internal law can thus be considered as settled in the Portuguese legal order, the same issue[22] remains unresolved, however, as regards the relations between international law and *constitutional* law.

III. THE SUPREMACY OF EC LAW IN THE CONSTITUTION

The same can be said when it comes to a different, though related, question in particular: the supremacy of Community law over national law.

In that regard, the constitutional amendment of 1982, by adding a new third paragraph to Article 8, sought, without explicitly saying so (the legislator referred broadly to the 'international organisations to which Portugal belongs'), to pave the way for the accession of Portugal to the European Communities, by accepting the direct or immediate applicability of secondary Community legislation.

It is open to doubt whether such clarification was actually necessary, given the principles already spelled out in the first two paragraphs of Article 8 regarding the reception of international law into the domestic legal order.

[19] Although application of such measures could trigger international liability of the State.

[20] J Mota Campos, *As relações da ordem jurídica portuguesa com o direito internacional e o direito comunitário à luz da revisão constitucional de 1982* (Lisboa, 1985) 387, and *Direito Comunitário II* (Lisboa, 1988) 357.

[21] *Tribunal Constitucional* (first chamber), judgment of 12 October 1988, Case 201/88 [1988] BMJ 380, 1980, 183. In this case, the first chamber of the *Tribunal Constitucional,* following its consistent line of case-law, declared itself competent to rule on the unconstitutionality of a national law contrary to an international convention. Conversely, the second chamber, in accordance with its own settled case-law, considered that the violation of an international convention by a national law does not fall within the jurisdiction of the Constitutional Court but comes within the competence of ordinary courts (see for instance, Case 198/85 [1985], in D.R. 2nd series, of 14 February 1986). Article 70(1)(i), of Law No 28/82, on the constitutional court and judicial review of the constitutionality of laws, as amended by Law No 85/89 of 7 September 1989 brought such divergence to an end by providing the Constitutional Court with express jurisdiction to control the conformity of a law with an international convention.

[22] G Canotilho and V Moreira (n 14) 92–93, speak, in this regard, of 'the degree of effectiveness and of the normative hierarchy of supranational law'.

Nevertheless, the addition of this new provision was useful in order to dispel any ambiguity concerning acceptance, by the Portuguese Constitution, of the principle of applicability of secondary Community legislation in the internal legal order, independently of any act of reception such as ratification, approval or publication. It also expresses, in the very text of the Constitution itself, the specificity of Community law that distinguishes it from international conventional law.[23]

It is possible, however, to detect in this provision related though distinct concepts such as 'direct effect' and 'direct or immediate applicability'.

Moreover, even if an express provision was necessary to ensure the incorporation of secondary Community legislation into the internal legal order, the fact that it was limited to what is *expressly* provided for in the Treaties is an obvious source of potential misunderstanding. Indeed, the question that immediately arises is whether the Article covers the provisions of directives, which have been recognised by the Court of Justice as capable of having direct effect in spite of the Treaties' silence on that point.

That is the reason why the 1989 constitutional amendment deleted the word 'expressly' from Article 8(3).

Even following that modification, however, the text of the Constitution still does not provide any clear answer regarding the hierarchical relationship between internal and Community law, nor therefore as to the supremacy of 'supranational law', in particular as regards those provisions arising from the legislative activity of the competent Community institutions. Portuguese academic opinion is also divided on that point, just as it is concerning the controversy surrounding the relationship between international law and national law.

It is worth noting that some authors who were previously opposed to the primacy of international or supranational law over subsequent internal legislation have, to some extent, reconsidered their positions.

Indeed, while arguing that the absence of a constitutional clause clearly providing for the supremacy of supranational law makes it difficult for the primacy of Community law to be fully recognised, Canotilho and Moreira concede that, were the supremacy of customary or conventional international law to be recognised, a similar solution should apply to the relationship between supranational and national law.[24]

The aforementioned judgment of the Constitutional Court of October 1988, by affirming the supremacy of international conventional law over *ordinary* domestic law, whether previous or subsequent, reinforces the case for the supremacy

[23] In that regard, see JC Moitinho de Almeida, *Direito Comunitário. A Ordem Jurídica Comunitária. As Liberdades Fundamentais na CEE* (Lisboa, Almedina, 1985) 102–03, stressing the need to 'distinguish Community law from the other international law'. The author takes the view that Article 8(3) of the Constitution supports the principle of supremacy of Community law over national law, with the exception of constitutional law.

[24] G Canotilho and V Moreira (n 14) 95.

of Community law over internal legislation, even where the latter is enacted subsequently.

However, as regards the position of constitutional law, there is virtual unanimity among legal writers[25] to the effect that the Portuguese Constitution confers absolute supremacy on constitutional law principles and provisions over any conflicting rules, whatever their origin.

Stemming from the principle of national sovereignty and provided for by certain constitutional provisions [eg, Article 277(1)], that view logically implies that 'supranational provisions' contrary to the Constitution should not be applied by the courts (Article 207) and should instead be subject to constitutional judicial review by the Constitutional Court (Articles 277, 280 and 281).[26]

It is true that successive amendments have brought the Portuguese constitutional system—designed in 1975, largely during the revolutionary period which followed the 'coup' of April 1974—more closely into line with the political and economic system established by the Treaties.

Nevertheless, the possibility, however marginal, of conflicts between the two legal orders should have been resolved, according to certain academic writers,[27] by an amendment to the Constitution clearly affirming the supremacy of Community law, as is required by the very nature of the Community legal system and in accordance with the case-law of the Court of Justice.

However, no such amendment was made in either 1982 or 1989, thus leaving the clarification of the constitutional status of Community law dependent on the attitude that might be taken in future by the Constitutional Court.

IV. THE FIRST CONSTITUTIONAL CASE ON EC LAW

That attitude recently began to take shape when the Constitutional Court was called upon for the first time[28] to deal with the relationship between national and Community law, in particular as regards the obligation to refer a question for a preliminary ruling in accordance with Article 177 EEC.[29]

[25] The exception is J Baptista Machado, *Introdução ao Direito e ao Discurso Legitimador* (Coimbra, Almedina, 1984)73, according to whom 'community law is not subordinate to sources of domestic law since it is placed at the top of the hierarchy (to which it belongs), in a position parallel to constitutional standards'.

[26] In this context, A Vitorino, *A Adesão de Portugal às Comunidades Europeias* (Lisboa, 1984) 57, pointed to the inferences that should be drawn from what he called 'the existential need' of the entire system of constitutional judicial review, that is the need to ensure compatibility of any provisions in force in the Portuguese legal order with the Constitution.

[27] See, in this respect, I Jalles, *Implications juridico-constitutionnelles de l'adhésion aux Communautés européennes: le cas du Portugal* (Brussels, Bruylant, 1981) 161; J Mota Campos (n 15) 269–76.

[28] Judgment of 23 May 1990, 2nd chamber, Case 154/89 [1990] not yet reported.

[29] The *Tribunal Constitucional* already had the opportunity to express its views on a specific issue relating to the links between Community and national law and concerning the implementation of Council Regulation (EEC) No 1787/84 of 19 June 1984, on the European Regional Development Fund [1984] OJ L169 (see judgment of 1 February 1989, Case 184/89 [1989] *Diário da República*,

An appeal was brought before the *Tribunal Constitucional* against a decision by the Court of Appeals of Porto (*Tribunal da Relação do Porto*) declaring inadmissible an action where the unconstitutionality of Article 678(1) of the Code of Civil Procedure (CPC) had been alleged, because that provision did not allow 'an ordinary appeal in cases whereby the amounts claimed do not exceed those that fall within the jurisdiction of the court whose decision is subject to appeal'.

The competent court at first instance had ruled in favour of the applicants in a case concerning rights to groundwater. Given the value of the claim (50,000 escudos) and the wording of Article 678(1) CPC, the defendant was prevented from lodging an appeal to a higher court. The defendant therefore sought to rely on the incompatibility of that prohibition with the Constitution.

Among the grounds of appeal invoked before the Constitutional Court, the plaintiff referred, inter alia, to 'the fundamental right to a double level of judicial scrutiny', which, in its view, stemmed from Article 20(1) of the Constitution and which was also enshrined in the EEC Treaty by Article 168A as a general principle of Community law 'binding upon all EEC Member States, and which the latter should transpose into their domestic law'.

The appellant therefore requested that the Constitutional Court should refer a question for preliminary ruling to the Court of Justice in order to know whether such a general principle could be inferred from the abovementioned provision of the Treaty 'for the protection of fundamental rights and only on matters of law'.

The judgment of the *Tribunal Constitucional* is worthy of attention for several reasons:

(a) It is the first judgment where the Court has examined the relationship between national law and Community law as regards application of the latter by national courts.
(b) The Court was requested to refer a question for a preliminary ruling by one of the parties in the main action. Indeed, private parties, assisted by their lawyers, often play a decisive role in prompting national courts to apply Community law, since that law constitutes a powerful tool for protecting their client's rights and interests.
(c) The question at issue concerned a new Treaty provision, added by the Single European Act, providing for the creation of the Court of First Instance.
(d) The judgment analyses in depth the obligation to refer, its function and the conditions governing its exercise.

No 57 [1989] 1044). In its judgment, the Constitutional Court ruled that when an EEC regulation needs adoption of internal implementing provisions, the enactment of such provisions is governed by the Portuguese constitutional rules concerning allocation of competence and the form of the acts. However, the Constitutional Court did not state its position as regards the status in the internal legal order of such 'domestic community law'. For an overall view of the questions raised in this case, as well as the first judgments of Portuguese courts regarding community law, see A Pinto, 'L'application du droit constitutionnel au Portugal' (1990) 6 (6) *Revue française de Droit administratif.*

Taking as its starting point the wording of Article 177 of the EEC Treaty, the Court recalled that

> where a question of interpretation of Community law is raised in a case pending before a court or a tribunal of a Member State against whose decisions there is no judicial remedy under national law it shall bring the matter before the Court of Justice.

The Constitutional Court therefore acknowledged the existence in such situations of an obligation to refer without expressing any reservation in respect of the fact that it was itself bound by that obligation.

The preliminary ruling mechanism appears then, in accordance with the reasoning of the Court, as a tool for ensuring the supremacy of the Community legal order, with a view to ensuring the uniform interpretation and application of Community law throughout the Community.

The Constitutional Court then went on to question the limits of the obligation to refer. After recalling the CILFIT case-law of the Court of Justice,[30] it stressed that this obligation only exists when the national court considers that the question of Community law raised before it is relevant to the solution of the dispute, thus requiring a ruling by the Court of Justice on the interpretation of the applicable provisions of Community law.

Furthermore, the Constitutional Court recalled that, although the parties to the proceedings may raise the possibility of making a preliminary ruling before the national court, it is only the latter that can decide to refer the question to the Court of Justice.

In that context, the Constitutional Court, after expressing doubts as to whether the question raised by the applicant was truly one of interpretation of a Community law provision, stated that no such question was relevant to the dispute at hand since that dispute did not raise any issue concerning the protection of fundamental rights.

In theory, it would have been possible for the Constitutional Court to exercise its power to reformulate the question proposed by the interested party in broader terms covering a possible generalised right to a double degree of judicial scrutiny.

The Constitutional Court did not do so and it is hard to see how, in this context, the reference to Article 168 A of the Treaty could ever have been anything more than a clearly doomed attempt to apply Community law in a case to which it bore no relation.

Furthermore, the fact is that for more than three decades the Community legal order has functioned with just one court and that, even after the creation of the Court of First Instance, the benefit of a second level of judicial decision-making was granted only to individuals and companies within the limited field of competence of that Court.

[30] Case 283/81 *CILFIT v Ministero della Sanità* [1982] ECR-3415.

In any event, and in the circumstances of that case, the Constitutional Court did not need to rule on the hierarchical relationship between Community law and Portuguese constitutional law.

Nonetheless, the remarkably clear reasoning employed by the Constitutional Court in its judgment leads me to predict that it will not depart in the future from the general principles laid down by the Court of Justice as regards the relationship between Community law and national constitutional law.

2

Are there Substantive Limits to the Amendment of the Treaties?[*]

WITH NUNO PIÇARRA[**]

I. INTRODUCTION

A. Article 236 of the EEC Treaty

ARTICLE 236 OF the Treaty establishing the European Economic Community (hereinafter the 'EEC Treaty' or the 'Treaty')[1] lays down the rules governing the procedure for the revision of that Treaty:

> The government of any Member State or the Commission may submit to the Council proposals for the amendment of this Treaty.
>
> If the Council, after consulting the European Parliament and, where appropriate, the Commission, delivers an opinion in favour of calling a conference of representatives of the governments of the Member States, the conference shall be convened by the President of the Council for the purpose of determining by common accord the amendments to be made to those Treaties. The European Central Bank shall also be consulted in the case of institutional changes in the monetary area.
>
> The amendments shall enter into force after being ratified by all the Member States in accordance with their respective constitutional requirements.

* First published in French under the title 'Y a-t-il des limites matérielles à la révision des traités instituant les Communautés européennes?' (1993) 1-2 *Cahiers dr eur* 4–37. A slightly different English version of the same article was published by the Zentrum fur Europäisches Wirtschaftsrecht, Rheinische Friedrich-Wilhelms Universität Bonn, 43, October 1995. The text as it is published now owes to both versions of the article.

** Legal secretary in the Chambers of the President of the Court of First Instance of the European Communities.

1 Article 236 of the EEC Treaty corresponds to Article 204 of the Treaty establishing the European Atomic Energy Community (EURATOM) and is similar to Article 96 of the Treaty establishing the European Coal and Steel Community (ECSC). All those provisions were subsequently repealed by the Treaty on European Union and replaced by Article N of the same Treaty, which became Article 48 of the EU Treaty post-Amsterdam. Our analysis is focused on the EEC Treaty, thus leaving in principle the other two founding Treaties aside. We kept in this publication the original wording and numbering of the EEC Treaty, which was still in application at the time when the article was first published. However, some references may be made, when appropriate, to the subsequent evolution of the relevant Treaty provisions and the case-law of the Court of Justice.

B. Nature and Holders of the Revision Powers

Some introductory remarks may be made as regards the above quoted Treaty provisions.

It appears, first of all, that the Member States are still the holders of the revision powers. Each one of them shares the initiative with the Commission and no amendment of the Treaty is possible without their unanimous agreement. The refusal by one Member State to ratify the amendments agreed during an intergovernmental conference makes it impossible for those amendments to enter into force.

Secondly, the powers of revision are exercised according to a classical intergovernmental technique. Once the first phase of the procedure, dominated by the Community institutions, is completed, it is for the representatives of the governments of the Member States, meeting in conference, to decide, by unanimity, what modifications shall be introduced in the Treaty. The procedure is, thus, of a diplomatic, not of a constitutional, character.

Next, since all Member States are democratic nations governed by the rule of law, the participation in the revision procedure of their respective parliaments, or even of their electorates by means of a referendum, has a decisive constitutional dimension, namely from the point of view of the democratic legitimacy of the Community itself.

Lastly, it should be emphasised that the abovementioned Treaty provisions lay down specific requirements that must be met, as concerns both the forms and the procedure to be followed by the Member States in exercising their revision powers.

C. Community Phase of the Revision Procedure

The first requirement relates to the mandatory participation of certain Community institutions—the Council, the Commission and the European Parliament—in the revision of the Treaty. That constitutes the so-called 'Community phase' of the revision procedure.

Other treaties establishing international organisations also provide for the participation of common institutions in the procedure for their amendment.[2] However, the tasks entrusted to the Community institutions by the Treaty are particularly relevant in that context. On the one hand, the European Parliament, and the Commission, if it hasn't taken the initiative with the proposal, must be consulted. On the other hand, the opinion which the Council is called upon to give in favour of initiating the procedure for revision constitutes in fact a decision to

[2] See, in this respect, J Smit and P Herzog, *The Law of the European Community* 6 (New York, Matthew Bender, 1989) 346.

call a conference of the representatives of the governments of the Member States[3] and not a mere 'opinion' within the meaning of Article 189 of the EEC Treaty. The Community intervention in the procedure goes therefore clearly beyond a mere consultation and constitutes a necessary pre-condition for launching an intergovernmental conference.[4]

D. Characteristics of the Revision Mechanism

Quite often multilateral international treaties, in particular those establishing international organisations, do contain provisions concerning their amendment.

However, Article 236 of the EEC Treaty has the ability to produce such binding effects that clearly help to distinguish the Treaty from other international agreements establishing international organisations.

Indeed, the Treaty is designed as a kind of 'framework' or 'constitutional' agreement whose substantive provisions set the objectives that must be pursued by the institutions and establish the principles that govern their action. In order to carry out their mission, those institutions have been empowered by Article 189 to adopt acts of a legislative nature.

A reading of Article 189 in conjunction with Articles 173 and 177(1)(b) of the EEC Treaty,[5] highlights the supremacy of the Treaty over ordinary Community legislation. Article 236 must be understood in that same context. By establishing a complex procedure of revision, which differs from the ordinary legislative procedure, Article 236 confirms not only that the Community legislature must respect the Treaty, but also that the same legislature cannot modify it.[6] It is the mission

[3] Pursuant to Article 148(1) EEC, the Council shall act by a majority of its Members.

[4] See Vedder, in E Grabitz, 'Kommentar zum EWG-Vertrag', Article 236, (Munich, Beck, 1991)7. However, for a consultative reading of the intervention of the Community institutions, see M Waelbroeck, 'Peut-on parler d'un droit constitutionnel européen?' (1964) 2 *Travaux et Conférences de la Faculté de droit de l'Université libre de Bruxelles* 80. The author considers, nevertheless, that such an intervention, even if it is merely consultative, 'enables the Community institutions to make known their views, to give an authoritative opinion and to pave the way for a customary evolution leading to a more active role for those institutions'—our translation (in the original: 'permet aux institutions des Communautés de faire entendre leur voix, de donner un avis qui jouira nécessairement d'une autorité considérable, et de paver ainsi la voie d'une évolution coutumière au terme de laquelle elles auront un rôle plus actif à jouer'). It is worth noting that the Council acts in this context as a Community institution itself, entrusted with the task to 'ensure that the objectives set out in this Treaty are attained' (Article 145 of the EEC Treaty), distinct from the conference of representatives of the Member States (see Vedder (n 4) 6).

[5] See J Mertens de Wilmars, 'Annulation et appréciation de validité dans le traité CEE: convergence ou divergence?' in WG Grewe, H Rupp and H Schneider (eds), *Europäische Gerichtsbarkeit und nationale Verfassungsgerichtsbarkeit*, Festschrift zum 70. Geburtstag von Hans Kutscher (Baden-Baden, Nomos, 1981) 238.

[6] See, in this respect, Opinion of Advocate General Jacobs, in Case C-343/89 *Witzemann* [1990] ECR I-4488 para 20. According to the Advocate General, the Treaty provisions are binding on the legislature and can be altered only by an amendment of the Treaty.

of the Court of Justice, in its capacity as a constitutional court, to ensure that the supremacy of the Treaty is respected.

By adopting Article 236, the authors of the Treaty made it a 'rigid', not a 'flexible' body of law.[7] But at the same time, they showed their willingness to make the Treaty adaptable to a changing reality, thus preserving its binding force, without prejudice to its own identity.

The 'rigidity' of the Treaty regarding its revision is confirmed by Article 228(1), second subparagraph, relating to the matter of external relations of the European Community, in particular to its treaty making power.[8] It provides that:

> The Council, the Commission or a Member State may obtain the opinion of the Court of Justice as to whether an agreement envisaged is compatible with the provisions of this Treaty. Where the opinion of the Court of Justice is adverse, the agreement may enter into force only in accordance with Article 236.

That provision[9] constitutes indeed an expression of the supremacy of the Treaty in the Community legal order. That supremacy is ensured by the Court of Justice, which is empowered with a competence similar, in terms of constitutional law, to the prior control of constitutionality of international agreements.[10] A negative opinion of the Court thus prevents a draft international agreement concluded by the Community from entering into force, at least so long as it is not modified.[11]

E. The Real Test: The Court's Opinions on the EEA

In this context, the question of the substantive limits to amending the Treaty may be formulated as follows: when the Court of Justice has given an adverse opinion on a draft international agreement in pursuance to Article 228(1), second subparagraph, may any modification, which would result in a fundamental change to the

[7] The classical reference book in this respect is James Bryce, 'Flexible and Rigid Constitutions', *Studies on History and Jurisprudence* (New York, Oxford University Press, 1901).

[8] On the treaty making power of the Community, see E Stein, 'External Relations of the European Community: Structure and Process' I, 1 *Collected Courses of the Academy of European Law* (Florence/London, European University Institute/Martinus Nijhoff, 1991) 115.

[9] The original version of the EEC Treaty, Article 238, third paragraph, also provided that where an association agreement concluded by the Community called for amendments to the Treaty, 'these amendments shall first be adopted in accordance with the procedure laid down in Article 236'. That provision actually contributed to reinforce the constitutional dimension of the Treaty. However, Article 238, third paragraph, of the EEC Treaty was repealed by Article G (84), adopted in Maastricht.

[10] Reference can be made, in this regard, to Article 54 of the French Constitution and to Article 91(3) of the Dutch Constitution.

[11] See R Kovar, 'La compétence consultative de la Cour de justice et la procédure de conclusion des accords internationaux de la Communauté économique européenne' in *Mélanges offerts à Paul Reuter: le droit international, unité et diversité* (Paris, A Pedone, 1981) 369. It must be stressed, however, that a declaration of incompatibility offers three solution possibilities: either a revision of the Treaty or the withdrawal of the draft agreement, or its renegotiation in order to eliminate the clauses incompatible with the Treaty.

existing Treaty, or even in a new treaty, be adopted in order to allow the agreement which has been declared incompatible with the Treaty to enter into force?

The Court of Justice itself had the opportunity to make known its views on that question in two opinions—Opinion 1/91 of 14 December 1991[12] and Opinion 1/92 of 10 April 1992[13]—delivered on the draft agreement between the European Community and its Member States, on the one hand, and the countries of the European Free Trade Association, on the other hand, relating to the creation of the European Economic Area (hereinafter, the 'EEA').

The agreement, which was finally signed on 2 May 1992, in Porto, was decisively influenced by those two opinions. In fact, on the one hand, the provisions that had been declared incompatible in the first Opinion were repealed. On the other hand, the new mechanisms that were renegotiated thereafter were upheld, under certain conditions, in the second Opinion.[14]

It follows from the Court's reasoning in those two opinions that, in certain circumstances, an international agreement which has been considered incompatible with the Treaty cannot enter into force as it stands, since that would require amendments to the Treaty that would not be possible to adopt even in accordance with the procedure laid down in Article 236. In other words, our view is that the two opinions paved the way for the recognition by the Court of the existence of certain implied substantive limits to the revision of the Treaty.

F. Substantive Limits: A Constitutional Issue

The issue of substantive limits only becomes relevant by reference to a text of a constitutional nature, inherent to which there is a material and temporal 'claim to validity' ('*Geltungsanspruch*') of any other normative instrument belonging to the same legal order.

That issue thus acquires a real significance only by reference to the process of 'constitutionalisation' of the Treaty. Such process led to the conversion of the Treaty into a 'constitutional charter of a Community governed by the rule of law',[15] as well as to the gradual development of a new legal order, autonomous *vis-à-vis* both the international order and the national legal orders of the Member States.

[12] [1991] ECR I-6079.

[13] [1992] ECR I-2821.

[14] See, in this respect, HG Schermers, 'Commentary on Opinions 1/91 and 1/92' (1992) 29 *Common Market Law Review* 1004: 'Today, the standing of the Community as such is that its Court of Justice can prevent 19 sovereign states from accepting particular rules in an international agreement. This shows how much the sovereignty of the Member States has been limited over the years, also in the field of external relations.'

[15] See Opinion 1/91 (n 12) para 21. That expression goes back to the judgment in Case 294/83 *Les Verts v Parliament* [1986] ECR 1365. However, Advocate General Lagrange had already used the expression in his Opinion in Case 8/55 *Fédération Charbonnière Belgique v High Authority* [1954–1956] ECR 260.

We will therefore start by examining the meaning and the scope of the process of 'constitutionalisation' of the Treaty and the concomitant process of building an autonomous Community legal order. The case-law of the Court of Justice played in this context the decisive role, in particular as concerns the interpretation of Article 236 and the conditions for amending the Treaty.

Opinions 1/91 and 1/92 will provide the framework to answering the question of whether, and to what extent, the concept of substantive limits to the amendment of the Treaty already forms part of the Community legal order.

II. THE REVISION OF THE TREATY, THE PROCESS OF 'CONSTITUTIONALISATION' AND THE BUILDING OF AN AUTONOMOUS COMMUNITY LEGAL ORDER

A. Building a Constitutional Order

The term 'constitutionalisation' refers, in the Anglo-American literature, to a circular or spiral process in which a treaty such as the EC Treaty is interpreted by a court such as the Court of Justice in accordance with a systematic, teleological and, above all, dynamic method, similar to that used by the constitutional courts of the Member States and different from that characterising the approach usually taken by international courts and arbitrators for the interpretation of an international convention.

As both a cause and an effect of such process, the Treaty has gradually taken on the characteristics which are inherent in a 'fundamental law' of a constitutional kind.[16] As a matter of fact, that represented a process of constructive case-law ('*Rechtsfortbildung*'), which found its basis in the text of the Treaty, as an instrument of international law distinct from any other classical international agreement.

[16] On the process of constitutionalisation, see E Stein, 'Lawyers, Judges and the Making of a Transnational Constitution' (1981) *The American Journal of International Law* 1 ff; GF Mancini, 'The Making of a Constitution for Europe' (1989) *Common Market Law Review* 595 ff; J-P Jacqué, 'Cours general de droit communautaire' (1990) I, 1 *Collected Courses of the Academy of European Law* 265 ff; JHH Weiler, 'The Transformation of Europe' (1991) *The Yale Law Journal* 2413; H Rasmussen, 'The Court of Justice of the European Communities and the Process of Integration' in E Orban (ed), *Fédéralisme et cours suprêmes* (Brussels, Bruylant, 1991) 199 ff; J Temple Lang, 'The Development of European Community Constitutional Law' (1991) *The International Lawyer* 455 ff. On the methods of interpretation of the Court of Justice, see H Kutscher, 'Méthodes d'interprétation du droit communautaire vues par un juge à la Cour', *Cour de justice des Communautés européennes*, Rencontre judiciaire et universitaire, 27–28 September 1976, Luxembourg, 1976.

B. First Stage: Direct Effect

The first stage of that process of constitutionalisation, inaugurated by the well-known judgment in *Van Gend en Loos*,[17] was to recognise that the provisions of the Treaty that are clear, precise, complete and unconditional have direct effect, even when they contain only obligations for the Member States. A provision with direct effect enables the individuals to rely on it before the national courts, which are required to protect the individual rights that derive therefrom.

The specific feature of Community law in that regard is that direct effect was spelled out as a general principle of Community law by virtue only of the content of its provisions, regardless of the will of the Contracting Parties,[18] whereas in international law such an effect is just the exception.[19]

In this context, the impact of the Treaty on individuals goes beyond the boundaries of classical international law and may be compared with what happens with a constitution to which the courts have 'direct access', irrespective of any intervention of the legislature.[20]

C. Second Stage: Primacy

The second stage of the constitutionalisation process conducted by the Court of Justice derived as a natural consequence from the first stage.[21] We refer to the recognition of the principle of precedence or primacy of Community law over the national law of Member States, including constitutional law.

[17] Case 26/62 *Van Gend & Loos v Netherlands Inland Revenue Administration* [1963] ECR-1. The Court stated therein for the first time that 'the Community constitutes a new legal order of international law for the benefit of which the States have limited their sovereign rights, albeit within limited fields, and the subjects of which comprise not only Member States but also their nationals'.

[18] See, in this respect, P Pescatore, 'The Doctrine of 'Direct Effect': An Infant Disease of Community Law' (1983) *European Law Review* 155. In Pescatore's view, the discussion about the direct effect was the consequence of a kind of 'infant disease' of Community law, which was a necessary step before reaching the conclusion that every rule pertaining to the Community legal order must be fully effective not only between the Contracting States but also as regards the relations between the States and the individuals and even the relations among individuals themselves.

[19] That is the case of the so-called self-executing treaties.

[20] The concept of 'constitutionalisation' was originated in the United States where the Constitution, in particular its provisions on fundamental rights, have been, from earlier times, regarded as endowed with direct effect and capable of being relied upon by individuals before the courts, including to oppose the application of laws that are not in conformity with the Constitution. Conversely, constitutionalism in continental Europe, failing to fully recognise the normative value of the Constitution, started by regarding action by the legislature as indispensable for the effectiveness of the constitutional provisions relating to fundamental rights. A process of 'constitutionalisation of the constitutions' had to be conducted in some Member States, leading to the embodiment in those constitutions of the principle of direct effect of the provisions relating to fundamental rights and of the principle of direct access by judges to the Constitution (as in Germany, Spain, Italy and Portugal).

[21] See GF Mancini (n 16) 600.

Such principle of 'internal primacy' has, in Community law, a prospective dimension, entailing an obligation 'to do', which differs from the principle of precedence in international law. The latter merely requires the Contracting States to comply with their international obligations, subject to their retrospective liability, leaving it to their constitutional law to determine the status of international law in the internal legal order, so as to satisfy that requirement.[22]

As is shown by the case-law, in particular in *Costa v ENEL*,[23] *Simmenthal*[24] and *Factortame*,[25] the Court of Justice, despite the absence in the Treaty of any provision stating the primacy of Community law, has laid down the principles that govern the relationship between Community law and the law of Member States in a federal-like manner. In a way, the constitutional rules of the Member States that applied, in the beginning, to that relationship have been, as a consequence of the case-law, 'enshrined' in the legal order of the Community, which now determines the content and the scope of the principle of primacy.[26]

In spite of the strong reservations initially raised by some national courts, it is possible to say that nowadays that doctrine is widely accepted by the courts in all Member States.[27]

D. Third Stage: An Unwritten Catalogue of Fundamental Rights

The 'discovery' in the Treaty, by the Court of Justice, of an unwritten catalogue of fundamental rights constitutes another step in the process of 'constitutionalisation' of the Treaty. Such a contribution to a 'constitution of Europe' was triggered by the pressure exerted by certain constitutional courts, in particular the *Bundesverfassungsgericht*, as a pre-condition for the gradual acceptance of the primacy of Community law.[28]

That catalogue of fundamental rights owes as much to the general principles common to the constitutions of the Member States as to the European Convention for the Protection of Human Rights and Fundamental Freedoms. Formulated step by step since *Stauder*,[29] it offers individuals a protection, which was not originally

[22] See B de Witte, 'Retour à Costa. La primauté du droit communautaire à la lumière du droit international', in W Maihofer (ed), *Noi si mura: Selected working papers of the European University Institute* (Florence, European University Institute, 1986), 257.

[23] Case 6/64 *Flaminio Costa v ENEL* [1964] ECR-585.

[24] Case 106/77 *Amministrazione delle Finanze dello Stato v Simmenthal SpA* [1978] ECR-629.

[25] Case C-213/89 *The Queen v Secretary of State for Transport, ex parte: Factortame Ltd and others* [1990] ECR I-2433.

[26] See D Simon, 'Les exigences de la primauté du communautaire: continuité ou métamorphoses?' *L'Europe et le droit—Mélanges en hommage à Jean Boulouis* (Paris, Dalloz, 1991) 498.

[27] In that context, see the judgment of 28 January 1992 where the *Bundesvarfassungsgericht* stated that the principle of primacy is embodied in an unwritten provision of the basic Community law.

[28] See GF Mancini (n 16) 611.

[29] Case 29/69 *Erich Stauder v City of Ulm—Sozialamt* [1969] ECR-419 para 9: the Court is entrusted with the protection of fundamental human rights, which are among the general principles of Community law.

envisaged by the Treaty,[30] and constitutes a standard of appraisal of the validity of the acts of the institutions, both of a legislative and of an administrative nature, as well as of national measures adopted within the field of application of Community law.[31]

Another aspect that is worth mentioning in that same regard concerns the application of the regime of fundamental rights to the 'four fundamental freedoms' enshrined in the Treaty: goods, persons, capital and services. Indeed, the notion that those fundamental freedoms express the fundamental rights of citizens of the Member States of the Community to carry out an economic activity and to choose the place and orientation of their occupation or vocational training entails recognition that the relevant provisions of the Treaty[32] ensure the appropriate protection of those citizens against any undue interference from Member States.[33]

The Court of Justice appeared to uphold such an understanding in that it stated that the rules of the Treaty on freedom of trade, freedom to exercise an economic activity and free access to employment, which may be construed as prohibiting Member States from setting up restrictions or obstacles to the entry into their territory of nationals of other Member States, have the effect of conferring fundamental rights directly on all persons to which the abovementioned articles may apply.[34]

[30] On the recent evolution of the case-law relating to fundamental rights, see H Rasmussen (n 16) 221 ff; GF Mancini and D Keeling, 'From CILFIT to ERT: The Constitutional Challenge facing the European Court' (1991) *Yearbook of European Law* 11. The Maastricht Treaty has ratified the outcome of this evolution. Article F(2) of the EU Treaty states that '[t]he Union shall respect fundamental rights, as guaranteed by the European Convention for the Protection of Human Rights and Fundamental Freedoms signed in Rome on 4 November 1950 and as they result from the constitutional traditions common to the Member States, as general principles of Community law'.

[31] See, in particular, Case C-4/73 *Nold v Commission* [1974] ECR 491, para 13, Case 44/79 *Hauer v Land Rheinland Pfalz* (1979) ECR 3727, Joined Cases C-60 and C-61/84 *Cinéthèque v Fédération Nationale des Cinémas Français* [1985] ECR 2605, para 25, Case C-222/84 *Johnston v Chief Constable of the Royal Ulster Constabulary* [1986] ECR 1651, para 18, Case 12/86 *Demirel v Stadt Schwäbisch Gmünd* [1987] ECR 3719, para 28, Case 5/88 *Wachauf v Bundesamt für Ernährung und Forstwirtschaft* [1989] ECR 2069, para 19, C-260/89 *Elliniki Radiophonia Tiléorassi and Others(ERT) v Dimotiki Etairia Pliroforissis and Others* [1991] ECR I-2951,paras 41-42 and C-159/90 *The Society for the Protection of Unborn Children Ireland Ltd v Stephen Grogan a o* [1991] ECR I-4655, para 31.

[32] As laid down, respectively, in Articles 30, 48, 61, 52 and 59 of the EEC Treaty.

[33] The recognition of such freedoms as fundamental rights may be found in the constitutions of some Member States, namely Article 12 of the *Grundgesetz*. See, in this respect, G Ress, 'La libre circulation des personnes, des services et des capitaux' European Commission, *Trente ans de droit communautaire* (Luxembourg, Office for Official Publications of the European Communities, 1982) 304. A Bleckmann, 'Considérations sur l'interprétation de l'article 7 du traité CEE' (1976) *Revue trimestrielle de Droit europeen* 481, underlines the fact that such understanding is not the mere expression of an ideology but is indeed required by the principles inherent in a State or Community based on the rule of law.

[34] Case 118/75 *Watson and Belmann* [1976] ECR 1185 para 12. The Court also stressed (para 16 of the same judgment) that those Treaty provisions and the implementing rules of secondary Community law give effect to the fundamental principle contained in Article 3(c) of the EEC Treaty, 'which states that, for the purposes set out in Article 2, the activities of the Community shall include the abolition, as between Member States, of obstacles to freedom of movement for persons, services

E. Next Step: Autonomy Vis-à-Vis International Law

The stages of 'constitutionalisation' of the Treaty which we have just considered led essentially to establishing the autonomy of the Community legal order *vis-à-vis* the legal orders of the Member States. Indeed, at stake was, first, to ensure the effective and uniform application of Community law in all Member States as a necessary condition for the existence of the Community legal order and, second, the need for a catalogue of fundamental rights without which a true constitution cannot come to exist.[35]

Conversely, the next step of 'constitutionalisation' of the Treaty, which is related to its revision,[36] concerns essentially the autonomy of the Community legal order *vis-à-vis* the international legal order. To this effect, the main question is to determine the extent to which relations between the Community and the Member States are governed by an 'internal law' of a constitutional nature, to the exclusion of any rules of international law.[37]

In that regard, the problems are more complex and the answers are still being worked out. Not only were the Member States fully sovereign States when the Community was set up, but they still are so today and have preserved their capacity as entities subject to international law.[38] For that reason, it is more difficult to establish the independence of the Community as regards international law than as regards the domestic law of the Member States.[39]

and capital'). See also Case 240/83 *Procureur de la République v ADBHU* [1985] ECR 531 para 9 ('the principles of free movement of goods and freedom of competition, together with freedom of trade as a fundamental right, are general principles of Community law of which the Court ensures observance'), and Case 222/86 *UNECTEF v Heylens* [1987] ECR 4097 para 14 ('free access to employment is a fundamental right which the Treaty confers individually on each worker in the Community'; the requirement of effective protection for that right 'reflects a general principle of Community law which underlies the constitutional traditions common to the Member States and has been enshrined in Articles 6 and 13 of the European Convention for the Protection of Human Rights and Fundamental Freedoms'). However, in Joined Cases C-267 and 268/91 *Keck and Mithouard* [1993] ECR I-6097 paras 14–18, the Court underlined the idea that the scope of Article 30 is not to ensure the commercial freedom of traders as such but only insofar as it affects trade between Member States. In this respect, see the commentary by W-H Roth (1994) 31 *Common Market Law Review* 851.

[35] See Article 16 of the Declaration of the Rights of Man and of the Citizen, of 26 August 1789.

[36] As M Waelbroeck (n 4) 78–79, put it, 'the fundamental distinction between a constitution and an international treaty concerns the procedure that must be followed in order to periodically modify or repeal either of them'—our translation (in the original: 'la distinction fondamentale entre constitution et traité international tient à la procédure qui doit être mise en œuvre pour pouvoir, régulièrement, modifier ou abroger l'une ou l'autre').

[37] A similar view is expressed by U Everling, 'Sind die Mitgliedstaaten der Europäischen Gemeinshaft noch Herren der Verträge?' *Das Europäische Gemeinshaft im Spannungsfeld von Politik und Wirtschaft* (Baden-Baden, Nomos, 1985) 89.

[38] In that regard, it must be recalled that, as E Stein noted (n 8) 130, '[t]aking into account the general features of the Community and its unique attributes in external relations, the label of international organization can be explained only by the extraordinary penury in the conventional taxonomy of international persons'.

[39] See, in this connection, P Dagtoglou, 'La nature juridique de la Communauté européenne' in *Trente ans de droit communautaire* (n 33) 36.

The general principle of international law governing the amendment of treaties, which finds its expression in the Vienna Convention on the Law of Treaties, may be stated as follows: the States parties to any international agreement are the 'masters of the treaty' and may at any time amend and revoke it, whether formally or not, in principle by unanimity (see Articles 39, 54 and 57 of the Vienna Convention). Moreover, even when an international treaty lays down provisions establishing a specific procedure for its amendment, the Contracting Parties may, by common accord, disregard such provisions.

In view of that, it is not surprising that the discussions among academics about Article 236 of the EEC Treaty have been centred on the question of whether its provisions are optional ('*Sollvorschrift*') or instead binding for the Member States. If the former were true, those States would be entitled, by application of the international law principles of the *actus contrarius* and the freedom to choose the form, to amend the Treaty without regard to the formal and procedural limits set out in Article 236.[40]

Article 169 of the EEC Treaty is of particular importance for an interpretation of Article 236 that goes in the direction of an autonomous and binding meaning. By virtue of Article 169, the Court may, on application by the Commission, find that Member States have failed to comply with their obligations under Article 236 and, therefore, that any amendment provisions adopted in breach of the requirements laid down in that article are inapplicable.[41] In those circumstances, it is impossible to maintain that the provisions on revision contained in Article 236 are merely optional and do not prohibit alternative recourse to the general rules of international convention law. On the contrary, those cannot but be mandatory provisions whose application is subject to review by the Court.[42]

It follows from the foregoing that Article 236 of the EEC Treaty operates, *vis-à-vis* the general principles of international law, as a *lex specialis*: since the Treaty lays down, and guarantees, a specific system for its own amendment, there

[40] In favour of the legality of a Treaty revision outside the boundaries of Article 236, see M Deliege-Squaris, 'Révision des traités européens en dehors des procédures prévues' (1980) *Cahiers dr eur* 550; G Gaja, 'Fonti Comunitarie' VI, *Digesto delle Disciplina Pubblicistiche*, (Milan, UTET Giuridica, 1990) 437; H Steinberger, 'Der Verfassungsstaat als Glied einer Europäischen Gemeinschaft', H Steinberger, E Klein, D Thürer (eds) *Veröffentlichung der Vereinigung der Deutschen Staatsrechtslehrer* (Berlin, De Gruyter, 1991) 16–17.

[41] Moreover, according to Article 171 of the EEC Treaty, if the Court of Justice finds that a Member State has failed to fulfil any of its obligations under the Treaty; such State shall take the measures required for the implementation of the judgment.

[42] It was on the basis of Article 169 that the Court of Justice ruled, in Joined Cases 90 and 91/63, *Commission v Luxembourg and Belgium* [1964] ECR 625, that, by establishing a new legal order which governs the powers, rights and obligations of the natural and legal persons to whom it is applicable, as well as the necessary procedures for taking cognizance of and penalising any breach of it, the Treaty is not limited to creating reciprocal obligations between the said persons. On the contrary, as the Court stated, the basic concept of the Treaty requires that Member States shall not fail to carry out their obligations and shall not take the law into their own hands. It follows that recourse to the rule *inadimplenti non est adimplendum*, applicable, though with reservations, in international law, is excluded within the Community legal order.

can be no question of applying those general principles to any such amendment. In other words, the Member States cannot by common accord rely upon the principles governing the modification of treaties in international law so as to disregard the formal and procedural limits to the revision of the Treaty as laid down in Article 236.[43]

Not surprisingly, the Court of Justice did fully uphold the understanding that the provisions of Article 236 are mandatory for the Member States. In *Defrenne*,[44] the Court ruled that 'apart from any specific provisions, the Treaty can only be modified by means of the amendment procedure carried out in accordance with Article 236'. It also declared in Opinion 1/92[45] that 'the powers conferred on the Court by the Treaty may be modified pursuant only to the procedure referred to in Article 236 of the Treaty'.

Furthermore, in *United Kingdom v Council*,[46] the Court pointed out that the rules regarding the manner in which the Community institutions arrive at their decisions are laid down in the Treaty and are not at the disposal of the Member States or of the institutions themselves.

It must also be recalled, in that regard, that the Court considered it competent to review the compatibility with the Treaty of agreements concluded by the Member States between themselves or with third parties, which introduce modifications or derogations in the Treaty or which may hinder its effective application in any way.

The Court therefore ruled that a convention concluded by the Member States to implement Article 220 of the EEC Treaty must be interpreted with regard both to its principles and objectives and to its relationship with the Treaty.[47] Moreover, the Court admitted that Article 5(2) of the same Treaty may serve as a reference framework for the appraisal of measures taken to implement any agreement concluded between Member States outside the scope of the Treaties, which are liable to impede the effective application of a Treaty provision or the functioning of the Community institutions.[48]

[43] In this connection, see J-P Jacqué (n 16) 273. See also W Meng, 'Artikle 236' in H von den Gröben, J Thiesing and C-D Ehlermann (eds), *Kommentar zum EWG-Vertrag*, 4th edn (Baden-Baden, Nomos, 1991) 5842–43, who rightly points out that the Member States cannot derogate by common accord, without regard to Article 236 and in breach of the principle of legal certainty, from the law that they have themselves made and which constitutes the basis of a legal order whose rules are mandatory for individuals and undertakings in the Community.

[44] Case 43/75 *Defrenne v Sabena* [1976] ECR 455 para 58. See also the opinions of Advocate General Dutheillet de Lamothe of 13 January 1971 in Case 37/70, *REWE v Hauptzollamt Emmerich* [1971] ECR 41, and of Advocate General J-P Warner of 25 October 1979 in Case 34/79 *Regina v Maurice Donald Henn and John Frederick Ernest Darby* [1979] ECR 3932.

[45] Opinion 1/92 [1992] ECR I-2843 para 32.

[46] Case 68/86 *United Kingdom v Council* [1988] ECR 900 para 38.

[47] Case 12/76 *Industrie tessili italiana v Dunlop AG* [1976] ECR 1485 para 9.

[48] Case 44/84 *Hurd v Jones* [1986] ECR 81 para 39.

Concerning agreements between Member States and third countries, the Court found, in *AETR*,[49] that

> to the extent to which Community rules are promulgated for the attainment of the objectives of the Treaty, the Member States cannot, outside the framework of the Community institutions, assume obligations which might affect those rules or alter their scope.

As the Court explained in its Opinion 2/91,[50] 'the authority of the decision in that case cannot be restricted to instances where the Community has adopted Community rules within the framework of a common policy' and applies in 'all the areas corresponding to the objectives of the Treaty'.

However, since the Member States are the Contracting Parties to those agreements, the Court has no jurisdiction to annul their provisions by virtue of Article 173 of the EEC Treaty or to declare them invalid and inapplicable under Article 177(1)(b).[51]

The Court may only, by way of Article 169, declare that a Member State has failed to fulfil its obligations under the Treaty or, on a reference for preliminary ruling in interpretation, by virtue of Article 177(1)(a), consider any provisions in the agreement as contrary to the Treaty and therefore inapplicable.[52] It is therefore not impossible that individuals, by means of Article 177, indirectly claim application of Article 236.[53]

As a matter of fact, the Court could have been called upon to rule on the possible disregard for the amendment procedure set out in the Treaty on only two occasions where Member States have agreed to modify the ECSC Treaty. These were, on the one hand, the Treaty between France and Germany, of 27 October

[49] Case 22/70 *Commission v Council* [1971] ECR 275 para 22.

[50] [1993] ECR I-1061 para 10.

[51] In Joined Cases 31 and 35/86 *Laisa and CPC España v Council* [1988] ECR 2285 para 18, the Court ruled that the provisions set out in the act of accession of a new Member State adjusting acts adopted by the institutions do not constitute an act of the Council but provisions of primary law which may, in principle, not be suspended, amended or repealed otherwise as by means of the procedures laid down for the amendment of the original treaties. Consequently, they cannot fall within the category of acts of the institutions open to an action for a declaration that is void under Article 173 of the EEC Treaty. However, it seems possible for the Court to declare void, for breach of an essential formality, a decision to open an intergovernmental conference for the revision of the Treaty adopted by the Council without regard to the consultation procedure provided for in Article 236. Such is the conclusion that follows from para 33 of the judgment in Case 138/79 *Roquette Frères* [1980] ECR 3333, by which the Court declared void an act of the Council adopted in the framework of the ordinary legislative process without the prior consultation of the European Parliament.

[52] Without prejudice to the possibility of interpreting those provisions in conformity with the Treaty. See C-3/91 *Exportur* [1992] ECR I-5529. Where third countries are parties to the agreement, the fact that its provisions cannot be relied on against a Community obligation may lead to engaging the international responsibility of the Member States. See, as regards this latter aspect, R Joliet, 'Le droit institutionnel des Communautés européennes' (Liège, Faculté de droit, 1983) 209; J-V Louis, 'La révision des traités et l'Union européenne' in André Miroir (ed), *Pensée et construction européennes* (Brussels, Émile Van Balberghe, 1990)196; J Rideau, 'Les accords internationaux dans la jurisprudence de la Cour de justice des Communautés européennes' (1990) *Revue générale de Droit public* 289.

[53] See W Meng (n 43) 5842.

1956, that modified the weighing of votes of Member States as established in Article 28(5) of the ECSC Treaty, following the accession of Saarland to the Federal Republic of Germany, and, on the other hand, the Convention on certain institutions common to the European Communities, signed in Rome on 25 March 1957, which modified the provisions of the ECSC Treaty concerning the composition and the working of the Assembly and the Court of Justice. Those two agreements were immediately subject to severe criticism.[54]

In all the other cases where the Treaties have been subject to revision—eight cases, including the Maastricht Treaty—the Treaty provision laying down the applicable procedure has, in substance, been complied with. In fact, Member States seem to have become definitively aware of the fact that they are not the absolute masters of the amendment procedure.

The evolution described so far shows that the rules of international law which apply to the amendment of treaties are formally excluded as regards the revision of the Treaty, thus allowing for the conclusion that the latter has been 'constitutionalised'[55] as concerns the *formal and procedural limits* to its amendment and the Community legal order has, to that extent, become autonomous *vis-à-vis* the international legal order.

It is now time to examine the question of whether there are any *substantive limits* to the amendment of the Treaty. Opinions 1/91 and 1/92 are of the utmost importance in this regard.

III. OPINIONS 1/91 AND 1/92 OF THE COURT OF JUSTICE: A NEW STEP IN THE PROCESS OF CONSTITUTIONALISATION OF THE TREATY?

A. The Judicial System in the Draft EEA Agreement

The Draft Agreement on the EEA submitted to the Court of Justice for an Opinion pursuant to Article 228(1), second subparagraph, of the EEC Treaty, envisaged in particular the establishment of a judicial system intended to guarantee the objective of uniform interpretation and application of the law within the EEA. That concerned the fundamental freedoms (goods, persons, capital, establishment and services) as well as the rules on competition, which are identical to the corresponding provisions of the EEC and the ECSC Treaties and with the measures adopted to implement those Treaties.

[54] The Dutch Parliament held a debate introduced by MP VG van Naters, who subsequently published a study on the subject entitled 'La révision des traités supranationaux', *Liber Amicorum Jean Pierre François* (Leyden, 1959) 120. The abovementioned agreements were subsequently considered 'youthful sins' due to the lack of experience. See JHH Weiler and J Modrall, 'The Creation of the European Union and its Relationship to the EEC Treaties' in R Bieber, J-P Jacqué and JHH Weiler (eds), *An Ever Closer Union—A Crtitical Analysis of the Draft Treaty Establishing the European Union* (Luxembourg, Office for Official Publications of the EC, 1985) 161.

[55] See J-P Jacqué (n 16) 269.

The judicial system set up in the Draft Agreement established an EEA Court and an EEA Court of First Instance partially composed of members of the Court of Justice and the Court of First Instance of the European Communities respectively.

It was envisaged (Article 96(1)(a) of the Draft Agreement) that the EEA Court would have jurisdiction to adjudicate, in particular, on disputes between the Contracting Parties upon application by one of them, on condition that the dispute had been submitted to two consecutive meetings of a Joint Committee without being resolved.

By virtue of Article 6 of the Draft Agreement, the EEA Court was to interpret the provisions of the Agreement in conformity with rulings of the Court of Justice on the corresponding provisions of Community law which were given prior to, but not subsequent to, the date of signature of the Agreement. The EEA Court of First Instance, for its part, was to have jurisdiction in particular to ensure judicial review of decisions of the European Free Trade Association (EFTA) Surveillance Authority relating to competition rules.

Moreover, the Draft Agreement allowed the EFTA States to authorise their Courts, when they found it necessary, to refer to the Court of Justice, for a preliminary ruling, questions on the interpretation of the provisions of the EEA Agreement regarding the free movement of goods, persons, services and capital and the rules on competition. However, the Court's rulings were not to be binding on the courts of the EFTA Member States.

The last question that was put to the Court for an opinion and the one that is of most interest for our study was whether Article 238, first paragraph, of the EEC Treaty[56] permitted the creation of a judicial system of the type envisaged by the Draft Agreement. In the event of the Court's finding that the system of EEA courts as laid down in the Draft Agreement was incompatible with the Treaty, the Commission admitted the possibility of activating the procedure for amendment provided for in Article 236 of the EEC Treaty, with a view to amending Article 238, first paragraph, so as to permit the conclusion of the EEA association agreement without modifying the system of courts then envisaged.

B. The Three Questions Examined by the Court

The Court of Justice examined the compatibility with the Treaty of three aspects of the judicial system envisaged in the Draft Agreement[57]: (i) the jurisdiction of

[56] According to that provision: 'The Community may conclude with a third country, a union of States or an international organisation agreements creating an association embodying reciprocal rights and obligations, joint actions and special procedures.'

[57] In two opinions previously delivered in pursuance of Article 228(1), second subparagraph (Opinion 1/75 [1975] ECR 1355, and Opinion 1/78 [1979] ECR 2871), the Court of Justice held that the compatibility of an agreement with the Treaty must be assessed in the light of all the rules

the EEA Court to settle disputes between the Contracting Parties; (ii) the objective of guaranteeing legal homogeneity within the EEA; (iii) the lack of binding effect to be attached to the answers given by the EEA Court following a reference for preliminary ruling from a court of a country member of EFTA.

As regards the first aspect, the Court of Justice held that the jurisdiction which the Draft Agreement conferred on the EEA Court, by virtue of Article 96(1)(a), to settle disputes between the Contracting Parties, as defined in Article 2(c) of said Draft Agreement, was not compatible with the jurisdiction conferred on the Court by the Treaty. In fact, since, according to that latter provision, the expression 'Contracting Party' may cover the Community, the Community and its Member States or simply the Member States, the EEA Court 'would have to rule on the respective competences of the Community and the Member States as regards the matters governed by the provisions of the agreement'. In other words, the EEA Court would have to decide on the balance of powers within the Community and to determine, in the light of the Treaty, whether or not a given competence had been conferred on the Community.

The Court of Justice took the view that conferring such competence on the EEA Court would be incompatible with Article 164 of the EEC Treaty and in particular that it would hinder the autonomy of the Community legal order.[58]

With regard to the second aspect, the Court of Justice emphasised that the objectives pursued by the Community legal order differed from those of the EEA: whereas the latter aims at applying rules on free trade and competition in economic and commercial relations between the Contracting Parties, as an end in itself, the same system of rules in the Community has been conceived as a means of achieving integration leading to the establishment of a single market and an economic and monetary union.[59]

The Court inferred from there that the objective of homogeneity in the interpretation and application of the law in the EEA not only was not secured by the identity or similarity of content or wording between the Community law provisions and the corresponding provisions of the EEA Agreement but also was frustrated by the divergence between the aims and context of the agreement *vis-à-vis* those of Community law.[60] Nevertheless, with the entry into force of the EEA

of the Treaty, both those rules which determine the extent of the powers of the institutions of the Community and the substantive rules.

[58] See Opinion 1/91 (n 12) paras 31–36.

[59] See Opinion 1/91 (n 12) paras 15–19, and Opinion 1/92 (n 13) para 17.

[60] In that respect, the Court of Justice, after referring to *Van Gend en Loos* (n 17) noted that whilst the Treaty creates rights and obligations for nationals of Member States and provides for a transfer of sovereignty from those Member States to the Community, the EEA Agreement 'merely creates rights and obligations as between the Contracting Parties and provides for no transfer of sovereign rights to the inter-governmental institutions which it sets up' (Opinion 1/91 (n 12) para 20). In fact, according to Protocol 35 to the EEA Agreement, the commitment of the Parties is restricted to introducing into their respective legal orders a provision of a legislative nature ensuring the precedence of the Agreement over contrary national legislation. On that point, see O Jacot-Guillarmod, 'Préambule, objectifs et principes (art. 1er-7 EEE)' in O Jacot-Guillarmod (ed), *Accord EEE—Commentaires et*

Agreement, its provisions, similar to the Community rules on free movement and competition, would be embodied in the Community legal order[61] and 'juxtaposed' to its corresponding rules.

In those circumstances, Article 6 of the Draft Agreement allowed the EEA Court to interpret the latter rules in a manner incompatible with the relevant case-law of the Court of Justice subsequent to the date on which the Agreement was signed. The autonomy of the Court of Justice in interpreting the Community law would thus be affected. In fact, with regard to the objective of uniform application of the Agreement throughout the EEA, the Court of Justice would have to take account of the possibly divergent case-law of the EEA Court on such fundamental rules of Community law as those on freedom of movement and competition.[62]

On those grounds, the Court of Justice held that Article 6 of the Draft EEA Agreement was incompatible with Article 169 of the EEC Treaty and 'more generally with the very foundations of the Community'.

Lastly, concerning the third aspect of the judicial system under consideration, the Court of Justice stated that to admit that the institutions set up by the Agreement were empowered to disregard the binding nature of the Court's decisions would adversely affect the autonomy of the Community legal order, respect for which the Court is required to assure by virtue of Article 164 of the EEC Treaty. The Court then made clear that, although the powers conferred on the Court by the Treaty may be modified pursuant to the procedure provided for in Article 236 of the Treaty, an international agreement concluded by the Community may only confer new powers on the Court, including jurisdiction to interpret the provisions of such an agreement provided that, in so doing, it does not change the nature of the function of the Court as conceived in the EEC Treaty, in particular the binding nature of its decisions.[63]

C. The EC Legal Order and its Autonomy

It follows from the aforementioned that Article 164 has been interpreted in Opinions 1/91 and 1/92 as conferring on the Court of Justice the essential mission of safeguarding the autonomy of the Community legal order, which is an order of integration, distinct from the international legal order, which is essentially an order of cooperation.

reflexions (Zürich, Schulthless Polygraphischer, 1992) 54, 58–59; A Saggio, 'L'incidence de l'accord EEE sur le système communautaire', report to the Association amicale des référendaires de la Cour de justice, 20 November 1992.

[61] The Court observed (Opinion 1/91 (n 12) para 37) that the provisions of international agreements concluded by means of the procedure set out in Article 228 of the Treaty and the measures adopted by institutions set up by such agreements become an integral part of the Community legal order when they enter into force.

[62] See Opinion 1/91 (n 12) paras 37–46, and Opinion 1/92 (n 13) para 16.

[63] See Opinion 1/92 (n 13) paras 22, 32, 33.

It also follows from those Opinions that Article 164 confers on the Court an exclusive and unconditional jurisdiction of last instance to interpret and to determine the scope of application of Community law,[64] in particular the boundaries of competence between the Community and the Member States.[65] From that point of view, Article 164 can only be regarded as one of the very foundations of the Community.

In those circumstances, it is no surprise that the Court, in answering the last question submitted to it, has stated that 'Article 238 of the EEC Treaty does not provide any basis for setting up a system of courts which conflicts with Article 164 of the Treaty and, more generally, with the very foundations of the Community'.[66]

By contrast, the second part of the Court's answer, according to which, for the same reasons, an amendment to Article 238 could not cure the incompatibility with Community law of the system of courts to be set up by the agreement, cannot be so easily understood. Indeed, the Court admits, in principle, the compatibility with the Treaty of a system of courts established by an international agreement concluded by the Community, since the Community's competences in the field of international relations and its capacity to conclude international agreements necessarily entails the power to submit to the decisions of a court created or designated by such an agreement as regards the interpretation and application of its provisions.[67] Such a system of courts may indeed be considered as a 'special procedure' authorised by Article 238, first paragraph.

As a matter of fact, the relevant question seems to be a different one, not related to the possibility, or the effectiveness, of an amendment to Article 238. The explanations given in that regard by the Court in the two Opinions under analysis show that the real problem concerns mainly the nature and the scope of the provisions that the system of courts provided for in the EEA Agreement would be empowered to apply, which are mostly identical to those provisions that constitute the main object of the Court's case-law.[68]

[64] The Court sees confirmation of that exclusive jurisdiction in Article 219 of the EEC Treaty, pursuant to which the Member States undertake not to submit a dispute concerning the interpretation or application of the Treaty to any method of settlement other than those provided for in the Treaty (Opinion 1/91 (n 12) para 35).

[65] According to JHH Weiler (n 16) 2414–15, the Court was 'implicitly, but unquestionably, asserting its "*Kompetenz-Kompetenz*", its exclusive competence to determine the competence of the Community', ie 'which norms come within the sphere of application of Community law'. This had a notable expression in 314/85 *Foto-Frost* [1987] ECR 4199, where the Court reserved for itself the exclusive power to declare the invalidity of secondary Community law. See also H Rasmussen (n 16) 202.

[66] See Opinion 1/91 (n 12) paras 69–72.

[67] ibid para 40.

[68] See, in that respect, J-G Huglo, 'L'incompatibilité de l'accord sur l'Espace économique européen au regard du traité de Rome' (1992) 78/79 *Gazette du Palais* 5.

D. A New Step Towards 'Constitutionalisation'?

The fundamental question underlying the reasoning of the Court of Justice, which does not, however, find a clear and unequivocal answer in the two Opinions, is the following: when the Court considers, so radically, that the system of courts envisaged by the Draft EEA Agreement is incompatible with Article 164 of the EEC Treaty, and more generally with the very foundations of the Community, to what extent may Article 164 be amended in pursuance with the procedure laid down in Article 236 so as to permit the Agreement to enter into force without its content being modified?

A negative answer to that question would apparently be tantamount to prohibiting an amendment to Article 164 so as to render the Agreement compatible with that Article, since such an amendment would necessarily bring into question the very foundations of the Community or the autonomy of the Community legal order. In other words, the question is whether Article 164, a corner-stone of the Community judicial system and a very foundation of the Community, may normally be revised under Article 236 or whether, on the contrary, it constitutes an implied substantive limit to the revision of the Treaty.[69]

That question reminds us of the classical notions of constitutional law, where the foundations or the characteristic features of a constitution are recognised as implied substantive limits to the exercise of the amending powers.

In that context, it is difficult to interpret Opinions 1/91 and 1/92 otherwise than implying that 'Article 164 and, more generally, the very foundations of the Community' may *not* be modified in pursuance of the procedure provided for

[69] For a similar view, see J Boulouis, 'La jurisprudence de la Cour de justice des Communautés européennes relative aux relations extérieures des Communautés' (1978) *Recueil des cours de l'Académie de droit international* 355: 'Incompatibilities may also lead to a revision of the Treaty or, if that seems uncertain or too difficult, the withdrawal of the project. When, on the basis of its negative opinion, the Court relies on such fundamental grounds as "a change in the internal constitution of the Community" (Opinion 1/76) and refers to the risk of progressive and irreversible disintegration of the Community structure, the question arises whether a revision of the Treaty is still conceivable or whether the negative opinion, as a genuine veto, does not prevent both a revision of the Treaty and the entry into force of the agreement'—our translation (in the original: 'Les incompatibilités peuvent aussi conduire à une révision du traité ou, si celle-ci se révèle aléatoire ou trop malaisée, à l'abandon du projet. Lorsque, pour fonder son avis négatif, la Cour invoque des motifs aussi fondamentaux qu'une "modification de la constitution interne de la Communauté" (Opinion 1/76) et qu'elle évoque le risque de désintégration progressive et irréversible de l'œuvre communautaire, on est justifié à se demander si une révision du traité est encore envisageable ou si l'avis négatif, prenant valeur d'un véritable veto, ne fait pas échec tout autant à une révision du traité qu'à l'entrée en vigueur de l'accord'). Boulouis refers to para 12 of Opinion 1/76, of 26 April 1977, on the Draft Agreement establishing a European laying-up fund for inland waterway vessels (ECR 1977 p 741), which was also delivered in pursuance to Article 228(1), second subparagraph. The 'change in the internal constitution of the Community' was linked to 'the alteration of essential elements of the Community structure as regards both the prerogatives of the institutions and the position of Member States *vis-à-vis* one another'.

in Article 236,[70] in the same way as any other provision which has the character of a foundation of the Community can be.[71] From that point of view, what both Opinions bring out is the existence of a 'hard core' of Treaty provisions and principles that constitute a substantive limit to its amendment. Such a hard core of provisions and principles restricts the exercise of any power to amend the Treaty, which corresponds, to that extent, not to a 'constituent' but to a 'constituted power'.[72] Regarding these revision powers, the 'foundations of the Community' would thus possess in a certain way a 'supra-constitutional value'.

In such circumstances, we have reached a new and important stage in the process of constitutionalisation of the Treaty characterised by the elaboration by the Court of Justice in the performance of its duties of a constitutional nature[73] (although in somewhat sibylline terms) of a reference framework for the drawing up of implied substantive limits to the amendment of the Treaty.

[70] Interpreting the Opinions of the Court to the effect that it is impossible to amend Article 164 and thus in favour of the existence of implied limits to the revision of the Treaty, see J-G Huglo (n 68) 6 ('principes métacommunautaires auquels même une révision du traité ne pourrait porter atteinte'—'meta-Community principles which cannot be adversely affected even by a modification of the Treaty'—our translation); J Boulois, 'Les avis de la Cour de justice des Communautés sur la compatibilité avec le Traité CEE du projet d'accord créant l'Espace économique européen' (1992) *Revue trimestrielle de Droit europeen* 462 ('dispositions du traité qui ne sont pas révisables'—'provisions of the Treaty which cannot be revised'—our translation); J Dutheil de la Rochère, 'L'Espace économique européen sous le regard des juges de la Cour de justice des Communautés européennes' (1992) *Revue du Marché commun* 607 ('supra-constitutionalité communautaire'—'Community supra-constitutionality'—our translation); A Reinisch, 'Kritische Bemerkungen zum EWR-Gutachten des EuGH' (1992) *Osterreichische Juristen-Zeitung* 325, although the author criticises 'the apodictic and scarcely reasoned position of the Court of Justice' (our translation); JHH Weiler, 'Journey to an Unknown Destination: A Retrospective and Prospective View of the European Court of Justice in the Arena of Political Integration' (1993) *Journal of Common Market Studies* 418, fn 2 ('legal principles which even Treaty amendments could not violate').

[71] However, interpreting the Opinions as indicating the need for a revision of Article 164, see W Hummer, 'Vorder- und Hintergründe des des Gutachtens des EuGH zum EWRV' (1992) *Wirtschaftsrechtliche Blätter* 39; N Burrows, 'The Risks of Widening without Deepening' (1992) *European Law Review* 360 ('although the Court does not state this in so many words, in order to set up the proposed system, an amendment to Article 164 itself would be required'); T Trautwein 'Anmerkung zum Gutachten des EuGH vom 1991-12-14 1/91 zum Entwurf eines Abkommens zwischen EG und EFTA über die Schaffung des Europäischen Wirtschaftsraumes' (1992) *Zeitschrift für Rechtsverleichung internationales Privatrecht und Europarecht* 126-128 (the author admits that the Opinions are capable of two interpretations but discards any reading that might suggest the recognition of substantive limits to the modification of the Treaty). The possibility, in principle, of revising Article 164 seems also to be accepted by MA Gaudissard, 'La portée des avis 1/91 et 1/92 de la Cour de justice des Communautés européennes' (1992) *Revue du Marché unique européen* 130; D Simon and A Rigaux, 'L'avis de la Cour de justice sur le projet d'accord CEE/AELE portant création de l'Espace économique européen (EEE)' (1992) *Éditions Techniques Europe* 4.

[72] A different view, according to which the Member States would be free to amend the substance of the Treaty, provided that they followed the forms and the procedure laid down in Article 236, is expressed by J-P Jacqué (n 16) 262; T Oppermann, *Europarecht* (Munich, Beck, 1991) 164; T Trautwein (n 71).

[73] On the constitutional role of the Court of Justice, see GC Rodriguez Iglesias, 'Der Gerichtshof der Europäischen Gemeinschaft als Verfassungsgericht' (1992) *Europarecht* 225; O Due, 'A Constitutional Court for the European Communities' in D Curtin and D O'Keeffe (eds), *Constitutional Adjudication in European Community Law and National Law* (Dublin, Butterworths, 1992) 3.

The Court, having already set out the principle that the Treaty is the 'constitutional charter of a Community based on the rule of law', has this time drawn, somewhat hesitantly, legal consequences similar to those which the constitutional law of the Member States normally draws from the concept of constitution of 'un État de droit'.[74]

As Vlad Constantinesco puts it,[75]

> portraying the Treaty as a constitution in the material sense of the expression also amounts for the Court to describing itself as a constitutional court and to giving a clear indication that the Community is evolving into a novel legal order borrowing some of its structural features much more from national legal systems than from the international order, since it is above all a Community based on the rule of law.[76]

As if to corroborate the Court's line of reasoning, in a somewhat 'simultaneous and joint action' with Opinions 1/91 and 1/92, the Maastricht Treaty on European Union renders explicit a certain number of substantive limits to its own amendment. We shall proceed to consider that topic.

IV. DOES THE MAASTRICHT TREATY CONTAIN SUBSTANTIVE LIMITS TO THE AMENDMENT OF THE EU TREATY?

A. Amendment Provisions in the Maastricht Treaty

An analysis of the modifications to the European Community brought about by the Maastricht Treaty[77] might lead one *a priori* to believe that the general provisions on the procedure for amending the Treaty are substantially different from those of Article 236 of the EEC Treaty. This is not the case.

Article N(1) of the Treaty of Maastricht, which has been inserted in Title VII, Final Provisions, repeated verbatim the provisions of Article 236 of the EEC Treaty as regards the procedure for amendment. It adds, however, a paragraph 2, according to which:

> A conference of representatives of the governments of the Member States shall be convened in 1996 to examine those provisions of this Treaty for which revision is provided, in accordance with the objectives set out in Articles A and B.

[74] In this regard, see A Bleckmann, 'Komentar über Gutachten 1/92', (1993) *Juristenzeitung*, 793, who takes the view that the characterisation of the Treaty as the 'constitution of the Community' allows for a 'prudent deepening' of the analogy with the constitutions of the Member States.

[75] V Constantinesco, 'Commentaire de l'avis 1/91' (1992) *Journal du Droit international* 425.

[76] Our translation. In the original: 'caractériser le traité de constitution au sens matériel du terme est aussi pour la Cour se désigner comme juridiction constitutionnelle et marquer fortement l'évolution de la Communauté vers un ordonnancement juridique inédit qui emprunte certains de ses éléments structurels bien d'avantage aux ordres juridiques internes qu'à l'ordre international, puisqu'elle est avant tout une communauté de droit'.

[77] On those modifications, see for instance J Rideau, 'Le Traité de Maastricht du 7 février 1992 sur l'Union européenne: aspects institutionnels' (1992) *Revue des affaires européennes* 21.

That provision refers to a specific revision, the date and purpose of which have been determined in advance. That does not mean, however, that the scope of such a revision could not be extended to provisions other than those expressly mentioned.

Article N(2) applies to two categories of provisions. On the one hand, it refers to a number of provisions for which revision is expressly envisaged, such as those provisions relating to policies and forms of cooperation established by the Maastricht Treaty, in particular those of Article J.4 concerning the common foreign and security policy.

On the other hand, and more importantly, it refers to certain common provisions whose objectives must be taken into consideration. These are Article A, which refers to the European Union established by the Treaty as 'a new stage in the process of creating an ever closer union among the peoples of Europe', and Article B, which sets the objectives of the Union, namely 'to promote economic and social progress which is balanced and sustainable, in particular through the creation of an area without internal frontiers, through the strengthening of economic and social cohesion and through the establishment of economic and monetary union' and moreover 'to strengthen the protection of the rights and interests of the nationals of its Member States through the introduction of a citizenship of the Union'.

B. Preservation of the Acquis Communautaire

In that connection, the fifth indent of Article B(1) is particularly relevant since it refers expressly to the amendment of the Treaty. It sets the Union the objective

> to maintain in full the 'acquis communautaire' and build on it with a view to considering, through the procedure referred to in Article N(2), to what extent the policies and forms of cooperation introduced by this Treaty may need to be revised with the aim of ensuring the effectiveness of the mechanisms and the institutions of the Community.

This provision, whose clarity is not beyond any doubt, raises two points of the greatest importance. First, the amendment effected by virtue of Article N(2) is linked to the objective sought. In fact, the revision of the policies and forms of cooperation established in the Treaty must be regarded as instrumental and subordinate to the primary objective of 'ensuring the effectiveness of the mechanisms and institutions of the Community'. This may be understood as an express substantive limit, at least as regards the specific revision envisaged for 1996.

Moreover, the Union has been given the objective of maintaining in full and building on the '*acquis commnautaire*'. It is difficult not to perceive there to be a kind of 'prohibition of regression' or of 'principle of no return', which may also be understood as a substantive limit to the revision of the Treaty.[78]

[78] Article K.9 of the Treaty of Maastricht, together with Article B and 100C of the EC Treaty, as amended, seem to confirm that principle. Indeed, they provide for the possibility of transferring to

The question then arises of what is to be understood in this context as the '*acquis communautaire*', all the more so as this is the first time such expression has been enclosed in a European Treaty. Resorting to a classification proposed by P Pescatore, it is possible to say that this does not cover an '*ordinary acquis*' but only a '*fundamental acquis*', that is to say, a legal heritage of a constitutional ranking, composed of 'rules the disregard of which would call in question the unity, the identity and even the existence of the European undertaking'.[79] Those rules concern 'the institutional structure of the Community and its legal order as well as its economic and social condition'.[80] In other words, it is a question of 'the very foundations of the Community',[81] of both a material and a formal nature.

It does not seem questionable that the concept of 'fundamental *acquis*' covers the 'fundamental freedoms' inherent in a common market, as well as the principle of free competition. It also encompasses the principles of equal treatment of all nationals of Member States and of non-discrimination between men and women as regards conditions of work and, more generally, fundamental rights and freedoms.[82]

But the concept also comprises, in our view, the institutional balance underlying the distribution of competences and prerogatives between the Member States and the Community institutions and within each of those two groups.[83] It covers equally the principles of direct effect and primacy of Community law and the foundations of the Community judicial system, as laid down in Article 164 of the Treaty.

That being said, only the case-law of the Court of Justice can establish, in the last resort, the precise scope of those concepts.

the Community certain matters included in the field of cooperation on justice and home affairs that constitute the third pillar of the European Union. In compliance with the principle of subsidiarity, as set out in Article 3B of the EC Treaty, it seems that once transferred to the sphere of competence of the Community, those matters cannot be sent back to the intergovernmental pillar. See, in this respect, CWA Timmermans 'Communication' in J-V Louis and Peter Praet (eds) *L'Union européenne après Maastricht, Journées d'études* (Bruxelles, *Institut d'études européennes de l'Université libre de Bruxelles* 1992) 52.

[79] Our translation. In the original version, 'règles dont la méconnaissance mettrait en cause l'unité, l'identité et jusqu'à l'existence de l'entreprise européenne'.

[80] P Pescatore, 'Aspects judiciaires de l'acquis communautaire' (1981) *Revue trimestrielle de Droit europeen* 620. Our translation. In French: 'tant la structure institutionnelle de la Communauté et son ordre juridique que sa condition éconmique et sociale'.

[81] Or the 'philosophy' and the 'general principles' of the Treaty, as R Bernhardt, 'Les sources du droit communautaire: la "Constitution" de la Communauté' in *Trente ans de droit communautaire* (n 33) prefered to call them.

[82] Article F(2) of the EU Treaty codified the case-law in this matter. It provides that: 'The Union shall respect fundamental rights, as guaranteed by the European Convention for the Protection of Human Rights and Fundamental Freedoms, signed in Rome on 4 November 1950, and as they result from the constitutional traditions common to the Member States, as general principles of Community law'.

[83] In particular, no discrimination or formal differentiation between Member States or groups of Member States should be allowed except on a temporary basis and for objective reasons.

C. A New Stage in the Constitutionalisation Process

It follows from the foregoing that the EU Treaty represents a new stage in the process of constitutionalisation, related to the establishment of a reference framework for the substantive limits to its revision. Whether, and to what extent, those substantive limits may themselves be subject to revision is another question, which we will briefly address below.

In any event, the process of constitutionalisation of the Treaty, from the point of view of its revision, cannot be considered to have been closed. In fact, it is unusual for the drawing up of a constitution to resort to a diplomatic procedure, as it is, to a large extent, the case regarding the revision of the Treaty.[84] Only the gradual conversion of that procedure in a constitutional one will finally permit to achieve the complete autonomy of the Community legal order *vis-à-vis* the international legal order.

It should however be added that the difficulties which beset the expression of a common constituent will of a 'European people' shall inevitably influence such an autonomous constitutional procedure and leave on it a mark of originality, as compared with any known procedure for drafting and revising a State constitution. In particular, insofar as the European Parliament does not represent a 'European people', it cannot be granted the constituent powers that would correspond to such a status.

V. THE PRESENT STATE OF THE ISSUE OF SUBSTANTIVE LIMITS

A. Constitutional Identity and Implied Limits

The fact that the EEC Treaty did not expressly provide for any substantive limits to its revision is not surprising given that it was concluded in the form of an agreement under international law.

However, if we accept that, as the Court put it, the Treaty is the 'constitutional charter of a Community based on the rule of law', the existence of substantive limits to the revision cannot be excluded simply because the Treaty did not expressly provide for those limits to exist.

Constitutional law reminds us that a constitution may contain implied limits to its revision and, moreover, that the presence of express limits[85] in a constitution does not preclude the existence, in addition, of implied limits to the revision.

It is thus from constitutional law that we must draw the necessary inferences concerning, first, the meaning and the scope of the substantive limits to the revision of the fundamental law of a democratic State governed by the rule of law and,

[84] See J-V Louis (n 52) 113.

[85] Only five constitutions of the Member States contain such types of provision: Germany, Article 79(3); France, Article 89(5); Greece, Article 110(1); Italy, Article 139; Portugal, Article 288.

second, the status of the provisions that contain such limits.[86] In this regard, four points should be emphasised.

Firstly, the material limits do not have, and cannot have, the purpose of preventing constitutional dynamics. Their objective is solely to preserve the stability and identity of the constitution. Such identity must not be characterised by rigidity but rather by a kind of 'evolutionary autonomy within contingency'.[87]

Secondly, the notion of implied substantive limits is closely linked with the concept of constitutional identity, which may be defined as the set of essential characteristics that determine the *ethos* of the constitution, the modification of which would mean a change of identity. A provision expressly reaffirming those limits will thus be, by its nature, merely declaratory and not constitutive. The meaning of such a provision would be to reinforce the strength of those limits by clarifying and confirming them.

Thirdly, the substantive limits aim at guaranteeing certain fundamental principles irrespective of their specific constitutional configuration. They do not aim at preserving the specific formulation of each principle, still less the inviolability of the provisions relating thereto. This being a question of minimal, not maximal limits, the actual revision of these principles cannot be entirely excluded, as long as it conforms to the political and philosophical foundations of the constitution.

Fourthly, the constitutional principles relating to the revision of the constitution also represent in themselves a substantive limit to the revision, even if the constitution does not state so expressly.

As concerns the provisions on the revision of the Treaty, it must be stressed that Article N gives a specific expression to a characteristic feature of the same Treaty, which is its 'rigidity' *vis-à-vis* ordinary Community legislation, in the sense that the latter cannot be used to change the Treaty.

'Rigidity', must therefore be considered as part of the hard core of the Treaty, thus constituting a substantive limit to its revision. Consequently, it would be unlawful to make the Treaty flexible by way of a revision, ie to make it capable of amendment by ordinary Community legislation.

To that extent, Article N should be regarded as a (further) implied substantive limit to the revision of the Treaty, but this should not prevent the possibility of revising the formal and procedural limits which it expressly lays down. In this regard, the only issue which might prove problematic would be an amendment of

[86] On the substantive limits to the revision of a constitution, see P Kirchhof, 'Die Identität der Verfassung in ihren unabänderlichen Inhalten' in J Isense and P Kirchhof (eds), *Handbuch des Staatsrechts I* (Heidelberg, CF Müller, 1987) 775; J Miranda, 'Sobre os Limites Materiais da Revisão Constitucional' (1990) *Revista Jurídica* 7; JJ Gomes Canotilho and V Moreira, 'Fundamentos da Constituição' (Coimbra, Coimbra Editora, 1991) 293.

[87] That expression was proposed by J Baptista Machado, 'Participação e Descentralização, Democratização e Neutralidade na Constituição de 76' (Coimbra, Almedina, 1982) 24. P Kirchof (n 86) 802, has recourse in this context to the subtle comparison with a tree 'whose roots remain immobile, whose branches resist the fury of the wind when it rages in their direction but not in the opposite direction, and which regularly renews its substance with foliage whilst keeping the same general appearance'.

Article N which would prevent the Community institutions from taking part in the procedure for revision of the Treaty.

B. The Prohibition of Regression and its Meaning

The fact that, as already stated,[88] the EU Treaty contains a prohibition of undertaking revisions leading to a move backwards in the achievement of the common market does not mean that, following a formal Treaty revision, the Community could not be deprived of certain powers which have been conferred on it or that the matters to which those powers relate could not be restored to the sphere of competence of the Member States alone.[89]

Indeed, the prohibition of regression, as an implied substantive limit to revision, seems to apply only to the establishment and the operation of the common market, based on the four freedoms having the status of fundamental rights.[90] Such principle can, in particular, not be applied to the powers which have been conferred upon the Community by means of Article 235 of the EC Treaty and which are not directly connected with the common market.

In that regard, one should emphasise the roles that the principle of subsidiarity, on the one hand, and the duty of sincere cooperation, on the other hand, are called upon to play when it comes to conferring new powers on the Community or to define the limits that constrain the exercise of the powers conferred upon the Community institutions or that are otherwise kept within the sphere of the Member States.

The former (principle of subsidiarity), set out in Article 5 EC, works not only as a guide as to how powers have to be exercised at the Community level, but also as a political principle governing the actual conferral of powers on the Community.

The latter (duty of sincere cooperation), enshrined in Article 10 EC, aims at ensuring fulfilment of the obligations arising out of the Treaties for both the Community and the Member States and at facilitating the achievement of the Community tasks. In particular, the Member States shall 'refrain from any measure which could jeopardise the attainment of the Community's objectives', thus implying to accept limits to the exercise of their prerogatives.[91]

[88] See section IV. B.

[89] See, in this respect, J-P Jacqué (n 16) 306. See also the judgment of the Court of Justice in Case 7/71 *Commission v France* [1971] ECR 1018 para. 20, where it is stated that powers transferred from the States to the Community 'could not [...] be withdrawn from the Community, nor could the objectives with which such powers are concerned be restored to the field of authority of the Member States alone, except by virtue of an express provision of the Treaty'.

[90] See section II. D. See also IV. B on the notion of 'fundamental acquis'.

[91] See, in this regard, V Constantinesco, 'L'article 5 CEE, de la bonne foi à la loyauté communautaire' in *Liber Amicorum Pierre Pescatore* (Baden-Baden, Nomos, 1987)112 ff; A Bleckman, 'Artikle 235' in H Groeben et al (n 43) 120.

In this context, from the point of view of Community law, there seems to be no reason why a revision pursuant to Article N should not result in widening the objectives of the Treaty or of the powers of the Community and its institutions.

C. The Constitutional Laws of the Member States

Nevertheless, the constitutional laws of the Member States may, as a consequence of the limits they impose on the transfer of sovereignty to supranational organisations, raise obstacles to an amendment of the Treaty that may lead to any unrestricted widening of powers of the Community.

In fact, the constitutional laws of the Member States have been conceived as allowing only specifically determined integration projects and transfers of sovereignty restricted to certain fields. As it generally stands, national constitutional law seems to prohibit the Member States from joining supranational organisations endowed with undetermined or unlimited powers.[92]

From that point of view, the principle of conferral, as a characteristic feature of the Community, must be regarded as another substantive limit to the revision of the Treaty. It is thus for the Member States to ensure respect of that principle in the framework of the ratification procedure provided for in the third subparagraph of Article N(1).[93]

It must be added, in this regard, that any amendment to the constitutions of the Member States with the purpose of allowing some modification to the identity of the Community in regards to its powers and competences, as well as the position of the Member States *vis-à-vis* one another, would come up against the substantive limits which those constitutions may lay down to their own revision. Whilst it is true that, 'as the Court of Justice has consistently held, the Community Treaties established a new legal order to the benefit of which the States have limited their

[92] See, in this regard, C Tomuschat, 'Die Rechtsetzungsbefugnisse der EWG in Generalermächtigungen, insbesondere in Art. 235 EWG' (1986) *Europarecht* 61.

[93] It is worth citing, in this regard, Article 88-1 of the French Constitution, as amended by Constitutional Law No 92/554 of 25 June 1992: 'Sous réserve de réciprocité, et selon les modalities prévues par le traité sur l'Union européenne signé le 7 février 1992, la France consent aux transferts de compétence nécessaires à l'établissement de l'Union économique et monétaire européenne ainsi qu'à la détermination des règles relatives au franchissement des frontières extérieures des États membres de la Communauté européenne' ('Subject to reciprocity and in accordance with the procedures envisaged by the Treaty on European Union signed on 7 February 1992, France consents to the transfer of the powers necessary for the establishment of the European Economic and Monetary Union and for the determination of rules relating to the crossing of the external frontiers of the Member States of the European Community'—our translation). The *Bundesverfassungsgericht* also expressed its views in this regard: 'Since the peoples of the States constitute [...] the source of democratic legitimation through the intermediary of the national parliaments, the democratic principle set limits to the extension of the Community's powers and competences' (judgment of 12 October 1993, in *Europäische Grundrechte*, 49 ff, especially C, I and II).

sovereign rights in ever wider fields',[94] such limits may nevertheless encounter clear 'counter-limits' in the constitutional law of the Member States.

D. Constitutional and Legal Difficulties

We cannot ignore other constitutional and legal difficulties that may arise in connection with the acceptance of implied substantive limits to the revision of the Treaties. Such difficulties relate, in particular, to the absence of objective legal criteria allowing for a clear definition of those limits, thus ensuring effective judicial review in case of infringement.

Those difficulties can however not justify claims that the existence of implied substantive limits is a theoretical impossibility. The idea that such limits cannot exist is based mainly on arguments relating to the stubborn opposition of Member States,[95] to the exceptional nature of limits of this kind in the constitutions of the Member States or to the unproved assertion that, in the current state of European integration, the Member States are, collectively, still the 'masters of the Treaties'. Therefore, as long as they comply with the form and the procedure set out in Article N, the Member States would be entirely free to change the substance of the Treaty.[96]

That idea disregards the obvious fact that the Treaty not only creates rights and obligations for the Member States but also confers individual rights on their nationals, such as those relating to free movement of persons, goods and services and freedom of establishment. Therefore, the Treaty is not, and neither could it be, wholly at the disposal of the Member States, no more so than the rights enshrined in their constitutions as States based on the rule of law. The extent of this 'non-disposability' is determined precisely by the scope of the material limits to the revision of the Treaty.

Ultimately, to argue against that would correspond to overlooking the fact that

> the structure of integration, in so far as it includes individuals, has been erected with a sturdy legislative hierarchy, a system of conferred powers and, finally, a Court which guarantees respect for this structure based on the rule of law.[97]

Of course, we cannot ignore that, after all, a unanimous decision of the Member States would meet, *de facto*, the conditions for bringing the European Community

[94] See Opinion 1/91 (n 12) para 21.

[95] See, in this connection, C-D Ehlermann, 'Mitgliedschaft in der Europaïschen Gemeinschaft—Rechtsprobleme der Erweiterung, der Mitgliedschaft und der Verkleirung' (1984) *Europarecht* 123, according to whom to circumscribe the freedom to amend the Treaties by setting unwritten material limits would be tantamount to inviting the Member States to rely on ordinary public international law concepts in order to circumvent those limits by a consensus arrived at outside the boundaries of Community law.

[96] See J-P Jacqué (n 16) 262; T Oppermann (n 72) 164; T Trautwein (n 71) 127.

[97] C Tomuschat (n 92) 55. Our translation.

and its legal order to an end or for radically changing its nature. Nor can we deny that a Member State might denounce the Treaty unilaterally and withdraw from the Community, much to the detriment of Community law, notwithstanding the fact that the degree of integration already attained would place major difficulties in the path of any attempt to reconstitute the economic frontiers that have been eliminated.

Such a political move would however be incapable, on its own, of conferring legal validity on the termination of the Community or on a radical change of its identity. To argue along such lines on the basis of the will of the Member States would amount to confusing might and right. As Rudolf Bernhardt put it, such a decision by the Member States 'would certainly be a revolutionary act not based on prevailing law'.[98]

Furthermore, the fact that the Community does not meet the conditions for thwarting any such measure on the part of the Member States would not suffice to validate it *de jure*. Similarly, the States themselves are not always in a position to avoid a revolution and their constitutions cannot, at the last resort, prevent their own violation: they can only deny any semblance of legality to such a violation.

Finally, the fact that, for the abovementioned reasons, the Member States can no longer entirely dispose of the Treaties shows that, from that specific point of view, the Community is approaching a situation similar to that of a State governed by the rule of law, where such a situation does not need to be raised or, if raised, cannot have any other answer but that 'no-one is the master of the constitution'. Only if this state of affairs continues shall we still be able to speak of a Community based on the rule of law.

E. Who are the 'Masters of the Treaties'?

The final destination of European integration is not defined once and for all in the EU Treaty. It is for future generations to decide, at each moment, which steps to take and which advances to accept. What matters in this regard is to ensure that appropriate mechanisms of democratic expression of the general will are available at any time. If that is the case, answering the question of whether the Member States are still the 'masters of the Treaties' loses much of its apparent dramatisation.

It is in this context that the fundamental question of whether the legality of Treaty amendments, carried out by means of a protocol or otherwise, may be reviewed by the Court of Justice on grounds that they allegedly breach any substantive limit to the revision of the Treaty, which must be examined. As a matter of fact, unlike the constitutions of certain Member States regarding their

[98] R Bernhardt (n 81), 81. Our translation. In the original: 'serait assurément un acte révolutionnaire qui ne se fonderait pas sur le droit en vigueur'.

constitutional courts,[99] neither the original Treaties nor the EU Treaty explicitly entrust the Court of Justice with powers to carry out judicial review of a Treaty amendment.

Nevertheless, it ought to be possible for the Court to decide, in its capacity as a constitutional court, on the compatibility of any Treaty modification with the fundamental *acquis communautaire*, which all the Community institutions are required to respect. As recourse to Article 173 of the EEC Treaty is foreclosed in this area[100] and Article 169 does not seem a suitable procedural means, the only approach available would be based on Article 177, by way of a request for preliminary ruling for interpretation of the amending provisions so as to ensure, to the extent possible, their conformity with the fundamental *acquis*.

In this connection, it is worth recalling the observations made by Deirdre Curtin:

> This kind of discussion immediately raises questions in many people's minds about the legitimacy of what can be effectively characterized as '*gouvernement des juges*', or the 'undemocratic nature' of judge-made higher law. But in a context where we are talking about a Community Treaty amendment process characterized by a singular lack of transparency and real 'democratic' choice, then it is suggested that the guarantee of judicial control by a Court concerned to protect the rights of individuals and their fundamental freedoms may be essential to fulfil the characterization of the EC Treaty as 'a constitutional charter based on the rule of law'.[101]

An important issue in this context is to what extent the establishment and the definition of substantive limits by the constitutions of the Member States may influence the definition of limits to the revision of the 'constitution' of the Community.

On that point, we submit that the interaction between the two levels is perfectly normal and desirable. Since the Community has always been based on the existence of sovereign States, which decided to pool part of their sovereignty with the purpose of attaining common objectives, it is quite normal that each State wish to ensure that the structure and working principles of the supranational Community that those States decided to create correspond to the basic principles underlying their own legal and social orders. That should not raise any serious problems in a Community whose constituent parts share essentially identical values and in which several decades have enabled those concepts to be brought closer still as far as their essential core is concerned.

[99] The *Bundesverfassungsgericht* decided on several occasions on the compatibility of constitutional amendments with the substantive limits to the revision of the *Grundgesetz*, as provided for by Article 79(3). See judgments of 15 December 1970, BVerfGE 30, p 1; of 26 July 1972, BVerfGE, 34, p 9; and of 23 April 1991, BVerfGE, 57, p 20.

[100] See Order of the CFI T-584/93 *Roujansky* [1994] ECR II-587 (Summary) para 15, where that Court held that it had no jurisdiction to decide on the legality of any provision of the EU Treaty by way of an application for annulment under Article 173.

[101] D Curtin, 'The Constitutional Structure of the Union: A Europe of Bits and Pieces' (1993) *Common Market Law Review* 65.

From that point of view, it may properly be considered that a substantial part of the constitutional core of the Community ultimately coincides with the fundamental principles shared, to a greater or a lesser degree, by the various national constitutional orders, and that therefore the substantive limits to be preserved in the Community legal order simply derive from the transposition into the Community level of those, identical or similar in nature, which are laid down by the national constitutions.

An example may be given: when the German Constitutional Court examined the compatibility of the law ratifying the EU Treaty with the democratic principle enshrined in Article 38 of the *Grundgesetz* and required that legitimisation by both the national parliaments and the European Parliament be secured, that Court did no more than to reflect that convergence of principles. In that respect, it is not easy to answer the question of to what extent, in so doing, the *Bundesverfassungsgericht* was still ensuring the observance of a national constitutional principle or already in the process of examining compliance with a democratic principle, which is itself a constitutional principle of the European Union.

Ultimately, that convergence is the expression of the creative cooperation between the national supreme and constitutional courts and the Community courts, which complement one another in ensuring the protection of fundamental rights.[102]

[102] The main propositions contained in this chapter as it was first published in 1993 and 1995 appear to have been upheld by the Court in its Opinion 1/2009, of 8 March 2011, [2011] ECR I-1137, on the compatibility with the EC Treaty of a draft agreement creating a unified patent litigation system. In that Opinion, the Court emphasised, on the one hand, the significance of the essential characteristics of the EU legal order and the fundamental elements of the judicial system designed by the founding Treaties and, on the other hand, the importance of the Court of Justice and the courts and tribunals of the Member States as the guardians of that legal order and judicial system and, in particular, of the role of the Court of Justice in ensuring respect for the autonomy of such legal order (Opinion 1/2009, paras 64–67). After stating that the European and Community Patents Court, whose creation was envisaged by the Draft Agreement and which was to be vested with exclusive jurisdiction in respect of a significant number of actions brought by individuals in the field of patents, to the detriment of the courts of Member States (Opinion, para 72), is outside the institutional and judicial framework of the European Union and is not part of the judicial system provided for in Article 19(1) TEU (Opinion, para 71), the Court recalled that while an international agreement concluded with third countries may confer new judicial powers on the Court of Justice or even affect its own powers, it must not change the essential character of the function of the Court or produce adverse effects on the autonomy of the EU legal order (Opinion, paras 75–76). The Court then took the view that since the tasks attributed to the national courts and to the Court of Justice respectively are indispensable to the preservation of the very nature of the law established by the Treaties, any solution that would deprive the courts of the Member States of their powers in relation to the interpretation and application of EU law and the Court of its powers to reply, by preliminary ruling, to questions referred by those courts would alter the essential character of the powers which the Treaties confer on the EU institutions and on the Member States and which are indispensable to the preservation of the very nature of EU law (Opinion, paras 85, 89). It follows necessarily from that that the EU Treaties are irremediably incompatible with an international agreement that would set up a parallel judicial structure, which would reduce the courts of the Member States to a residual role as regards the interpretation and application of EU law. On the significance of Opinion 1/2009 in this context, see Nuno Piçarra, 'Três Notas sobre a Identidade do Sistema Jurisdicional da União Europeia' in J Miranda et al (eds) *Estudos em Homenagem a Miguel Galvão Teles I* (Lisboa, Almedina, 2012) 767–89.

3

*Reflections on Judicial Review of the Constitutionality of EU Legislation**

I. THE COURT OF JUSTICE AS A CONSTITUTIONAL COURT

THERE CAN BE no democratic constitution without a mechanism for judicial review of the constitutionality of the laws and other acts adopted by public authorities, ie a mechanism that ensures that all such acts are compatible with the constitutional provisions.

That function is the defining characteristic of any constitutional court. According to Ole Due, former President of the Court of Justice,[1] 'a minimal condition for qualifying a judicial body as a constitutional court must be that it has jurisdiction to interpret and apply the provisions of the national Constitution or to define and apply constitutional principles where no written constitution exists'.

Advocate-General Francis Jacobs[2] has described the role of a constitutional court as generally consisting in

> judicial review of legislation to ensure its conformity with the constitution or other fundamental law; and in particular to ensure the observance of fundamental rights. More generally, it may also adjudicate in disputes over the respective powers of the organs of the State. Where, as in a federal system, power is divided between central authorities and those of the component States or regions, the respective limits to the powers of those authorities will also be considered a constitutional issue.

In a number of constitutional systems those tasks are not entrusted to a specialised court.[3] By contrast, such a specialised constitutional court has been set up

* A French version of this article was published under the title 'Le contrôle juridictionnel de la constitutionnalité: quelques réflexions' in L Serena Rossi (ed), *Vers une nouvelle architecture de l'Union européenne* (Brussels, Bruylant, 2004).

[1] O Due, 'A Constitutional Court for the European Communities' in D Curtin and O'Keeffe (eds), *Constitutional Adjudication in European Community and National law—Essays for the Hon. Mr Justice T. F. O'Higgins* (Dublin, Butterworths, 1992) 4.

[2] FG Jacobs, 'Is the Court of Justice of the European Community a Constitutional Court?', ibid, 25.

[3] See, for example, the United States, where 'constitutional review' is undertaken by the US Supreme Court in the context of a federal system; or Ireland, where compliance with the State's written constitution is ensured by non-specialised courts and specific powers have been granted to the Supreme Court on constitutional matters. See also the case of the United Kingdom where the 'judiciary' is entrusted with 'constitutional' functions in the absence of a written constitution.

in several Member States of the European Community.[4] Within the Community, however, it is the Court of Justice that has always performed that role.

One may certainly wonder whether it is appropriate to talk of a constitutional court in the absence of a 'constitution', in the formal sense, particularly when it comes to a legal order which transcends the limits of the constitutional framework of the Nation State.

In fact, some believe that a treaty, which is a legal instrument characteristic of public international law, is not a suitable vehicle for the genesis of a constitution; for others, the notions of constitution and State are inextricably linked; still others consider that the Community legal order does not meet all of the substantive requirements inherent in the concept of a constitution; finally, it can be argued that a 'constitutional subject' or a 'European nation' that could provide a sociological basis for a European constitution is still missing in the Community legal area.

None of those objections appears to be conclusive or insurmountable and, in any event, they appear irrelevant for the purposes of the present analysis.[5]

To begin with, I submit that there is no reason why a constitution could not be created by means of a treaty. Modern constitutions have been enacted according to a variety of procedures: approved by a popular convention or a constituent assembly, by referendum or by plebiscite; granted by an absolute monarch or adopted unilaterally by the sole political party in a one-party system; imposed by victors in war, sometimes by means of 'quasi-judicial' procedures. Should the above arguments be given any credence, it would mean denying constitutional status to the Constitution of the United States, which was established by a treaty (or a 'convention') signed between former colonies reconstituted as states and which went on to be the successful constitution of the world's most powerful federal State.

Secondly, the association between the Nation State and the concept of a Constitution is an historical phenomenon which is not rooted in any rule of natural law. The movement towards globalisation has in fact made it necessary, in many respects, to set aside the notion that the exercise of power and the adoption of legislation are the exclusive preserve of States. Constitutional law is no exception to that evolution.

Thirdly, the essential features of a constitution are already present in the Treaties, in particular in the Treaty establishing the European Community and the Treaty on the European Union: they spell out the fundamental tasks of the Communities and the Union; they lay down the main principles underlying the division of powers between the Community and its Member States (conferred powers, subsidiarity, proportionality); they entrust the various Community institutions with the necessary powers to pursue their tasks within a framework

[4] This is the case in several Member States, notably Belgium, Spain, France, Italy and Portugal.

[5] See C Closa, 'Constitution and Democracy in the Convention Draft', *CIDEL Project Citizenship and Democratic Legitimacy in Europe*, working paper presented to the seminar 'O Tratado Constitucional da União Europeia', Law Faculty of the Nova University of Lisbon, 15–26 September 2003.

of complex institutional balance; they establish the fundamental principles that govern the implementation of the Community policies (non-discrimination, the single market, freedom to pursue an economic activity, competition); they confer legislative powers on the institutions and set out the types of act that Community institutions may adopt; they establish judicial remedies within the framework of a specific and autonomous judicial system; and they include rules governing the revision of their own provisions.

Finally, as constitutional law academics have stressed,[6] the occurrence of a 'constituent event' does not necessarily imply the prior existence of a well-established 'constituent subject'. The exercise of constituent power, as such, is an 'extra-legal' fact which, if successful in historical terms, will be acknowledged *a posteriori* in the new constitutional order.[7]

The Treaties establishing the European Communities did not establish a specialised constitutional court. This is not surprising given that the 'founding fathers' did not pursue an immediate and explicit constitutional aim.

Consequently, a genuine constitutional mission was inevitably conferred, explicitly or implicitly, on the Community judicial system established in the Treaties.

It was indeed unavoidable that the Court should assume that role, given the broad scope of its jurisdiction as laid down in Article 164 EEC (now Art 220 EC): 'The Court of Justice shall ensure that in the interpretation and application of this Treaty the law is observed.' Such a wide definition of the Court's jurisdiction makes it impossible to identify any specific, substantive criterion capable of distinguishing certain matters of a constitutional nature from other issues arising under Community law.

The Court has willingly taken up its constitutional role, adopting a 'federal' perspective and relying on its own interpretation of its powers and responsibilities. On the one hand, it has pushed close to their outer limits the scope of the judicial remedies provided for by the Treaties, in order to better review the conformity of the acts of the institutions and of Member States with those Treaties, guided by the need to ensure that they are interpreted in accordance with commonly-accepted general principles of law. On the other hand, acting as the guardian of an evolving legal order, whose final aims were as yet only indistinctly defined and whose rules were often incomplete or too general in nature to be truly effective, the Court developed a method of teleological interpretation that fostered integration and strengthened the autonomy of that legal order, but which also made it vulnerable to accusations of judicial activism.

Finally, the Court has also set in train a process of gradual 'constitutionalisation' of the Treaties that has further strengthened its own role as a true constitutional court. This was achieved through an evolving process involving establishment

[6] See C Closa (n 5) 2.

[7] See also JHH Weiler, *The Constitution of Europe. Do the New Clothes Have an Emperor?* (Cambridge, Cambridge University Press, 1999) 238.

of the basic principles of direct effect and supremacy, the judicial drafting of a catalogue of fundamental rights, the definition of the principles governing the division of powers between the Community and its Member States and, finally, the recognition of formal and material limits, both explicit and implicit, to the revision of the Treaties.[8]

At the present time, when the Convention on the Future of Europe is drafting its Treaty establishing a Constitution for Europe, the remaining gaps in the constitutional organisation of the Union are beginning to be filled.[9] I submit that, at this stage, any opposition to the process of 'constitutionalisation' of the Treaties effected by the Court of Justice is increasingly moot, in formal terms at least.

II. IS THERE ANY NEED FOR A NEW CONSTITUTIONAL COURT?

The considerations set out in the previous section may provide a partial answer to the question of which court(s) or institution(s) should ultimately be entrusted with the powers necessary for ensuring that the institutions of the Union and the Member States comply with any new European constitutional treaty.

At previous intergovernmental conferences, proposals have been put forward for the establishment of new mechanisms for the constitutional review of EU legislation.

Some authors expressed a preference for leaving the review of constitutionality outside the jurisdiction of the courts and for submitting it instead to procedures of a political nature.[10] According to this line of thinking, since the Treaties, and the Court itself, have been increasingly driven to deal with political matters, notably those affecting the division of competences between the Union and the Member States, the interpretation of the relevant Treaty provisions ought not to be left to the Court—a body which, according to its detractors, is not impartial on such matters, is composed of unelected judges and holds 'unlimited' powers—but should instead be carried out under a procedure that is political in nature and is subject to the scrutiny of national parliaments.

[8] See, in that regard, the seminal works of E Stein, 'Lawyers, Judges, and the Making of a Transnational Constitution' (1981) 75 *American Journal of International Law* 1; JHH Weiler, ibid, 10; F Mancini, 'The Making of a Constitution for Europe' (1989) 26 *Common Market Law Review* 595; LS Rossi, 'La Carta dei diritti come strumento di costituzionalizzazione dell'ordinamento dell'UE' (2002) 3 *Quaderni costituzionali*, 565; K Lenaerts, 'Constitutionalism and the Many Faces of Federalism' (1990) 38 *American Journal of Comparative Law* 205; A Barav, 'The Judicial Power of the European Economic Community' (1980) 53 *Southern California Law Review* 461. See also JL da Cruz Vilaça and N Piçarra, 'Y a-t-il des limites matérielles à la révision des traités instituant les Communautés européennes?' (1993) 1 *Cahiers Dr Euro* 2.

[9] One significant gap was the absence of an explicit catalogue of fundamental rights. The adoption of the European Charter of Fundamental Rights is thus a major step forward in that regard.

[10] See in this sense, F Vibert, 'A Core Agenda for the 1996 Inter-Governmental Conference (ICG)', *European Policy Forum*, London, 1995.

I have already had the opportunity to refute that position.[11] Should such an approach be followed, it would represent an important step backwards on the road to consolidating the European Union as an entity governed by the rule of law and might even herald the dismantling of the institutional system set up by the Treaties. No complex institutional system—whether of a federal or of a supranational type—can survive without a single impartial arbitrator, empowered to establish a uniform interpretation of the rules which govern the division of powers between the federation or the Union, on the one hand, and the federal States or the Member States, on the other hand. It seems obvious that a political procedure involving national parliaments would inevitably lead to a Union or Community characterised by some form of 'variable-geometry', or even to multiple, disparate communities unable to counter the centrifugal forces of disintegration. If the rationale underlying those proposals is based simply on the undoubted need to strengthen the independence and the legitimacy of those who are entrusted with such a vital constitutional mission within the Union, then the answer should be sought elsewhere. The focus of the debate should not be the constitutional nature of the Court of Justice as such, but rather the procedures governing the nomination and appointment of its members.

Proposals have also been put forward to set up a specialised constitutional court alongside the Court of Justice. The great majority of commentators have rejected any such proposal.[12] I have also expressed criticism of that idea.[13]

To the extent that the Court of Justice already undertakes the functions of a constitutional court within the Community legal order, the need to create a new court with a similar function would only seem to be reasonably justified if the Court of Justice were no longer in a position to carry it out adequately. That is not the case, however, especially since that Court is now assisted in administrative law cases by the Court of First Instance, thus being able to focus its full resources on its core tasks of ensuring the uniform interpretation and application of Community law and of preserving the right balance between the Community institutions.

It must be said that the objections raised by some commentators, supposedly on account of a perceived lack of 'democratic legitimacy' of EU judges, actually seem to hide an ideological reluctance on their part *vis-à-vis* the 'constitutional' case-law of the Court of Justice, which they consider to be impregnated with

[11] See JL da Cruz Vilaça, 'Le système juridictionnel communautaire' in A Mattera (ed), *La Conférence intergouvernementale sur l'Union européenne: répondre aux défis du XXI siècle* (Paris, Clément Juglar, 1996) 219.

[12] See, in this context, GC Rodriguez Iglesias, 'Der Gerichtshof der Europässchen Gemeinschaft', (1992) *Europarecht* 225; O Due (n 1) 3; FG Jacobs (n 2) 25; W Van Gerven, 'The Role and Structure of the European Judiciary Now and in the Future', report presented during the *Conference on Suggestions for Revision of the Treaty on European Union* (The Hague, TMC Asser Instituut, 1995), as well as my 'Commentary' on that report.

[13] JL da Cruz Vilaça, ibid, 228.

'pro-integration' activism. It is in fact a shift in the substantive case-law that they seek to achieve through the creation of a new constitutional court.

Mention should also be made of a different and most realistic proposal, suggested by a team led by JHH Weiler, at the request of the European Parliament, with a view to the 1996 intergovernmental conference (IGC).[14]

That working Group proposed the creation of some sort of Constitutional Council of the European Community whose jurisdiction would be limited to those issues affecting the division of competences between the Community and its Member States (including the principle of subsidiarity) and which would adjudicate on the 'constitutional' conformity of Community acts at the stage when they are already approved but are yet to enter into force. A ruling by the Constitutional Council could be requested by the Commission, the Council, a Member State or the European Parliament, acting on a decision of the majority of its members.[15] The Constitutional Council would be headed by the President of the Court of Justice and composed of members selected from the constitutional courts, or equivalent bodies, of Member States.

According to the authors of this proposal, it would, if adopted, on the one hand, discharge the Court of Justice of a politically sensitive task, thereby reducing the political sensitivity of any *ex post* interpretation undertaken by the Court. On the other hand, it would ensure that one single Community law body was charged with enforcing *ex ante* compliance of Community acts with the legal principles governing the division of powers between the Community and the Member States, while at the same time reassuring the sceptics through the involvement of judges from national constitutional courts.[16]

The innovative character of that proposal on a matter as politically sensitive as this does not make it easy to accept. A number of difficulties might arise, notably in relation to the achievement of consistency between the *ex ante* case-law of that new body and the *ex post* case-law of the Court of Justice and objections that could be raised as to the preservation of the judicial autonomy of the latter. Regardless of those considerations, the proposal shared the same fate as the others, and was adopted neither by the 1996 IGC, nor at Nice, nor by the constitutional Convention.

In any event, it should be observed that the Court is already experienced in the review of constitutionality, so that the establishment of any new institution with the same remit would be pointless.

In the light of the Court's case-law, I would venture to suggest that it has adapted in a near-perfect manner to the constitutional role that it has been called upon to play. And if I use the qualifier 'near', it is merely because the authors of

[14] JHH Weiler, A Balmann, U Haltern, H Hofman and F Mayer, 'Certain Rectangular Problems of European Integration', Project IV/95/02, *Directorate General for Research*, European Parliament.

[15] Perhaps also by the parliaments of Member States.

[16] It is interesting to note that this mode of composition was chosen for the Benelux Court of Justice whose members are also judges of the Supreme Courts of the three Member States of the Benelux.

the Treaty did not conceive the Community judicial institution as a true constitutional Court, in a legal order whose autonomy remained to be established.

As a consequence, the constitutional case-law of the Court has evolved in spite of the Treaties' silence, using concepts and legal remedies not designed specifically for constitutional purposes.

Therefore, the action for annulment (Article 173 of the EC Treaty, now Article 230 EC), which was primarily designed to carry out judicial review in administrative matters, served as a tool in the hands of the Court to deal with constitutional issues raised notably in the context of inter-institutional disputes, particularly as regards the legal basis for the adoption of a Community act or the division of powers between the institutions. Similarly, the Court issued a number of judgments of constitutional significance on actions for infringement of Community law by a Member State (Article 169 of the EC Treaty, now Article 226 EC). Nevertheless, it is the preliminary ruling procedure on the interpretation or on the validity of Community law that has become the principal procedural means for effecting constitutional control. Since it requires the intervention of national courts, under the guidance of the Court of Justice, that mechanism has developed into a tool of decentralised judicial review as to the compatibility of secondary Community legislation and of national law with the Treaty.

III. THE NEW INSTITUTIONAL CONTEXT

The question that should now be asked is whether the draft Constitutional Treaty will radically change the legal framework in which the Court performs its constitutional task. Under the draft constitution, the political structure and the institutional machinery of the Union are structured in a more transparent and consistent way. The federal purpose of the Union is not, however, strongly affirmed. Similarly, the critical step of converting the judicial system of the Union into a true federal judiciary has not yet been taken. National courts—rather than new Union courts[17]—are set to remain the principal judicial bodies empowered to apply Union law. Moreover, the Court of Justice does not have hierarchical

[17] For example, regional Community courts, a possibility put forward by Weiler and Jacqué a few years ago. Notwithstanding the difficulties that the establishment and organisation of such courts would create, it cannot be excluded that such a reform will later become necessary by reason of the Union's enlargement and the increasing obstacles that the Union will face in ensuring a uniform application of Union law throughout the whole of its territory. Alternatively, the setting up of information offices or helpdesks on Union law matters—with a Union nature and structure but which would operate within each Member State's judicial system—might provide a temporary solution and help to fill the significant organisational and informational gaps that, in certain Member States, still impede the full effectiveness of Union law. The latter solution was proposed in the Report of the Working Party on the Future of the European Communities' Court System (Brussels, January 2000, available at: http://ec.europa.eu/dgs/legal_service/pdf/due_en.pdf), chaired by the former President of the Court O Due, as well as at a number of academic conferences.

authority over them and the relationship is still conceived in terms of judicial cooperation, achieved through the preliminary ruling mechanism.

It is submitted that the option that has been chosen is clearly the most appropriate one taking into consideration, on the one hand, the current state of the institutional development of the Union and, on the other hand, the proven efficacy of the preliminary ruling mechanism in ensuring the uniform application of Community law. Nevertheless, it is clear that, despite its success, the preliminary ruling mechanism needs to be refined, especially in view of the forthcoming enlargement of the Union to 25, or more, Member States. The Constitutional Treaty does not provide for any such improvement but neither does it exclude the possibility of adapting that mechanism in the future.

Moreover, the new judicial architecture of the Union—comprising, since the Treaty of Nice, the so-called judicial panels that may be set up to hear and determine at first instance certain classes of actions or proceedings in specific areas, as well as mechanisms of referral and of exceptional review of decisions by the 'General Court' should jurisdiction be conferred on that court to rule on certain subject matters in the context of preliminary rulings[18]—reinforces the role of the Court of Justice as the supreme and constitutional court of the Union, the ultimate guarantor of uniformity in the application of Community law, in particular as regards those legal questions that are of crucial importance for the Community legal order.[19]

However, no new judicial remedy has been set up specifically for the protection of fundamental rights within the Community legal order in cases where the existing judicial remedies do not offer sufficiently effective protection. Such a judicial remedy could have been established in conjunction with a filtering mechanism requiring, for example, prior submission of a complaint to the European Ombudsman.

The fact that the criteria for admissibility of actions brought by individuals against regulatory acts will apparently be less stringent in the new constitutional text[20] does reduce the deficit in judicial protection present in the current system.[21]

[18] Or on an appeal brought against the decisions of the judicial panels. Details regarding the conditions under which such exceptional review or reappraisal proceedings might be filed shall be laid down in the Statute of the Court of Justice. Their implementation will at times entail delicate technical choices and possibly the establishment of new and innovative mechanisms, eg appeals 'in the interest of the law' (*pourvois dans l'intérêt de la loi*). Such mechanisms would be needed, in essence, to ensure the coherence of the case-law and the uniform application of Union law.

[19] See K Lenaerts, D Arts and I Maselis, *Procedural Law of the European Union*, R Bray (ed), 2nd edn (London, Sweet & Maxwell, 2006) 22–28.

[20] The change may simply consist in no longer requiring, in the context of appeals brought against regulatory acts, that the applicant shows that he is 'individually concerned', but only that he is 'directly concerned'.

[21] However, the proposed text maintains the current ambiguity as to the admissibility of an action for failure to act whose objective is to obtain the adoption of an act that is not addressed to the plaintiff but that may concern him (individually and/or directly).

However, it will only be possible to assess the effectiveness and completeness of the new rules when they come to be applied in practice.

It would have been possible to create a system whereby the compatibility of new legislation with the Constitution would have been appraised by the Court before its entry into force, perhaps taking as a model the procedure for obtaining an opinion of the Court of Justice as to whether an international agreement envisaged is compatible with the Treaties (provided for in Article 300(6) EC and which is likely to be retained in the constitutional text).[22] Such a system could have contributed, as it does in several of the Member States, to removing uncertainties as to the constitutionality of normative provisions of the Union in advance, before they become legally binding. Legal certainty within the Union would thus have been strengthened and unnecessary litigation avoided.

It is true that an early warning mechanism concerning compliance with the principle of subsidiarity is contemplated, but only national parliaments may invoke it (as well as the principle of proportionality) before the institutions involved in the legislative procedure. It appears that the Court of Justice may only become involved by means of an action for annulment after the act has already been adopted.[23] Apart from that action (used in combination, where necessary, with a plea of illegality under Article 241 EC), the review of the constitutionality of Union legislation will continue to be undertaken through the preliminary ruling procedure with national courts raising questions as to the validity of acts of the EU institutions.

It follows that the constitutional review of acts of the Union will continue to rely to a great extent upon a system of private enforcement, which depends on the bringing of actions by individuals at national level and thus, to a considerable degree, on the ability of national courts to respond and on their willingness to apply the law of the Union.

The institutions of the Union and the constitutional authorities of the Member States will not therefore have specific judicial mechanisms at their disposal[24] in order to trigger, in a quick, efficient and flexible way, a ruling by the Court of Justice as a constitutional court.

It has undoubtedly been by means of preliminary rulings that the Court of Justice has developed the bulk of its constitutional case-law. Nevertheless, that route has its limitations and, once again, the efficacy of such a decentralised mechanism depends on how both individuals and national courts decide to use it.[25]

[22] See Article III-222.

[23] See the Protocol on the application of the principles of subsidiarity and proportionality, point 7.

[24] The action for annulment and the action for failure to act are forms of action that were not specifically designed for the constitutional review of legislation.

[25] It is of the utmost importance that investments are made in education and continuous training as regards EU law in every Member State in order to improve the functioning of the preliminary ruling procedure and to enhance the role of national courts in ensuring the uniform application of European Union law.

Finally, compliance with the European Constitution by Member States may also be secured through the action for infringement of EU law (it is also envisaged that the European Investment Bank Board and the European Central Bank Council shall have power to bring such actions under certain conditions and in relation to specific matters),[26] together with the preliminary ruling procedure for the interpretation of EU law, the latter by reason of the *erga omnes* effects that the Court's case-law has conferred on such rulings.

IV. WHAT STRUCTURE SHOULD THE CONSTITUTIONAL COURT HAVE?

The composition and the organisation of the Court should, in any case, be adapted to enable it to better fulfil its constitutional role.

First of all, a Court composed of as many judges as the number of Member States (soon to be 25 and yet more in the future) is not well suited to carry out the tasks of a constitutional court.

A constitutional chamber should therefore be set up within the Court, whose role should be defined in a clear and predictable manner, in accordance with the principle of the 'legal judge', and whose composition should ensure the presence of judges representing the different legal traditions and national legal orders on the basis of an equal system of rotation. In addition, provision should be made to ensure the presence of the judge from the national legal order involved in the case at hand so that the Court is able to understand fully all the legal implications of the case and in order to increase the chances that its decision gains acceptance within the national order concerned.

Secondly, with regard to the rules applicable to the appointment of the members of the Court of Justice and of the General Court, the constitutional draft follows the solution advocated by the Due Group of making the appointment of new members subject to a prior opinion of a selection committee of independent lawyers on the suitability of the candidates to perform the duties of Judge or Advocate General.

I consider this a positive move as it should ensure that the members of the two main Union courts are truly chosen among those having the requisite experience and independence, as well as the necessary legal and personal qualities, required to perform the highest judicial functions in the European Union. Ill-considered decisions or nominations motivated by criteria other than those pertaining to the higher interest of the Union should thus be avoided. In my view, this is a better solution than one conferring a direct role on the European Parliament (however, it is envisaged that one member of the Committee should be proposed by the Parliament) or, alternatively, one involving the adoption of a uniform selection

[26] The action for infringement of EU law may also be brought by one Member State against another. The Draft Constitution maintains that possibility in spite of having been rarely used thus far.

procedure at national level (each Member State has its own established procedures and constitutional traditions).

Nevertheless, I am of the view that, if only for symbolic reasons, it would be preferable to spell out in the constitutional text, rather than simply in the Statute, the rules governing security of tenure and immunity of the members of both Courts.

As regards the duration of the mandates of judges at the Court of Justice[27] (currently appointed for a term of six years, with the possibility of reappointment), I would personally be in favour of a single non-renewable term of office with a longer duration (eg nine years). I believe that this change would enhance judicial independence and ensure a regular renewal of the Court's membership without, however, jeopardising the necessary continuity.

Lastly, it seems to me that the proposed changes to the names of the Union courts seem appropriate to their respective roles and functions. In particular, it is widely recognised that the Court of First Instance should be considered as the administrative court having general jurisdiction within the Union.

V. CONCLUSION

A new chapter in the constitutional history of the Community judiciary is set to begin. In my view, this certainly does not mean that the past will be discarded. Indeed, there is clearly no intention that the EU judiciary should break with its history and existing case-law. The precedents set in decided cases will therefore continue to provide guidance and to serve as a source of inspiration to the Court.

Nevertheless, the significantly different institutional context that is likely to emerge will still require appropriate adjustments in the structure and the functioning of the courts of the Union. It will, in any case, be extremely interesting to watch how the Court of Justice performs its role as supreme and constitutional court within the framework of a true Constitution of the European Union.

[27] The reappointment of Judges of the General Court does not give rise to the same objections since it is not a constitutional court. Similarly, the office of Advocate General does not necessarily need to be subject to the same constraints since the Advocates General express a personal opinion and do not take part directly in the actual decision of the Court.

Part II

The EU Judicial Architecture

4

The Setting Up of a New Community Court—The First Year of the Court of First Instance[*]

I. INTRODUCTION

A. A New Court for the Community

THE COURT OF First Instance (hereinafter the 'CFI') was established by a Council Decision of 24 October 1988 (hereinafter, the 'Council Decision'),[1] in order to 'improve the judicial protection of individual interests', notably 'in respect of actions requiring close examination of complex facts', and 'to enable the Court of Justice to concentrate its activities on its fundamental task of ensuring uniform interpretation of Community law'.[2]

Less than a year and a half has elapsed since the setting up of the CFI, in September 1989. This is still too short a period of time for a comprehensive assessment of the new court to be undertaken. Nevertheless, given the uniqueness of this project from the point of view of the Community judicial order and its importance for the future it is worth providing a first account, at this early stage, of the CFI's first steps.

As a matter of fact, the last time a Community court was set up was in 1957, 33 years ago, when the Court of the European Coal and Steel Community (hereinafter the 'ECSC') became the new Court of Justice of the European Communities (hereinafter also the 'Court'). However, that change did not involve the creation of a new entity from scratch, but rather the transformation of an existing one, following the creation of the two new Communities (the EEC and EURATOM),

[*] This article was first published in French under the title 'Le démarrage d'une nouvelle jurisdiction communautaire—Le Tribunal de première instance un an après' in *L'Europe et le Droit, Mélanges en hommage à Jean Boulouis* (Paris, Dalloz, 1991) 47–74.

The author acknowledges the assistance of his legal secretary LM Pais Antunes in the preparation of the original version of this chapter.

[1] Council Decision of 24 October 1988 establishing a Court of First Instance of the European Communities (88/591/ECSC, EEC, Euratom) [1998] OJ L319/1 and Corrigendum [1999] OJ L241/4.

[2] ibid, third and fourth recitals.

which made necessary the re-establishment of the Court as a single judicial organ for all three Communities.

By contrast, the establishment of the CFI was, by its very nature, a new departure within the institutional framework of the Community judicial system.

B. The Establishment of the CFI

Following on from the Single European Act (hereinafter the 'SEA'), the establishment of the CFI did not create a new 'institution' in addition to those already mentioned in Article 4 of the EEC Treaty, charged with carrying out 'the tasks entrusted to the Community'. Rather, it introduced a new, independent judicial body within the existing judicial institution that was—and continues to be—known as the Court of Justice.

The SEA achieved that objective in its Articles 4, 11 and 26,[3] each of which inserted the following text into the founding Treaty of one of the three Communities:

> At the request of the Court of Justice and after consulting the Commission and the European Parliament, the Council may, acting unanimously, attach to the Court of Justice a court with jurisdiction to hear and determine at first instance [...] certain classes of action.

The Council Decision implemented this major reform in the Community judicial system when it determined that a court of first instance would be 'attached' to the Court of Justice.

From a single, unitary institution comprising just one court, the Court of Justice became a more complex one, comprising two independent judicial bodies linked by a hierarchical relationship, in jurisdictional terms.

Wisely enough, this creation of a new judicial body within the existing Community judicial institution was not accompanied by any disruption to or radical change in the structure of the existing Community court. Moreover, the institution has also retained its original name, 'Court of Justice of the European Communities' which is *also* the name of the court of last instance.

Another difficulty that arose as a result of this reform concerns the terminology used in Community law and, in particular, in Community legislation: each time the expressions 'Court' or 'Court of Justice' are used it will be necessary to determine whether they should be read as referring to the Court as an institution or to the Court as a judicial body.

The question is relevant in relation to the interpretation of the Treaties themselves as they may use the same expression in contexts where they have different meanings.

[3] The aforementioned provisions inserted, respectively, Article 32 *quinto* in the ECSC Treaty, Article 168 A in the EEC Treaty, and Article 140 A in the Euratom Treaty. Hereinafter I will refer only to the new provisions inserted in the EEC Treaty.

Indeed, whereas Article 164 EEC must clearly be taken to refer to the Court as an institution, since it relates to a task now shared by both courts,[4] the same does not hold true as regards Articles 165 and 168 EEC, which govern the composition and organisation of the Court of Justice *qua* judicial body.

Indeed, it is clear that in referring to 13 judges and six Advocates General those provisions must necessarily concern the 'Court-judicial body'. Similarly, the Registrar to whom reference is made in Article 168 cannot but be the Registrar of the 'Court-judicial body' since a different provision, Article 45 of the Statute,[5] inserted by Article 7 of the Council Decision, applies to the Registrar of the CFI.

By contrast, Articles 169 EEC and following, which provide for different forms of action that may be brought by individuals, relate either to the 'Court-judicial body' or to the 'Court-institution' depending on whether the relevant form of action falls within the exclusive competence of the 'Court-judicial body' (which is notably the case as regards Articles 169, 170, 171 or 177) or within the areas of jurisdiction now shared by the two courts (Articles 173(2), 175(2), 178 and 179).[6]

A similar problem may arise in relation to the interpretation of secondary legislation.

The recently-adopted Merger Control Regulation[7] exemplifies that problem. Indeed, Article 16 of that Regulation, which concerns judicial review, identifies the 'Court of Justice' as the competent court to review the legality of the Commission's decisions taken in application of that Regulation.

Although it is unlikely that the legislator of the Merger Control Regulation, which was 16 years in the drafting, actually foresaw the possible creation of the CFI when framing Article 16, that provision has to be understood as referring to the 'Court-institution' since any other reading would ignore the transfer of competences effected in the meantime by virtue of Article 3(1)(c) of the Council Decision.[8]

This terminological ambiguity reflects, in substance, an institutional context which is still somewhat unclear. It might also be taken as meaning that the Court of Justice still remains the same institution as before, the creation of the CFI

[4] That task is to 'ensure that in the interpretation and application of the Treaties the law is observed'.

[5] Corresponding to Article 45 of the ECSC Statute, as inserted by Article 5 of the Council Decision, and Article 46 of the Euratom Statute, as inserted by Article 9 of the Council Decision.

[6] Pursuant to Article 3 of the Council Decision. See also Articles 172, 174, 176, 184 to 187 and 192 of the EEC Treaty—as well as the corresponding provisions of the ECSC and the Euratom Treaties—applicable to the CFI by virtue of Article 4 of the Council Decision.

[7] Council Regulation (EEC) No 4064/89 of 21 December 1989 on the control of concentrations between undertakings [1989] OJ L395/1 and Corrigendum [1990] OJ L257/13.

[8] It follows from Article 3(1)(c) of the Council Decision that the argument that some have drawn from the fact that Article 235 of the EEC Treaty, together with its Article 87, constitutes the legal basis for the Regulation, does not support the conclusion that the CFI has no jurisdiction to rule at first instance on actions brought by individuals and legal persons against Commission decisions adopted under the Merger Control Regulation. See, in that regard, my article (with LM Pais Antunes) 'The Court of First Instance of the European Communities—A Significant Step towards the Consolidation of the European Community as a Community Governed By the Rule of Law', 10(1) (1990) *Yearbook of European Law* 1–56.

having simply established a new, additional judicial body whose institutional position within the Community judicial system is only just beginning to take shape.

C. Administrative Arrangements

In administrative and organisational terms, it must be noted that the solution retained by the SEA was to 'attach' the new Court of First Instance to the Court of Justice.

For obvious reasons of economy, the Council did not wish to set up the CFI with a complete and separate array of administrative and service departments, thereby duplicating those that already existed within the Court.

For that reason, Article 45(2), first sentence, of the Statute of the EEC Court states that the 'officials and other servants attached to the Court of Justice shall render their services to the Court of First Instance to enable it to function'. It is only to a limited extent, as will be seen below, that 'certain officials or other servants shall be responsible to the registrar of the Court of First Instance under the authority of the President of the Court of First Instance' (Article 45(2), *in fine*).

D. A Gradual Implementation

It should also be emphasised that the legislature has opted for a piecemeal approach to the setting up of the CFI and to the expansion of its jurisdiction.

First, the SEA did not create the CFI but merely authorised the Council to establish it, following the procedure set out therein. Second, it was left to the Council to determine, within the general framework of Article 168 A, the specific jurisdiction to be exercised by the CFI.

In setting up the CFI, the Council has necessarily granted that Court, at first instance, competences that had previously been exercised, in accordance with the Treaties, by the Court of Justice. A transfer of competences has thus taken place between the two courts, subject to the possibility for the parties to appeal to the Court of Justice, on points of law only, against judgments of the CFI.

As will be seen in more detail below, that mechanism for allocating competences has naturally affected the initial allocation of cases to the CFI and, consequently, the workload of that Court.

E. Object of the Present Chapter

This chapter aims to explore the most important issues raised by the creation of this new Community court. More specifically, it intends, on the one hand, to describe the main difficulties faced by the founding members of the CFI when they took office and how they dealt with them and, on the other hand, to assess the extent to which, one year on, the CFI has achieved its two main goals of:

— relieving the Court of Justice of part of its workload through the partial transfer of competences in order to speed up the administration of justice and to allow the Court of Justice to focus on its core function of ensuring the uniform interpretation of Community law, and
— improving the judicial protection of individuals and undertakings by instituting a double degree of judicial control, particularly in those areas of litigation that require the assessment of complex facts, notably litigation of an economic nature.

This contribution also affords me the opportunity, as an academic, to pay tribute to a great professor of Community law, Jean Boulouis, and, as President of the CFI, to account publicly for that Court's performance during its first year of operation.

II. PROBLEMS LINKED TO THE ESTABLISHMENT OF THE CFI

A. First Steps

The adoption of the Council Decision establishing the CFI[9] set in train the process leading to the actual setting up of the new Court.

After a number of practical issues had been sorted out,[10] a conference of representatives of the Member State governments met, on 18 July 1989, to appoint those who would become the first members and the President of the CFI, as of 1 September 1989.[11]

All the new members arrived in Luxembourg in early September and were able, with the assistance of the Court's administrative services, to immediately begin to perform their duties and to plan the working regime of the CFI.

The offices of the new members and the Registrar were located in the building next to the 'Palais de la Cour', inaugurated the previous year, which was

[9] See n 1 above. An initial decision on the principle of setting up a new Court was taken on 25 July 1988, in accordance with the request put forward by the Court of Justice on 29 September 1987.

[10] On 19 December 1988, the Council approved the Council Regulation (ECSC, EEC, Euratom) No 4045/88 of 19 December 1988 laying down the emoluments of the President, Members and Registrar of the Court of First Instance of the European Communities [1988] OJ L356/1. A supplementary budget was also adopted for the last four months of the financial year 1989, in order to meet the initial needs of the CFI ([1989] OJ L132/1).

[11] Decision of the Representatives of the Governments of the Member States of the European Communities, 89/452/EEC, Euratom, ECSC, of 18 July 1989 appointing the Members of the Court of First Instance of the European Communities and Decision of the Representatives of the Governments of the Member States of the European Communities, 89/453/EEC, Euratom, ECSC; of 18 July 1989 appointing the President of the Court of First Instance of the European Communities [1989] OJ L220/76.

refurbished so that it could accommodate the new Court on a temporary basis. Later, by joint decision of both courts, the building was named after the great Renaissance humanist, Erasmus of Rotterdam.[12]

On 25 September 1989, the President and the members of the CFI were sworn in before the Court of Justice, thus allowing the President of the Council, as provided for by Article 12 of the Council Decision, to designate, by the drawing of lots, those six members of the CFI whose terms of office would expire at the end of the first three-year period of operation. A few days later, on 10 October, the CFI appointed its first Registrar.

The setting up of the CFI's registry, following the recruitment of its first officials, enabled the President of the Court to issue a declaration stating that the CFI was regularly constituted, in accordance with Article 13 of the Council Decision.[13] Article 3 of the Council Decision, stipulating the competences to be exercised by the CFI at first instance, thus entered into force, enabling the Court of Justice, as provided for by Article 14 of the Council Decision, to refer to the CFI those cases pending before it that fell within the jurisdiction of the latter, provided that the preliminary report in that case had not yet been submitted by the judge-rapporteur at the Court of Justice.

On that basis, 153 cases were transferred to the CFI, of which 73 were competition cases, two were ECSC cases and 78 were staff cases. Among the competition cases, three groups of actions were particularly important in terms of the number and the size of the applicants, the amount of the fines imposed by the Commission, the factual complexity of the files and the importance of certain legal issues that they raised. Those three series of cases concerned the main producers of polypropylene (14 applicants), of polyvinyl chloride (PVC) (16 applicants) and of low density polyethylene (13 applicants), all of which had been found by the Commission to have breached Article 85 of the EEC Treaty.

In the meantime, on 6 November 1989, the first action was lodged directly before the CFI.[14]

B. Rules of Procedure

One of the first tasks the CFI had to undertake was to prepare its draft Rules of Procedure, as provided for in Article 11 of the Council Decision. For that purpose, a working group was set up within the CFI.

However, given that the Rules of Procedure of the Court of Justice were applicable *mutatis mutandis*, by virtue of Article 11, in fine, of the Council Decision,

[12] Following an internal competition to find a name launched by the Staff committee, whose result was confirmed by the Court and the CFI.

[13] Decision of the President of the Court establishing a Court of First Instance of the European Communities [1989] OJ L317/48.

[14] T-154/89 *Vidranyi v Commission* [1990] ECR II-445.

until the entry into force of the CFI's own rules, a separate working group examined the questions raised by the application of those existing rules. As a result, some important conclusions were drawn that were useful for the task of drafting the new Rules of Procedure of the CFI.

The draft Rules of Procedure prepared by the CFI were ready by the end of January 1990. Meetings were then held within a contact group involving representatives of both courts with a view to the adoption, by consensus, of a final draft to be submitted to the Council for its approval, unanimity being required for that purpose, as set forth in Article 168 A(4) of the Treaty.

The draft was sent to the Council on 4 April 1990[15] and the Rules of Procedure of the CFI were finally adopted on 21 December 1990. They will enter into force shortly.

The CFI considered from the outset that its Rules of Procedure should depart from those of the Court of Justice only in the three following situations:

i. where a departure was justified by the composition and internal organisation of the CFI as set forth in Article 2 of the Council Decision;
ii. where the particular characteristics of the disputes dealt with by the CFI and the nature of the judicial review to be undertaken by the CFI required it;
iii. where the previous experience of the Court of Justice in applying its own Rules of Procedure indicated that certain specific modifications in the rules of procedure of both courts would be desirable.

In addition, it was necessary to establish appropriate rules for the procedure to be followed by the CFI following a ruling of the Court of Justice on an appeal setting aside, in whole or in part, the judgment at first instance and referring the case back to the CFI for a new decision.

i. New Rules Required by the Specific Composition and Organisation of the CFI

Contrary to the provisions set out in Article 165(2) of the EEC Treaty in respect of the Court of Justice, the CFI normally sits in chambers, the plenary session being the exception. Indeed, Article 2(4) of the Council Decision states that 'the Court of First Instance shall sit in chambers of three or five judges' and it may sit in plenary session 'in certain cases governed by the Rules of Procedure'.

The CFI therefore had to determine not only 'the composition of the chambers and the assignment of cases to them', but also the criteria for referring a case to the plenary session.

As to the chambers, the CFI decided to establish two chambers of five judges and three chambers of three judges.[16]

[15] The draft was published in the Official Journal ([1990] OJ C136/1), for the information of all interested parties.

[16] Decision of the CFI of 4 October 1989 ([1989] OJ C281/12).

All 12 judges, including the President of the CFI, who is also the president of the first chamber, sit in a chamber of five judges, which means that each of the 'large' chambers is in fact composed of six judges. For each case, one of the judges (with the exception of the President of the chamber) must therefore withdraw, in turn, from taking part in the deliberations.

As concerns the 'small' chambers, only one is composed of three judges, the other two having four judges who also sit on a rotational basis.

This mechanism gives each judge, with the exception of the President,[17] who does not sit in a small chamber, the opportunity to sit in both a large and a small chamber.

Since, in light of the current state of the CFI's competences, each type of chamber deals, in principle, with different, specific fields of litigation (large chambers for competition matters, small chambers for staff cases), the fact that each judge sits in both a small and a large chamber means that the judges of the CFI are not 'specialised' in just one type of case, which would, it is submitted, be undesirable and unjustified.

Indeed, Article 12(1) of the Rules of Procedure provides that 'disputes between the Communities and their servants shall be assigned to Chambers of three Judges', whereas 'other cases shall, subject to the provisions of Article 14, be assigned to Chambers of five Judges'.

In practice, the latter category currently comprises actions concerning the application of the rules of competition applicable to undertakings (EEC and ECSC), as well as actions brought by undertakings and associations of undertakings regarding market-regulating measures under the ECSC Treaty.

Article 14 of the Rules of Procedure provides, however, that

> whenever the legal difficulty or the importance of the case or special circumstances so justify, a case may be referred to the Court of First Instance sitting in plenary session or to a Chamber composed of a different number of Judges.

The wording of that provision is sufficiently flexible to enable the Court to choose the formation of the court that it considers most appropriate in light of the specific characteristics of each case.

Up to the end of 1990 the mechanism established by Article 14 has been used twice: the first situation related to the only case so far referred to the plenary session; the second concerned a series of actions brought by civil servants which, given their importance, were transferred from a chamber of three judges to a chamber of five judges.

[17] During the first judicial year of the CFI, the President of the second chamber did not sit in a small chamber. Only one of those chambers was thus composed of four judges. Experience has however shown that it would be appropriate, in the interests of a better distribution of work, to allocate the President of the second chamber to sit in one of the small chambers. That change has already been made for the judicial year 1990/1991. See Decision of the CFI of 5 July 1990 ([1990] OJ C199/9).

The case referred to the plenary session—*Tetra Pak v Commission*[18]—was a competition case in which the CFI held its first public hearing, on 14 December 1989, and whose particular characteristics justified the referral. Indeed, the case raised an important legal issue concerning the respective scope of application of Articles 85(3) and 86 of the EEC Treaty, which had not yet been settled by the Court of Justice. Moreover, the facts of the case were not disputed and there was therefore no difficulty in establishing them.

Indeed, factual complexity is not, in itself, considered to be an appropriate reason for referring a case to a panel composed of a greater number of judges, since to do so might risk clogging up the plenary session with the onerous task of establishing and assessing complex sets of facts. A panel of three or five judges is therefore more appropriate. For that reason, it was decided that the 'polypropylene cases' should remain before the first chamber, notwithstanding the importance of the legal issues that they raised.

The cases that have been transferred from a chamber of three judges (the third chamber) to one of five judges (the second chamber) constitute a series of actions brought against the Commission's decisions concerning the financial adjustment—to take account of the local cost of living—applied to the salaries of officials and other servants posted in certain Member States; the Regulation adopted following the most recent five-yearly revision of the relevant weightings had been annulled, in the meantime, by the Court. The cases raised important questions of principle affecting the salary regime of the European civil service.[19]

Pursuant to Article 14, last sentence, read in conjunction with Article 51 of the Rules of Procedure, the decision to refer a case to a panel comprising a different number of judges is taken by the CFI at its plenary meeting, following a proposal from the chamber hearing the case, either of its own initiative or at the request of one of the parties. In any case, the CFI shall not take its decision in this regard, without previously hearing the parties[20] and the Advocate General, where one has been appointed.

Given that the work of the CFI is mainly carried out within the chambers, it was necessary to adopt working methods that avoided the judicial activity of the court being excessively compartmentalised.

That objective is pursued by means of plenary meetings of all the CFI judges,[21] which normally take place once each month, as well as through coordination

[18] T-51/89 *Tetra Pak v Commission* [1990] ECR II-309.

[19] T-16/89 *Hans Herkenrath and Others v Commission* [1992] ECR II-275 and Joined Cases T-17/89 *Brazzelli Lualdi and Others v Commission*, T-21/89 *Bertolo and Others v Commission* and T-25/89 *Alex and Others v Commission* [1992] ECR II-293, referred to the second chamber by decision of the CFI of 6 December 1990.

[20] The obligation to hear the parties before the decision on the referral was not included in the initial draft of the Rules of Procedure submitted by the CFI and was added by the Council when it approved the final version of those Rules.

[21] Corresponding to the Administrative Meeting of the Court of Justice.

meetings that are regularly held between the President of the CFI and the presidents of the chambers.

The appointment of Advocates General also required the adoption of specific rules. In that regard, the Council Decision represents a compromise between the proposal of the Court of Justice (which did not envisage that there should be Advocates General at the new first instance court) and the contrary proposals put forward by other stakeholders (European Parliament, some Member States, European Bar Associations).

Thus, as stated in Article 2(3) of the Decision, 'the members of the Court of First Instance may be called upon to perform the task of an Advocate-General' in accordance with the criteria laid down in the Rules of Procedure.

According to Article 2(1) of those rules, 'every Member of the Court of First Instance shall, as a rule, perform the function of Judge'. However, pursuant to Article 2(1), 'every Judge, with the exception of the President, may, in the circumstances specified in Articles 17 to 19, perform the function of Advocate-General in a particular case'.

As provided for in Article 17 of the Rules of Procedure, 'when the Court of First Instance sits in plenary session, it shall be assisted by an Advocate-General designated by the President of the Court of First Instance'. Since the CFI is, in any event, bound to deliberate on its judgments with an uneven number of judges, 11 judges will normally sit in the plenary session whilst the 12th performs the function of Advocate General.

A CFI chamber may also be assisted by an Advocate General 'if it is considered that the legal difficulty or the factual complexity of the case so requires' (Article 18 of the Rules of Procedure).

According to Article 19, 'the decision to designate an Advocate-General in a particular case shall be taken by the Court of First Instance sitting in plenary session at the request of the Chamber before which the case comes'.

As of February 1991, the CFI has decided to designate an Advocate General, in addition to the aforementioned *Tetra Pak* case, in 16 cases assigned to a chamber of five judges (14 of which formed part of the 'polypropylene' litigation). No case assigned to one of the 'small' chambers has required the appointment of an Advocate General.

It is submitted that certain inferences and conclusions may already be drawn from the practice that has been followed regarding the criteria for the designation of an Advocate General:

- as a rule, the President chooses an Advocate General among the members of a chamber to which the case has not been assigned; this practice ensures that the Advocate General operates at a greater 'distance' vis-à-vis the other judges to whom he is to deliver his Opinion, as they are not the ones with whom he usually sits;
- the proposal of the chamber to which the case has been assigned must be reasoned in order to enable the plenary meeting to understand and to

consider the legal and factual circumstances justifying the proposal; the practice adopted by the CFI in this regard offers the additional advantage of enabling the designated Advocate General to know in detail the reasons why the chamber asked for his assistance, thus allowing him, if he so wishes, to focus his Opinion on the most difficult and controversial aspects of the case;

— the compromise solution adopted by the Council has genuine advantages: it is fairly flexible, the specific characteristics and difficulties of each case may be taken into account and it avoids the drafting of an Advocate General's Opinion where the case does not truly raise any difficulties or new legal issues, whilst ensuring that the judges deciding the case can benefit from the assistance of an Advocate General whenever that appears to be justified;

— nevertheless, the system also has its shortcomings, mainly because of the excessive workload that it represents for the judges when they are called upon to perform the functions of an Advocate General in cases which, by definition, are bound to be complex or difficult, since otherwise no Opinion would be necessary; this makes it difficult to organise the Court's judicial work, particularly as each judge is currently assisted by just one Legal Secretary or '*référendaire*'.

Article 46, third paragraph, of the Statute of the ECC Court, inserted into the relevant Protocol by Article 7 of the Council Decision, provides that 'notwithstanding the fourth paragraph of Article 18 of this Statute, the Advocate-General may make his reasoned submissions in writing'.

That provision was implemented by Article 61(1) of the Rules of Procedure of the CFI, pursuant to which 'where the Advocate-General delivers his opinion in writing, he shall lodge it at the Registry, which shall communicate it to the parties'.

ii. New Rules Required By the Particular Characteristics of the Disputes that Come Before the CFI and By the Nature of the Judicial Review Entrusted to that Court

The nature of the litigation transferred to the CFI called for effective and flexible mechanisms for establishing and appraising the relevant facts, in order to ensure effective case management and a quick and efficient administration of justice.

Thus, alongside the traditional measures of inquiry (Article 65), adopted by means of an order, possibly after hearing the parties (Article 66), the Rules of Procedure provide for the adoption of measures of organisation of the procedure in order 'to ensure that cases are prepared for hearing, procedures carried out and disputes resolved under the best possible conditions' [Article 64(1)].

Pursuant to Article 64(2), those measures

> shall, in particular, have as their purpose:
>
> (a) to ensure efficient conduct of the written and oral procedure and to facilitate the taking of evidence;
>
> (b) to determine the points on which the parties must present further argument or which call for measures of inquiry;

(c) to clarify the forms of order sought by the parties, their pleas in law and arguments and the points at issue between them;
(d) to facilitate the amicable settlement of proceedings.

Thus, measures of organisation of the procedure may consist of putting questions to the parties, inviting the parties to make written or oral submissions on certain aspects of the proceedings, asking the parties or third parties for specific information or further particulars, asking for the production of any documents or other evidence that may be relevant to the case, or summoning the parties' agents or the parties in person to informal meetings [Article 64(3)].

More flexible and less formal than measures of inquiry, measures of organisation of the procedure may be adopted at any stage of the proceedings, on the court's own motion or at the request of one of the parties; once the competent formation has taken the decision to adopt the measures, they shall be carried out by means of a simple letter from the Registrar rather than by the notification of a formal order [see Article 64(4)].

The effective implementation of those provisions is only possible where the judge-*rapporteur* keeps track of the proceedings from a very early stage so that he is in a position to suggest that the CFI take steps, where necessary, to ensure proactive management of the case.

For that purpose, the CFI's practice is not to fix the time-limit for the reply immediately, in order to enable the judge-*rapporteur* to propose to the competent formation, after the defence is lodged, the adoption of any measures of organisation of procedure that he may consider necessary in light of the pleadings already filed.

On a practical level, the main obstacle that may prevent the court from making extensive use of this possibility relates to the time taken to have the documents in the file translated in those cases where the judge-*rapporteur* is not in a position to work directly in the language of the particular case.

Nevertheless, these new measures have already proven to be useful in practice as, for example, in *La Cinq v Commission*,[22] where the applicant challenged a Commission decision rejecting its request for interim measures following its complaint in respect of alleged anti-competitive conduct of the European Broadcasting Union.

In its defence, the Commission, without formally raising an objection of inadmissibility, questioned whether the applicant had an interest in bringing proceedings.

Before allowing the written procedure to proceed any further, the first chamber, on a proposal of the judge-*rapporteur*, decided to summon the parties to an informal meeting, primarily with the aim of enabling the applicant to make known its position with regard to the arguments put forward by the Commission concerning its interest in the proceedings.

[22] T-44/90 *La Cinq v Commission* [1992] ECR II-1.

The meeting that took place between the CFI and the parties, held in public, made it possible for them to agree to waive their right to submit additional pleadings (reply and rejoinder), thus reducing the duration of the written procedure, as the circumstances of the case required, given the urgency of the particular measure whose adoption the applicant sought.

Also in the context of measures adopted with a view to improving the conduct of the proceedings, in *Wartenburg v European Parliament*,[23] on the initiative of the fifth chamber, the parties were summoned to a hearing whose aim was to reconcile their respective positions and thus to reach an amicable settlement of the dispute. As a result, following an adjournment of the hearing, the parties informed the CFI that they had reached an agreement, including on the issue of costs, thus enabling the immediate removal of the case from the register.

Finally,[24] the measures of organisation of the procedure adopted in the 'polypropylene cases' are worth mentioning.[25] Given the overall number of applicants in the 14 cases, which had been joined for the purposes of the oral procedure, and the number and importance of the factual and legal issues raised, some of which were specific to one case, whilst others were common to all or at least to several of them, the first chamber decided to organise a meeting with the lawyers and agents of the parties in order to prepare for the hearing. At that meeting, the CFI informed the parties of the questions it intended to put to them, either for an oral or a written reply, the different procedural steps to be taken were identified and the time available for pleading was shared out among the parties' representatives.

The meeting was followed by a further exchange of letters. Taken together, this preparatory work enabled the hearing, which lasted for a whole week (from 10 to 15 December 1990), to proceed in an efficient and coordinated manner.[26]

iii. New Rules Intended to Clarify the Rules of Procedure

Among the innovations that the CFI suggested in its draft Rules of Procedure in order to eliminate doubts as to the interpretation of, or to overcome shortcomings that had previously been identified in, the Rules of Procedure of the Court of

[23] Order of the CFI, T 59/89 *Wolfdieter von Wartenburg v European Parliament* [1990] ECR II-25.

[24] Other measures of organisation of the procedure were adopted, in particular, in Joined Cases T-33/89 and T-74/89 *David Blackman v European Parliament* [1993] ECR II-249, and in T-140/89 *Hilaire Della Pietra v Commission* [1990] ECR II-717.

[25] Cases joined for the purposes of the oral procedure T-1/89 to T-4/89 and T-6/89 to T-15/89 *Rhône-Poulenc SA and others v Commission* [1990] ECR II-637.

[26] Some specific features of the Rules of Procedure of the CFI have are the direct consequence of the fact that its decisions are subject to an appeal. This issue will be dealt with more fully below. Some of these specificities justified variations as compared to the equivalent provisions in the Rules of Procedure of the Court of Justice. An example of this may be found in the duty to give reasons for rejecting a request for intervention, which is not required by the Rules of Procedure of the Court of Justice but is required from the CFI since its decisions on those requests may be challenged before the Court.

Justice, I will mention, by way of example, only those that concern the calculation of procedural time-limits.[27]

Those calculations have at times given rise to significant difficulties and created considerable legal uncertainty, thus harming the legitimate interests of the parties. The application of Article 80 of the Rules of Procedure of the Court of Justice, on the calculation of procedural time-limits, which stated that 'the day of the event from which the period is to run shall be excluded' (*dies a quo*), is just such an example.

In its judgment in *Misset v Council*,[28] the Court of Justice interpreted that provision in a way that eliminated some of the doubts that had arisen in that regard. The Court's interpretation is explicitly reflected in the wording of Article 101(1)(b) of the Rules of Procedure of the CFI.

However, there were also other difficulties of interpretation concerning, in particular, the calculation of time-limits where the period was expressed in months or years. Specific provisions were therefore necessary in order to take account of the different number of days in each month.

The new Article 101 of the CFI's Rules of Procedure has therefore clarified the situation, as follows: '[i]f, in a period expressed in months or in years, the day on which it should expire does not occur in the last month, the period shall end with the expiry of the last day of that month.'

Moreover, the CFI's experience brought to light the fact that certain rules were clearly out of date. For example, Article 80 of the Rules of Procedure of the Court of Justice extended time-limits until the end of the first working day following where they fell on a Sunday or on an official holiday, but not where they fell on a Saturday.

As the registries of both courts are closed on Saturdays, it is not difficult to imagine the unfortunate situations to which the application of such a provision could give rise.[29]

In order to deal with that anachronism, Article 101(2) of the Rules of Procedure of the CFI now provides that if the date when a time-limit ends would otherwise fall on a Sunday or on an official holiday but also on a Saturday, then it shall be extended until the end of the first working day following that date.

Those amendments, which were, it is submitted, necessary to ensure that the requirements of legal certainty and the interests of a proper administration of justice were met, have subsequently also been incorporated in the Rules of

[27] Reference should also be made to the possibility, provided for in Article 116(5), of establishing a time-limit for the main parties to reply to the observations submitted by the interveners in a case. Indeed, the observations of the interveners are often submitted at a time when all or some of the main parties have already filed their written submissions and are therefore prevented, contrary to the interests of a proper organisation of the procedure, from taking into consideration, within the written procedure, the pleas and arguments put forward by the interveners.

[28] Case 152/85 *Rudolf Misset v Council* [1987] ECR 223.

[29] That is what occurred in T-125/89 *Filtrona Española SA v Commission* [1990] ECR II-393.

Procedure of the Court of Justice, thus harmonising this important aspect of the procedural regimes applicable before both courts.

iv. Procedure before the CFI Following a Judgment of the Court of Justice on Appeal Setting Aside a Decision of the CFI

The provisions inserted in the Statute of the Court by the Council Decision concerning the referral of a case back to the CFI, following a successful appeal against its initial judgment, merely state that the CFI 'shall be bound by the decision of the Court of Justice on points of law'.

As the procedural issues that may arise in this context were not clarified when the Rules of Procedure of the Court of Justice were amended, on 7 June 1989, in order to determine how appeals against the decisions of the CFI should be dealt with,[30] it fell to the CFI to include the necessary provisions in its own Rules of Procedure and, in particular, to determine the appropriate chamber to rule on the case for a second time.

The solution adopted is intended to achieve both flexibility and efficiency. Article 188 of the CFI's Rules of Procedure provides that where the Court of Justice sets aside a judgment or an order of a chamber, the President of the CFI may assign the case to another chamber composed of the same number of judges. However, where the Court of Justice sets aside a decision made by the CFI sitting in plenary session, the case must be assigned once again to the plenary session.

It would have been possible to adopt, *mutatis mutandis*, the system in place in some Member States where, following a successful appeal before a higher court, the case is referred to a different court of the same rank or to a different chamber of the same court.

It is, however, often appropriate to refer the case to the same chamber that has already ruled on the case at first instance where, for example, the Court of Justice quashes an order that was limited to the question of admissibility or where, in a complex case, that Court sets aside the CFI's decision only in part and upholds its ruling on other points.

Article 118(3) also aims to ensure flexible and efficient case-handling, enabling the chamber that would otherwise have re-heard a case, in which the Court of Justice has overturned the first instance judgment and which it has referred back to the CFI, to propose that a different judicial formation rule on the case.

Pursuant to Article 117 of the Rules of Procedure, where the Court of Justice sets aside a decision of the CFI and refers the case back to it, the CFI is seized of the case by the appeal judgment so referring it. The parties are not therefore required to submit a new application to the CFI. The procedure is subsequently conducted in accordance with the provisions of Title II of the CFI's Rules of Procedure (Articles 43 *et seq*) as provided for by Article 120.

[30] Amendments to the Rules of Procedure of the Court of Justice [1989] (OJ L241/1).

A number of specific features of the procedure before the CFI after its initial decision has been overturned and referred back to it are also worth mentioning. First, Article 119(2) provides that where the written procedure before the CFI had not been completed—ie where the decision that was appealed had been adopted before all the stages of that procedure were complete—at the time when the judgment referring the case back to the CFI was delivered, it shall resume at the stage which it had reached, by means of measures of organisation of the procedure adopted by the CFI pursuant to Article 64 of the Rules of Procedure. That scenario may occur, in particular, where the judgment of the Court of Justice adjudicates only on a part of the merits of the dispute or when it rules on an objection of inadmissibility or of lack of competence and the proceedings on the merits have been suspended before the CFI while awaiting the judgment of the Court of Justice.

Conversely, Article 119(1) provides that where the written procedure before the CFI has already been completed at the time when the judgment referring the case back to it is delivered, the applicant may lodge a statement of written observations, within two months from the service upon him of the judgment of the Court of Justice. The defendant may also lodge a statement of written observations in the month that follows the communication to him of the applicant's statement. The time allowed to the defendant for lodging that statement may in no case be less than two months from the service upon him of the judgment of the Court of Justice. The same provisions apply to interveners.

Although the applicant may no longer modify the claims sought in its application, the procedure on appeal before the Court of Justice may, in fact, bring to light new factual or legal elements that might be used by the applicant to raise new pleas in law before the CFI. According to Article 119(3) of the Rules of Procedure, if the circumstances so justify, the CFI may allow supplementary sets of written observations to be lodged, in order to make possible a comprehensive treatment of the case at hand.

C. Administrative Issues

The particular circumstances that surrounded the creation and establishment of the CFI have affected the way in which its services are set up.

Given the deadlines applicable to the budgetary procedure, both the supplementary budget for the last four months of 1989 and the part of the institution's 1990 budget providing for the needs of the CFI, were drawn up by the services of the Court at a time when the members of the CFI had not yet taken up their posts.

The drawing up of the 1991 budget is therefore the first opportunity that the CFI has had to play a role in the planning of its own budgetary needs.

The CFI has done that by submitting to the budgetary authority a plan, to be implemented over several years, enabling it to take on the minimum staff required in order to properly exercise its current competences.

Given the administrative structure chosen for the institution by the legislator following the CFI's creation,[31] the abovementioned plan covered only those officials and other servants who, according to the last sentence of Article 45 of the Council Decision, 'shall be responsible to the Registrar of the Court of First Instance under the authority of the President of the Court of First Instance'.

That provision of the Council Decision does not specify which officials and servants are included. It is for the budget authority to determine, in the annual budget, on a case by case basis, the practical effect to be given to those words.

As may be deduced from the budgets approved since the creation of the CFI, this issue concerns only the small group of officials and other servants directly attached to the members' chambers (*référendaires* and secretarial staff) and to the Registrar of the CFI.[32]

Indeed, the core of personal staff allocated to both the judges and the registrar is intimately involved in the performance of the CFI's judicial tasks and represents the irreducible minimum necessary to ensure the independence of the Court.[33]

The conditions under which the exercise of the powers conferred on the AA (the 'appointing authority', which is responsible for all staffing decisions under Community civil service law) with regard to these officials and servants have been set out in an amendment to the Decision of the Court of Justice of 11 September 1987 on the powers of the AA[34] and in an equivalent decision of the CFI[35] specifying the division of powers, as AA, between the CFI as a whole, its President, its Registrar and, as appropriate, other officials, and laying down the conditions under which those powers may be delegated.

As regards the other services whose contribution is necessary to the activity of the CFI—research and documentation, the library service, translation, interpretation, the financial and accounting departments, the personnel department and the infrastructure service—the CFI is, as provided for by Article 45 of the Statute, assisted by the officials and other servants attached to the Court of Justice.

The system could, of course, have been set up in a different way. It follows, however, from the first sentence of Article 45(2) that the legislator did not wish to share between the two courts the powers of the AA in respect of the staff working

[31] See section I. C. above.

[32] The budget for 1991 anticipates a very small staff contingent for the CFI, consisting of one *référendaire* and one secretary or assistant in each cabinet, a judgment reviser (*lecteur d'arrêts*), four typists and 11 posts at the registry.

[33] This notion of means strictly necessary to ensure the exercise of judicial autonomy of the CFI was inserted in the Council Decision, thus replacing the proposal formulated by the Court of Justice which merely provided that the two presidents *could* decide to allocate to the CFI a number of officials and servants ('*Ils peuvent décider…*'). The Council has therefore opted for a formulation similar to that used in Article 11 of the Statute in relation to the officials and other servants responsible to the Registrar of the Court of Justice under the authority of the President of the Court.

[34] Decision of the Court of Justice of 10 May 1990 (nyr).

[35] Decision of the CFI of 13 June 1990 (nyr).

for those institution-wide services, thereby creating a kind of joint administration of the institution.[36]

Thus, the Court of Justice alone exercises the powers of the AA vis-à-vis the administrative departments of the institution. However, according to the Statute, the presidents of both courts 'shall determine, by common accord' the conditions under which officials and other servants attached to the Court of Justice shall render their services to the CFI. This means that the efficiency of the system as a whole relies, to a great extent, on close and effective cooperation between the two presidents.[37]

Future experience will undoubtedly provide guidance as to the most appropriate means for improving the system, in particular as regards the management and budgetary autonomy of the CFI, as has already happened in other Community bodies, such as in the Social and Economic Committee, for example.

III. THE WORKLOAD OF THE COURT OF JUSTICE

The steady increase in the number of cases brought before the Court of Justice over the years has led, despite strenuous efforts to improve working methods and to speed up procedures, to an increase in the number of pending cases and to the lengthening of the average duration of procedures.

Whereas in 1970 only 79 new cases were brought before the Court of Justice, the figure rose to 279 in 1980 and continued to increase rapidly thereafter, reaching 433 in 1985. Those statistics mean that the number of cases registered increased more than fivefold between 1970 and 1985 whilst the number of members of the Court did not even double during the same period (from seven judges and two Advocates General in 1970 to 11 judges and five Advocates General in 1985).

Despite the significant increase in the number of judgments delivered each year,[38] the rise in the number of new cases led to an increase in the number of pending cases from 106 on 31 December 1976 to 318 on 31 December 1980 and 605 at the end of 1988.

As a result, the average duration of proceedings also saw a significant increase, from nine months, for direct actions, and six months, in preliminary ruling cases, in 1978, to 24 and 18 months, respectively, in 1988.

[36] Either by means of a joint administrative meeting or by establishing a common management or administrative board.

[37] Given that a significant share of the powers relating to the administration of the institution are exercised, at the Court of Justice, by the administrative meeting or by an administrative committee exercising delegated powers, the effort required to achieve sound, coordinated management is even greater in some areas.

[38] In 1970, 63 judgments were rendered, 211 in 1975 and 238 in 1988. Of course, this number cannot be increased exponentially; indeed, the maximum capacity for the delivery of judgments may already have been reached.

The transfer of 153 cases from the Court of Justice to the CFI on 15 November 1989, by virtue of the competences conferred on the new Court, necessarily brought about a corresponding reduction in the number of cases pending before the Court of Justice, to 501 on 31 December 1989.

However, although 302 cases were disposed of by the Court of Justice in 1990, the number of cases pending before it just one year later was 583 and that figure reached 618 on 31 January 1991, ie more than before the setting up of the CFI (611 on 31 July 1989).

During the same period, the CFI made a final ruling in 82 cases; since 59 new cases were filed, 145 cases were therefore pending at the end of 1990.

If one adds to this figure the 583 cases pending before the Court of Justice, a grand total of 728 cases were pending before the institution as a whole on 31 December 1990, that is, 58 more than at the end of the previous year.[39]

It can therefore be concluded, at the end of the first full year of activity of the CFI that the volume of litigation before the institution as a whole has continued to rise during that period. At the same time, the average duration of proceedings before the Court of Justice also increased, from 19.1 months in 1989 to 22.6 months in 1990.

Of course, 1990 was the new Court's very first full year of operation. Although it was able to dispose of a significant number of cases and thus reduce its stock between late 1989 and 31 December 1990, it must be borne in mind that the judge-*rapporteurs* inevitably needed some 'reading in' time to carry out an initial examination of each of the cases that had been transferred from the Court of Justice and assigned to them in the previous year. Furthermore, one must also take into account the time required to work on the file and the inevitable time lag between the closing of the written procedure, the preparation of the preliminary report and the holding of the public hearing.

Moreover, in a number of cases, the written procedure was already completed by the time the case was transferred and some of them, in particular those concerning the application of the rules on competition, were extremely voluminous and complex. That is one reason why the CFI, despite its considerable efforts, which enabled it to dispose of 21 cases (11 judgments and 10 orders) during the first quarter of 1990, was not able truly to operate at full capacity until mid-1990.[40]

One conclusion that may be drawn from the foregoing is that the setting up of the CFI with the competences that it currently exercises has not been sufficient in itself to reverse the trend of a rising backlog of cases, notwithstanding the positive contribution that the new Court has undoubtedly made. In any event, the

[39] At the end of 1989, 670 cases were pending before the two courts, of which 501 before the Court of Justice and 168 before the CFI, 153 of which had been transferred from the Court of Justice pursuant to the Council Decision of 24 October 1988.

[40] In June–July 1990, 14 judgments were delivered, compared to 15 during the preceding five months.

CFI has been able to work at full capacity from the very beginning of 1991 and a significant increase in the number of cases dealt with each year may therefore be expected.

Assuming that the CFI were to double its judicial output, a total number of judgments in the range of 120 would be delivered each year, which is slightly more than the number of judgments delivered by the Court of Justice before a second *référendaire* was assigned to each member and at a time when that Court comprised nine judges and four Advocates General.

Even though that objective may appear difficult to achieve—given the nature of the competences assigned to the CFI, covering cases that often require a careful examination of myriad complex facts, the fact that a judge may sometimes be called upon to perform the functions of Advocate General in certain cases and the fact that each judge has only one *référendaire* at his disposal—the presence of several 'series' of cases that are likely to be decided either this year or in early 1992 may indeed facilitate the achievement of that objective, in the short term.

Nevertheless, that will not suffice, on its own, to settle all the problems arising from the Community judiciary's heavy and increasing workload. Indeed, if the number of new cases brought before the CFI in the current year is similar to that registered in 1990 (around 60 cases) the CFI's judicial capacity will soon be underutilised and thus its contribution to achieving faster and more efficient justice at Community level will be considerably diminished.

I therefore believe that measures should be taken to effect further transfers of jurisdiction to the CFI in order to achieve maximum efficiency of the Community judicial system.

Indeed, even if, as provided for by Article 3(3) of the Council Decision, the competence to rule at first instance on cases concerning antidumping measures is transferred to the CFI in short order, that will have a relatively small impact as the number of those cases brought before the Court of Justice has significantly decreased in the last few years (from almost 20 in 1987 to just three in 1990).

Moreover, even if the possibilities afforded by Article 168 A were exploited to the maximum, that would, at present, concern barely 30 cases per year,[41] a small number of them concerning extra-contractual liability,[42] the others pertaining to a wide array of fields (agriculture, State aid, social funds).[43]

It should therefore be observed that, in order to deal effectively with the increasing workload of the Court of Justice, serious thought needs to be given to the possibility of granting the CFI jurisdiction beyond the scope currently allowed

[41] It is not possible to determine with accuracy the number of cases that may be covered by Article 168 A. The figure given above is thus merely an estimate.

[42] Based on the average from recent years, one should expect five cases to be brought each year. Although 98 non-contractual liability actions were brought in 1990, 95 of these cases concern the same question (milk quotas).

[43] Moreover, it should be noted that these cases often do not proceed beyond an appraisal of issues of admissibility.

for by Article 168 A, including preliminary rulings and/or actions brought by the Member States and the institutions.

The intergovernmental conferences currently taking place may provide an ideal opportunity for that debate to take place. For its part, the CFI has already put forward for consideration a number of ideas concerning the future of the Community judicial system.[44]

IV. THE CASE-LAW OF THE CFI AND THE JUDICIAL PROTECTION OF INDIVIDUALS—ONE YEAR AFTER

To complete this overview of the work of the CFI at the end of its first year of operation, I would like to make a few remarks on the way in which the case-law of the CFI has already contributed to the objective of strengthening the protection of individuals' rights.

A. The Length of the CFI's Judgments

The first point I would like to examine concerns the length of judgments.

Academics and practitioners have noted that the first judgments and orders rendered by the CFI are, in general, relatively long and contain a very detailed assessment of the different factual and legal issues raised in each case.

There are, I believe, three main reasons for that.

The first relates to the particular nature of the cases falling within the scope of the CFI's competences, which often require a meticulous analysis of complex facts. The CFI should indeed carry out a particularly thorough review of decisions adopted by the institutions, thus obliging them, not least the Commission when it takes decisions in the field of competition law, to establish carefully the facts in each case.

The second reason is that the decisions of the CFI are subject to an appeal before the Court of Justice. They must therefore be duly reasoned in law in order to enable the parties to understand the grounds for the decision and to exercise their right of appeal, should they wish to do so, and for the Court of Justice to conduct its review.

The third reason relates to the fact that the right of appeal is limited to points of law, meaning that the CFI has the duty to establish the facts without, in principle, any further right of appeal.

This requires not only that the examination and establishment of the facts be as complete and accurate as possible, but also that the description of the facts be

[44] See CFI, 'Éléments de réflexion sur l'évolution de la juridiction communautaire' of 3 December 1990, in Bulletin of the European Parliament [1991] SpecED 1/S-91.

included in the judgment itself,[45] since the Court of Justice has to rely on the facts established by the CFI when it comes to rule on any appeal.

Moreover, the fact that an appeal may lie on grounds of 'breach of procedure before [the CFI] which adversely affects the interests of the appellant',[46] further requires that the different procedural steps followed by the CFI be clearly indicated in its judgment or order.

As is well-known, the distinction between points of fact and points of law is one of the most delicate questions facing an appellate court such as the Court of Justice. Indeed, issues such as the legal qualification of facts or the relationship between facts and findings of law are grey areas that are neither unambiguously in one category, nor in the other.

It is ultimately for the higher Court, when interpreting the provisions laying down the grounds for appeal, to set out the limits and conditions of admissibility for appeals and, to that extent, the scope of its own powers of review, thus defining, in turn, the effective field of application of the principle of double judicial control.

B. Appeals against CFI's Judgments

Up until now, there has not been a decision of the Court of Justice on appeal that might provide us with a clear indication as to the direction that the Court might take in that regard.[47]

Sixteen appeals were, however, brought against judgments and orders of the CFI during the year 1990, out of 44 decisions that could have been appealed

[45] Contrary to the practice followed by the Court of Justice for the past few years, which is to describe the facts only in a separate document, the 'report for the hearing'. At the CFI, the report for the hearing is not published together with the judgment and its only purpose is to enable the parties to verify, before the hearing, that all their pleas and arguments have been fully understood and examined by the Court. Nevertheless, the report for the hearing normally serves as the basis for the part of the judgment stating the facts of the case.

[46] See Article 51 of the Statute of the Court, inserted by Article 7 of the Council Decision of 24 October 1988.

[47] So far, the President of the Court has made only two interim orders in the context of appeals brought against decisions of the CFI. See the Order of the President of the Court C-242/90 P-R *Commission v Albani and others* [1990] ECR I-4329, rejecting an application for suspension of the execution of the judgment of the CFI in Case T-35/90, *Albani and Others v Commission*, and the Order of the President of the Court C-345/90 P-R *Parlement v Hanning* [1991] ECR I-231, ordering the suspension of the execution of the judgment of the CFI in T-37/90 *Hanning v Parlement*. In the latter judgment, the CFI had annulled a decision of the European Parliament on the appointment of the head of the information office in London. The President of the Court held that, on the one hand, the reasoning of the CFI raised questions of principle concerning the limits to the judicial review of the AA's decision, which the Court of Justice had not yet had the opportunity to determine. Thus, the pleas in law relied upon by the appellant were, *prima facie*, not without merit. On the other hand, the vacancy of the post following the annulment of the appointment decision could give rise to serious and irreparable damage to the functioning of the Parliament's services.

and for which the time-limit to bring an appeal had expired before the end of the year.[48]

Two of those appeals concern competition cases whereas the other 14 relate to staff cases.[49]

The two appeals on competition matters concern, respectively, an order dismissing the application as inadmissible[50] and an order of the President of the CFI on an application for interim relief.[51] The first of those appeals was removed from the register of the Court on 16 January 1991, after the applicant withdrew its application.[52]

C. Important Judgments in Competition Cases

Five decisions of the CFI delivered during the year 1990 in cases concerning the application of the Treaties' competition rules thus became *res judicata*, once the time-limit to bring an appeal expired. A number of those cases raised important questions on the interpretation of the EEC Treaty and/or of secondary Community law. I will mention two examples.

Firstly, in its judgment in *Tetra Pak v Commission*,[53] the CFI ruled on the combined interpretation of Articles 85(3) and 86 of the EEC Treaty.

In response to the arguments put forward by the applicant, which contested the legality of the decision of the Commission in that it had found an agreement to be contrary to Article 86 of the EEC Treaty, notwithstanding the fact that the agreement in question benefited from an exemption under Article 85(3) of that same Treaty, the CFI found that 'in the scheme for the protection of competition established by the Treaty the grant of an exemption, whether individual or block exemption, under Article 85(3) cannot be such as to render inapplicable the prohibition set out in Article 86.'[54]

Following the *Continental Can* line of case-law[55] and after recalling that Articles 85 and 86 'are independent and complementary provisions designed, in general, to

[48] On 17 February 1991, 20 appeals had been brought, out of a total number of 62 judicial decisions that could have been appealed.

[49] In this area of litigation, 10 appeals were brought by officials in cases where the CFI dismissed the application, whereas four others were lodged by the institutions following the annulment of the contested measure by the CFI.

[50] C-268/90 P *Norsk Hydro v Commission*, concerning the annulment of the order of the second chamber of the CFI in T-106/89 *Norsk Hydro v Commission* [1994] ECR II-419.

[51] C-372/90 P *SEP v Commission* [1991] ECR I-2043 concerning the annulment of the order of the President of the CFI in T-39/90 R *SEP v Commission* [1990] ECR II-649.

[52] Order of the Court of Justice C-268/90 P (n 50).

[53] *Tetra Pak* (n 18). See also the Opinion delivered on 21 February 1990 by Judge H Kirschner acting as Advocate General [1990] ECR II-309.

[54] Judgment in *Tetra Pak* (n 18), para 25.

[55] Case 6/72 *Continental Can v Commission* [1973] ECR 215, para 25.

regulate distinct situations by different rules', the CFI found that 'in principle, the grant of exemption cannot preclude application of Article 86.'[56]

Secondly, in the *Automec* case,[57] the CFI was called upon to rule on the nature and scope of administrative acts pertaining to the examination of complaints submitted to the Commission under Article 3(2) of Regulation No 17,[58] referred to in Article 6 of Regulation No 99/63;[59] in doing so, it emphasised the existence of three distinct stages of the administrative procedure.[60]

Furthermore, a number of cases raising important questions of principle on the interpretation and application of the Community competition rules are currently pending before the CFI.

Among those questions it is worth mentioning, in particular, the distinction between agreements and concerted practices, the protection of copyright in relation to TV listings, the interpretation of the notions of abuse of a collective dominant position or of an activity equivalent to resale and the conditions governing the application of Article 85 to cooperative associations.

In light of that list, the near future will inevitably bring a significant enrichment of the case-law of the CFI on competition law matters.

D. An ECSC Case

In addition, the ECSC Treaty, in particular the quota system that it lays down, continues to raise interesting legal issues. The CFI's Advocate General has just delivered his Opinion in the *Stahlwerke Peine-Salzgitter* case,[61] which concerns the Community's extra-contractual liability regime in the context of the ECSC Treaty, and, more particularly, the relationship between Articles 34 and 40 thereof.

E. CFI's Case-law in Staff Cases

Finally, some aspects of the CFI's case-law in staff matters are worth mentioning. Indeed, such cases may raise interesting and novel legal issues that are of considerable importance for the organisation of the Community civil service, in particular

[56] ibid, para 26.

[57] T-64/89 *Automec v Commission* [1990] ECR II-367.

[58] Council Regulation (EEC) No 17: First Regulation implementing Articles 85 and 86 of the Treaty [1962] OJ SpecEd 13/204.

[59] Regulation No 99/63/EEC of the Commission of 25 July 1963 on the hearings provided for in Article 19(1) and (2) of Council Regulation No 17 [1963] OJ SpecEd 127/2268.

[60] *Automec* (n 57) paras 43 ff.

[61] T-120/89 *Stahlwerke Peine-Salzgitter v Commission* ECR II-279. Opinion delivered on 31 January 1991 by Judge J Biancarelli acting as Advocate General in the case.

as regards the interpretation of the Staff Regulations applicable to officials and other servants of the Communities.[62]

The cases pending before the CFI or on which it has already adjudicated concern a whole array of different matters including provisions on social security, the location where tasks are to be performed and changes in the post to which an official is assigned, remuneration, staff committee elections, resignations, termination of temporary staff employment, the duty to state reasons in administrative decisions, etc.

On a number of occasions, the CFI has had to rule on the interpretation of provisions in the Staff Regulations whose content and scope had yet to be clarified. For example, the CFI has interpreted the notion of a 'person treated as if he were a dependent child' referred to in Article 2(4) of Annex VII to the Staff Regulations,[63] and the notion of 'centre of interests' in order to determine an official's place of origin, within the meaning of Article 7(3) of Annex VII to the Staff Regulations.[64]

In other situations, the CFI has had recourse to general principles of Community law in order to interpret the Staff Regulations. In particular, the CFI applied the principle of equal treatment to the calculation of the study allowances provided for in Article 27 of the Staff Regulations, in a situation where the Commission had calculated those allowances on the basis of the 'transfer rate' used for the purpose of transferring part of an official's remuneration outside the country where he/she is employed, as provided for by Article 17(3) of Annex VII to the Staff Regulations.[65]

F. A Positive Experience So Far

It follows from the foregoing that it is still too soon to assess fully the impact of the setting up of the CFI, leading to the establishment of a two-tier system of judicial review, and, it is hoped, to an improvement in the judicial protection available to litigants before the Community courts.

It is already apparent, however, that, judging by the relatively limited number of appeals filed with the Court of Justice, and even though the latter has not yet

[62] Staff Regulations of Officials and the Conditions of Employment of Other Servants of the European Communities laid down by Regulation (Euratom, ECSC, EEC) No 259/68, as last amended by Regulation (Euratom, ECSC, EEC) No 2258/90 Regulation (Euratom, ECSC, EEC) No 3736/90 of the Council of 24 November 2010 amending the Staff Regulations of Officials of the European Communities and the Conditions of Employment of Other Servants of those Communities [1990] OJ L 360/1.

[63] T-48/89 *Beltrante and Others v Council* [1990] ECR II-493, T-49/89 *Mavrakos v Council* [1990] ECR II-509 and T-52/89 *Piemonte v Council* [1990] ECR II-513.

[64] T- 44/90 *Gouvras-Laycock v Commission* [1990] ECR II-217.

[65] T-167/89 *De Rijk v Commission* [1991] ECR II-91.

ruled on the merits of those appeals, the decisions of the CFI have, in general, been extremely well received.

It is therefore no longer possible to claim, as some feared prior to the setting up of the CFI, that the possibility for the parties to bring an appeal against the decisions of the CFI would necessarily entail a significant increase in the workload of the Court of Justice, liable to outweigh the benefits arising from the reduction in the number of cases handled by the latter at first instance following the transfer of jurisdiction to the CFI.

Actually, the opposite is true. Indeed, the statistics noted above show that, at the end of the CFI's first year of activity, the number of cases under appeal had in fact fallen in relation to the total number of cases.

More specifically, whereas the stock of cases transferred to the CFI in 1989 (153) represented around a quarter of the total number of cases pending before the Court of Justice, the number of cases pending before the CFI at the end of 1990 (145) represented less than one fifth of the total number of cases pending before the two courts put together.

Of course, these figures must be treated with caution given the considerable fluctuations to which judicial workflows may be subject, sometimes even over the course of a single one-year period.

In any event, the allocation of new competences to the CFI on the basis of Article 168 A of the Treaty will, to a certain extent, enable the legislator to broaden the scope of the system of two-tier judicial control.

That principle may be further strengthened if, as has been suggested,[66] the CFI is entrusted with the task of judging, under conditions yet to be determined, cases that relate to new areas of litigation at the edge of Community law's current scope and that concern the protection of private interests.[67]

It must, however, be stressed that the allocation of new jurisdiction to the CFI should not simply become an exercise in resolving the Court of Justice's workload problems by means of a wholesale transfer to the CFI of all the cases that are regarded as problematic or time-consuming. Any significant further transfer of competences should be gradual and should take into consideration both the CFI's ability to deliver justice and the specific nature and the respective roles of each of the two courts.

[66] See CFI, 'Éléments de réflexion sur l'évolution de la juridiction communautaire' (n 44).

[67] This is the case in respect of trade marks (see Draft Council Regulation on the Community trade mark [1984] OJ C230/1) and of the Community patent (89/695/EEC: Agreement relating to Community patents [1989] OJ L401/1), as well as of the interpretation of the Convention on the law applicable to contractual obligations, opened for signature in Rome on 19 June 1980 [1980] OJ L266/1.

5

The Development of the European Judicial System Before and After Maastricht*

I. THE FIRST STEP: THE SINGLE EUROPEAN ACT AND THE COURT OF FIRST INSTANCE

A. Setting up the CFI

FOR 37 YEARS the Treaties establishing the European Communities[1] have entrusted the essential mission of ensuring that the European Community under construction is a 'Community of law' to a judicial system based on two pillars.

The first one was composed of the Court of Justice, the only judicial body set up by the Treaties, which has been charged with the task of guaranteeing that Community law is observed across the whole Community. The second pillar comprises the national courts or tribunals, the ordinary judicial institutions for applying Community law, which are linked to the Court of Justice by a mechanism of legal cooperation, within the framework of the system of reference for preliminary ruling, provided for in Article 177 of the EEC Treaty.[2]

The system reached new dimensions following the establishment of the Court of First Instance of the European Communities. That step was made possible by Article 11 of the Single European Act, which inserted Article 168(1) in the EEC Treaty. The Court of First Instance was actually established by a decision of the Council of 24 October 1988[3] and started to operate on 1 September 1989.

* Published in 'Collected Courses of the Academy of European Law—Florence' V 1, *European Community Law* (The Hague, Kluwer Law International, 1996) 21–54.

[1] Articles 4, 164 ff of the EEC Treaty (renamed the EC Treaty following the Treaty on European Union) and the corresponding provisions of the Treaty establishing the European Coal and Steel Community (ECSC) (Articles 7, 31 ff).

[2] And the corresponding provisions of the other Treaties. Hereinafter I shall refer exclusively to the Treaty of the European Community (EC Treaty) unless the contrary is expressly indicated.

[3] Council Decision No 88/591/ECSC, EEC, Euratom of 24 October 1988 establishing a Court of First Instance of the European Communities [1988] OJ L319/1 and [1989] OJ L241 (amendments).

The aims prompting the setting up of the Court of First Instance were twofold. First and foremost, it aimed at meeting the constant increase in the number of cases coming before the Court of Justice, with the inevitable consequence of delaying the proceedings and augmenting the caseload. One need only recall in this connection that the number of cases registered each year (23 in 1960) rose from 79 in 1970 to 433 in 1985. In 15 years, it therefore rose by a factor of five, whilst the number of Members of the Court did not even double over the same period.

Experience has shown that—despite the effort made, the increase in the number of Members and the measures of rationalisation adopted—the maximum annual production of judgments by the Court of Justice, as presently composed, is between 200 and 220. Therefore it is hardly surprising that the number of cases pending has risen sixfold between 1976 and 1985, from 106 to 605.

It is generally agreed that the administration of justice must be effected with the speed necessary to bring illegal situations to an end and restore any legitimate rights or interests infringed. The necessary swiftness of justice must, however, be reconciled with the care which must be taken in establishing the facts and reviewing the decisions of administrative authorities; it must, moreover, preserve a rigorous and well-reasoned application of the law.

It is particularly difficult to reconcile such requirements in cases where complex facts are to be established, particularly those of an economic nature, and requiring the application of wide discretionary powers by the administrative authorities. That is exactly what happens in the field of Community litigation with cases arising from the application, *inter alia*, of the rules of the Treaty on competition, State aid and commercial policy, in particular the anti-dumping regulations.

In setting up the Court of First Instance, the Community provided itself with a new court, with which the Court of Justice has since been able to share its judicial task.

From the outset, the Court of First Instance was given jurisdiction to decide certain categories of cases brought by natural or legal persons on matters which very often require in-depth consideration of complicated facts: competition, ECSC cases and litigation on Community staff cases. The hope was that the judges of the new court would have the time, which the Court of Justice no longer had, to devote to disputes of that kind and, moreover, that their decisions would be sufficiently well-accepted so that the Court of Justice would not be subsequently inundated by an avalanche of appeals that might finally hamper the other essential aim bound up with the setting up of the Court of First Instance: that of improving the judicial protection of individuals by introducing a two-tier judicial review.

Indeed, Article 168a(1) of the Treaty provides that the decisions of the Court of First Instance shall be subject to a right of appeal 'on points of law only'. In practice, and up to now, the percentage of appeals has been around 22 to 25 per cent of the final decisions of the Court of First Instance.

B. A Gradual Improvement in Judicial Protection

How has the Court of First Instance so far lived up to the expectations, which inspired its inception? To what degree has it helped to achieve the task for which it was introduced?

It should be remembered in the first place that, in view of the narrow field of jurisdiction allocated to it at the outset, its contribution to alleviating the workload of the Court of Justice could only be a limited one. In 1989, when it began functioning, the Court of First Instance took over a stock of 153 cases, transferred from the Court of Justice, representing less than a quarter of the total number of cases then pending before that Court. This gave, no doubt, some small degree of relief to the judges of the Court of Justice and those assisting them in their daily work. In fact other cases further down the registry list simply took the place of the cases transferred and awaiting judgment.

The idea of 'de-concentration', which brought the Court of First Instance into being, should then be pursued farther along the field of jurisdiction envisaged by the Treaty for that Court. That was achieved by a Council Decision of 8 June 1993,[4] supplemented later by a Council Decision of 7 March 1994[5] on the transfer of jurisdiction in respect of cases concerning the application of measures to protect trade in the case of dumping and subsidies. Those two decisions practically exhausted the field of possibilities opened up by Article 168(a), by transferring to the Court of First Instance jurisdiction to deal with all cases brought by individuals—natural and legal persons—whatever the subject at issue.

It should be noted that the transfer of jurisdiction in anti-dumping cases took place only after a long period during which discussions within the Council were blocked.

The cases in question, although there are not many, generally raise delicate problems of a factual and economic nature, associated in particular with the determination of the market price and the normal value of goods, the calculation of the margin of dumping, the analysis of the structure of the various markets and the like. Those are consequently cases, which, by their very nature, are perfectly suited to the role of the Court of First Instance.

It should be, in any event, explained that the reasons for initially excluding anti-dumping litigation from the sphere of jurisdiction of the Court of First Instance had nothing to do with the actual nature of the Court or its capacity for dealing with such disputes. The reasons were rather more political and lay outside the influence of Community jurisdiction, whose role in this field was merely that of a spectator at an arm-wrestling match between a number of Member States, as well as between those States and the Commission with regard to the revision of

[4] Council Decision No 93/350/Euratom, ECSC, EEC of 8 June 1993 [1993] OJ L144/21.
[5] Council Decision 94/149/ECSC, EEC, Euratom of 7 March 1994 [1994] OJ L66/29.

the basic regulation on the matter and to the distribution of powers between the various institutions, in particular the Council and the Commission.

The new transfers of jurisdiction have already made possible a considerable reduction in the workload of the Court of Justice, since 465 cases were involved, of which 380 were actions for a declaration of invalidity and actions concerning non-contractual liability of the Community legislation on milk-production quotas within the framework of the common agricultural policy (CAP). As a result of these transfers, the ratio of cases pending before each of the Courts has been reversed: whilst the number of cases pending before the Court of Justice has fallen from over 700 to fewer than 400, those pending before the Court of First Instance have risen from some 200 to some 650 (800 on 31 May 1994).

That is, however, only one of the aspects from which we may evaluate the contribution made by the Court of First Instance to achieving the aims of reforming the Community system of administration of justice, which was conceived at its inception.

One may in fact also consider to what extent the introduction of a second tier of jurisdiction has managed to 'improve the judicial protection of individual interests' as envisaged in the Decision of 24 October 1988.

The first point to note is that the parties to cases transferred from the Court of Justice to the Court of First Instance at the time of its creation have of course in general had the benefit of having their cases considered immediately, without having to await their turn on the Court of Justice waiting list. This is a kind of automatic effect of the assignment of the first cases to a new court starting with a clean slate.

Furthermore, the lasting effects of this new distribution of jurisdiction should be considered from a medium and long-term point of view. In that respect, some thought needs to be devoted to the working methods adopted by the Court of First Instance, bearing in mind the aims pursued.

The innovative nature of these methods may be seen above all in the provisions of Article 64 of the Rules of Procedure of the Court of First Instance, adopted on 2 May 1991.[6] That Article lays down the measures of organisation of procedure, which differ from measures of inquiry inasmuch as they are more informal. They may be adopted at any stage of the procedure upon a proposal from one or another of the parties, or upon the initiative of the Court of First Instance, and are intended to ensure the preparation of cases for the hearing and the efficient conduct of procedures, to facilitate the taking of evidence, to clarify the points at issue as well as the pleas in law and arguments of the parties, and finally, to facilitate an amiable settlement of proceedings.

In practice, although it cannot be said that the Court of First Instance has yet availed itself of all possibilities offered by that provision, it may already be stated

[6] [1991] OJ L136/1 and [1991] OJ L317/34 (amendment).

that some of the measures taken within that field have actually made it possible to improve the administration of justice and to speed up the proceedings.

C. The Initial Case-Law of the CFI

The case-law of the Court of First Instance has, from the outset, been guided by a concern to make a scrupulous review of the facts as they have been established by the authority responsible for the contested act, whilst not appearing to usurp the role of the administration in inquiring into the facts or producing evidence.

That concern to make a thorough review of the facts is reflected in particular in the quantity and depth of the questions put in writing and in the number and nature of the documents and information requested before the hearings, both from the parties, and from others. It is also reflected in the frequent use of oral testimony and statements by the parties, and then again in the relatively lengthy oral procedures which in certain cases have lasted more than a week (such as the cases known as the *Polypropylene*[7] and *PVC*[8] cartel cases).

Such thoroughness in the preparation and organisation of the cases inevitably somewhat slows down the pace of proceedings. For that reason, in several cases, the Chamber concerned has asked the Judge-Rapporteur to undertake measures of organisation of the procedure. He has thus examined, together with the parties at informal meetings (sometimes lasting several hours), the evidence produced and the content of the documents and has established their importance and relevance for the case in question. In certain complicated cases where there was a great deal of evidential material (for example the *Flat Glass* cases[9] or the *English Tractors* cases[10]), that method has enabled the Chamber dealing with the case to use a slimmed down version of the file, based on the Report of the Judge-Rapporteur, even before the oral procedure with the parties, which has then been able to progress free from ambiguities and with optimum speed and clarity.

It must also be said that the Court of First Instance has been able to carry out its judicial task in a relatively flexible manner since it generally sits in Chambers of three or five judges, sittings in plenary sessions being an exception[11] (so far

[7] Cases T-1-4/89 and T-6-15/89 -*Rhône-Poulenc and Others v Commission* [1991] [1992] ECR II-867.

[8] Cases T-79/89, T-84/89, T-85/89, T-86/89, T-89/89, T-91/89, T-92/89, T-94/89, T-96/89, T-98/89, T-102/89 and T-104/89 *BASF and Others v Commission* [1992] ECR II-315.

[9] Cases T-68/89, T-77/89 and T-78/89 *SIV a o v Commission (Flat Glass)* [1992] ECR II-1403.

[10] Cases T-34/92 and T-35/92 *1994, Fiatagri and Others v Commission (English Tractors)* ECR [1994] II-905.

[11] Article 2(4) of the Council Decision of First Instance of 24 October 1988 provides: 'The Court of First Instance shall sit in Chambers of three or five Judges. (...) In certain cases governed by the Rules of Procedure the Court of First Instance may sit in plenary session.' See also Articles 10 ff of the Rules of Procedure.

only three cases have been heard in plenary session).[12] Moreover, in contrast to the Court of Justice, no Advocate General is in principle heard in cases coming before the Court of First Instance. The judges may indeed be called upon to perform the task of an Advocate General in specific cases,[13] but such a possibility has been used on only four or five occasions.[14]

D. Amicable Settlement of Proceedings

The other aim of the Court of First Instance, sought by the adoption of such measures of organisation of procedure as those mentioned above, is 'to facilitate the amicable settlement of proceedings' (Article 64(2)(d)). That aim has been achieved most frequently in the field of staff cases, but also in the field of competition litigation.

Attempts are made to reach agreement between the parties either during the oral procedure or at informal meetings of the Chamber with the lawyers. Where the Court of First Instance wishes to take the initiative, on the basis of the information contained in the file, the representatives of the parties are informed in advance that the Court is considering the possibility of attempting conciliation and are asked to obtain the necessary powers for reaching an agreement.

Finally, on this same subject, it may be appropriate to recall the importance assumed, in the Court's practice, by the special form of procedure for interim measures (laid down in Article 104 to 110 of the Rules of Procedure) as a factor for simplifying proceedings, for swiftly settling urgent matters and for the amicable settlement of the dispute. The President of the Court of First Instance, who is responsible in principle (under Article 106 of the Rules of Procedure) for deciding on all applications for the adoption of interim measures (suspension of the operation of the decision at issue and other interim measures), was thus able, in the case concerning ferry services between England and Ireland,[15] to bring the positions of the parties so close together that, by the agreement reached between them at the hearing, they discontinued both their application for interim measures, the main action, as well as the complaint previously submitted to the Commission.

The Order of the President of the Court of First Instance,[16] made in proceedings brought by several milk producers, where (because of undertakings not to

[12] Case T-51/89 *Tetra Pak v Commission* [1990] II-309, T-28/90 *Asia Motor France and Others v Commission* [1992] ECR II-2285 and T-24/90, *Automec v Commission (Automec II)* [1992] ECR II-2223.

[13] In the conditions set out in Article 2(3) of the Decision of 14 October 1988 and in Articles 17, 18 and 19 of the Rules of Procedure.

[14] Apart from the cases heard in plenary session, cited above, the cases in point are T-120/89 *Stahlwerke Peine-Salzgitter v Commission* [1991] ECR II-279 and T-1-4, 6-15/89 *Polypropylene* (First Chamber) (n 7).

[15] T-42/92R *Sealink Stena Line v Commission* (not published in the ECR).

[16] Order of the President of the Court of First Instance of 1 February 1994, T-278/93R and T-555/93R *David Alwyn and Others v Council of the European Union.*

market milk entered into under Council Regulation No 1078/77[17]) they were not granted reference quantities under Council Regulation No 857/84,[18] is of similar significance and even broader scope. The decision taken in the light of the information provided by the parties during the hearing, and in particular regarding an explanatory statement by the Council and the Commission, made it possible to clarify one particularly important point in dispute, concerning the application of the provision in Article 43 of the Statute of the Court of Justice on the limitation of actions brought against the Community in matters arising from non-contractual liability. Following that Order, many producers involved in such proceedings withdrew their claims for declaration of invalidity or for compensation, which made it possible to put an end, at least provisionally, to a significant part of a vast proportion of litigation involving some 450 cases which for the most part had been transferred from the Court of Justice to the Court of First Instance.

Even when agreement between the parties, although very close, proves to be impossible, the information submitted to the President, in connection with applications for the adoption of interim measures, sometimes enables him to take a decision instituting an 'intermediate *modus vivendi*' reflecting a balance between the various opposing interests. That constitutes in practice a step on the way to settling the dispute which might, if appropriate, be followed up by the Chamber dealing with the case. In this connection reference may be made to the Orders made in the German ice-cream cases (Orders of 8 May 1992, 16 June 1992 and 16 July 1992, *Langnese Schöler v Commission*)[19] and the Netherlands building firms (Order of 16 July 1992, *Spo v Commission*).[20]

The procedure with regard to applications for the adoption of interim measures seems to be, by virtue of its speed and flexibility, naturally destined to assume considerable significance in the field of economic litigation, where speed is of paramount importance for the business world. This is particularly evident in the legal fields of competition law, concentrations between undertakings, State aids, and commercial policy.

Moreover, due to the way it is organised by the Rules of Procedure and the use to which it may be put, the procedure in connection with applications for the adoption of interim measures makes an excellent testing ground for certain reforms which might be envisaged and introduced into other fields of Community litigation.

[17] Council Regulation (EEC) No 1078/77 of 17 May 1977 introducing a system of premiums for the non-marketing of milk and milk products and for the conversion of dairy herds [1977] OJ L131/1.

[18] Council Regulation (EEC) No 857/84 of 31 March 1984 adopting general rules for the application of the levy referred to in Article 5c of Regulation (EEC) No 804/68 in the milk and milk products sector [1984] OJ L90/13.

[19] T-24/92R *Langnese-Iglo and Schöller Lebensmittel v Commission* 1992 ECR II-1713 and II-1839.

[20] T-29/92R *SPO a o v Commission* [1992] ECR II-216.

E. Length and Accessibility of Judgments

To end this section there are two other aspects, which are worth mentioning.

The first aspect relates to the average length of judgments of the Court of First Instance. The most frequent criticism towards the case-law of the Court of First Instance concerns the excessive length of its judgments. It must indeed be recognised that those judgments are, in general, noticeably longer than those of the Court of Justice, which sometimes makes life harder for regular readers of Community case-law.

There are three main reasons for this. First, it is inherent in the complex nature of the litigation, which involves above all economic cases, coming before the Court of First Instance. Second, the fact that the decisions of this Court may be subject to appeal on questions of law means, not only that the statement of the grounds of judgment must be particularly detailed and complete, but also that the findings of fact—which are final—must be stated fully, precisely and clearly, in the judgment itself and not only in the report for the hearing. Finally, it must be acknowledged that certain habits of drafting—and possibly the personality or the national tradition of one or other Judge-Rapporteur—have helped to lengthen the case-law of the Court of First Instance beyond what might be desirable.

The Court of First Instance therefore recently adopted extremely clear internal guidelines[21] on its working methods, aimed at restricting as far as possible the volume of its judgments, recording only the decisive features of the grounds of judgment and examining only the principal arguments put forward by the parties to the dispute.

That is also a way to help to alleviate another problem, concerned with the publication of the Community case-law—one which has been constantly growing worse over the past few years. That is to say, the growing bulk of the Reports of Cases before the Court—now including that of both Courts—which in 1992 reached almost 10,000 printed pages in each language. Even though that figure demonstrates a noteworthy productivity, it does nevertheless raise considerable difficulties: apart from the space occupied in libraries and the costs involved in the publication and distribution of such Reports, it must be acknowledged that it is becoming more and more difficult to follow all the case-law and to pick out its essential aspects. Moreover, the problems of translating Reports into all the Community languages have continued to grow, bringing longer delays in publication of the different linguistic versions, hence threatening the principle of equal treatment for the various Community languages.

For those reasons—and following the decision taken by the Court of Justice not to publish the report of the hearing for each case, which formerly accompanied

[21] Plenary Conference of 13 January 1994. These guidelines are the sequel to other measures rationalising working methods and speeding up proceedings, which were adopted by the Court to keep pace with the development of litigation, to take account of the experience acquired and to put right any errors of method.

the judgment—the Court of First Instance has decided no longer to publish in the general Reports the judgments delivered in the staff cases of the Community public service, but to put them instead in a separate publication, comprising a set of specialised multi-lingual reports which will include all the judgments in that sphere in the individual language of the case, accompanied by sufficiently complete and clear summaries in all the other official languages.

With the help of such measures, it will be possible not only to make up for any remaining backlog in the publication of the case-law of the Court of Justice and the Court of First Instance, but also to ensure that all judgments in matters other than the civil service are available in all the official languages on the day on which they are delivered, or at least within a week, so that they may all be published six months after they are delivered at the latest.

If it is to be effective and meet the expectations of those for whom it is intended, the activity of a Court covering the whole territory of the Community requires a considerable effort as regards publication and transparency. For that very reason the Court of First Instance has adopted, four years after it was established, its 'Instructions to the Registrar', as provided by Article 23 of its Rules of Procedure. That document, which is available in all of the official languages and is published in the Official Journal,[22] is of course intended for the Registrar, but it is mainly of interest to the lawyers and agents of the parties, since it codifies the practices for the administration of justice adopted by the Court of First Instance and the procedural consequences arising from the way the parties conduct their relations with the Court. The existence of such a document ensures that such relations are in line with the best conditions of legal certainty.

It should be noted that the Court of Justice has also for many years had its own Instructions to the Registrar.[23] In addition to its own experience, the Court of First Instance has been able to reap the benefit of the long experience of the Court of Justice, in order to better meet the new requirements of Community litigation, particularly in the phase coming to pass as the Treaty on European Union comes into force.

The second part of this chapter will be devoted more specifically to the description, and a brief discussion, of the changes in the structure and operation of the judicial system introduced by the Treaty of Maastricht, so as to have a better framework for our subsequent reflections on the future of the system after Maastricht.

[22] 'Instructions to the Registrar of the Court of First Instance' of 3 March 1994 [1994] OJ L78/32.

[23] Adopted on 4 December 1974 [1974] OJ L350/33 and amended on 3 October 1986 [1986] OJ C286/4.

II. THE TREATY ON EUROPEAN UNION AND THE COMMUNITY JUDICIAL SYSTEM

A. Access to Court and Allocation of Cases

The Treaty on European Union[24] introduced a number of changes in the organisation and operation of the Community system of administration of justice. However, they vary in importance and in any event do not bring about any revolution in the structure of the system, which would anyway be undesirable.

In certain cases, the new Treaty merely recorded the evolution operated in the case-law of the Court of Justice during recent years. Thus the amendments made to Articles 173 and 175 of the Treaty embodied in the text of the Treaty the procedural position the Court had already accorded to the European Parliament.

In one case—Article 165—the amendment made related to the internal workings of the Court of Justice, which has been granted almost complete freedom in the assignment of cases to the Chambers, save for cases where the Member States or the institutions which are parties to the proceedings ask that a case be heard in plenary session. The measure in question is not without importance since it allows the Court to improve its organisation in order to meet the increase in litigation.[25]

B. Sanctions in Infringement Proceedings

Next, reference should be made to the new wording of Article 171. This provision allows the Court of Justice, on proposal of the Commission, to impose pecuniary sanctions, in the form either of a lump sum or of a penalty payment, on Member States failing to comply, within the time limit laid down, with judgments declaring that a State has failed to fulfil an obligation under the Treaty. That new provision is an answer to the widely-expressed concern over the absence, in the text of the EC Treaty,[26] of any machinery for effective sanctions for infringements of Community law by Member States, as well as to the risk that findings of a failure to fulfil obligations, if not followed by enforcement, might be regarded as

[24] Treaty on European Union, signed at Maastricht on 7 February 1992.

[25] It may be mentioned also, as regards the internal workings of the Court, that, following objections raised by one Member State, the inter-governmental conference did not approve another proposal of the Court, namely that of amending Article 167 of the Treaty in order to allow Advocates General to take part in the same way as judges in the election of the President of the Court (although not to be elected as President).

[26] In contrast to the European Coal and Steel Community (ECSC) Treaty, Article 88 of which already provided that in the event of a Member State's omitting to implement a decision of the High Authority declaring a failure to fulfill an obligation under the Treaty, the High Authority might, with the assent of the Council acting by a two-thirds majority, impose the appropriate sanctions: suspend the payment of any sums due to the State in question; take measures or authorise the other Member States to take measures by way of derogation from the Treaty in order to correct the effects of the infringement in question.

hollow. Such a concern was also reflected in the text of Declaration No 19 annexed to the final act of the Treaty of Maastricht relating to the implementation of Community law.

In spite of its relatively innovative content, doubts have been expressed with regard to the need for effectiveness and operational nature of such a provision. In fact (a) it is not possible to say that the failure to fulfil obligations by Member States are systematic, reiterated or extremely serious; (b) certain indirect mechanisms make it possible to ensure the effectiveness of a finding of failure to fulfil an obligation: the *Francovich* judgment[27] has made it possible for such findings to be more compelling; (c) other alternative or cumulative methods of sanction might prove more effective (for example suspension of payment of Community funds, the possibility of adopting specific measures), notably if it were provided that they should be adopted from the first judgment finding a failure to fulfil an obligation; (d) the rare cases of repeated failure have their origin in institutional (eg, of a constitutional nature) domestic bottle-necks, rather than in any generalised anti-Community attitude; (e) the application and determination of the amount of the pecuniary sanction provided for will inevitably raise certain delicate problems.[28]

C. Extending Jurisdiction of the CFI

The most important innovation from the point of view of the development of the Community judicial system is, however, the amendment made to Article 168a(1) of the EC Treaty which, in its new version following the Treaty on European Union, extends the jurisdiction of the Court of First Instance to all classes of action, regardless of the applicant—natural or legal person, Member State or Community institution—and the field of Community law that is concerned. Only questions referred to the Court of Justice for a preliminary ruling under Article 177 are expressly excluded from the jurisdiction of the Court of First Instance.

Article 168a(2) provides that the Council, acting unanimously, shall at the request of the Court of Justice, and after consulting the European Parliament and the Commission, determine the classes of action, which are within the sphere envisaged in paragraph 1, to be subject to the jurisdiction of the Court of First Instance. The train will therefore be able to depart again as soon as it is thought appropriate to bring into play the machinery provided by the said provisions. The question that immediately springs to mind is naturally in what terms, according to which criteria and at what tempo the power conferred on the Council by the new Article 168a is to be used. I will deal with that question in the following section.

[27] C-6/90 and C-9/90 *Francovich and Bonifaci and Others v Italy* [1991] ECR I-5357.

[28] See in particular XVth Congress FIDE—II 'La sanction des infractions au droit communautaire' (Lisbon, APDE, 1992), especially the General Report by Advocate General Giuseppe Tesauro 425 ff.

D. The Three Pillars and the Protection of Rights

First, however, it is appropriate to recall that, according to Article L in the Final Provisions of the Maastricht Treaty, the powers of the Court of Justice (and those of the Court of First Instance as well) apply only to the provisions of the Community Treaties, excluding *inter alia* the provisions relating to the common foreign and security policy (CFSP) (second pillar) and the cooperation on justice and home affairs (third pillar).[29]

In that connection, three comments may be made. First, in the present state of Community law development, the solution embodied in the Treaty will come as no surprise. In fact, since the two pillars in question are subject to purely inter-governmental logic, there is nothing wrong in submitting judicial review in these fields to mechanisms which are distinct from those provided for by the Treaty as regards the areas of Community integration.

Second, in spite of the above, it must be recognised that the solution adopted by the Treaty represents a weakening in the degree of protection of rights and of the review of acts of government. It must be remembered that in those closely associated with internal security—CFSP, cooperation on justice and police affairs, in particular the latter—action by the Union may directly affect not only the protection of rights of the citizen, but also the fundamental principles of free movement within the Community territory.

Moreover, it must not be overlooked that whilst review by the Court is in principle excluded, parliamentary control over these two pillars of the Union action is also perceptibly reduced. It is true that the European Parliament is informed and consulted on the principal aspects and fundamental options of these policies. In addition it organises an annual debate and Members of the Parliament may put questions and submit recommendations to the Council.

However, the European Parliament's opinions are simply 'duly taken into consideration', which leaves the essential part of parliamentary control back with national parliaments. In such circumstances, since important aspects of those policies have been removed from the national sphere and 'inter-governmentalised', without being brought under the Community system, the risk of a 'democratic retreat' is a real one.[30] What might help to reduce it, at least at declamatory level, is the express reference in Article K.2 to the application in the field of cooperation on justice and police affairs, of the European Convention for the Protection of

[29] Except for Article K.3(2)(c), which refers to the jurisdiction which may be conferred on the Court of Justice to interpret the conventions adopted between the Member States in these areas and rule on any disputes regarding their application.

[30] See in this context D Curtin, 'The Constitutional Structure of the Union: A Europe of Bits and Pieces' (1993) 30 *Common Market Law Review* 20.

Human Rights and Fundamental Freedoms and the Geneva Convention relating to the Status of Refugees.[31]

Finally, it should be stressed that the coexistence within the framework of the Union of three pillars governed by such different philosophies, one subject to judicial control by the Court while the others are not, means that the province of each needs to be clearly delineated. That will inevitably entail difficulties of implementation and problems in linking together the various parts of the Treaty.[32] Such ambiguity is aggravated by the fact that the new Article 100c, inserted in the EC Treaty by the Treaty of Maastricht, subjected a part of the visa policy to the Community system and that Article K.9 of the same Maastricht Treaty makes it possible to extend that system to other aspects of the policies in the areas of cooperation on justice and home affairs.

Such ambiguities reflect the transitional stage in which the institutional structure of the Community, or of the Union, is placed, and with it its judicial system.

[31] The reference to the European Convention for the Protection of Human Rights makes more explicit in this field the general declaration set out in Article F(2) of the Treaty on European Union, according to which '[t]he Union shall respect fundamental rights, as guaranteed by the European Convention for the Protection of Human Rights and Fundamental Freedoms signed at Rome on 4 November 1950 and as they result from the constitutional traditions common to the Member States, as general principles of Community law'. Such references naturally help to strengthen the idea of the European Union as a union based on a Community of Law. It is true that the Treaty does not include, as had been proposed, a detailed catalogue of fundamental rights; but the case-law of the Court of Justice has already undertaken to embody them as a key component in the Community legal order. It is nevertheless surprising that Article F, coming under Title I (Common Provisions) is formally excluded from judicial review by Article L. The question is, however, purely formal since fundamental rights as a whole are an integral part of the *acquis communautaire* and are therefore, as such, safeguarded by the actual text of the Treaty (Articles M and N(2)). It may be added that the machinery for the defence of the rights of the citizen in the Community is enhanced in the Treaty of Maastricht by the inclusion of the right to petition the European Parliament (first subparagraph of Article 8d, in conjunction with Article 138d of the EC Treaty) and the right to apply to the Ombudsman (second subparagraph of Article 8d, in conjunction with Article 138e).

[32] An interesting example of the type of problem, which may arise in connection with the interaction between the Communities and the Union relates to the European Council and its institutional position within the new system of the Treaties. In fact the European Council appears to be conceived in Article D of the Treaty of Maastricht as an important body which forms part of the institutional machinery of the Union, however it is not included among the institutions of the Community listed in Article 4 of the EC Treaty, which casts doubt on the relevance of the statement in Article C that '[t]he Union shall be served by a single institutional framework'. Moreover it is astonishing that, while it is for the European Council to 'provide the Union with the necessary impetus for its development and … define the general political guidelines thereof' (Article D), Title VI on Cooperation in the fields of Justice and Home Affairs, unlike Title V on the CFSP, does not mention it in any of its provisions. Moreover, whereas by virtue of Article L the acts of the European Council are excluded from review by the Court of Justice, the Court may nevertheless be called upon to consider indirectly the compatibility with the Treaty of the political guidelines defined by the Council when required to assess the validity of decisions of the other institutions based on those guidelines. In this connection, see U Everling, 'Reflections on the Structure of the European Union' (1992) 29 *Common Market Law Review* 1061, 1062.

III. FUTURE OF THE COMMUNITY JUDICIAL SYSTEM FOLLOWING THE ENTRY INTO FORCE OF THE TREATY ON EUROPEAN UNION

A. The New Regulation on the Community Trade Mark

The first point to be considered under this section relates not to the Treaty of Maastricht itself, but to the implementation of the judicial system, inserted in the EEC Treaty (Article 168a) by the Single European Act, after the adoption of a legal framework for the protection of trade marks at the community level.

In fact, once the issue of the seat of the Office for Harmonisation in the Internal Market (hereinafter the 'Office'), set up at Alicante, was settled and the choice of the working languages of the Office was made, Council Regulation (EC) 40/94 of 19 December 1993 on the Community trade mark was approved and published.[33]

The implementation of that Regulation will very likely give rise to abundant litigation of a type, which is new in the Community context. A special system of legal remedies is established by the Regulation, both to ensure that parties that are affected by decisions made by the Office are entitled to legal protection in a manner that is suited to the special characteristics of trade mark law, and to strengthen the protection of Community trade marks and their unitary character throughout the whole Community territory.

The Regulation provides, on the one hand, that, once the set of appeals available within the Office has been exhausted, the parties may apply to the Court of First Instance seeking that the contested decision of the Board of Appeals of the Office is annulled or altered (Article 63), with a possible appeal, limited to questions of law, to the Court of Justice. The possibility, provided for in the draft Regulation, that the Member States and the Community institutions might bring an action 'in the interest of the law' against the decisions of the Office, has been deleted from the final version of the Regulation.[34]

The Regulation provides, on the other hand, that the Member States are to designate in their territories a number of 'Community trademark courts', which have exclusive jurisdiction for infringement actions relating to Community trade marks and actions for declaration of non-infringement, as well as for actions for compensation in respect of matters arising after the publication of a Community trade mark application and after publication of the registration of the mark, and for counterclaims for revocation or for declaration of invalidity of the Community trade mark (Article 91 et seq). These Community trade mark courts, and the other national courts before which a question of interpretation of the

[33] Council Regulation (EC) 40/94 of 19 December 1993 [1994] OJ L11/1. The Regulation on the Community trade mark was followed some months later by Council Regulation (EC) No 2100/94 of 27 July 1994 on Community plant variety rights [1994] OJ L2271, which institutes appeal procedures similar to those established in the trade mark Regulation.

[34] The usual legal remedies, in particular Article 173 of the Treaty, may certainty be used by those privileged applicants; but in view of the private or commercial type of litigation in this field, it is hard to see how such a possibility may materialise in practice.

Regulation is brought, may refer questions to the Court of Justice for a preliminary ruling pursuant to Article 177 of the Treaty.

i. Amendments to the Rules of Procedure

The implementation of the various legal remedies just mentioned might raise new problems of either a procedural nature or otherwise connected with the organisation of the Community judicature.

Problems of the first type arise from the fact that two different types of proceedings before the boards of appeal are envisaged. In the first place, there are proceedings of an administrative nature, which are *ex parte* proceedings opposing a private party and the Office in respect of a decision taken by the latter (for example, a decision to refuse to register a Community trade mark). A different category of proceedings concerns cases of a civil nature: it involves proceedings *inter partes*, between two natural or legal persons before the Office, which has the task of settling the dispute (following, eg, applications for revocation or for a declaration of invalidity of the Community trade mark).

The Community judiciary (Court of First Instance and Court of Justice) therefore has the problem of organising the procedure to be followed when an application is lodged against a decision of the Office. In view of the nature of the legal remedies established by the Treaty and the Regulation itself (Article 63), the procedure can only be conceived as an application for annulment of the type envisaged in Article 173 of the Treaty, in which the Office is in the defendant's position. But the quasi-judicial nature of the boards of appeal and the purely private nature of the opposing interests require adaptations to the Rules of Procedure, in particular, that special treatment is accorded to the position of an intervener.

In order to deal with the issues arising from the new procedural situation, the Court of First Instance has just prepared a draft amendment to its Rules of Procedure, designed to insert a new chapter containing appropriate provisions of a procedural nature.

ii. The Increase in Litigation and Possible Solutions

The second group of problems is connected with the likely volume of this new litigation. In fact, estimates made by the Commission a few years ago suggest that between 750 and 1000 appeals might be filed per annum with the boards of appeal, which might entail some 200 to 250 actions[35] brought annually before the Court of First Instance. As this will involve a new field of Community law and enforcement of new individual rights in the Community sphere, thus giving

[35] These estimates have recently been revised upwards.

rise to novel legal issues, appropriate solutions must be found to deal with it. The Court of First Instance has also been giving thought to this matter.

An increase in the number of judges of the Court of First Instance is one of the possible answers to the problem. Another, which has moreover been envisaged as from the first discussions within the Court, might consist of the creation of a new type of specialised 'judge-assessor', responsible for the preparation of cases for hearings and for taking part in the decision together with the judges of the Court of First Instance and under the presidency of one of the latter, according to appropriate procedures.

Such judge-assessors would basically correspond to the development of the concept of 'assistant rapporteurs', provided for in Article 12 of the Statute of the Court. Although that provision has never been applied, the main reason for that is the powers of such assistant rapporteurs would not make it possible for them to be anything more than qualified 'legal secretaries'.[36] In any case, it is certain, in my view, that the judge-assessor formula would raise delicate problems for the internal cohesion and the organisation of the Court.

The Court of First Instance has therefore tended, at least initially, towards a form of judicial organisation, which, whilst not disrupting its structures or composition, would enable it to give judgment more quickly so as to cope without delay with growing volumes of litigation.

Thus the decision has been taken to have as large a number of cases as possible decided by Chambers consisting of three judges, which would become the normal way of judging all cases not falling within categories which generally raise problems of special complexity (competition and concentrations of undertakings, State aid, anti-dumping, ECSC, Euratom). Even in those fields there should be more flexible rules for assigning cases to Chambers of three judges than the present scheme of Articles 14 and 51 of the Rules of Procedure.

With a view to achieving these aims, the Court of First Instance has submitted to the Council, with the agreement of the Court of Justice, a proposal to amend Article 12 of its Rules of Procedure allowing it to lay down, by a decision to be published in the Official Journal, the criteria for the allocation of cases between the Chambers composed of different numbers of judges (three or five).[37]

[36] In particular, according to the Statute, those assistant rapporteurs would take part only in the organisation of the cases and in preparatory inquiries, which would mean that a Judge-Rapporteur would still need to be appointed. Although physically present, they would not take part in the deliberations and would not therefore share responsibility for the decisions to be taken. U Everling, 'L'organisation juridictionnelle de l'Union européenne' in G Vandersanden (ed), *La réforme du système juridictionnel communautaire* (Brussels, Ed Université Libre de Bruxelles, 1994) 22, called them 'second class judges' ('*juges de seconde catégorie*'), which might be a source of tension within the Court.

[37] The proposal was unanimously adopted by the Council and published in [1994] OJ L249/17. See also the new paragraph 5a added to Article 44 and paragraph 2 added to Article 51. In its initial version, Article 12 of the Rules of Procedure, only staff cases were automatically allocated to a Chamber composed of three judges, all the others being assigned to chambers of five judges.

So as to put these guidelines into practice immediately, the Court of First Instance has decided to apply them as from the beginning of the judicial year 1994/5, therefore putting to the test the effectiveness of the new solutions.

iii. Limiting the Number of Appeals

The search for appropriate solutions to this type of litigation—and to others, which may make their appearance[38]—might also be pursued as regards the judicial relationship between the two Community Courts. In fact, regard being given to the considerable number of cases and the nature of the questions at issue, which will rarely be of general interest, and to the fact that the boards of appeal of the Office for Harmonization in the Internal Market have already reached a decision about them prior to their submissions for a decision of the Court of First Instance, it is doubtful whether, in the majority of cases, there will be any justification for appeals to the Court of Justice as a third instance court.

A screening system or mechanism of leave to appeal might therefore have a part to play with the object of restricting access to the Court of Justice in this field to cases where such a step is justified by their importance for the case-law or by their general impact. As no provision is made for machinery of this kind in the present system of Community law, it will be necessary to make arrangements for inserting it into the Treaty, possibly at the time of the amendment envisaged for 1996.

The results of an experience of this kind in this specific sphere of intellectual property law will make it possible to learn many lessons for or against the possible extension of the system to other fields of Community law.[39]

B. A General First Instance Administrative Court

The new version of Article 168a set out in the Treaty on European Union gives the Council power to assign to the Court of First Instance, in addition to cases brought by natural or legal persons, jurisdiction to hear actions brought by Member States and Community institutions.

Although that development seems perfectly logical, the whole problem lies in the choice of rhythm and the detailed arrangements for using such an authorisation. It is clear, in fact, that it cannot be used immediately and without careful consideration of what the Court of First Instance should be in the future.

It does not seem appropriate to regard it as a court of first instance generally empowered to deal with all Community litigation, a kind of necessary stage

[38] See in this connection the proposal, submitted by the Commission on 3 December 1993, for a regulation on Community designs ([1994] OJ C29/20).

[39] See, in this regard, U Everling (n 36) 31.

through which all and any action must pass before any intervention by the Court of Justice.

In particular, litigation of a constitutional nature must continue to be reserved for the Court of Justice. It should be pointed out that all constitutional courts, in the countries that have them, consist of but a single instance. The question of a two-tier judicial review does not arise, as far as they are concerned, with the same degree of necessity as when the question at issue is the protection of private interests in civil lawsuits, a review of the legality of acts of the administration or the exercise of rights of defence against punitive sanctions.

The Court of First Instance, in my opinion, must be regarded in the future as an administrative court of first instance with generalised jurisdiction within the Community legal system.

From that point of view it is possible to envisage the assignment to it—in addition to cases brought by natural or legal persons—of actions brought against acts of the institutions by the Member States as addressees of such acts as any natural or legal person could be.[40] In this respect, no reason seems to justify making a distinction between individual and normative acts. In fact, it is current practice in those judicial systems which admit individual actions against acts having the character of laws or regulations to handle them by way of administrative rather than constitutional litigation.

It must be acknowledged that an important ambiguity subsists in the Community legal order when it comes to drawing a distinction between rules laid down by law or by regulation. In the national legal systems the difference between these two types of rule is in general clear, so that it is possible to distinguish with reasonable precision between the legislative and the administrative field. It is however to be hoped that, as provided by Declaration No 16 annexed to the Treaty of Maastricht, the inter-governmental conference to be convened in 1996 will undertake a revision of the classification of Community acts with a view to establishing an appropriate hierarchy between the different categories of acts. Any ambiguity should then be removed so that any objections against extending the concept of administrative litigation to regulations may be withdrawn.

Of course a difference exists, as regards the nature of the interests directly protected, between actions brought by natural or legal persons and actions brought by Member States. In the latter case the interests of individuals are concerned only indirectly insofar as the State is acting on behalf of the citizens. However, the position of the parties to the proceedings (Community institutions, on the one side, and entities, either private or public affected by measures taken by the former, on the other) are the same in both cases, which justifies their being treated by the same courts and according to identical rules of procedure.

In this context, the transfer of jurisdiction to the Court of First Instance might include, in particular, actions brought by Member States in fields such as State

[40] On this point, see ibid 27.

aid, fishing quotas, clearance of European Social Fund and European Agricultural Guidance and Guarantee *Fund* accounts, CAP regulations and others of the same content and importance. Only with a great effort would it be possible to discern, in such administrative litigation, elements of a constitutional nature that might give grounds to claim that it should continue to be subject in the first and last instance to the jurisdiction of the Court of Justice alone.

The great advantage of including it in the field of jurisdiction of the Court of First Instance—apart from allowing the Member States the opportunity to benefit from two-tier jurisdiction—is the fact that, in a considerable number of such cases (like those relating to State aid or Community funds), general interests (in particular those of a budgetary nature) and private interests are interwoven in such a way that very often the same measures (of individual or general nature) are challenged simultaneously in proceedings brought by undertakings and by Member States.

In the present state of affairs such proceedings—although related and often seeking annulment of the same decision—must be decided by different courts. Such a situation, in spite of the existence of appropriate procedural means (see in that connection Article 47 of the Statute of the Court) nevertheless raises delicate problems.

The same reasoning does not apply to proceedings between institutions or to proceedings brought by the institutions against Member States (in particular actions for failure to fulfil an obligation under the Treaty), which must be regarded as being of a constitutional nature, in particular because they concern the institutional balance within the Community or the division of powers between the Community and the Member States. Those are, of course, to be reserved to the jurisdiction of the Court of Justice.

C. A Supreme and Constitutional Court

As a result of such a development the Court of Justice will gradually establish itself as the 'Supreme and Constitutional Court within the Community legal order'.

The qualitative and quantitative importance of its intervention as a Supreme Court will increase in proportion to the extension of the jurisdiction of the Court of First Instance, and thus of the field of application of the principle of two-tier judicial review. It will grow still further following the enlargement of the frontiers of Community litigation to new fields of Community law. After the entering into force of the Merger Control Regulation[41] and of the Regulation on the Community trade mark, that might be the case, for example, with the system of Community design, when the proposal for a regulation put forward by the

[41] Council Regulation (EEC) No 4064/89 of 21 December 1989 on the control of concentrations between undertakings [1989] OJ L 395/1.

Commission has been adopted and comes into force;[42] the same must be said with regard to patents, for which a EC regime may come into force in the form of a Convention between the Member States.

As regards the role as a Constitutional Court, it should be remembered from the outset, that the importance of this role has grown in recent years, since the Court of Justice has increasingly been called upon to arbitrate on conflicts of competences between the Community institutions in fields in which their respective powers, as laid down by the Treaties, impinge upon one another. By these indirect means the Court of Justice has been led to encroach frequently upon the field of the internal political law of the Community and consequently upon the barely perceptible dividing line between the legal and the political spheres, which is the province of all constitutional law relating to the powers of the State. This is, however, not a reality which is unknown to the Court: that is shown by the earliest case-law, whether as concerns the balance of powers between the various institutions or the relations between the latter and the Member States.

Moreover, institutional developments within the European Union should strengthen the constitutional role of the Court of Justice. First of all, by establishing a joint decision-making procedure for the adoption of legislative acts in addition to the procedure of cooperation established by the Single European Act, the Treaty of Maastricht significantly enhances the participation of the European Parliament in the legislative process. Second, it is clear that, in terms of the inter-institutional balance, the European Union is still in a transitory phase, where the powers of the various institutions are far from being consolidated within the Community system. Besides, the principle of subsidiarity, now enshrined in the Treaty, introduces in this system a new concept and a new dynamic; it will naturally fall to the Court of Justice to ensure compliance with it by the Community legislature.

In this respect, contrary to those who consider it to be a principle of a merely political nature, I believe that such a task constitutes an inescapable aspect of the Court's constitutional duties. In fact, it is hard to see how, in view of the legal nature of any provision of the Treaty, however imprecise it may be, the Court of Justice could refrain from carrying out its duty of 'ensuring that in the interpretation and application of this Treaty the law is observed' (Article 164). Resorting to appropriate legal concepts and the theory behind them—eg the concept of discretionary power of the administration or that of the wide margin of appreciation of the author of the act and their respective limits, as balanced against the limits of the Court's judicial discretion—will make it possible to overcome the difficulties arising from the use, in the Treaty, of vague or imprecise concepts, however inconvenient that may be for the Court.

The Court might still be called upon to play an important constitutional role on the occasion of the next revision of the Treaties, planned for 1996. Following

[42] See n 35 above.

a line of constitutional reasoning defined in the Court's Opinions on the draft agreements establishing the European Economic Area (EEA),[43] it should be a crucial task for the Court to ensure that the fundamental *acquis* and the core principles of the 'Community constitution' are preserved in case of any profound revision of the Treaty.[44]

In brief, the process of gradual 'constitutionalisation' of the Community Treaties which has established itself throughout the years, and is at present facing serious threats, implies the growing entrenchment of the Court of Justice as a true Constitutional Court of the Union.

D. Reforming the Preliminary Ruling Mechanism

Within the framework of the Community legal order, and for the purpose of ensuring the effective and uniform application of its rules and principles throughout the Community, Article 177 of the Treaty has assigned to the Court of Justice the critical task of answering questions referred to it for a preliminary ruling by the national courts or tribunals. In the present state of construction of the Community that machinery for judicial cooperation remains indispensable and the most suited mechanism to ensure realisation of the aims of the Treaties.

The Treaty of Maastricht (following the example of the Single European Act) has expressly reserved that role to the Court of Justice, excluding any intervention by the Court of First Instance.

Admittedly, the task of ensuring uniform application of Community law must be entrusted, at Community level, to one (or more) judicial bodies endowed with jurisdiction extending to the whole Community.

It is not impossible for such a task to be shared, in appropriate terms, between two Community courts, provided that their respective powers and areas of intervention are mutually exclusive. For some commentators,[45] this is not only a possible but also a desirable development. This was also the line advocated by the Court of First Instance in the document 'Reflections on the Future Development of the Community Judicial System', which it prepared and submitted in December 1990 to the inter-governmental conference which led to the adoption of the Treaty on European Union.[46]

The problem is certainly not a pressing one and developments in this matter are certainly not to be foreseen in the short or medium term. However, the subject is not taboo and we do not necessarily need to bury it or draw a veil over it.

[43] Opinion 1/91 of 14 December 1991 [1991] ECR I-6079, and Opinion 1/92 of 10 April 1992 [1992] ECR I-2821.

[44] On this topic, see JL da Cruz Vilaça and N Piçarra, 'Y a-t-il des limites matérielles à la révision des traités instituant les Communautés européennes?' (1993) 1–2 *Cahiers dr eur* 4–37.

[45] See U Everling (n 36) 30–31.

[46] The document was published by the European Parliament, Doc EP 147.830, of 4.2.1991, as well as by several law reviews.

On the one hand, the evolution of the workload of each of the two Community courts may in the future require serious thought on the problem. On the other hand, it may turn out to be appropriate to assign to another court—or to specialised Chambers within the same court—jurisdiction to reply to questions for a preliminary ruling in cases which, by their very nature, do not justify the ponderous intervention of a supreme and constitutional court, above all when that court has already provided a clear and consistent line of case-law on the subject. That might be the case with the interpretation of the Common Customs Tariff or regulations on agricultural matters or social security; it might also be the case as regards the interpretation by the Court of Justice of Conventions peripheral to Community law (Brussels Convention of 27 September 1968 on Jurisdiction and the Enforcement of Judgments on Civil and Commercial Matters; Convention of Rome on Contractual Obligations).[47]

It is also possible to envisage that, in certain areas, the Court having jurisdiction to hear direct actions is empowered, in principle, to answer references for preliminary ruling on the same matters. That would allow the establishment of 'homogeneous sets of jurisdiction' assigned to each Court, with obvious advantages for the consistency of the case-law. As regards the Court of First Instance, that would make it possible to allocate to it questions on matters such as competition law and concentrations of undertakings, State aid, and anti-dumping policy.

Whatever view one may have of this, it must be borne in mind that a number of preliminary questions would still have to be settled before the establishment of any system for sharing jurisdiction for preliminary rulings between the two Community Courts. Such a division of competences would have to be based, above all, on an objective definition of the matters to be subject to the jurisdiction of the Court of First Instance.[48] It would also be necessary to exclude, in principle, the possibility of an appeal against decisions at first instance so as to avoid the delays, which would negatively impact on the proceedings before the national court. However, important questions of principle, or of a constitutional nature, may sometimes arise concerning an apparently unimportant reference for a preliminary ruling; then it would be necessary to provide machinery for transfer of the issue to, or for consideration by the Court of Justice, or even the possibility of the institutions or the Member States to bring an action 'in the interest of the law', with no bearing on the case at stake.

The political importance and the technical complexity of the problems to be settled in this field justify the problem being dealt with from a pragmatic point of view and free from dogmatism.

[47] See U Everling (n 36) 31–32.

[48] I strongly oppose, both on practical grounds and for reasons of principle, alternative systems of sharing jurisdiction based either on transfers on a case-by-case basis from one court to another, or on a criterion relating to the level of the national court raising the question (references for a preliminary ruling from supreme courts to go to the Court of Justice, those from other courts to the Court of First Instance).

E. Regional Community Courts?

The inter-governmental conference, which led to the signing of the Treaty on European Union encouraged interesting reflections on the development of the EU judicial system, among them the following suggestion, which has been put forward by Professor Jean-Paul Jacqué and Professor Joseph HH Weiler with a view to the setting up of Community regional courts.[49]

According to that proposal, four regional courts[50] would have jurisdiction to decide upon references for a preliminary ruling raised by the national courts within the relevant geographical zone, as well as on applications for annulment, for failure to act and for compensation brought by natural or legal persons within the region concerned. The authors' proposal was that the Commission should be entitled to demand transfer of the case to the Court of Justice; they also advocated that it should be open to the parties in every case, to the Member States and to the institutions, to appeal against all decisions of the regional courts (including replies to references for a preliminary ruling) and that the Court of Justice should have discretion to decide as to the admissibility of such appeals.

Admittedly, the setting up of Community regional courts would raise a series of important questions with regard to the jurisdiction of the various courts and the links between them, the uniformity of the case-law, the force of *res judicata* to be attached to the various judgments and the composition and seat of each court, of which the authors were aware but preferred to leave for subsequent consideration.

However attractive the proposal may appear, it nevertheless seems to have been inspired by a model of judicial organisation of a consolidated federal type, as in North America, which does not necessarily match the present structure of the European Union.[51]

The negotiators at the inter-governmental conference did not, in any event, seize the suggestion, but it is not excluded that it may one day have to be revisited.

F. Final Remarks

To conclude, certain final remarks should be made with regard to three specific questions.

[49] J-P Jacqué and JHH Weiler, 'On the Road to European Union—A New Judicial Architecture' (1990) *Common Market Law Review* 185–207.

[50] Corresponding to the four 'judicial regions' in which the present territory of the 12 Member States could be divided. They would cover the following groups of countries: the United Kingdom, Ireland and Portugal; France, Spain and Belgium; Italy, Greece and the Netherlands; Germany, Denmark and Luxembourg. However, the authors agree that not only is such a division not the only possible one but also that it is not based on any magic formula.

[51] That was also the opinion of G Vandersanden and U Everling in the proceedings of the *Journée d'études sur la réforme du système juridictionnel communautaire* (n 36) 13, 28–29.

The first concerns the status of the Community judges and proposals made in this connection. One such proposal was made in the Rothley Report,[52] approved by the European Parliament, to the effect that the Parliament and the Council should elect the members of the Court of Justice for a non-renewable period of nine years.[53]

As Judge Federico Mancini recently wrote, '[f]ew supreme courts in the western world are so lacking in links, direct or indirect, with the symbol of democratic government and in few countries is the judiciary so bereft of formal guarantees of its independence.'[54]

That being the case, and whatever the formula to be adopted for the Parliament's intervention, it would have to be organised in such a way as to strengthen and not to weaken the independence and dignity of the function of judge. From that point of view a sufficiently long,[55] non-renewable period of office, as proposed by the Parliament, is an essential condition of independence. It should be emphasised, however, that the formula proposed by the Parliament involves the Council in the appointment, whereas at present it is the Conference of the Representatives of the Member States (not the Council as an institution), which proceeds, by common accord, to appoint the members of both courts.

If the reform proposed by the Parliament is adopted, it might prove appropriate to discuss the possible introduction into the Community judicial system of the method of open voting and of dissenting opinion, combined with a change in the system of appointment of the Judge-Rapporteur. It is true that some of the reasons, which originally prompted the present system of secret deliberations, would by then have lost some of their *raison d'être*; but it is not clear that the specific nature of the Community has changed so substantially that the system has lost all of its justification.

The second remark is prompted by the recent report of the House of Lords' Select Committee on the European Communities on 'The Enforcement of Community Competition Rules', of 7 December 1993. Among the recommendations set out therein with regard to a possible revision of Regulation No 17, which has been since 1962 the main Regulation for the application of EC competition rules,[56] is that of conferring on the Hearing Officer, whose duty it is to conduct hearings during the administrative proceeding, power to take certain decisions

[52] 'Report of the Committee on Institutional Affairs on the Role of the Court of Justice in the Development of the Constitutional System of the European Community', Rapporteur: Mr Willi Rothley, EP 155441/fin, 6.7.1993.

[53] The proposal does not apply to the members of the Court of First Instance, which is explained by the position occupied by that Court in the hierarchy of the Community Courts (it is not the Supreme Court) and by the nature of the litigation before it (not constitutional but merely administrative).

[54] F Mancini and D Keeling, 'Democracy and the European Court of Justice' (1994) *Modern Law Review* 175–90.

[55] Judge Everling (n 36) 23, suggests 12 years.

[56] Council Regulation No 17 of 6 February 1962, First Regulation implementing Articles 85 and 86 of the Treaty [1962] OJ 13, 204/62.

to settle procedural disputes between the parties, particularly with regard to the statement of objections, access to files or the setting of time-limits.

The Select Committee proposes that the parties should be able to bring an action before the Court of First Instance against such decisions of the Hearing Officer, and that a single judge should give a decision on the matter according to a simplified procedure.

By analogy with the decisions on interim measures applications, which are taken by the President of the Court, the extension of such a system to other categories of decisions might not only be justified but also result in speeding up proceedings and personalising the administration of justice in the Community.

One last question relates to terminology. The Rothley Report to the European Parliament suggests that the new adjudication of powers between the two EC Courts justifies their being given new names. Thus it proposes that the Court of First Instance be called 'Court of the European Union' and the Court of Justice 'Court of Justice of the European Union'. Jacqué and Weiler for their part had proposed that the latter be called the 'European High Court of Justice'.

The name is certainly not the most important thing about an institution. But for words to have any sense they must correspond to reality. Thus it is becoming less and less realistic to attach the name 'Court of First Instance' to a judicial body, which from now on has jurisdiction to hear appeals, as is the case with the Community trade mark.

However, for the Parliaments' proposal to have any meaning, the whole field of application of the Treaties would have to be subject to review by the Courts: only then shall we have real Courts of the European Union.

In any event, whatever developments there may be, and whatever names they take, one essential value must be preserved: that of the independence of the Community Courts. The Community/Union does not rigorously obey all of the conditions typical of a State governed by the rule of law with a separation of powers according to the strictest criteria applied in the Member States. Hence the independence of the Community Courts must continue to be an indispensable support for the gradual realisation of the community governed by the rule of law, characterised by complying with rules having democratic legitimacy and with fundamental rights, which must be given full expression throughout the whole of the territory of the Union.

6

The New Judicial Architecture of the European Union and the Intergovernmental Conference[*]

I. NEED FOR REFORM AND CHALLENGES AHEAD

THE 1996 INTERGOVERNMENTAL conference (IGC) that has recently convened provides a welcome opportunity to discuss the current state of the Community judicial system and its preparedness to meet the challenges to which the development of the European Community and the imminent reform of its institutions will certainly give rise.

The debate started a few years ago, in particular in the early stages of the previous IGC that led to the adoption of the Maastricht Treaty on the European Union. The discussion began primarily in legal and academic circles. It paved the way for a debate concerning this crucial aspect of the European project which had previously been ignored in official circles and, in particular, for rectifying the disappointing lack of interest shown in the Court of Justice, and indeed the Community judicial system as a whole, at the European Council meeting of June 1990, in Dublin.

At the time, the Court of First Instance presented, in December 1990, a document entitled 'Éléments de réflexion sur l'évolution de la juridiction communautaire' and the Court of Justice also submitted to the IGC, some months later, a number of suggestions intended to improve its own internal operation.

It has to be recognised that the few innovations brought about in this field by the Treaty on the European Union have, thus far (with the possible exception of the amendment to the third paragraph of Article 165 of the Treaty), had very limited practical effect. Moreover, recent developments and the increased seriousness of certain existing problems have made necessary a more in-depth review of the situation and made urgent the adoption of effective measures.

A number of significant individual contributions have been put forward and several prominent institutions—the European Parliament, the House of Lords, the *Institut d'Études européennes* of ULB, the TMC *Asser Instituut* in The Hague,

[*] This chapter was published in French as an Editorial to (1996) 1–2 *Cahiers de droit européen* 3–8.

the *Cahiers de Droit Européen*, among others—have taken important initiatives in this area leading to a number of interesting proposals. Also, both the Court of Justice and the Court of First Instance brought to the attention of the Reflection Group set up by the Corfu European Council, held in June 1994, their own reports on the current situation and on the future development of the Community judiciary, within the context of the 1996 IGC.

It is submitted, without prejudice to any further ideas and suggestions that may emerge, that the aforementioned initiatives and proposals would lead, if implemented, to the adoption of effective reform measures that would reinforce the Community judiciary's capacity to cope with the most serious challenges it will have to face. With respect, it is unclear whether the Reflection Group has devoted to this topic the attention that it deserves and whether it has examined all of its implications. Although the implementation of most of the measures that might be adopted would not require any changes to the Treaty, it is of the utmost importance that the political authorities be aware of the new tasks conferred on the Community judiciary and of how they may impact on its organisation in future, in order to ensure the continued proper functioning of the judicial system as a whole and thereby preserve its credibility.

II. GOOD IDEAS, BAD SOLUTIONS?

Some of the solutions put forward, that aim to enhance the rule of law within the Community, deserve careful analysis. A critical look must be taken at each proposed solution on its merits and particular attention must be paid to its viability.

In particular, decentralising the Community judicial system through the creation of *regional courts*, a proposal that seems to have been inspired by the well-established model of judicial federalism, such as that existing in the United States, would raise a number of delicate issues regarding practical organisation, geographical delimitation of jurisdiction and the coherence of future case-law, each of which appears difficult to overcome.

Neither do I believe that the time has yet come to set up *specialised courts* or *tribunals of first instance* with jurisdiction in respect of particular substantive areas of Community competence. In any event, following that route would give rise to a number of risks which would present the Community judicial system with some formidable obstacles. The creation of such specialised courts should not therefore be pursued unless it is demonstrated that the advantages of that solution clearly outweigh the disadvantages. My alternative suggestion would be to introduce into the treaties the necessary provisions empowering the Council to decide, under the procedure set out in Article 168 A of the EC Treaty, on the creation of such new courts or tribunals as may be required by the number and complexity of different types of dispute that arise in the future and by the increase in the workload of the existing courts.

Academics and lawyers are increasingly calling for a relaxation of the *conditions for admissibility* of actions brought by individuals under the fourth paragraph of Article 173 of the EC Treaty as a means of ensuring effective judicial protection. Caution is also necessary in this matter. It is submitted that the emphasis should be placed on strengthening the system of judicial protection established in the Treaties as a whole. That system relies heavily on a decentralised review, by national courts, of the legality of the action of the Community institutions and of the national authorities when applying Community law, under the supervision of the Court of Justice acting through the preliminary ruling procedure. From that perspective, it is necessary, firstly, to identify clearly any shortcomings in national systems of judicial protection of Community law rights and to take all necessary corrective measures and, secondly, to take action to boost recourse to and increase the effectiveness of the preliminary ruling mechanism in a way that is systematic and comprehensive. As regards the right of individuals to bring direct actions before the Community courts, greater access should be promoted by the case-law so that the conditions of admissibility set out in the fourth paragraph of Article 173 of the EC Treaty do not give rise to situations where substantive and effective justice is denied.

An alternative solution might be to grant individuals the possibility of bringing an action against legislative acts of the institutions to the extent necessary for the *protection of their fundamental rights*, both within the current scope of the Community and also under the second or third 'pillars' of the European Union. A new type of direct action for the protection of fundamental rights could simply be added to the system of existing judicial remedies established by the Treaties, provided that adequate safeguards were put in place, in particular the definition of a hierarchy of norms, identifying precisely the fundamental rights to be protected within the Community legal order and ensuring that the mechanism was not abused where it was clear that no breach had occurred.

Proposals have also been made for the creation of a *constitutional court* alongside the Court of Justice. That idea should be dismissed as undesirable and unnecessary. Given that the Court of Justice has for decades undertaken the functions of a constitutional court within the Community legal order, the creation of a new court with jurisdiction for constitutional matters would only be reasonably justified if the Court of Justice were no longer able to properly carry out that task. That is not the case, particularly at a time when a significant share of the judicial burden regarding actions brought by individuals has been transferred to the Court of First Instance. The beneficial impact of such a transfer could be increased by granting the Court of First Instance—as is provided for by Article 168 A, in its current post-Maastricht Treaty version—jurisdiction to rule, at first instance, on *actions brought by Member States*, in certain areas, against acts of the institutions that may simultaneously be challenged by individuals, such as in the areas of State aid or in respect of antidumping measures.

The Court of Justice should therefore retain its core functions, including those of a constitutional nature, regarding the interpretation and the application, as a sole and impartial arbitrator, of the rules governing the division of powers between the Community and the Member States. Any attempt to undermine or limit the exercise of those competences by the Court would constitute a serious step backwards in the process of consolidating the European Community as a community based on the rule of law and, sooner or later, might even imperil its very existence.

Furthermore, the current status of the members of the Court confers on them—as well as on those of the Court of First Instance—full independence and impartiality in the exercise of their functions. The gradual consolidation of the constitutional role of the Court may, however, justify enhancing the democratic legitimacy of its members, which would call for the participation in the procedure leading to their appointment—through appropriate mechanisms but not, it is submitted, for the reasons mentioned by the Court in its report for the IGC, the organisation of hearings before parliamentary commissions—of the European Parliament and, if appropriate, of national parliaments.

III. TO STRENGTHEN A COMMUNITY OF LAW

The real 'revolution' that took place in the Community judicial system actually goes back to its initial establishment by the authors of the Treaty who designed a *sui generis* mechanism suited to the specific characteristics and requirements of the Community and which reflect the principle of subsidiarity, recently enshrined in the text of the Treaty. When tinkering with that system it would be wise to avoid any major structural disruption that might undermine the foundations of the Community itself. It would be preferable to adopt a reformist, gradualist and pragmatic approach, in order to take advantage of the inherent flexibility of the system and to develop it gradually.

It was with this in mind that the Court of First Instance set out, in its contribution to the 1996 IGC, a number of measures which could, in the short or medium term, strengthen its ability to tackle the most serious issues arising from the changes in the case-law and from its increased workload.

One of the measures proposed was a small increase (but certainly not a doubling) in the *number of judges* which would make it possible to set up a greater number of chambers and thus enable the Court of First Instance to deal more rapidly with a greater number of cases.

Such an increase in the number of judges could be accompanied by measures of internal specialisation within the Court of First Instance in order to handle the growing and increasingly diversified case-law. The creation of *specialised chambers* would be the most appropriate measure as the idea of '*specialised judges*' should, it is submitted, be ruled out. The appointment of *assistant rapporteurs*, an option already envisaged in the Statute of the Court, could also enable the Court to benefit from the combined wisdom of generalist judges and specialist legal experts.

The involvement of assistant rapporteurs would be particularly useful if accompanied by reforms allowing simple cases of relatively minor importance in specific fields to be heard by a *single judge*, that is, a member of the Court of First Instance sitting alone, most likely the judge-rapporteur appointed to deal with the case. The introduction of *simplified procedures* in certain fields should also be part of this package of measures intended to expedite the administration of justice.

Moreover, since the Court of First Instance no longer appoints judges to perform the functions of Advocate General, the judges are now free to focus all of their energies on their essential task of judging cases. Nevertheless, the appointment of a small number of *advocates general* to deliver Opinions in certain specific cases that raise particularly sensitive issues would, I believe, contribute to the development of the case-law, thus paving the way for a swift and fully-informed judicial decision in the most difficult cases.

As regards the procedures for the *appointment of judges* of the Court of First Instance, the scope of its jurisdiction and the fact that it is not a supreme court justify the absence of any parliamentary scrutiny. Given the specific and technical nature of the work carried out by the Court of First Instance, the possibility for judges to serve multiple terms, thus ensuring an appropriate degree of continuity in the exercise of judicial functions, should continue to be available.

Finally, taking into consideration the competences and the role of the Court of First Instance within the Community legal order, it would seem appropriate to change its current name and to include it in the list of institutions and organs of the Community set out in Article 4 of the Treaty.

In conclusion, the 1996 IGC should acknowledge the decisive role of the Community's judicial system in the establishment of a fully-functioning Community of law and should therefore seek to enhance its independence and to strengthen its efficiency.

7

The Court System of the European Communities*

I. INTRODUCTION—THE MAIN CHALLENGES

As the 1996 intergovernmental conference (IGC-96) takes place, the judicial system of the European communities faces three main challenges.

A. The First Challenge: A Growing Litigation

The first challenge is a quantitative one and relates to the advent of a larger and more diverse caseload, as may be confirmed by an analysis of changes in the number of incoming and pending cases since the creation of the Court of First Instance (CFI). In November 1989, when that Court began its work, the number of cases pending before the European Court of Justice (ECJ) was approximately 600, a quarter of which (153 to be precise) were transferred to the CFI in accordance with the jurisdiction initially conferred on it.

By the time the jurisdiction of the CFI was extended, in 1993–1994, the total number of cases pending before the two courts was over a thousand. Immediately after the transfer of around 450 cases which took place following the delegation of new competences to the CFI, the number of pending cases was roughly 400 for the ECJ and 650 for the CFI.[1]

Since then, the pace at which new actions have been brought before the two courts has accelerated further. At the ECJ, the number of new cases brought each year rose from 313 (excluding the milk quota cases) in 1993 to 354 in 1994 and 415 in 1995. From January to March 1996, 104 new cases were brought. At the CFI, the number of new cases, which had increased gradually between 1990 and

* Published in French as 'Le système juridictionnel communautaire' in A Mattera (ed), *La Conférence intergouvernementale sur l'Union européenne : répondre aux défis du XXI siècle* (Paris, Clément Juglar, 1996) 219–34.

[1] Of which 380 were actions for annulment or damages relating to the application of Community legislation in the field of milk production quotas under the common agricultural policy (CAP).

1993,[2] saw a sudden increase in 1994[3] to almost 400; the equivalent figure was 244 in 1995 and 47 in the first three months of 1996.

As a consequence of this increase in workload, the total aggregate number of cases pending before the ECJ and the CFI put together reached 1130 on 31 March 1996.

Among the types of litigation that saw the greatest growth are competition, State aid and antidumping cases, all of which require a thorough examination of complex issues. Sometimes such actions form large groups of related cases, with the combined judicial or administrative files amounting to thousands of pages.

The fact that several groups of such cases were pending at the same time naturally raised difficult issues concerning the organisation of the Community courts' work, especially for the CFI as the Court that had to deal with them at first instance, an onerous task requiring an intensive effort in order to satisfy the competing requirements of a high-quality examination of the facts and the need for judicial proceedings to reach a rapid outcome compatible with the proper administration of justice.

Reference should also be made to the substantial increase in the number of interim measures applications initiated by individuals as a means for obtaining, on a provisional basis, a decision that protects their rights and interests against the risk of serious and irreparable harm caused by the immediate application of a Community act whose legality is subject to challenge. While between 1991 and 1993 the number of orders issued in interim measures proceedings before the CFI varied from seven to 12 per year, that number rose to 35 in 1994 and remained higher, at 19, in 1995.

In addition, account should also be taken of the future growth that may be anticipated in a new area of litigation, that concerning trade marks.[4] In this connection, the estimates made by the relevant services within the Court of Justice suggest that approximately 100 applications in trade mark cases will be brought before the CFI in 1996 (the first full year of activity of the Office for Harmonisation in the Internal Market, known as 'OHIM') and 400 applications per year from 1997. Reality has, however, already overtaken those estimates, since by the end of April 1996 more than 18,000 requests for registration (ie double the number which served as the basis for such estimates) had already been received by the Office.[5]

[2] Fifty five in 1990, 93 in 1991, 116 in 1992 and 138 in 1993 (excluding the cases which were transferred to the ECJ).

[3] This number excludes the cases which were transferred to the ECJ but includes 173 milk quota cases.

[4] Council Regulation (EC) No 40/94 of 20 December 1993 on the Community trade mark [1994] OJ L 11/1.

[5] It should be added that an unknown, but certainly high, number of additional requests for registration were undoubtedly made before the relevant national trade mark offices, which are subsequently required to transfer them to the Community Office in Alicante.

One cannot ignore the effects of the enlargement of the Union to include new Member States, not only as regards direct actions, but also in terms of the increase in the preliminary references made by national courts to the ECJ. Developments such as those briefly described above naturally call for an appropriate response in terms of reviewing the structure and functioning of the Community judicial system, in order to achieve the greatest possible degree of effectiveness in the administration of justice within the Union. The credibility of the Community legal system depends on it.

B. A Need for Legitimacy and Protection of Rights

Indeed, that system is faced with challenges arising from the pressing need both for increased democratic legitimacy at an institutional level and for enhanced protection of citizens' rights in a society that is ever more open and complex. The members of European societies are gradually becoming more aware of their rights and of the need to ensure that those rights are respected at all levels, by means of appropriate and effective mechanisms.

On the one hand, the process leading to the ratification of the Maastricht Treaty has raised the level of interest among the peoples of Europe in the development of the European institutions and in the latters' relationship with Europe's citizens. On the other hand, the Community courts have progressively applied pressure to raise the standard of protection of fundamental rights within the Community legal order. The warnings issued by certain constitutional courts in this respect give voice to that same shift in attitudes which also inspired the framers of the Maastricht Treaty itself to include within it Article F, paragraph 2. The central focus for reform has moved, at both the European and national level, from an emphasis on the '*raison d'État*' to a broader conception embracing individual freedom from unwarranted interference by public authorities and the idea that the citizen may be an agent of change.

C. The Treaty of Maastricht and the Court

For the ECJ, in particular, another major change has been brought about by the 'qualitative' transformation made to the Community system by the Maastricht Treaty, a change that had already begun with the Single European Act: the switch from an approach based purely on economics to one that raises the importance of politics is reflected in and has been consolidated by the superimposition of the EU structure on top of the existing European Community. From being a construction whose sole aim was 'merely' to pursue an economic integration process, which is still ongoing, the Community has developed into a Union with broader objectives and with political contours that are still being clarified and whose institutions are progressively being endowed with powers that fall within the constitutional sphere.

In that context, the role played by the ECJ over the years as an engine of integration has sometimes been questioned. Today, more than ever, the Court is called upon to play its constitutional role as guarantor of the institutional balance of power, as prescribed by the Treaty, not only in terms of relations among the European institutions, but also as between the Community and its Member States.

The insertion into the Treaties of the subsidiarity principle both reflects and reinforces this new state of affairs. In spite of the reluctance expressed by some, who believe that the political role of the ECJ is an undesirable, if inevitable, corollary of its judicial tasks, the Court will not be able to ignore the calls that will now be made for it to contribute to the interpretation of the subsidiarity principle and to exercise judicial review of its application by the Community legislator and administration.

One should not underestimate the difficulties that the Court will face in this new context, nor the ambiguities that its role entails. Even the interpretative principles traditionally used by the Court will have to be applied within a new framework. Some believe, in this respect, that the recognition of the subsidiarity principle jeopardises the possibility for the ECJ to continue to carry out a teleological interpretation of the Treaties' provisions. From that perspective, this situation could be compared to a problem of linear programming, the objective being to maximise the functions defined by the different Treaty objectives whilst remaining within the relevant limits which, in light of the subsidiarity principle, have become even stricter. Thus, in order to achieve the appropriate balance between dynamism and inertia, the Court will have to search for a new equilibrium that avoids the twin pitfalls of excessive activism, on the one hand, and of sterile paralysis, on the other.

II. PROPOSALS THAT SHOULD BE EXAMINED WITH CAUTION

Certain solutions proposed in consideration of the changes to the caseload described above and in order to make the Community justice system work properly should be regarded with a degree of circumspection. Indeed, they do not seem, in my view, perfectly suited to the particular problems faced, or to the very specific Community context in which those problems arise.

A. Regional Courts

In the first place, the creation of regional Community courts (a well-known idea proposed by Weiler and Jacqué some years ago[6]) seems to be inspired by a

[6] JP Jacqué and JHH Weiler, 'Sur la voie de l'Union européenne—une nouvelle architecture juridictionnelle européenne' (1990) 26 *RTDE* 441.

federal model of judicial organisation, akin to the US model, which finds no ready parallel in the current structure of the European Union.[7]

Furthermore, the creation of regional Community courts would raise a number of delicate issues which would have to be resolved—either beforehand or subsequently—and to which there does not appear to be an obvious answer. For example, it is hard to see how adequate mechanisms could be put in place to ensure the uniformity, or at least the coherence, of the case-law, without creating a plethora of appellate bodies; other problems would include the definition of each regional court's jurisdiction, the scope of *res judicata* enjoyed by their judgments and the determination of the composition and location of each regional court.

B. Specialised Courts

It has also been suggested that specialised courts of first instance might be created with jurisdiction to decide cases relating to certain fields of law that are sufficiently specific and homogenous to enable them to be defined (civil service law, intellectual property, customs matters, social or company law).[8]

This solution should not be rejected outright as it may be necessary in future, should the caseload evolve in such a way that the CFI is unable to cope with it. Nevertheless, it appears to me that the time when the disadvantages of this solution will be clearly outweighed by its advantages still lies in the distant future.

The CFI, in its 'Contribution to the ICG-96', has expressed its doubts regarding this proposal. The CFI's position results from its concern to avoid disruption to the cohesion and balance of the Community's judicial system, as well as to the coherence of the case-law. There would be a serious risk of such disruption if several such specialised first instance courts were to be created in short order.[9]

Moreover, it would be necessary to ensure that each of the specialised courts created was properly organised, as a true judicial body, and staffed by independent judges, in order to prevent those courts from tending, by virtue of their specialised character, towards a 'corporatist' model, which would inevitably prevent them

[7] Cf JL da Cruz Vilaça, 'L'évolution du système juridictionnel communautaire avant et après Maastricht' in O Due, M Lutter and J Schwarze (eds), *Festschrift für Ulrich Everling I* (Baden-Baden, Nomos, 1995) 200.

[8] Cf T Koopmans, 'The Future of the Court of Justice of the European Communities' (1991) 11 *Yearbook of European Law* 24; W Van Gerven, 'The Role and the Structure of the European Judiciary Now and In the Future', working paper to the '*Conference on Suggestions for Revision of the Treaty on the European Union*' (TMC Asser Institute, The Hague, September 1995), as well as my 'Comment' on the same working paper. Cf also PJG Kapteyn, 'The Court of Justice of the European Communities after the Year 2000' (1994) 2 *Institutional Dynamics of European Integration, Essays in Honour of Henry G Schermers* 139.

[9] The same concerns were expressed by the Council of Bars and Law Societies of Europe (CCBE) in its document entitled 'Contribution du CCBE en vue de la Conférence intergouvernementale de 1996'. The CFI, for its part, has also pointed to the administrative and budgetary costs which the creation of new courts would entail.

from playing the desired role in improving the quality of judicial review within the Union.[10]

In any case, in light of the still fragile nature of what has been built at Community level, it would be wrong to undertake any structural upheaval of the Community judicial system whose necessity is not proven beyond doubt.

Thus, it would appear more sensible to follow a gradualist approach, based on the potential improvements that may be made, in the short term, within the institutional framework of the current system, in order to maximise, as far as possible, that potential before taking any more drastic steps. Such an approach would make it possible to take account of changes in the Community courts' caseload, particularly in the new fields of activity that are likely to give rise to additional litigation, in order to adopt, on a piecemeal basis, tailor-made solutions that are designed to resolve the specific problems that arise in those fields.

In that same spirit, one solution might be simply to insert into the Treaties provisions allowing for decisions to be taken by the Council subsequently, in the light of the CFI's experience with the new types of litigation, under the procedure provided for by Article 168a of the EC Treaty.

C. Access to Courts by Individuals

Some academic writers, in particular those with experience of appearing before the Community courts, are also in favour of an amendment to the fourth paragraph of Article 173 of the Treaty, with a view to broadening the access of individuals to the Community courts, especially as regards the review of the legality of normative acts.[11]

In my view, that suggestion needs to be approached with extreme caution. In the first place, the admissibility conditions for individual applications, as currently defined in that Treaty provision, form a coherent part of the overall system of judicial protection provided for by the Treaties, which is based on a largely decentralised system of review of the legality of the acts of the institutions and of the authorities of Member States in the light of Community law.

From this perspective, it is important that conditions are put in place to enable national courts to perform that decentralised judicial review and that the preliminary ruling mechanism should function in such a way that it can play its

[10] The same reservation was voiced by Ole Due, 'The Court of First Instance' (1988) 8 *Yearbook of European Law* 10, in reaction to the views expressed by the Commission in its Opinion to the Council concerning the proposal of the Court for the creation of a court of first instance, according to which that court should be composed of 'experts', specifically in competition law.

[11] See D Waelbroeck and AM Verheyden, 'Les conditions de recevabilité des recours en annulation des particuliers contre les actes normatifs communautaires à la lumière du droit comparé et de la Convention des droits de l'homme' (1995) *Cahiers de Droit européen* 399; G Vandersanden, 'Pour un élargissement du droit des particuliers d'agir en annulation contre des actes autres que les décisions qui leur sont adressées', (1995) 5-6 *Cahiers de Droit européen* 535. See also CCBE (n 9) 8 ff.

fundamental role, which is to ensure the uniform interpretation of Community law and to serve as a focal point for the judicial system created by the Treaties.

It is in the light of this dual system of judicial control, operating both at national and at Community level, that one should analyse the adequacy and completeness of the system of judicial protection created by the Treaties. From that perspective, as regards the EC Treaty, Articles 169–71 (infringement proceedings), Articles 178 and 215 (extra-contractual liability of the European Community) and Article 184 (objection of illegality) must be read in conjunction with Articles 173 and 175, on the one hand, and Article 177, on the other.

Secondly, it is important to note that the admissibility conditions for applications by individuals (natural and legal persons), formulated in generic terms in the Treaty, have been further specified by the Community courts. Those courts have been responsible, in spite of the vagueness and conservatism of which they have sometimes been accused, for a relaxation of the strict requirements found in the older case-law, which has resulted in a gradual opening up of access to judicial review.

That move towards wider access for litigants is particularly evident in the interpretation of the requirement for direct and individual concern of an applicant in actions for annulment against decisions addressed to third parties,[12] as well as in the definition of *locus standi* for applicants more generally.[13] However, it may also be observed in relation to actions directed against measures of general application.[14]

Notwithstanding the overall scheme of complementary remedies described above, the system of judicial protection is neither complete nor absolute and gaps may be identified in certain specific situations.[15]

[12] See, eg, the ECJ cases C-26/76 *Metro v Commission* [1977] ECR 1875; C-191/82 *Fediol v Commission* [1983] ECR 2913; C-210/81 *Demo-Studio Schmidt v Commission* [1983] ECR 3045; C-11/82 *Piraiki-Patraiki v Commission* [1985] ECR 207; C-169/84 *Cofaz v Commission* [1986] ECR 391. See also the CFI cases T-3/93 *Air-France v Commission* [1994] ECR II-121; T-2/93 *Air-France v Commission* [1994] ECR II-323; T-96/92 *Comité Central d'entreprise de la Société générale des grandes sources/Commission* and T-12/93 *Comité central d'entreprise de la Société anonyme Vittel v Commission* [1995] ECR II-1213; T-435/93 *Association of Sorbitol Producers v Commission* and T-442/93 *Association des amidonneries de céréales (AAC) v Commission* [1995] ECR II-1285 and ECR II-1329; and lastly T-447, 448 and 449/93 *AITEC and Others v Commission* [1995] ECR II-1971.

[13] See ECJ cases C-67, 68 and 70/85 *Van der Kooy v Commission* [1988] ECR 219; CFI cases T-37/92 *BEUC et NCC v Commission* [1994] ECR II-285, and T-114/92 *BENIM v Commission* [1995] ECR II-147.

[14] See ECJ cases C-358/89 *Extramet Industrie v Council* [1991] ECR I-2501 and C-309/89 *Codorniu SA v Council* [1994] ECR I-1853.

[15] See G Tesauro, 'The Effectiveness of Judicial Protection and Cooperation between the Court of Justice and the National Courts' in (1994) *Festskrift til Ole Due* 356; CWA Timmermans, 'Judicial Protection against the Member States: Articles 169 and 177 revisited' 2 *Essays in Honour of Henry G Schermers* (n 8) 391; A Arnull, 'Private Applicants and the Action for Annulment under Article 173 of the EC Treaty' (1995) *Common Market Law Review* 7; JC Moitinho de Almeida, 'Le recours en annulation des particuliers (article 173, deuxième alinéa, du traité CE): nouvelles réflexions sur l'expression "la concernent … individuellement"' in *Festschrift für Ulrich Everling I* (n 7) 849.

Professor G Vandersanden[16] has suggested that, in the fourth paragraph of Article 173 (and, *mutatis mutandis*, in Article 175), the notion of direct and individual concern should be replaced by a criterion of 'sufficient effect' ('*affectation suffisante*') on the interests of the person wishing to bring an action.

With respect, I find it hard to support that proposal, even though I agree with the starting point for Vandersanden's analysis. On the one hand, I do not believe that the suggested form of words is apt to provide litigants with greater legal certainty and, on the other hand, I fear that it would lead us to open a Pandora's box of unintended consequences that would be hard to control.

I also believe that in reforming the judicial system of the Communities, with a view to filling any possible gaps in judicial protection and to correcting any pernicious effects of the current rules, we should not place all the emphasis solely on the question of direct access to the Community courts. On the contrary: the inherent logic of the system created by the Treaties urges us rather to focus our attention and efforts for reform on the functioning of the preliminary ruling mechanism.

All measures capable of enhancing the efficiency of that latter mechanism should be adopted without hesitation, whether they relate to the Court's functioning or to that of national courts. Indeed, various reports and academic studies have highlighted possible steps that might be taken in order to improve the efficiency of the system.[17] The ECJ has, in its case-law on the application of Article 177, set down very precise guidelines reinforcing the judicial protection available at the national level for the enforcement of individual rights derived from Community law, and making the preliminary reference mechanism as efficient as possible.[18]

[16] G Vandersanden (n 11) 551–52.

[17] See T Koopmans, 'La procédure préjudicielle victime de son succès ?' (1987) *Du droit international au droit de l'intégration, Liber Amicorum Pierre Pescatore* 347; R Kovar, 'L'évolution de l'article 177 du traité CE' in G Vandersanden (ed), *La Réforme du système juridictionnel communautaire* (Brussels, Université de Bruxelles, 1994) 35; JA Usher, 'Les renvois à titre préjudiciel', ibid, 59; W Van Gerven (n 8).

[18] As an example, one may cite, in addition to the 'founding' case law (*Van Gend en Loos* (Case 26/62, *Van Gend en Loos v Nederlandse Administratie der Belastingen* [1963] ECR 1), *Costa/ENEL* (Case 6/64 *Flaminio Costa v ENEL* [1964] ECR 585), *Simmenthal* (Case 106/77 *Amministrazione delle Finanze dello Stato v Simmenthal SpA* [1978] ECR 629), more recent cases such as *Delimitis* (Case Case C-234/89 *Delimitis v Henninger Brau AG* [1991] ECR I-935), *Rewe* (Case 33/76 *Rewe-Zentralfinanz eG et Rewe-Zentral AG v Landwirtschaftskammer für das Saarland* [1976] ECR 1989), *Zuckerfabrik* (Case C-143/88 and C-92/89 *Zuckerfabrik Süderdithmarschen AG v Hauptzollamt Itzehoe and Zuckerfabrik Soest GmbH v Hauptzollamt Paderborn* [1991] ECR I-415), *Factortame* (Case C-213/89 *The Queen v Secretary of State for Transport, ex parte Factortame Ltd and Others* [1990] ECR I-2433) and *Francovich* (Cases C-6 and 9/90 *Francovich and Bonifaci v Republic of Italy* [1991[ECR I-5375). See, in this respect, P Nihoul, 'La recevabilité des recours en annulation introduits par un particulier à l'encontre d'un acte communautaire de portée générale' (1994) 30 *Revue trimestrielle de Droit européen* 169; D Curtin, 'The Decentralised Enforcement of Community law Rights. Judicial Snakes and Ladders' (1992) *Constitution Adjudication in European Community and National Law—Essays for the Hon. Mr. Justice TF O'Higgins* 33; G Bebr, 'Court of Justice: Judicial Protection and the Rule of Law' 2 *Essays* in *Honour of Henry G Schermers* (n 8) 303. For a critical assessment of the shortcomings of the preliminary reference mechanism for questioning a Community law measure's validity, see D Waelbroeck and AM Verheyden (n 11) 433–36.

In the present context I would merely like to underline, on the one hand, the importance of teaching and training Community law in the Member States, in particular as judges and lawyers are concerned, and, on the other hand, the imperative need for the IGC to resist all political pressure and sectorial lobbying aimed at limiting the possibility for national jurisdictions to make references for a preliminary ruling. In its 'Report on certain aspects of the application of the Treaty on European Union',[19] the ECJ clearly insisted on this particular point.

As regards the right of individuals to act directly before the Community courts, I think that we should allow the trend of increasing openness to run its course through the development of the case-law. It would, however, be desirable to open up a right of intervention for individuals in disputes between Member States and Community institutions,[20] which is currently precluded by Article 37 of the Statute of the ECJ. In certain cases (such as, for instance, those concerning State aids) the current rule leads to unjustified restrictions on the judicial protection of individual rights and legitimate interests.

In any case, if a modification of the system allowing individuals to challenge acts that are genuinely regulatory (and not only 'acts in the form of a regulation') were to become inevitable, it would also be necessary to review the hierarchy of Community norms itself, so as to resolve the current confusion, within the EU legal system, between the 'legislative' and the 'regulatory' levels.[21] In that case, however, one should exercise the utmost caution in order to avoid putting the Community courts in a situation where they would face an unmanageable caseload. Most probably, in any event, the debate on the creation of new Community courts exercising specialised competences (possibly even regional competences) will be overtaken by events since a reform of that sort will be essential in order to prevent the CFI from being completely overcome by its workload.

D. Protecting Fundamental Rights

One specific aspect dealt with in the proposals to relax the rules on admissibility for actions brought by individuals relates to the protection of fundamental rights within the Community legal system. In that respect, it has been suggested that a new form of direct action for individuals before the Court, akin to the German

[19] Luxembourg, May 1995. Available at: http://europa.eu/en/agenda/igc-home/eudoc/justice/cj_rep.html.

[20] As recommended by the CCBE (n 9) 3.

[21] See G Vandersanden (n 11) 551.

'Verfassungsbeschwerde', could be included in the system of remedies established by the Treaties.[22]

The ECJ, in its report for the IGC-96, recalls in this regard that, in exercising its current competences, it already ensures respect for fundamental rights by the Community institutions in their exercise of legislative and executive power, as well as the Member States when they act in a field that falls within the scope of Community law. However, the ECJ also recognises, in that same report, that one might legitimately ask whether the annulment action provided for by Article 173 of the EC Treaty is sufficient to provide individuals with effective judicial protection against violations of their fundamental rights that may result from the legislative activity of the institutions.

Should the Conference address this fundamental aspect of the judicial protection of individuals within the Community system, it is submitted that three key points should be borne in mind for the purposes of those discussions: (a) this question cannot be dissociated from the definition of a hierarchy of norms; (b) it is difficult to imagine the implementation of such a remedy without the establishment (either directly in the Treaties or by reference to the European Convention on Human Rights) of a precise catalogue of fundamental rights to be protected in the Community legal order; (c) there would need to be a filter mechanism in order to avoid a proliferation of manifestly unfounded or vexatious procedures.

The question of fundamental rights protection also affects the second and third pillars of the Union. In these areas (especially justice and home affairs), which touch directly upon individual rights, significant powers have been removed from national parliaments' control and transferred to the intergovernmental decision-making mechanism that exists at Union level, without a corresponding mechanism for oversight having been created, either by the Community courts (Article L of the TEU) or by the European Parliament (which is to be merely 'informed' and 'consulted' in these fields—Article K.6).

As long as these areas of Union activity remain subject to a system of intergovernmental cooperation, it seems unlikely that these problems relating to the judicial protection of individuals—whether EU citizens or not—can be resolved through the extension to those pillars of existing Community court competences, in particular the possibility of bringing the forms of direct action established by the Treaties. In fact, these competences, created in the context and with the objective of fostering integration, do not seem to fit with a mechanism for mere intergovernmental cooperation.

As long as these areas of Union activity do not fall within the scope of the Community, a review will have to be carried out through a combination of different organs and instruments: oversight by national parliaments and courts, an increase in the European Parliament's powers, recourse to Article K.3, paragraph 2, c),

[22] See J Mischo, 'Un rôle nouveau pour la Cour de Justice?' (1990) 342 *Revue du Marché commun* 681. See also D Waelbroeck and AM Verheyden (n 11) 439–41.

complaining to the European Court of Human Rights and possibly creating some form of constitutional appeal for fundamental rights protection.

E. A New Constitutional Court?

Another suggestion which keeps surfacing, originating in political circles which are more sceptical concerning the pursuit of European integration, is that of the creation of a constitutional court, alongside the ECJ. This idea has already been fiercely criticised by many authors.[23] I shall address it only briefly.

Bearing in mind that the ECJ already acts as a constitutional court within the Community legal order, the creation of a new court would be only justifiable if the ECJ were no longer capable of duly fulfilling its constitutional functions. That does not seem to be the case, especially at a time when a significant part of the ECJ's work relating to individual actions has been reallocated to the CFI, specifically in order to enable it to focus on its essential duties as guarantor of the uniform interpretation and application of Community law, as well as of the institutional balance at Community level.

One must therefore look for other reasons in order to understand why this proposal has been made. Indeed, those promoting it do not hide their concerns regarding the constitutional case law of the ECJ, which they consider to be characterised by 'pro-integration activism'. In fact, their real objective in suggesting the creation of a new constitutional court is to bring about a change in that case-law, which they dislike.

This leads me to make two further points. On the one hand, it would be a very bad start for a new court, whose strength can be drawn from its independence, to be associated with the pursuit of politically predetermined objectives as regards the content of the case-law. On the other hand, it is somewhat surprising that such a suggestion should emanate from precisely those circles which are the most strongly opposed to the 'constitutionalisation' of the Treaties.

In any event, the problems that would inevitably be created concerning the delimitation of competences as between the ECJ and any new constitutional court constitute, in themselves, an additional reason to reject that idea.

The line of thinking expressed in the reflections of the European Policy Forum also comes close to that idea of creating a new constitutional court.[24] According to those reflections, the fact that the ECJ, in response to Treaty changes, is called upon to deal with questions that are increasingly political in nature, particularly

[23] See GC Iglesias, 'Der Gerichtshof der Europäischen Gemeinschaft' (1992) *Europarecth* p 225; O Due, 'A Constitutional Court for the European Communities' in *Constitution Adjudication in European Community and National Law—Essays for the Hon. Mr. Justice TF O'Higgins* (n 18) 3; FG Jacobs, 'Is the Court of Justice of the European Communities a Constitutional Court?', ibid, 25; W Van Gerven (n 8).

[24] See F Vibert, 'A Core Agenda for the 1996 Inter-Governmental Conference (IGC)' (London, May 1995).

those concerning the division of powers between the Union and the Member States, means that the interpretation of the rules governing those questions ought not to be left to the ECJ (which, allegedly, is neither impartial nor democratic and wields unlimited powers), but should rather be carried out by means of a political procedure, subject to the oversight of national parliaments.

That suggestion should be firmly rejected. Were it to prevail, the ongoing process of establishing the European Union as an entity based on a Community of law would suffer a serious setback. Indeed, any such change would be an important step towards dismantling the institutional system created by the Treaties.

No complex institutional system—whether federal or of a community type—can survive without an impartial arbiter having power to interpret the rules governing the distribution of powers between the federation or community, on the one hand, and its federal or Member States, on the other. In that respect, a political procedure involving national parliaments would necessarily give rise to a 'Communauté à géometrie variable', or even to several communities incapable of resisting the effects of centrifugal forces. Moreover, it cannot seriously be claimed that any other judicial or quasi-judicial body or constitutional court that might be created would act with greater impartiality than the ECJ in the pursuit of this objective. Quite the reverse: there would be good reason to fear the contrary.

As regards the independence of individual members of the ECJ, it should be recalled that they are appointed by the Member States' governments to perform a task on behalf of the Community as a whole and that they enjoy all possible guarantees of their independence and impartiality. To reinforce the democratic character of the appointment process, it would certainly be possible to give the European Parliament a role. Furthermore, since the Member States are currently free to organise as they see fit the national procedure culminating in the proposal of a candidate to be judge, in accordance with their own constitutional, political and legal mechanisms, then they could, if they deemed it appropriate, involve their own national parliaments—notably through the relevant parliamentary committees—in that national procedure.[25]

Finally, it should be emphasised that the Court has always seen itself as being bound by the Treaties and, as such, as the guarantor of the institutional balance upon which they are based.

[25] As regards the suggestion that the involvement of national parliaments in the appointment of judges to the ECJ should be obligatory, the latter held that 'a reform involving a hearing of each nominee by a parliamentary committee would be unacceptable. Prospective appointees would be unable adequately to answer the questions put to them without betraying the discretion incumbent upon persons whose independence must, in the words of the Treaties, be beyond doubt and without prejudging positions they might have to adopt with regard to contentious issues which they would have to decide in the exercise of their judicial function.' ('Report on certain aspects of the application of the TEU' (n 19)).

III. POSSIBLE REFORMS—A GRADUAL AND PRAGMATIC APPROACH

In order to prepare the Community courts, in the short and the medium term, for the role that they will be called upon to play in light of the changes that have taken place in their caseload, and to improve their efficiency more generally, a number of measures could be adopted, either together or separately.

A. Reforming the CFI

Regarding the CFI specifically, its individual contribution to the IGC-96, submitted in May 1995, contains a series of suggestions. Before mentioning any other measures that might be envisaged, I would just like to recall the main proposals contained in that contribution, in no particular order.

i. Increase in the Number of Judges

Since the CFI sits in chambers (of three or five judges), the arrival of new judges could be easily managed and would make possible a substantial acceleration of the judicial decision-making process at first instance, by means of an increase in the number of chambers. Administratively, the increase in the number of members would certainly require a strengthening of the CFI's structure, organisational capacity and judicial management, but most issues could be resolved relatively easily using internal changes to current working methods and administrative arrangements.

Naturally, a strict insistence on the unwritten rule that the number of judges should correspond to the number of Member States, with each designating the same number of judges, would hinder this potential reform and make it unworkable. Indeed, a simple doubling of the number of judges should be avoided;[26] any increase in the CFI's size should be limited to what is reasonable and be implemented gradually and rationally. One way to achieve this would be to adopt a new and different appointment mechanism for additional judges joining the core of existing members of the CFI (for example, the choice could be made amongst the names contained in a list of candidates, one being put forward by each Member State).

ii. Specialisation

In view of the growth and diversification of the caseload, a certain degree of specialisation might be appropriate for a first instance court of general jurisdiction. That could be achieved through the creation of specialised chambers selected to deal with certain specific types of dispute, those disputes being identified by

[26] As was suggested by the Barreaux de France delegation (see 6651 *Agence Europe*, 24 January 1996).

reference to their subject matter in fields deemed appropriate for that purpose (industrial property, civil service cases, customs litigation).

Certainly, such specialisation at chamber level should not involve permanent specialisation of the judges themselves. An appropriate system of rotation, applied using the powers of internal organisation conferred on the CFI by the Statute of the ECJ and the CFI's own Rules of Procedure, would make it possible to avoid that undesirable result.

On the other hand, the use of assistant rapporteurs, an office provided for by Article 12 of the EC statute of the ECJ but never yet used, could provide a way to reconcile the principle that judges should be 'generalists' with the wish to have recourse to high-level specialists when necessary. Responsibility for deciding cases would continue to be reserved for the judges, but the research necessary to prepare cases and the drafting work could, in certain fields, be left to such experts, depending on their qualifications and fields of specialisation. Unlike the existing *référendaires* (legal secretaries), such rapporteurs might attend the judges' deliberations and their appointment could considerably help to unclutter the Court.

iii. Advocates General

Unlike the ECJ, the CFI does not include Advocates General among its members. Each judge (with the exception of the President) may, however, be called upon to exercise that function in certain cases, by virtue of Article 2(3) of the Council Decision of 24 October 1988[27] and of Articles 17, 18 and 19 of the CFI's Rules of Procedure.

The CFI's experience has shown, however, that, in every case where a judge is called upon to act as an Advocate General, that has inevitably led him to focus on the preparation and drafting of the necessary Opinion, thus delaying his work in other cases. This explains why that possibility has only been used by the CFI four or five times in the seven years since it was established.

The formula contained in the Council Decision of 24 October 1988 concerning Advocates General at the CFI was the result of a compromise between those who believed them to be superfluous in a first instance court and those who felt that their contribution played, and should continue to play, an essential role in the development of the case-law and in the public debate on the issues raised at Community level.

This compromise formula having become outdated, could conceivably be replaced by another solution, consisting in the designation of a small number of permanent Advocates General (two or three perhaps), responsible for giving Opinions in cases where the relevant chambers deemed it to be necessary, and only in respect of the most delicate and contentious issues raised in each of those

[27] Council Decision of 24 October 1988 of 24 October 1988 establishing a Court of First Instance of the European Communities [1988] OJ L 319/1.

cases. In that way, one could retain the advantages of the Advocates General system without causing delay to the handling of cases.

iv. Single Judge and Simplified Procedures

The CFI deals with a wide range of disputes whose complexity is extremely variable, to which new areas of litigation will be added in the near future (European trade marks, plant varieties, possibly industrial designs and models and even the European patent).

In this context, one may legitimately ask whether this is not the right moment to accept, within the Community legal order, that certain cases should be handled by a single judge who would deal with the large number of disputes that involve relatively simple questions of fact and law. That reform should not encounter any significant political opposition, since it would only be applicable in simple disputes involving individual interests, which do not in any event require chambers of more than three judges. The delegation of certain cases to a single judge in Community litigation could, moreover, be implemented in such a way as to meet all the principal concerns that have been raised in that regard. In particular, the use of that mechanism could be limited to those cases where a chamber deemed it to be appropriate, following a preliminary examination of the case, and the single judge could retain the option of referring the case back to a chamber should he come to believe that it actually raised more complex questions than an initial analysis suggested.

Moreover, a judge sitting alone could be supported by an assistant rapporteur, who would work with the judge in a transparent and professional way in order to help the latter to assess the case.[28] In cases capable of being dealt with by a single judge, one might envisage the application of simplified procedural rules that take into account the straightforward nature of the questions raised by the case and which make it possible to deal with such cases more expeditiously.

v. Division of Competences between the ECJ and the CFI.

The TEU made possible the transfer to the CFI of actions brought by the Member States or the institutions. Thus far, the ECJ has not made use of its right of legislative initiative in this respect. In any event, it would not be appropriate to undertake major changes in this field. A limited transfer of competences could be justified in areas where the same act of an institution, a Commission decision for example, is often challenged simultaneously before both courts: by one or more undertakings (before the CFI) and by a Member State (before the ECJ). Notwithstanding the existing procedural mechanisms provided for by the EC Statute of the ECJ, such

[28] A paper criticising the single judge proposal (except for civil service disputes), as well as the proposal concerning the nomination of assistant rapporteurs, was produced by the CCBE (n 9) 3; it prefers the creation of specialised chambers.

situations raise difficult issues in terms of potential conflicts of jurisdiction, which may be detrimental to the parties' interests. This mainly occurs in the field of State aids and, more occasionally, also in cases concerning antidumping measures.

As for the possible transfer of jurisdiction to the CFI in some preliminary ruling cases, sometimes proposed by judges and academic writers,[29] this does not seem to be a live issue at the present time, which explains its absence from the IGC's agenda.

B. Measures Not Requiring Treaty Changes

One of the most significant advantages of the measures set out above is that their implementation would not require any change to the Treaties.

An increase in the number of judges at the CFI could be achieved by means of a change to Article 2(1) of the Council Decision of 24 October 1988, in accordance with the procedure set out in Article 168a(2) of the EC Treaty. The creation of Advocates General would also merely require the amendment of Article 2(1) and (3) of that same Decision while the possibility of using a single judge in the Community courts could be achieved by a modification of Article 2(4) of that Decision. The extension to the CFI of the (as yet unused) office of assistant rapporteurs, already envisaged for the ECJ, could be realised by applying *mutatis mutandis* Article 12 of the ECJ's Statute to the CFI and the creation of simplified procedural mechanisms would require amendments to the existing provisions of—or, in the alternative, the enactment of additional provisions complementing—the Rules of Procedure as well as, possibly, changes to Articles 18 and/or 36 of the EC Statute of the ECJ. The creation of specialised chambers is simply a matter of internal organisation of the CFI which that Court is free to determine for itself. Finally, the transfer of jurisdiction to hear certain applications brought by Member States to the CFI would require an application of the procedure set out in Article 168a(2) of the EC Treaty.

C. Amendments to the Treaties

Certain amendments will, however, still be needed in order to adapt the text of the Treaties to the real-world changes that have taken place since the CFI was set up.

In fact, the sole legal basis in the EC Treaty for the existence of the CFI is Article 168a, whose wording, even after the modifications introduced by the TEU, continues to follow a flawed legislative technique and to use ambiguous language ('A Court of First Instance shall be attached to the Court of Justice …').

[29] See U Everling, 'L'avenir de l'organisation juridictionnelle de l'Union européenne' in *La réforme du système juridictionnel communautaire* (n 17) 30, where it is stressed that relations between Community and national courts are of a cooperative, not hierarchical, type.

With a view to improving the clarity and readability of the 'founding' texts of the Community, it would be appropriate to refer to the CFI in Article 4 of the EC Treaty, since such a reference would better reflect its functions and role within the Community legal order. Indeed, that provision (together with Articles 4a and 4b) lists all the institutions and organs charged with the achievement of the Community's objectives.

It should be recalled that those provisions make reference to the Court of Auditors, now raised to the rank of an institution, to organs exercising purely advisory functions (the Economic and Social Committee, now joined by the Committee of Regions), to the European System of Central Banks and the European Central Bank, and to the European Investment Bank, whose existence was provided for by the EC Treaty from the outset (Articles 129 and 130).

It is therefore surprising, at the very least, that the European citizen, on opening the Treaty, should find no mention of the CFI in those Articles which, at the very beginning of the Community's founding text, list its institutions and principal organs. Indeed, the CFI is the only organ created by the Treaties themselves which is not mentioned in those provisions, in spite of the nature and importance of the judicial function it shares with the ECJ in ensuring that 'in the interpretation and application of this Treaty the law is observed' (Article 164).

That issue is closely connected to that of a possible change to the CFI's name, which has already been suggested on numerous occasions.[30] Indeed, as things stand, the CFI's name does not accurately reflect the nature of its functions and its position within the Community's judicial architecture, since it gives rulings that are final on issues of fact (hence, the ECJ is not an appeal court but rather a court of 'cassation').

The discussions on this subject have not, however, up to the present day, come up with a more appropriate name, in all the Community languages, which explains the absence of any concrete proposal by the CFI itself. An effort of imagination is required. I, for one, would suggest calling it the 'Court of the European Community', a simple designation which, in all of the official languages, would be sufficiently different from the expression 'Court of Justice of the European Communities'.

As regards a possible change to the provisions relating to the rules governing the appointment of judges to the CFI, the latter is of the view that (subject to modification of the system of replacing judges at the end of fixed terms, regardless of the date on which the appointment of that judge occurred) 'the current system of renewable mandates seems to be the most appropriate to the CFI's functional requirements'. In any event, any new rule should, in the interests of the requirements of the sound administration of justice, ensure an appropriate degree of stability in the exercise of judicial functions.

[30] See, for example, European Parliament, Committee on Institutional Affairs, 'Report on the Role of the Court of Justice in the Development of the Community's Constitutional System' (Rothley Report) 13 July 1993 (doc EP 155.441/def.).

Part III

Judicial Protection of Individuals

8

Interim Measures in Judicial Proceedings as an Instrument of Protection for Individuals in European Community Law[*]

I. INTRODUCTION

IN COMMUNITY LAW in general and in Community competition law in particular, applications for interim relief have become a relatively frequently-used and efficient means of provisional protection of individuals seeking to challenge administrative decisions in proceedings before the Community courts. As the relevant statistics appear to indicate, the setting up of the Court of First Instance (hereinafter the 'CFI') is one of the main factors that explain the recent increase in the use of this mechanism by individuals, especially in the field of antitrust and merger control law.

In fact, whereas during the first 37 years of the Court of Justice's activity (hereinafter the 'Court'), ie between 1952 and 1989, when the CFI was set up, the President of the Court, or his substitute, ruled on roughly 230 applications for interim relief by way of orders published in the European Court Reports, the President of the CFI, or his substitute, has already delivered, in approximately seven years, more than 100 orders on interim relief applications. The number of such judicial decisions has been particularly large since 1994: whereas, between 1991 and 1993, the number of orders made by the President of the CFI was between seven and 12 each year, it increased to 35 in 1994, 19 in 1995 and 22 in 1996.

In broad terms, roughly half of those CFI interim relief orders related to competition law matters.[1] The economic and financial significance of the sums of money at stake in such cases and the need for a swift ruling clarifying the parties'

[*] First published in French under the title: 'La procedure en référé comme instrument de protection juridictionnelle des particuliers en droit communautaire' in Fabio Monaco et al (eds), *Scritti in Onore di Giuseppe Federico Mancini*, II—Diritto dell'Unione Europea (Milano, Giuffrè Editore, 1998) 257–306.

[1] In 1996, of 22 orders, eight concerned competition law issues: four of those orders related to the application of Articles 85 and 86 of the Treaty, one to merger control and the remaining three to the application of Articles 92 and 93 (State aid).

legal position, in contrast to the slow pace of proceedings leading to a final ruling on the merits, serve to explain the practical value of interim measures for economic operators.

Without prejudice, where appropriate, to references to aspects of the regime applicable to these proceedings more generally, this chapter will mainly focus on interim measures sought before the Community judicature in the field of competition and merger control law.[2] Interim measures within the competence of the Commission[3] or of national judges[4] will not, in principle, be analysed in any depth.

[2] Examples will therefore be taken, where appropriate, from other areas of Community law: European Coal and Steel Community (ECSC), Euratom, common agriculture policy, staff cases.

[3] The landmark cases dealing with the Commission's powers to order interim measures in the field of competition law are 792/79 R *Camera Care v Commission* [1980] ECR 119; Joined Cases 229/82 R and 228/82 R *Ford et al v Commission* [1982] ECR 3091; and T-44/90 *La Cinq v Commission* [1992] ECR II-1. In the field of State aid, reference should be made to C-301/87 *France v Commission* (*Boussac*) [1990] ECR I-307. On *Camera Care*, see in particular R Joliet, 'Protection juridictionnelle provisoire et droit communautaire' (1992) *Rivista di Diritto Europeo* 253–84, in particular 262–63. Joliet's remark that the Court ruled on the merits in the order terminating the interim measures proceedings, instead of making that decision in the main proceedings, seems especially pertinent. On interim measures falling within the competence of the Commission, see: J Temple Lang, 'The Powers of the Commission to Order Interim Measures in Competition Cases' (1980) *Common Market Law Review* 49–61; LM Pais Antunes, 'Interim Measures under EC Competition Law—Recent Developments' (1993) *Yearbook of European Law* 83–95; L Idot, 'Les mesures provisoires en droit de la concurrence: un nouvel exemple de symbiose entre le droit français et le droit communautaire de la concurrence' (1993) *Revue trimestrielle de Droit européen* 581–600; G Tesauro, 'Les mesures provisoires dans le système communautaire' in M Pérez González (ed), *Hacia un Nuevo Orden Internacional y Europeo—Estudios en Homenaje al Professor Don Manuel Díez de Velasco* (Madrid, Tecnos, 1995) 1242–54.

[4] Regarding the competence of national courts in this field, see especially: C-213/89 *Factortame* [1990] ECR I-2433; C-143/88 *Zuckerfabrik Süderithmarschen* [1991] ECR I-415, C-465/93 *Atlanta Fruchthandelsgesellschaft et al* [1995] I-3761, and C-68/95 *T Port* [1996] ECR I-6065. The Court ruled in *Factortame* that a judge can suspend application of a national legislation until the Court has decided, following a reference for a preliminary ruling, on the compatibility with Community law of that legislation. In *Zuckerfabrik*, it held that the coherence of the system of interim judicial protection requires that national courts have power to grant interim measures in the context of the application of a national administrative act adopted on the basis of a Community regulation whose legality is subject to challenge and whose validity is the object of a reference for a preliminary ruling. The conditions for taking such measures were laid down in *Atlanta*, above. Lastly, in *Port*, above, the Court examined whether a national judge can grant interim protection to economic operators on the basis of the foreseeable adoption of an act by the Commission, pursuant to a Community regulation. The Court concluded that since the Treaty did not enable it to rule on an institution's failure to act by way of the preliminary ruling proceedings, national courts are not empowered to order interim measures while awaiting the action of the institution. The Court also stated, in this regard, that the competence to rule on a failure to act belongs exclusively to the Community judiciary. It is doubtful, however, whether the reasoning of the Court was absolutely correct and, in any case, whether the conclusion reached is the only one that could be drawn from those premises. First of all, whereas a national court cannot ask the Court, by means of a preliminary ruling, to find that an institution has failed to act, it can, however (as follows from the Court's answer to the first preliminary question put by the national court in this case), ask it to interpret the relevant provisions of Community law in order to ascertain whether they give rise to an obligation for the institution to act. Secondly, it is understandable that a national court may have serious doubts concerning the legality of an institution's failure to act. Two of the main conditions set in *Atlanta* (see para 48 of the judgment in *Port*) with regard to the examination of the validity of a positive act of the institutions could thus apply, *mutatis mutandis*, to the case of a failure to act. Thirdly, once the other conditions, especially the urgency, are met (in particular, when a breach of

II. THE LEGAL FRAMEWORK OF INTERIM RELIEF PROCEEDINGS AND ADMISSIBILITY CONDITIONS

A. General Remarks

A general overview of the legal framework applicable to interim relief proceedings in Community law is not difficult to provide.[5] By contrast, as will be seen below, the case-law does not provide clear guidance as to how future cases will be decided in this field, leading some legal scholars to identify a lack of coherence, or even outright contradictions, in the Community case-law.

Those criticisms do not appear justified: every single case is different and has therefore to be dealt with by the Court in the light of its precise and specific context. This area of litigation is indeed conditioned by the need to provide timely and pragmatic rulings to deal with urgent situations, the specific circumstances of

a fundamental right, such as the right to property or the freedom to pursue a professional activity, may be at stake: see para 40 of *Port*), it is necessary in order to ensure the coherence of the system of interim judicial protection that the two situations be treated in a similar way. In fact, as the Court recalled in paras 49 and 59 of *Port*, respectively, on the one hand, a preliminary reference concerning the validity of a measure is, like an action for annulment, a means of reviewing the legality of Community institutions' action and, on the other hand, Articles 173 and 175 of the Treaty constitute the expression of what is essentially one and the same legal remedy. Fourthly, as with a finding of invalidity of a Community measure, the adoption of interim measures by a national court is not of such a nature as to jeopardise the exclusive competence of the Community judiciary to review a failure to act. Lastly, the possibility mentioned in the *Port* judgment (para 59) that individuals may bring an action for failure to act against the institution which failed to adopt an act that would directly and individually concern them is not relevant when the act whose adoption is sought is of a normative nature or where it would require the prior adoption of an act of general application, in order to provide a sufficient legal basis. These *lacunae* hamper effective judicial protection in this context and it is precisely for this reason that national courts are often called upon to rule on the issue of failure to act, just as they would be in relation to the validity of a Community regulation. That question would merit an in-depth analysis that is beyond the scope of this chapter. On the topic of interim judicial protection of the rights of individuals by national courts applying Community law, see: A Barav, 'Enforcement of Community Rights in the National Courts: The Case for Jurisdiction to Grant an Interim Relief' (1989) *Common Market Law Review* 369–90; E Garcia de Enterria, 'El problema de los poderes del juez national para suspender cautelarmente la ejecución de las leyes nacionales en consideración al derecho comunitario europeo' (1989) *Revista Española de Derecho Administrativo*, 411–32; D Simon et A Barav, 'Le droit communautaire et la suspension provisoire des mesures nationales: les enjeux de l'affaire Factortame' (1990) *Revue du Marché commun* 591–97; R Joliet (n 3) 274 ff; L Papadias, 'Interim Protection under Community Law before the National Courts. The Right to a Judge with Jurisdiction to Grant Interim Relief' (1994) *Legal Issues of European Integration* 153–93; JM Sobrino Heredia, 'La incidencia del derecho comunitario sobre la facultad de los órganos jurisdiccionales nacionales de adoptar medidas cautelares de contenido positivo (comentario de la sentencia del TJCE de 9 Noviembre de 1995, *Atlanta Fruchthandelsgesellschaft y otros*, C-465/93)' (1996) *Revista de Instituciones Europeas* 779–97; G Tesauro (n 3) 1246–54.

[5] On the procedural aspects of interim measures and the applicable legal rules, see: B Pastor Borgoñon and E Van Ginderachter, *El procedimiento de medidas cautelares ante el Tribunal de justicia y el Tribunal de primera instancia de las Comunidades europeas* (Madrid, Civitas, 1993). See also: M Waelbroeck and D Waelbroeck, 'Articles 185 and 186' in M Waelbroeck et al (eds), *Commentaire Mégret*, 2nd edn (Brussels, Les éditions de l'Université de Bruxelles, 1993) 395–408, and J Rideau and F Picod, *Code des procédures communautaires* (Paris, Litec, 1994) 420–30, 569–75, 679–82.

each case playing a decisive role in relation both to the procedure to be followed and the decision to be taken.

The judge hearing the application for interim relief must therefore enjoy a considerable margin of discretion to assess the case and to take the decision that is most appropriate, as well as in managing the proceedings and making use of the relevant powers vested in the court.

B. Legal Framework

Interim measures are the object of two different provisions in the EC Treaty.

Article 185 provides that '[t]he Court of Justice may, [...] if it considers that circumstances so require, order that application of the contested act be suspended'. In addition, Article 186 provides that '[t]he Court of Justice may in any cases before it prescribe any necessary interim measures'.

An application for interim relief lodged with the Court or the CFI may thus seek the suspension, in whole or in part, of the application of the contested act or the adoption of other 'necessary measures' such as, in particular, the imposition of an injunction ordering a party to act or not to act, thus making possible a provisional *modus vivendi* as between the parties.[6]

In both situations the application should, by definition, aim at achieving a *temporary* outcome, as both the suspension of a measure's application and the other 'necessary measures' envisaged are intended to produce effects only until the Court or the CFI give their judgment in the main proceedings. Moreover, the

6 The case-law of both the Court and the CFI provide examples of the latter type of measure. They are particularly common in the field of civil servant disputes (staff cases). This may be illustrated by cases where the judge has ordered suspension of tests to be held as part of an open competition for admissions purposes, and where the act challenged in the main proceedings was the refusal to allow a candidate to participate in those tests (see the orders cited by R Joliet (n 3) 261, fn 37). Another striking example is the Order of the President of the CFI of 30 November 1994, T-379/94 R *Kessler v Commission*, not published, where the President ordered, for reasons of urgency and without even hearing the defendant, that a candidate excluded by the selection panel should be allowed to participate in the written tests, to be held two days later. The results of the correction of the tests of that candidate and his participation to the next stages of the proceedings were suspended pending the final decision in the main action. By Order of 21 November 1994, T-368/94 R *Blanchard/Commission* [1994] ECR II-1099, the President of the CFI while suspending the election procedure for a Commission Local Staff Committee and pursuant to the parties' agreement, established a set of provisional rules for the new electoral procedure. The suspension, either in whole or in part, of the operation of the contested decision is often accompanied, especially in the area of competition law, by an obligation for the Commission to monitor execution of the interim relief decision, on the basis of information to be provided by the applicants and/or the plaintiffs. See Order of the President of the CFI of 16 June 1992, Cases T-24/92 R and T-28/92 *R Langnese-Iglo* and *Schöller Lebensmittel v Commission* [1992] ECR II-1839. In certain cases, the obligation to pass information to the Commission is aimed at allowing the latter to monitor changes in the economic and financial situation of the applicant, thus enabling the Commission to intervene by taking, where necessary, the appropriate precautionary measures or by requesting the President to modify his Order, as provided for in Article 108 of the Rules of Procedure of the CFI (Article 87 of the Rules of Procedure of the Court). See Order of the President of the CFI, of 17 February 1995, T-308/94 R *Cascades v Commission* [1995] ECR II-267.

measure sought by the applicant is of a *protective* nature, inasmuch as it aims to protect the rights of one of the parties or of a third party or the Community's public interest, by preventing an irreversible situation from arising.

Article 36 of the Statute of the Court of Justice provides that the President of the Court or of the CFI may adjudicate on applications for suspension or other interim measures by way of summary procedure, which may, insofar as necessary, differ from some of the rules contained in the Statute and which are to be laid down in the Rules of Procedure of the Court (Articles 83 to 90) and of the CFI (Articles 104 to 110). Pursuant to Article 36 of the Statute and Article 85 of the Rules of Procedure of the Court (Article 106 of the Rules of Procedure of the CFI), it is the President of the Court or of the CFI who has jurisdiction to rule on applications for interim relief. However, the President may alternatively refer the interim measures case to the panel of judges (chamber or plenary session) to which the main case has been assigned.[7] In the event that the President is absent or is prevented from dealing with an application, he is replaced by the President of Chamber or by the most senior judge.[8] As spelled out in Article 36 of the Statute, the Order of the President or of the judge replacing him is of a provisional nature and does not prejudice the decision of the Court or of the CFI on the substance of the case.

The Rules of Procedure (Article 84(2) of the Rules of Procedure of the Court and Article 105(2) of the Rules of Procedure of the CFI) confer on the judge a wide margin of appreciation in handling the proceedings. In particular, the judge may order the opening of an enquiry, the production of documents and other information (statistics, sales figures, number of outlets, market data, contracts, internal and external communications, internal corporate communications).[9] He or she may also grant the requested measure even before the other party has had the opportunity to make known its views, whilst maintaining the possibility of modifying or revoking the Order thus made of his or her own motion. He or she is also competent to decide whether a hearing should be organised or whether the written submissions provide sufficient information to rule on the application without opening the oral phase of the proceedings.

[7] In accordance with a common practice, the President usually hears the Judge-Rapporteur and, where applicable, the Advocate-General appointed in the main action who may be present at the oral hearing.

[8] In the CFI, almost all interim relief orders (except for two or three) have been adopted by its President.

[9] See eg Orders of the President of the CFI of 8 May 1992, Joined Cases T-24/92 R and T-28/92 R *Langnese and Schöller* [1992] II-1713 paras 18–22, of 2 April 1993, T-12/93 R *CCE Vittel and CE Pierval v Commission* [1993] ECR II-449, and of 10 May 1994, T-88/94 R *Société commerciale des potasses et de l'azote and EMC v Commission* [1994] ECR II-263.

C. Conditions of Admissibility of Applications for Interim Relief

In Community procedural law, applications for interim relief are not autonomous actions. Indeed, it follows from both Article 83 of the Rules of Procedure of the Court and from Article 104 of the Rules of Procedure of the CFI that (i) a request to suspend the operation of a measure adopted by an institution is inadmissible unless the applicant is challenging that measure before the Court or the CFI and (ii) any application for interim measures of another kind is inadmissible unless it is submitted by a party to a pending case and relates to that case.

The case-law in this field has deduced some important rules from those provisions as to the *admissibility* of requests for interim measures.

i. Link with a Direct Action

First of all, it follows from the abovementioned provisions that interim relief proceedings must always be *ancillary* to one of the direct actions laid down in the Treaty, ie actions for annulment or for failure to act, actions against Member States for failure to fulfil an obligation under the Treaty, actions for damages or staff cases.[10]

[10] As regards the relationship between *preliminary ruling* proceedings and the competence of the Community courts to adopt interim measures, reference should be made to the observations of the President of the CFI in his Order of 12 February 1996, T-228/95 R *Lehrfreund v Council and Commission* [1996] ECR II-111 paras 60 and 61. In its request for interim measures, made in the course of an action for damages against the Community, the applicant sought to obtain a declaration interpreting Article 3, first indent, of Regulation No 3254/91. The President of the CFI considered this request incompatible with the particular nature of interim proceedings as well as, more generally, with the wider system of remedies of which they form part. In fact, in his Order, the President held that: 'Only in the [case of a request for preliminary ruling under Article 177] may the Court of Justice be asked to give a decision whose operative part itself relates directly to the interpretation of a rule of Community law. Such a decision cannot, therefore, be obtained in interim proceedings, which are necessarily an adjunct to a direct action'. One particular question that needs to be answered is whether it is possible to obtain interim judicial protection from the Community judicature in the context of preliminary rulings. The answer has to be negative, in spite of the reluctance of President Mertens de Wilmars (quoted by R Joliet (n 3) 274, fn 97). The issue to which Mertens de Wilmars referred has been resolved in the meantime in *Zuckerfabrik* (n 4). R Joliet (n 3) 274, saw two reasons for that impossibility: first, a reference for a preliminary ruling cannot be qualified as an action within the meaning of Article 185 of the Treaty; second, a 'case' has not been brought before the Court as is required by Article 186. I would add that interim protection, in that context, would neither be allowed under Article 83(1) of the Rules of Procedure of the Court, as the act whose suspension is requested has not been challenged by the applicant in an action brought before the Court, nor would it concern a party to a case before the Court. It is therefore only before the national court and under the conditions set out in *Zuckerfabrik* and *Factortame* that the parties to the main action can obtain the suspension of operation of a measure or any other interim relief in relation to a Community act or on the basis of Community law. Moreover, the wording of Article 177 and the specific nature of the reference for a preliminary ruling on the interpretation or on the validity of Community law preclude any interpretation of the Treaty that would make possible the adoption of interim measures by the Community courts in this context.

That does not mean that any application for interim measures is automatically admissible solely by reason of the fact that it makes reference to a direct action pending before the Court or the CFI.

A first distinction that must be drawn in this regard is between an application to suspend operation of an act and a request to obtain other interim measures: whereas the latter can be submitted in any case brought before the Community courts, the former is, in principle, only admissible if it concerns an action for annulment or a staff case. Indeed, given that, on the one hand, only the *contested act* can have its operation suspended and, on the other hand, only the *acts of the Community institutions* can be challenged before the Community courts, it would not appear possible to have the operation of a measure suspended in the context of an action for failure to act, of an action for damages which is not associated with an action for annulment, or of an action for failure to fulfil an obligation under the Treaty.

As regards the latter form of action, it should be pointed out that the distinction between the suspension of a measure's operation and other interim measures is, in practice, rather formalistic. Indeed, by its orders in the Italian Lotto case[11] and in the case concerning a German tax on heavy goods vehicles,[12] the Court suspended the operation of *national* measures. It is therefore clear that the effects of certain interim measures other than the suspension of a Community measure may be similar to those that follow from such a suspension.

However, even the existence of a 'contested measure' in the framework of an action for annulment or a staff case is not in itself sufficient to ensure the admissibility of an application for suspension of the operation of that measure. Indeed, it is still necessary that the contested measure should not constitute a negative decision, that is, a decision whereby the institution refuses to adopt the act that the applicant is seeking. Suspending operation of such a negative decision would not, in principle,[13] change the factual or legal situation in favour of the applicant.[14]

[11] Orders of the President of the Court of 31 January 1992 and of 12 June 1992 in C-272/91 R *Commission v Italy* [1992] ECR I-457 and I-3929, where the President of the Court ordered the Italian Republic to take (and to maintain) 'the measures necessary to suspend the legal effects' of a decree adopted by the Finance Minister awarding a public contract for the computerisation of the National Lottery. That suspension covered the operation of the contract that had been entered into in the meantime with one of the competing consortia.

[12] See C-195/90 R *Commission v Germany* [1990] ECR I-3351, where the Court ordered the Federal Republic of Germany to suspend, until final judgement, the collection of its tax on heavy goods vehicles insofar as it affected vehicles registered in other Member States.

[13] In fact, account should be taken of exceptional cases where the legal situation of the applicant has been modified by a decision dismissing the application. See Order of the Court in Case 76/88 R *La Terza v Court of Justice* [1988] ECR 1741, which suspended operation of a decision by the authorities refusing an extension of the authorisation to work part-time. That negative decision required the applicant to start working full-time and therefore modified her legal and factual situation (see R Joliet (n 3) 259).

[14] See C-206/89 *S v Commission* [1989] ECR 284, para 14; T-507/93 R *Branco v Court of Auditors* [1993] ECR II-1013, and T-164/96 R *Moccia Irme v Commission* [1996] ECR II-2261 paras 26–28.

It also follows from the case-law that, for similar reasons, the admissibility of an application for interim relief cannot rely merely on the likelihood that a challengeable act will be adopted or even on the announcement by a Community institution of its intention to adopt it. In an Order of 22 November 1995,[15] the President of the CFI thus ruled that a group of maritime transport companies, which had notified an agreement whereby they jointly set the rates for the provision of combined transport services,[16] could not request in advance, and in the absence of exceptional circumstances, the suspension of the operation of a possible future decision withdrawing the benefit of immunity from fines resulting from said notification, since no such decision had actually been adopted by the Commission. According to the President of the CFI, such a request does not, as a rule, meet the conditions for admissibility set out in Article 104(1) of the Rules of Procedure of the CFI.

Indeed, as underlined in that same Order (para 39), a mere declaration of intention on the part of the Commission does not have a binding effect on the applicants. As long as a decision to withdraw immunity from fines has not been taken and produces no legal effects, the applicants are not entitled to ask the CFI to adopt interim measures.

By contrast, the Court, relying, on the one hand, on the broadly-worded provision of Article 186 of the Treaty, which does not provide for any exception concerning special proceedings,[17] and, on the other hand, on settled case-law that, since 1977,[18] has made clear that interim measures can be ordered in the context of proceedings of a declaratory nature, has confirmed in *Port*[19] that the Community courts are competent to order, in the context of an action for failure to act, the interim measures provided for in Article 186 of the Treaty.

[15] T-395/94 R II *Atlantic Container a o v Commission* [1995] ECR II-2893. See below the analysis of other issues of admissibility raised in this Order.

[16] The so-called Trans-Atlantic Conference Agreement (TACA) replaced a previous agreement between the same parties, the Trans-Atlantic Agreement (TAA), which the Commission considered, by Decision No 94/980/EC [1994] OJ L376/1, to include several provisions that were contrary to Article 85(1) of the Treaty. An action for annulment was brought against that Decision in T-395/94 where the applicants sought interim relief. That request was partially granted by Order of the President of the CFI of 10 March 1995, T-395/94 R *Atlantic Container et al v Commission* [1995] ECR II-595, confirmed on appeal by Order of the President of the Court of 19 July 1995, C-149/95 P(R) *Commission v Atlantic Container et al* [1995] ECR I-2165. The new application for interim relief, dismissed by Order of the President of the CFI of 22 November 1995 (n 15) above, concerned a statement of objections addressed by the Commission to the parties to the TACA indicating that the Commission envisaged the adoption of a decision withdrawing the immunity from fines that resulted from the notification of the new Agreement.

[17] See C-120/94 R *Commission v Greece* (Former Yugoslav Republic of Macedonia) [1994] ECR I-3037 para 42.

[18] Cases 31/77 R and 53/77 R *Commission v United Kingdom* [1977] ECR 921.

[19] *Port* (n 4).

ii. Link with the Object of the Main Action

A further condition of admissibility that follows from Article 83(1) of the Rules of Procedure of the Court and Article 104(1) of the Rules of Procedure of the CFI pertains to the link that must exist between the measures sought and the *object of the main action.*

Indeed, it should be borne in mind that the rationale underlying an application for interim relief is to ensure that effective execution of the final judgment is possible in case the main action succeeds.[20]

Thus, according to well-established case-law,[21] in order to be admissible an application for interim relief must both (i) fall within the scope of the final decision which the judge hearing the main proceedings can make and (ii) concern the relations between the parties.

For this reason, the President of the CFI rejected as inadmissible one of the requests for interim measures made in the abovementioned *Gestevisión Telecinco* case, to the extent that the applicant sought to obtain from the CFI the suspension of the Eurovision system for joint acquisition of the television rights of international sporting events. As the Order points out, the decision that the CFI was asked to take in the main action could not have as its object the annulment of the agreement on the joint acquisition of the television rights concluded within the framework of the EBU (European Broadcasting Union) by companies that were not even parties to the main proceedings between the applicant and the Commission (para 25).

Similarly, the President of the CFI dismissed the application for interim measures made in the context of an action for annulment against the decision of the Commission on the TAA Agreement, already mentioned,[22] on the additional ground that the measure sought, insofar as it concerned the statement of objections issued against the new TACA Agreement[23] concluded between the same parties and replacing the TAA, could not be regarded as relating to the annulment of the contested decision since it formed part of a completely separate procedure.[24]

iii. The Competences of Other Institutions Must be Respected

The Community courts have always taken great care not to exceed the boundaries of their own jurisdiction to grant certain types of interim measures. In fact, it follows from the case-law that safeguarding the division of competences set out in

20 See B Pastor Borgoñon and E Van Ginderachter (n 5) 28.

21 See notably Orders of the President of the CFI of 14 December 1993, T-543/93 R *Gestevisión Telecinco v Commission* [1993] ECR II-1409 paras 25–26, of 2 December 1994, T-322/94 R *Union Carbide v Commission* [1994] ECR II-1159 para 28, and of 27 February 1996, T-235/95 R *A Goldstein v Commission*, paras 36, 38.

22 *Atlantic Container* (n 15).

23 Containing several clauses identical to those included in the previous Agreement. See n 16 above.

24 *Atlantic Container* (n 15) paras 42–45.

the Treaty and protecting the competences of the other institutions, in particular those of the Commission, has always been a concern of the Community courts in this type of proceeding.

In that context, those courts have stressed that, within the institutional framework of the Community, it is for the Commission, whenever it considers it necessary and within the limits of the powers granted to it in competition matters by Articles 85 and 86 of the Treaty and by Regulation No 17 of 6 February 1962, to adopt the interim measures sought by a plaintiff. In fact, rather than substitute itself for the Commission in the exercise of the powers conferred by those provisions, the role of the judge is to review the legality of the Commission's activity in this field.[25]

For that very same reason, the Community courts typically refuse to examine issues not yet addressed by the defendant institutions in order to avoid preempting the examination of the merits and so that the different procedural stages remain properly distinct, the administrative procedure coming first and the judicial thereafter. It is not therefore possible—save in exceptional circumstances—to preclude the Commission from exercising its powers of investigation and sanction by admitting an application for interim relief submitted immediately after the opening of the administrative procedure, at a time when the interlocutory or final acts, whose suspension is sought, have not yet been adopted.[26]

iv. The Main Action ought not to be Manifestly Inadmissible

Lastly, in order for an application for interim relief to be admissible, the main action must not be *manifestly inadmissible.*

This rule raises some delicate issues. According to Article 36 of the Statute of the Court, the decision of the judge in interim proceedings shall not prejudge the decision of the Court in the main proceedings. Nevertheless, by declaring the application for interim relief inadmissible by reason of the manifest inadmissibility of the main action, the judge hearing that application will inevitably appear to anticipate the admissibility decision in the main case.

It should be stressed, however, that the interim order may only be based on the information that the judge has in his or her possession at this preliminary stage of the procedure. Therefore, even where the interim decision relies on a finding that the main action is inadmissible—thus providing the parties with a strong indication as to the possible future course of the proceedings—the autonomy of the Court to rule on the main action remains intact and so the possibility of adopting a different view in the light of a new assessment remains entirely open.

[25] See Orders of the President of the CFI of 6 December 1989, T-131/89 R *Cosimex v Commission* [1990] ECR II-1 paras 11–12, and of 27 February 1996, T-235/95 R *A Goldstein* (n 21) para 40. See also Orders of the President of the Court, *Camera Care* (n 3), *Gestevisión Telecinco* (n 21) and *Union Carbide* (n 21).

[26] See Order of the President of the CFI of 12 July 1996, T-52/96 R *Sogecable v Commission* [1996] ECR II-797 paras 40–41.

In any event, both as regards this issue and the analysis of the *fumus boni juris*,[27] the judge deciding on the interim relief application is required to show great restraint, including as regards the wording used, in order not to cast any doubt on the provisional nature of the assessment made at this stage.

That concern explains why many interim orders—in addition to the traditional reference to the *provisional nature* of such measures, meaning that they shall not prejudge the decision in the main proceedings—make use of wording that is intended to convey caution, in the form of expressions such as: '*it is not apparent at this stage*'; 'a *summary* analysis of the provisions'; 'that interpretation *appears* to be borne out'; 'the procedure followed thus *appears* in accordance'; '*appears, at first sight*, to be intended to'; 'the contested act *does not appear*'; 'it follows that the applicant's argument is *prima facie* unfounded'; 'constitutes, *at first sight*, a preparatory measure'; 'does not *prima facie* constitute a decision'; 'the main application seeking annulment *appears at this stage* manifestly inadmissible'; 'this request is, *prima facie*, manifestly inadmissible'.[28]

Although one may be tempted to question the logic underlying the combined use of expressions such as '*at first sight*' and '*manifestly inadmissible*', as in 'does not appear manifest at first sight', it should be remembered that the judge ruling on interim measures applications is simply taking care, as indeed he or she must, to avoid giving the impression—whether to the parties to the dispute, to the general public or indeed to the panel of judges hearing the main action—that his or her interim findings in any way prejudge the decision on the merits.

Having said that, the judge, hearing the application for interim relief has, in reality, other ways open to him or her to deal with the issue of manifest inadmissibility:

— first, to avoid the problem by dismissing the request due to a lack of urgency, without ruling on the admissibility point;[29]
— second, to refer the request to the chamber having jurisdiction to rule on the main application so that the admissibility of that main application and the interim relief request may be decided at the same time;[30]
— third, to wait until the chamber has declared the main action inadmissible and to dismiss the interim proceedings thereafter on the basis that they have become devoid of purpose.

[27] See below section III/B.

[28] All these expressions can be found in the Order of the President of the CFI of 26 August 1996, T-75/96 R *Söktas Pamuk v Commission* [1996] ECR II-859.

[29] This is a common practice in orders for interim relief since the different conditions required for ordering such relief are cumulative; therefore, in the absence of one of those conditions, the request must be dismissed (see below section III). As the President of the Court put it in his Order of 19 July 1995 in *Atlantic Container Line* (C-149/95 P(R) (n 16)): 'the judge hearing the application enjoys a broad discretion and is free to determine, having regard to the specific circumstances of the case, the manner and order in which those various conditions are to be examined, there being no rule of Community law imposing a pre-established scheme of analysis within which the need to order interim measures must be analysed and assessed' (para 23).

[30] See C-66/91 and C-66/91 R *Emerald Meats/Commission* [1991] ECR I-1143, and T-192/93 and T-492/93 R *Nutral* [1993] ECR II-1023.

Too much emphasis should not, in any case, be placed on this issue given that the rejection of an application for interim relief on the basis of the manifest inadmissibility of the main action is somewhat exceptional. Thus far, in the field of competition law, the President of the CFI has only dismissed an application for interim relief on these grounds on one occasion, in the 'Cement' cases, where two applicants (*ENCI* and *VNC*) sought the annulment of the statement of objections addressed to them by the Commission.[31] In the related field of antidumping, the President of the CFI also dismissed an application for interim relief due to the manifest inadmissibility of the main proceedings in one case.[32]

III. CONDITIONS FOR INTERIM RELIEF

Pursuant to Article 104(2) of the Rules of Procedure of the CFI, interim measures may be granted if the two following cumulative conditions are met: *urgency* and the existence of sufficient grounds, in fact and in law, to justify the measure *at first sight*.

A. Urgency

The condition of urgency of the interim measure sought has to be assessed 'in relation to the necessity for an interim order to prevent serious and irreparable damage [or at least damage that is difficult to repair] to the party applying for it'.[33]

I will make only a small number of observations in this respect, starting with the *nature* and the *intensity* of the damage.

i. Nature and Intensity of the Damage

According to settled case-law, 'purely hypothetical damage based on uncertain future events' does not satisfy the urgency condition for ordering interim relief. For this reason the President of the CFI dismissed a request to suspend operation of a Commission decision where the latter institution, following a preliminary examination under Article 15(6) of Regulation No 17, lifted the immunity from fines in relation to clauses in an agreement providing for the exclusive sale of cosmetics in pharmacies, which had been previously notified to the Commission.[34]

[31] Joined Cases T-10/92-T-15/92 R *Cimenteries CBR and Others v Commission* [1992] ECR II-1571. In a Euratom context, see T-219/95 R *Danielsson et al v Commission* [1995] ECR II-3051.

[32] *Söktas Pamuk* (n 28).

[33] See Order of the President of the CFI of 7 November 1995, T-168/95 R *Eridania and Others v Council* [1995] ECR II-2817 para 33.

[34] See Order of the President of the CFI of 7 June 1991, T-19/91 R *Vichy v Commission* [1991] ECR II-265. This case should not be confused with the aforementioned *Atlantic Container* (n 16) case, in which the President found the interim relief application inadmissible (as well as unfounded)

Also pursuant to settled case-law, 'damage of a purely pecuniary nature cannot, save in exceptional circumstances, be regarded as irreparable or even as being reparable only with difficulty, if it can ultimately be the subject of financial compensation'.[35]

This statement applies, in particular, to the assessment of the urgency condition in the context of interim relief applications concerning Commission decisions imposing fines or other sanctions of a pecuniary nature for breach of the rules on competition. The Commission has started applying, as of a few of years ago, the practice of not collecting the fine whenever an application for annulment is brought before the CFI and the undertaking concerned provides a bank guarantee covering the fine and interest payments due.

Hence, the application for suspension of the operation of such a decision must, in effect, be understood as seeking to obtain a waiver of the obligation to provide the bank guarantee requested by the Commission as a condition for agreeing to delay the payment of the fine.[36] Pursuant to well-established case-law of the Court and of the CFI,[37] such a request can only be granted in exceptional circumstances under the conditions laid down in the Rules of Procedure for ordering interim relief.[38]

The exceptional nature of such waivers explains why it has only been granted, in whole or in part, on three occasions,[39] in consideration of the very specific characteristics of those particular cases, notably in order to avoid the liquidation of the applicant[40] and, where necessary, accompanied by additional conditions and guarantees.[41]

because the Commission merely expressed its *intention* to take a decision withdrawing the immunity from fines. Other examples in the same line as *Vichy* exist in various different fields, ie orders of the President of the CFI of 15 July 1994, T-239/94 R *EISA v Commission* [1994] ECR II-703 paras 20, 22, and of 16 February 1995, T-5/95 R *Amicale des résidents du square d'Auvergne v Commission* [1995] ECR II-255 paras 15 ff.

[35] See *Eridania* (n 33) para 42. See also Orders of the President of the CFI of 7 July 1994, T-185/94 R *Geotronics v Commission* [1994] ECR II-519 para 22, and of 24 February 1995, T-2/95 R *Industries des poudres sphériques v Council* [1995] ECR II-485 para 28.

[36] See Orders of the President of the CFI of 25 August 1994, T-156/94 R *Siderúrgica Aristrain Madrid v Commission* [1994] ECR II-715 para 26, and of 21 December 1994, T-301/94 R *Laakmann Karton v Commission* [1994] ECR II-1279 para 21.

[37] See Orders of the President of the Court of 6 May 1982, Case 107/82 R *AEG v Commission* [1982] ECR 1549 para 6, and of 15 March 1983, Case 234/82 R *Ferriere di Roé Volciano v Commission* [1983] ECR 725 paras 2, 8, and Orders of the President of the CFI of 21 December 1994, T-295/94 R *Buchmann v Commission* [1994] ECR II-1265 para 23, and *Laakmann Karton* (n 36) para 22, and of 11 August 1995, T-104/95 R *Tsimenta Halkidos v Commission* [1995] ECR II-2235 para 19.

[38] See *Aristrain* (n 36) para 28, and *Cascades* (n 6) para 43.

[39] See *Ferriere* (n 37), *Aristrain* (n 36) and *Cascades* (n 6).

[40] See, however, in the context of State aid granted under the ECSC Treaty, the Order of the President of the Court of 3 May 1996, Case C-399/95 R *Germany v Commission* [1996] ECR I-2441, where it was held that in the absence of an obvious illegality or a manifest error of assessment affecting the contested Decision, the arguments of the applicant pertaining to the bankruptcy or the imminent dissolution of the undertaking which was the addressee of the Commission's Decision, and therefore to the existence of serious and irreparable damage, could not on their own justify the measure sought.

[41] See *Cascades* (n 6).

Moreover, it follows from the case-law that when the undertaking concerned belongs to a group, the whole group has to be taken into account for the purpose of evaluating the ability of the economic operator to provide the guarantee required by the Commission.[42] Similarly, when the fine is applied to federations, associations or foundations bringing together several undertakings active in a given sector, the risk of serious and irreparable damage resulting from the immediate payment of the fines or the provision of bank guarantees must be assessed in view of the size and economic power of the undertakings in question, at least insofar as it is not proven that the interests of the federation, association or foundation are separate from those of its member undertakings.[43] Lastly, the possibility for partners and shareholders to assist the company concerned with the provision of a bank guarantee requested by the Commission should also be taken into consideration.[44]

The test applicable to the assessment of the urgency condition may, however, under certain circumstances, be less stringent. The Order of the President of the CFI in *Connelly v Commission*[45] illustrates that point. The damage at stake was merely potential and could be offset by pecuniary compensation. Nevertheless, given the risk of serious and irreparable damage to the honour and the professional reputation of the applicant, a 'soft' interim measure was ordered in the form of a *request* to the Commission to take the necessary measures to avoid any additional disclosure of certain elements of information that might harm the applicant.[46]

By way of conclusion, in the words of former judge Pierre Pescatore,[47] the concept of damage likely to justify the adoption of interim measures should be understood broadly to include any serious threat to one of the interests at stake in the case, regardless of its nature, whether tangible or intangible.

ii. Changes in Market Conditions

In competition law matters, the Community courts generally recognise the risk of serious and irreparable damage when the implementation of the Commission's

[42] See *Aristrain* (n 36) para 33, *Laakmann Karton* (n 36) para 26, and *Cascades* (n 6) para 46. See also Order of the President of the Court of 7 March 1995, C-12/95 P *Transacciones Marítimas and Others v Commission* [1995] ECR I-467 para 12.

[43] See Order of the President of the CFI of 4 June 1996, T-18/96 R *Stichting Certificatie Kraanverhuurbedrijf (SCK) and Federatie van Nederlandse Kraanverhuurbedrijven (FNK) v Commission* [1996] ECR II-407.

[44] See Order of the President of the Court of 7 May 1982, Case 86/82 R *Hasselblad v Commission* [1982] ECR 1555 para 4, Order of the President of the CFI of 26 October 1994, Joined Cases T-231/94 R, T-232/94 R and T-234/94 R *Transacciones Maritimas et al v Commission* [1994] ECR II-885, upheld on appeal by Order of the President of the Court of 7 March 1995 (n 42) para 12, and Order of the President of the CFI *Buchmann* (n 37) para 26.

[45] See Order of 12 December 1995, T-203/95 R *Connelly v Commission* [1995] ECR II-2919.

[46] The balance of interests (see below) has certainly played a role, at least implicitly, in this case.

[47] P Pescatore, 'Les mesures conservatoires et le référé' in Société Française pour le Droit International, *La juridiction internationale permanente* (Actes du colloque de Lyon, mai 1986) (Paris, A Pedone, 1987) 339.

decision is likely to cause market conditions to change in a particular way and where there are serious reasons to believe that it would be extremely difficult, or even impossible, to reverse those changes later should the main action succeed. That may happen, in particular, where the decision requires modification of an existing distribution system,[48] dismantles the procedural framework under which competition on the market takes place[49] or imposes price cuts that are virtually impossible to recoup.[50]

However, it does not follow that suspension of operation of any such decision will necessarily be granted. The *prima facie* examination of the merits of the pleas and arguments put forward by the applicants, on the one hand, and the balance of interests, on the other hand, may cause the judge to dismiss the interim relief application, in whole or in part. For example, in the aforementioned *SPO v Commission* case,[51] the President of the CFI agreed to suspend the operation of the Commission Decision only in relation to the provisions of the contested regulations that were not manifestly anticompetitive.

Furthermore, in order to avoid prejudging the decision in the main proceedings and to safeguard the provisional nature of the interim relief order, which could be undermined by potentially irreversible effects arising from the suspension of the contested act, the judge may, in certain circumstances, require *indisputable* urgency in order to grant interim relief.

Reference should be made in this respect to the reasons underlying the rejection, by Orders of 21 March 1997 of both Presidents,[52] of the applications seeking suspension of the operation of a Council Regulation[53] introducing safeguard measures with regard to the import of rice from overseas countries and territories (OCTs). Those safeguard measures took the form of a tariff quota valid for a period of four months, from 1 January to 30 April 1997, intended to maintain, during this period and until the planting of a new crop that would take place in April, imports of cheap rice from the OCTs within limits compatible with the stability of the Community rice market, thus enabling Community producers time to adjust to the new market conditions.

Had the suspension of the operation of the regulation at issue been granted in this case, the rice coming from OTCs would have been put on the market during the period of application of the safeguard measures. An interim order would thus

[48] See Order of the President of the Court of 13 June 1989, C-56/89 R *Publishers Association v Commission* [1989] ECR 1693, and Order of the President of the CFI of 19 February 1993, T-7/93 R and T-9/93 R *Langnese-Iglo and Schöller v Commission* [1993] ECR II-131.

[49] See Orders of the President of the CFI of 16 July 1992, T-29/92 R *SPO et al v Commission* [1992] ECR II-2161, and of 16 March 1995 *Atlantic Container Line* (n 15) para 55.

[50] See Order of the President of the II Chamber of the Court of 5 April 1976, Case 27/76 R *United Brands v Commission* [1976] ECR 425.

[51] *SPO* (n 49) paras 36, 39–42.

[52] Orders of the President of the Court, C-110/97 R *Netherlands v Council* [1997] ECR I-1795, and of the President of the CFI, T-41/97 R *Antillean Rice Mills v Council* [1997] ECR II-447.

[53] Regulation (EC) No 304/97 of 17 February 1997 introducing safeguard measures in respect of imports of rice originating in the overseas countries and territories [1997] OJ L51/1.

have given rise to definitive (or 'quasi-definitive', as the President of the Court put it) effects well before the two courts dealing with the matter had been able to take a final decision on the legality of the Regulation. Given the irreversible nature of the effects produced by the potential suspension, it would not have been possible to consider that the damage alleged, which was not of such a nature as to endanger the very existence of the undertakings concerned, which was unlikely to produce irreversible effects on the economy of the territories concerned and whose financial consequences could be indemnified, would justify undermining the competing Community interest in applying the safeguard measures and prejudging the final decision on the merits.

Ultimately, it was on the basis of a balancing of interests that the Court concluded that the suspension of operation sought did not give rise to *indisputable* urgency and confirmed that the grant of that interim measure would produce irreversible effects. This latter element—the *balance of interests*—is of vital importance in the context of the assessment of any interim relief application.

iii. Balance of Interests

The late judge René Joliet noted, in the aforementioned article published in 1992,[54] that in interim orders, the *balance of interests* 'appears either as a distinct condition, or as an element of the condition of urgency, and most often is simply used to corroborate the conclusion following the assessment of the *fumus boni juris* and the urgency'.[55] Notwithstanding the truth contained in that insight, the fact remains that the balance of interests is, as a rule, closely linked to the condition of urgency and more specifically to the requirement for serious and irreparable damage.[56]

Indeed, quite often the balancing of interests leads to the refusal of an interim measure which would otherwise be justified were it not for the serious consequences that its adoption would entail for the other party or for the public interest in the particular circumstances of the case, thus precluding any possibility for an acceptable and proportionate balance between the burden borne by that party or interest and the potential advantages flowing from the measure's adoption for the applicant.

It follows from the above that assessing the *balance of interests* actually amounts to little more than applying the *principle of proportionality* to interim

[54] R Joliet (n 3).

[55] My translation. In the original: 'apparaît tantôt comme une condition distincte, tantôt comme un aspect de la condition d'urgence, le plus souvent comme servant simplement à corroborer la conclusion qui se dégage de l'examen du *fumus boni juris* et de l'urgence'.

[56] See Order of the President of the CFI of 3 June 1996, T-41/96 R *Bayer v Commission (Adalat)* [1996] ECR I-381 paras 58 ff, and Order of the Court of 12 July 1996, C-180/96 R *United Kingdom v Commission (ESB)* [1996] ECR I-3903 paras 89 ff.

relief proceedings.[57] In other words, the judge needs to weigh the harm that the immediate operation of the contested act may cause to the applicant against the harm that may be inflicted on the other or a third party or to the public interest by the adoption of the interim measures.[58]

In order to protect the Community interest, the grant of interim measures is often accompanied by appropriate conditions: provision of a bank guarantee to ensure payment of the total sum due to the Commission should irregularities be found in the use of the subsidies awarded;[59] prohibition on enforcing the penalties provided for in an anticompetitive agreement, as a condition for suspending the operation of a Commission decision ordering the termination of certain practices under that agreement,[60] etc.

The balance of interests sometimes appears to be the decisive part of the interim order, in that it is carried out before the assessment of the *fumus boni juris* and the urgency, thus enabling the judge to decide how strict he should be as regards that assessment of those latter conditions.[61]

The outcome of the balance of interests carried out by the judge may influence the choice of the specific interim measure to be granted. The Order of the President of the Court of 24 September 1996, *United Kingdom v Commission ('social policy')*[62] provides a good example. After dismissing the plea concerning the manifest inadmissibility of the main action and acknowledging the *fumus boni juris* and the urgency, the President proceeded to balance the interests at stake. He

[57] In this context, the wording used by the President of the CFI in *Bayer (Adalat)*, ibid, para 60, is particularly significant: 'Comparison of the various interests involved shows that the damage likely to be caused to the applicant by immediate implementation of the provision in question would be disproportionate in relation to the interests' of the other party. See also P Pescatore (n 47) 351, where several examples of the balancing of interests in the case-law of the Court are given. See, in addition, N Emiliou, *The Principle of Proportionality in European Law. A Comparative Study* (London, Kluwer Law International, 1996) 188.

[58] The balance of interests is particularly relevant with regard to actions in the field of merger control, especially in the case of applications put forward by third parties, which are not parties to the notification. Indeed, the need for the parties to know as quickly as possible whether or not they may proceed with the transaction requires that the judge effect a particularly careful balancing of the interests at stake. In this regard, see, in particular, the orders of the President of the CFI of 15 December 1992, T-96/92 R *CCE Grands sources and Others v Commission* [1992] ECR II-2579, of 15 June 1994, T-88/94 R *Soc Com des Potasses et de l'Azote et EMC v Commission* [1994] ECR II-401, paras 28, 32–37, and of 2 December 1994, *Union Carbide* (n 21) para 36.

[59] See *Transacciones Maritimas* (n 44), where the President of the CFI, taking into account 'that one of the applicants has already been liquidated, the other applicants' assets and share capital and reserves are practically non-existent, and none of them has engaged in any activity during the past few years', ruled that suspension of operation had necessarily to be made conditional on the provision of collateral equal to the sums claimed, since otherwise 'there would be a real risk of it [the Commission] not being able to find sufficient assets to obtain repayment of the aid in question in the event of the applications in those proceedings being dismissed'.

[60] See Order of the President of the Court of 31 March 1982, Joined Cases 43 and 63/82 R *VBVB and VBBB v Commission* [1982] ECR 1241.

[61] See Order of the President of the CFI of 21 March 1997, T-179/96 R *Antonissen v Council and Commission* [1997] ECR II-425.

[62] Joined Cases C-239/96 R and 240/96 R *United Kingdom v Commission ('social policy')* [1996] ECR I-4475.

found that by simply suspending the contested procedures, relating to the grant by the Commission of financial support projects designed to promote the interests of older people and to combat poverty and social exclusion, an irreversible situation, with possibly serious consequences, would be created. The President concluded that the Commission should be authorised to commit the expenditure provided for under the procedures at issue but ordered it to make clear that such commitments were conditional upon the outcome of the judgment in the main proceedings and to make no actual payment before that judgment was delivered.[63]

B. *Fumus boni juris*

The second condition that must be met for interim relief to be granted by the Community courts is generally referred to by the Latin expression *fumus boni juris*.

What does it actually mean?

Should it be understood as 'a justification, in terms of urgency, of measures intended to maintain entirely open the possibility of a subsequent decision on the merits'?[64] Or must it instead be proved 'that the grounds put forward will very likely be upheld'?[65]

According to well-established case-law, this condition does not relate to the urgency of the matter but rather to the probability that the main action may be considered well founded.[66]

[63] ibid, paras 71–75. See also T-203/95 R *Connolly v Commission* [1995] ECR II-2919.

[64] P Pescatore (n 47) 340. My translation. In the original: 'une justification, au regard de l'urgence, des mesures destinées à maintenir ouvertes les possibilités d'une décision ultérieur sur le fond'. The author is particularly concerned that the analysis of the *fumus boni juris* might inevitably prejudge the merits of the case. However, in my opinion, as explained below, a *prima facie* assessment of the grounds of annulment put forward in the main action is indispensable once the judge decides to order the interim measures sought. In any case (see above, on the issue of manifest inadmissibility), the risk of prejudging any decision on the merits is only apparent.

[65] R Joliet (n 3) 269. My translation. In the original: 'que les moyens peuvent être considérés comme très probablement fondés'.

[66] It is true that the expressions used in the case-law give somewhat contradictory indications. In this context, see Order of the President of the Court, *Atlantic Container Line* (n 16) para 22, and Order of the Court, *Commission v United Kingdom* (n 18) para 44, according to which '[i]t is thus open to the judge hearing an application to order the suspension of the operation of an act, or other interim measures, only if it is established that such an order is justified, prima facie, in fact and in law'. It is possible to see behind this wording an understanding of the *fumus boni juris* based on an assessment of the interim measures application that is separate from the main application (as proposed by P Pescatore (n 47)), different from the assessment of whether the main action is or is not *prima facie* well founded. However, as we will see below (n 68), in light of the different wording used in para 26 of the Order in *Atlantic Container Line* (n 16), that reading must be treated with caution. In any case, it is my view that the interim measures application must be assessed in light of the application submitted in the main action, whose *prima facie* justification must necessarily be examined. In fact, the remainder of the abovementioned orders clearly show that the judge regarded the *fumus boni juris* as something separate from urgency, since it contains the words: 'and that it is urgent in so far as', etc.

However, a number of issues still need to be addressed. In fact, does the reference to the probability of success presuppose that the main action should appear *prima facie* well founded, which would imply that a 'strong presumption that the main application is well founded'[67] exists—the 'strong *prima facie* case' to which Advocate-General Slynn refers in his Opinion in *Ford*[68]—or does it suffice that the judge hearing the application for interim relief cannot exclude the possibility that the main action may be well founded or that the grounds put forward are not entirely without substance?

The answer to that question is that the judge hearing the application for interim relief must always check, at the very least, whether the grounds put forward by the applicant do *not* manifestly lack foundation.[69] In fact, if the application in the main proceedings is manifestly unfounded there is no reason to grant interim measures on the sole basis that urgency (or at least the appearance of urgency) is proven.

By contrast, it would not be correct to interpret the condition of *fumus boni juris* as requiring that the main action appears, at the stage of the interim measures application, as being a priori well founded, still less, as being very likely to be well founded. Any such requirement would imply that it should be possible to reach, at this preliminary phase of the proceedings, a degree of certainty that, as a rule, is only possible when a judgment on the merits is made. The risk of prejudging the outcome of the main action would then be very high.[70]

In practice, there are countless intermediary approaches that the court might adopt in order to assess the interim measures sought: indeed, experience shows that there are various different nuances and degrees of strictness in the assessment of the *fumus boni juris* requirement, among which the court must balance when hearing an application for interim relief.

Thus, if the urgency in favour of adopting a precautionary measure is manifest, the judge may rely on a less stringent version of the *fumus boni juris*

[67] Order of the President of the Court of 17 March 1986, Case 23/86 R *United Kingdom v European Parliament* [1986] ECR-1085.

[68] Opinion of Advocate-General G Slynn, Joined Cases 228 and 229/82 *Ford of Europe and Others v Commission* [1984] ECR-1129.

[69] This expression may be found in the Order of the President of the CFI *Bayer* (*Adalat*) (n 56) paras 42, 52, where it is stated: 'At this interim stage, the applicant's arguments do not appear *prima facie* to be manifestly lacking in foundation' (in French: '(...)n'apparaissent pas, à première vue, comme manifestement privés de tout caractère sérieux'). The Order of the President of the Court of 19 July 1995, *Commission v Atlantic Container Line* (n 16) para 26, confirms the appropriateness of such formula in that it 'shows that, in the opinion of the judge hearing the application, the arguments put forward by the applicant cannot be dismissed at that stage in the procedure without a more detailed examination'. In this regard, see also Lord Diplock, who wrote in *American Cyanamid v Ethicon Ltd* (1975) 2 WLR 316: 'The Court no doubt must be satisfied that the claim is not frivolous or vexatious; in other words that there is a serious question to be tried' (quoted by G Borchardt, 'The Award of Interim Measures by the European Court of Justice' (1985) *Common Market Law Review* 203–36, and subsequently referred to by LM Pais Antunes (n 3) 97).

[70] By the same token, although in the context of interim measures falling within the competence of the Commission, see *La Cinq* (n 3) paras 60–62.

requirement—a kind of *fumus non mali juris*—based on the lack of any evidence to suggest that the main action is, at first sight, unfounded.[71]

Nevertheless, when the balance of interests, carried out at the stage of assessing urgency, appears inconclusive, the decision of the judge will in fact rely more heavily on the probability of the main action being well founded. Conversely, when the balance of interests raises a serious doubt as to the reasonableness of the interim measure requested, the court, taking account of the nature and weight of the competing interests, in particular when the private interest of the applicant is balanced against a public interest of paramount importance, may require a particularly strong *fumus boni juris* or that the urgency invoked be manifest.[72]

That said, too much significance should not be attached to the wording chosen by the court.

As underlined by the President of the Court in his aforementioned Order in *Atlantic Container Line* on the basis of various precedents, 'a number of different forms of wording have been used in the case-law to define the condition relating to the establishment of a *prima facie* case, depending on the individual circumstances' (para 26), which may be regarded as identical or equivalent.

In summary, the question whether a *fumus boni juris* is established cannot be reduced to one of semantics. The judge must, first and foremost, take into account the specific characteristics of each case, and must not lose sight of the fact that, in this context, a decision, in order to be of any practical utility, has to be adopted quickly. The formal aspects of the procedure are therefore secondary.[73]

It should nevertheless be acknowledged that, similarly to the assessment of manifest inadmissibility of the main action, the analysis of the *fumus boni juris* may raise delicate issues in terms of the need to avoid prejudging the final decision on the merits. That is why the judge hearing the application for interim relief must, to the extent possible, refrain from analysing in detail issues that the judge hearing the main action will later have to address at the end of the proceedings, once he is in possession of all the relevant facts and arguments.

That is particularly true in complex cases on the application of Articles 85, 86, 90 or 92 of the EC Treaty. In these areas, only a complete and in-depth analysis, incompatible with the need to adopt a preliminary decision within a tight time-frame, as is the case in interim proceedings, will make it possible to assess whether the arguments raised are well founded. In this context, more than in any other, the

[71] See in this regard the reference made in the Order of the President of the Court *Atlantic Container Line* (n 16) para 25, to the arguments put forward by the Commission against the understanding of the *fumus boni juris* to which the President of the CFI had recourse in the contested order. The latter had used the following expression: '[the pleas in law put forward by the applicants] appear, prima facie, to be relevant and in any event not entirely ungrounded' (para 49). The President of the Court rejected the Commission's claim in this respect.

[72] On this topic, see below the particularly striking example provided by the Orders of the Presidents of the Court and the CFI in *Antonissen* (n 117 below).

[73] In this regard, see P Pescatore (n 47) 337, in fine.

test of plausibility of the pleas and arguments put forward must be effected on the basis of a broad, but rigorous, criterion of reasonableness 'at first sight'.

Given the intrinsically complex nature of these cases, it should not generally be difficult for the parties to pass this test. Indeed, arguments such as those relating to the effects of an agreement or concerted practice on intra-Community trade or to the effects on competition of a tax advantage granted to an undertaking or to the definition of the relevant product or geographic market normally require a thorough legal and factual analysis, which, as a rule, goes beyond the scope of the interim proceedings. In those circumstances, it is normally possible to hold that the condition relating to *fumus boni juris* is satisfied.[74]

In light of the above, it is generally appropriate that the court should begin with a careful assessment of the urgency condition. If it concludes that this condition is not met, the application may be rejected without an assessment of the *fumus boni juris*.[75] The rationale for that approach is easy to understand, given that the main justification for granting interim measures lies in the need to deal swiftly with a situation of urgency.

Pierre Pescatore suggests, in this context, that 'decisions of the courts should be read as they have been conceived, that is, backwards: one should first consider what the desired outcome was and from there try to understand the underlying reasoning'.[76]

A thorough analysis of the *fumus boni juris* will therefore, in principle, not be required unless the judge envisages granting any kind of interim measures, since any such decision requires all the necessary conditions to be met.

Nonetheless, even considering that it might be possible to dismiss the application by simply relying on the absence of one of the cumulative conditions, the court may decide, in particular circumstances (eg, the political implications or other specific characteristics of the case), to examine all the various conditions in detail, in order to strengthen the authority of its decision. Some interim relief orders therefore examine the *prima facie* merits of the main action first, before dismissing the application on the ground that the other conditions are not met.

The aforementioned Orders of the Court, in *Commission v Greece (former Yugoslav Republic of Macedonia)* and *United Kingdom v Commission (ESB or 'mad*

[74] This understanding, together with the corresponding expressions, is present in various Orders on interim relief in competition cases. See, for example, Order of the President of the CFI in *Cascades* (n 6) paras 49–50.

[75] See in this regard Order of the President of the CFI of 13 July 1993, T-24/93 R *CMBT v Commission* [1993] ECR II-543, or Order of 4 June 1996, *SCK and FNK* (n 43). Expressions such as 'without it being necessary to consider the prima facie merits of the pleas put forward by the applicant in its main application' (*CMBT*) or without there being any need to consider whether the pleas and arguments relied on by the applicant in support of the main action appear, prima facie, to be well founded' (*SCK and FNK*) may be found in those Orders.

[76] P Pescatore (n 47) 338. My translation. In the original: 'les décisions de justice méritent d'être lues comme elles ont été conçues, c'est-à-dire à rebours: il faut voir avant tout quelles ont été les dispositions prises et, à partir de là, essayer d'apprécier la portée des motivations'.

cow disease')[77] provide interesting examples of Decisions where the application for interim relief was dismissed but where the judge, as the circumstances of the cases objectively justified, carefully assessed the *prima facie* legality of the contested acts.

In those two cases, the President referred the application to the full Court under Article 85(1) of the Rules of Procedure of the Court.

In the first Order, the Court began by observing that the legality of Greece's behaviour 'requires thorough consideration of arguments from both sides' and that

> at the stage of the application for interim measures, it is sufficient to note that the arguments put forward by the Commission appear, at first sight, to be sufficiently pertinent and serious to establish a prima facie case justifying the interim measures.

Only thereafter did the Court examine the condition of urgency and conclude that none of the types of harm alleged by the Commission, even if established, would justify the adoption of the measure sought.

The Order in the 'mad cow disease' case offers an even more striking example. After examining in detail the *fumus boni juris*, the Court concluded, on the one hand, in relation to one of the pleas in the main action, that 'the arguments put forward both by the United Kingdom and by the Commission and the Council raise, at first view, complex questions of law which warrant detailed analysis after hearing argument from all parties' (para 81) and, on the other hand, that 'whilst some of the pleas in law put forward by the United Kingdom cannot be wholly ruled out at this stage, the Commission has none the less presented serious arguments as to the lawfulness of its decision as a whole'. Although the analysis was not conclusive, it nevertheless enabled the United Kingdom to meet the first condition that needed to be satisfied for the interim measure to be granted.

Nonetheless, the Court decided to devote around 40 paragraphs to the analysis of the *prima facie* merits of the main action before examining the condition of urgency. The Court followed an unusual line of reasoning that enabled it to more directly examine the balance of interests. Indeed, the Court considered that

> even assuming that the United Kingdom had fully established the existence of serious and irreparable harm, the Court would still have to balance the applicant's interest in a suspension of the ban [...] against the interest of the other parties in having that ban maintained.

The Court concluded that 'such a balancing of interests would, on any view, favour maintaining the Commission's decision, inasmuch as the interest in having the contested decision maintained is not readily comparable to the applicant's interest in having its operation suspended'.

It should be recalled that the balance of interests was between, on the one hand, the commercial and corporate interests of both the producers and the exporters

[77] *Commission v Greece* (n 17) and *ESB* (n 56).

and, on the other hand, the collective interest in public health, at a time when it had already been established that Creutzfeld-Jakob disease was deadly but the scientific evidence as to its causes remained very unclear. It should further be noted that in a case such as this, where the Commission's decision is taken in a situation where an emergency exists, the considerations on whether the main action is well founded and whether the measure is urgent are closely linked.

A similarly cautious line of reasoning may be found in the Order of the President of the CFI in *The National Farmers' Union and Others v Commission.*[78] Given that the case concerned the same decision of the Commission, the same facts and the same political context as *United Kingdom v Commission*, it is not surprising that the President of the CFI also decided to assess in detail all the conditions for the grant of interim relief, including whether all the grounds put forward in the main action were *prima facie* well-founded. After completing his analysis, he considered, first, that the pleas in law and the arguments raised by the applicants (and by the United Kingdom that intervened in support of them) could not justify, in principle, the suspension of the contested decision (para 97), second, that the information provided to the Court did not justify the conclusion that the applicants risked suffering serious and irreparable damage (paras 100–101) and, third, that the balance of interests favoured the effective implementation of the decision (para 105).

Finally, it is possible to find in the Order of the President of the CFI, *D v Commission*,[79] another example, this time in the context of civil service litigation, of a ruling that dismissed the application for interim relief on the basis that the urgency condition was not met, though concluding, in respect of the *fumus boni juris*, that 'the information available to him at this stage in the procedure is capable of constituting serious support for the arguments submitted by the applicant in support of his action for the annulment of the contested decision' (para 40). As we will see below, the President's intention was to draw the Commission's attention to various shortcomings both in the evidence produced and in the regularity of the disciplinary proceedings.

To conclude, as Advocate-General Tesauro has observed,[80] the analysis of the *fumus boni juris* shows 'the automony of the interim proceedings in relation to the main action',[81] which, 'as a result, makes possible and justifies different, if not opposing, approaches'.[82] As the two levels of review, preliminary and final,

[78] T-76/96 R *The National Farmers' Union and Others v Commission* [1996] ECR II-815.

[79] T-549/93 R *D v Commission* [1993] ECR II-1347.

[80] G Tesauro (n 3) 1244. See also the reference made by the author to the different legal traditions in both common law and continental law (1244–45).

[81] My translation. In the original: 'l'autonomie du jugement en référé par rapport au jugement au principal'. Once again, see below how this question was dealt with in the orders of the Presidents of the Court and of the CFI in *Antonissen* (n 117 below).

[82] My translation. In the original: 'par conséquent, permet et justifie des évaluations différentes, voire opposées'. A good example in this regard is given by the *Publishers Association—Netbook Agreement* case. After an application in the main action was lodged with the Court on 27 February 1989, the President of the Court ordered the suspension of Articles 2 and 4 of the contested Decision

are completely separate and mutually autonomous, the judgment in the main proceedings must not be seen as something that it is not, that is an appeal against the interim order that might 'overturn' the decision taken by the judge dealing with the application for interim relief.

IV. BRIEF ANALYSIS OF CERTAIN SPECIFIC QUESTIONS

This study would not be complete without a reference to certain specific questions that are examined below.

A. Interim Relief as an Instrument of Effective Judicial Protection

Administration of justice in the area of competition law often involves a conflict between, on the one hand, the undertaking's need to have the proceedings reach a rapid conclusion and, on the other hand, the sometimes rather long duration of judicial proceedings in this field. The pace at which business life must be conducted is often incompatible with the time required for the adoption of a thorough judicial decision in a factually complex case. As I have already noted above, this is one of the reasons for the steady increase in the number of applications for interim measures brought before the Community judiciary, in particular before the CFI.

Against that background, interim proceedings represent an important mechanism for achieving effective judicial protection, making it possible to achieve a rapid ruling within a time frame that is compatible with the need for the effective administration of justice.[83]

This is all the more relevant since the judge hearing the interim relief application may decide to immediately suspend application of the contested measure, on a precautionary basis, until the interim proceedings are themselves brought to a close either to avoid an imminent damage or because the judge does not have

(*Publishers Association* (n 48)). He noted in particular that '[i]n those circumstances, it must be stated that, at the present interlocutory stage, the application does not appear to be devoid of all foundation and that accordingly the requirement that a prima facie case must be established is satisfied' (para 31). The case having been referred to the CFI under Article 14 of the Council's Decision of 24 October 1988, the CFI (T-66/89 *Publishers Association v Commission* [1992] ECR II-1995) dismissed the appeal, in particular on the ground that 'in the application of Article 85(3) of the Treaty the Commission did not rely on incorrect facts or commit any error of law; nor did it make any manifest error of assessment' (para 116). Finally, following an appeal brought by the applicant, the Court (C-360/92 P *Publishers Association v Commission* [1995] ECR I-23) annulled the judgment of the CFI as it found that several errors of law had been made (para 32) and, pursuant to Article 53, first paragraph, second sentence, of the EEC Statute of the Court, also annulled Articles 2, 3 and 4 of the contested Decision.

[83] As P Pescatore (n 47) 323, put it, 'les mesures conservatoires ont pour fonction de tenir ouvertes les possibilités de solution, de maintenir l'égalité de chances entre parties et de permettre ainsi à la décision finale de déployer sa pleine efficacité' ('interim measures aim at keeping open different possible solutions, maintaining equality of arms between the parties and allowing the final decision to be fully effective'—my translation).

sufficient information to evaluate the risk alleged, thus making it necessary for the parties to produce additional elements of information.[84]

The issue of the duration of judicial proceedings is of the utmost importance in the context of merger control, where Community law itself imposes strict time-limits and time is also of the essence for commercial and regulatory reasons. As yet, no application has been brought by the parties to a merger against a decision of the Commission finding the concentration to be incompatible with the common market[85] or imposing remedies on them. It cannot be ruled out that the reason underlying this absence of litigation is exactly to be found in the tension between the commercial requirement for certainty and the likely duration of judicial proceedings.

If interim proceedings appear to have only a limited role to play in relation to decisions opposing an operation of concentration, since the judge hearing the application for interim relief cannot provisionally clear the merger operation prohibited by the Commission and allow it to proceed, they may however play an important role in relation to decisions imposing remedies, as the court may impose the suspension, in whole or in part, of the implementation of such remedies.[86]

B. Interim Relief as a Signal to the Parties

An order for interim relief contains only a preliminary assessment of the dispute. However, it cannot be denied that it constitutes a first act of administration of justice, which the parties may subsequently take into consideration in making their decision whether or not to pursue their substantive action.[87] Indeed, the part of the judgment concerning the 'chances' of success of the main application often

[84] In this respect, see Orders of the President of the CFI *Vittel and Pierval* (n 9), *Société commerciale des potasses et de l'azote* (n 9) and *Transacciones Marítimas* (n 42).

[85] An application for suspension of the 'decision' and for other interim measures has however been submitted against an alleged decision of the Commission considering that a concentration had a Community dimension, thereby initiating merger control proceedings. In this case, the application for interim measures was submitted even before the adoption by the Commission of a decision as to the compatibility or incompatibility of the merger with the common market. See Order of the President of the CFI *Sogecable* (n 26).

[86] See in this respect, Orders of the President of the CFI *Vittel and Pierval* (n 9) and *Société commerciale des potasses et de l'azote* (n 9).

[87] In the words of P Pescatore (n 47) 324: 'L'institution de mesures provisoires doit être vue comme une phase préliminaire ou intermédiaire dans le cadre d'une procédure engagée en vue d'aboutir à une décision de justice. Parmi toutes les mesures successives qui encourent à cette fin [...] le référé est sans doute un moment d'intensité majeure puisque [...] le juge ne peut pas prendre une décision sur des mesures conservatoires sans effleurer les problèmes de fond.' ('The adoption of interim measures must be seen as a preliminary or intermediary phase within proceedings instituted with a view to obtaining a judicial decision. Among all the steps that contribute to that end [...] the interim procedure is one of particular intensity as [...] the judge cannot take a decision on precautionary measures without touching on the merits of the case'—my translation.) See also 326–27.

draws the parties' attention either to the weakness of certain pleas or arguments,[88] or instead to the probability that the application may succeed.[89]

On occasion, in addition to giving an indication to the parties to the dispute, the interim order may also send a signal to third parties, in particular other Community institutions. This appears to have occurred in the abovementioned 'mad cow disease' cases, where the Orders of the Court and of the President of the CFI would appear to have influenced the position taken by the European Parliament in respect of this matter.[90]

C. Suspension of Operation of Interim Decisions

The application for interim relief may sometimes be directed against a decision by which an institution, notably the Commission, itself orders interim measures.

In this regard, the interpretation given by the CFI in *La Cinq*[91] to the conditions of *fumus boni juris* and urgency that must be met in the context of interim measures ordered by the Commission has made it somewhat easier to obtain interim relief from that institution in competition matters. It is therefore natural that the CFI has subsequently been called upon to rule on a number of applications for annulment of interim measures decisions adopted by the Commission, sometimes accompanied by applications for suspension.

The President of the CFI has thus been asked to rule on a number of applications to suspend interim measures decisions taken by the Commission, namely in *Ecosystem v Peugeot*,[92] in a case concerning the market for ice-cream in Germany,[93] as well as in the case relating to ferry-boats operating between the United Kingdom and Ireland.[94] In the first case, the application was dismissed as the urgency condition was not satisfied;[95] the second led to the adoption of

[88] See, in particular, Orders of the President of the CFI of 21 May 1990, T-23/90 *Peugeot v Commission* [1991] ECR II-195, and of 16 July 1992, *SPO* (n 49). See also the Order of 30 November 1993 *D v Commission* (n 79), where the President of the CFI drew the Commission's attention to a number of weaknesses in the disciplinary proceedings that preceded the contested Decision. During the proceedings pertaining to the main action, the information and arguments put forward by the Commission clarified the doubts raised during the interim proceedings as to the legality of the contested Decision.

[89] In this regard, see, for example, Order of 1 December 1994, T-353/94 R *Postbank v Commission* [1994] ECR II-1141 paras 27–29, where the President of the CFI called upon certain principles established by the case-law of the Court, as their application to the case at hand could cast doubt on the legality of the Commission's conduct. In its decision in the main action the CFI followed the path traced by the interim Order.

[90] See 'Recommandations pour l'avenir' (1997) 2024 *Europe Documents, Agence Europe*.

[91] *La Cinq* (n 3).

[92] Decision not published in the OJ. See Press release IP (90) 233.

[93] Decision not published in the OJ. See Press release IP (92) 222.

[94] Decision not published in the OJ. See Press release IP (92) 478. On this decision, see N Malty, 'Restrictions on Port Operations: Sealink/B&I—Holyhead' (1993) *European Competition Law Review* 223–25.

[95] *Peugeot v Commission* (n 88).

interim measures;[96] in the third case, the application was withdrawn after the parties reached an agreement during the hearing before the judge.[97] I will come back later to this latter example.

It must be emphasised, however, that applications for interim relief against decisions ordering precautionary measures may raise delicate issues. By their very nature, the effects of decisions ordering interim measures are limited in time. Usually, the effects of those decisions cease before the judge is able to rule on the merits of the case. Thus, in such circumstances, any decision taken by the judge hearing the application for interim relief, either suspending the operation of the decision or dismissing such a request, will, in practice, deprive the main action of its purpose. The judge must therefore look for *sui generis* temporary solutions that both prevent the factual situation from changing in a way that is irreversible and safeguard the interests of the parties until a decision on the merits is taken.

D. Interim Relief as a Dispute Resolution Mechanism

One of the main strengths of interim proceedings is the possibility that they offer for facilitating a provisional resolution of a case by means of an amicable settlement.

Judge Pierre Pescatore notes in this regard:

> Sometimes the judge hearing the interim measures application, instead of using his power of injunction or of suspension, seeks to extract from the parties an agreement on a provisional *modus vivendi*, which he takes into account, in one way or another, in his order. That is probably the best way of bringing interim relief proceedings to an end...[98]

He then wonders 'whether it might not be useful to insert in the different rules of procedure a provision intended to facilitate that sort of arrangement'.[99] As regards the Rules of Procedure of the CFI, it should be pointed out that they already make provision for a high level of flexibility in the organisation of proceedings with the aim of finding the best way of resolving the dispute, thus reducing the need for the insertion of such a clause.

In any event, the possibility of settling the dispute amicably must, whenever possible, guide the court when hearing the parties to proceedings for interim

[96] See Orders of the President of the CFI of 8 May 1992 and of 16 June 1992, T-24/92 R *Langnese-Iglo* [1992] ECR II-1713 and T-28/92 R *Schöller v Commission* [1992] ECR II-1839. For a brief commentary to this Order see L Idot (n 3) 599.

[97] See Order of the President of the CFI of 1 October 1992, T- 42/92 R *Sealink Stena Line v Commission*, not published.

[98] P Pescatore (n 47) 347. My translation. In the original: 'Parfois le juge du référé, plutôt que de faire usage de son pouvoir d'injonction ou de suspension, essaie d'obtenir des parties un accord sur un *modus vivendi intérimaire* dont il prend acte, sous une forme ou sous une autre, dans son ordonnance. C'est peut-être le meilleur moyen de terminer une instance de référé ...'

[99] ibid. My translation. In the original: 's'il ne serait pas utile d'insérer dans les divers règlements de procédure une clause destinée à faciliter de tels arrangements'.

relief. That approach enabled the judge hearing the case concerning ferry-boats operating between the United Kingdom and Ireland to broker an agreement between the parties that not only brought to an end the interim proceedings, but made possible a settlement of the main proceedings as well as the administrative proceedings before the Commission. The settlement entailed the withdrawal of the applications and of the complaint that had triggered the Commission's investigation and the adoption by it of interim measures.

The aforementioned examples highlight the important role that the judge, hearing the application for interim measures, can play as a mediator. Sometimes, as in the ferry-boats case, an attempt to reach agreement is made during the hearing and is achieved after one or more adjournments. In other cases, the parties are invited to continue their discussions outside the court with a view to reaching an agreement, and to convey the outcome of those discussions to the President so that he may decide whether an order disposing of the dispute is necessary.[100]

In the absence of an agreement on all contentious issues, the attempt to bring the parties together may, in any case, be of great use for the decision on the interim relief application. Indeed, such an attempt may provide the court with important information, which he may take into account when weighing the interests at stake, hence facilitating the adoption of a decision that meets the parties' expectations.[101]

Moreover, interim procedures are also extremely useful in ensuring a degree of legal certainty for economic operators. The Orders of the President of the CFI in *David Alwyn Jones and Mary Bridget Jones et al v Council and Commission*,[102] and in *Cimpor and Secil v Commission*,[103] are good examples of this in that they vested the administrative practice of the institutions as described by their agents in the course of the proceedings with the binding force inherent in a judicial decision.[104]

[100] In this context, see *Transacciones Marítimas* (n 42) para 4, and *Cascades* (n 6) para 7.

[101] This was the case in *Schöller* (n 96), and in *Cascades* (n 6).

[102] Cases T-278/93 R and T-555/93 R, T-280/93 R and T-541/93 R *David Alwyn Jones and Mary Bridget Jones and Others v Council and Commission* [1994] ECR II-11. The interpretative statement signed by the agents of the Council and of the Commission and included in the Order of the President bringing the case to an end reads as follows: 'The Agents of the Council and the Commission declared at the hearing that if the Court of First Instance and at last instance the Court of Justice should decide that Regulation (EEC) No 2187/93 had not correctly applied Article 43 of the Protocol on the Statute of the Court of Justice, this would constitute a new situation as the period for which compensation would be paid would, then, in principle, be calculated without taking into account the effect of the time bar. In such a case, in the opinion of the Agents, the flat-rate basis on which compensation is calculated could be reconsidered in favour for example, of actual losses' (para 51).

[103] Cases T-61/95 R and T-62/95 R *Cimpor and Secil v Commission* not published.

[104] The Order of the President of the CFI of 25 August1994, T-156/94 R *Siderúrgia Aristain v Commission* [1994] ECR II-715, is also worth mentioning. The Commission had indeed recognised the need to amend its Decision in order to take account of the fact that responsibility for the same infringement was shared between two companies in the same group. The President then ordered 'the partial suspension of the obligation to provide a security in so far as the fine is excessive in view of the applicant's position within the Aristrain group until the legal issue of the application of the fine is clarified by the CFI' (para 32).

E. Appeals against Interim Orders of the CFI

I would like to make just two observations in this regard.[105]

The first concerns the time-limit of two months set out in Article 50, second paragraph, of the Statute of the Court. Given that interim proceedings are by definition urgent, it is questionable whether it is appropriate for appeals against decisions in interim proceedings to be subject to the same time-limit that has been established for appeals against a decision of the CFI putting an end to the main action. However, that apparently excessive time-limit for interim measures appeals is mitigated, on the one hand, by the fact that only 'the parties to the proceedings' may bring an appeal and, on the other hand, by the fact that the President of the Court must rule on such appeals by way of the summary procedure set out in Article 36 of the Statute and in the Rules of Procedure of the Court for interim relief applications.

The second observation concerns the grounds of appeal. Pursuant to Article 168 A of the Treaty and Article 51 of the Statute, the right of appeal to the Court is confined to points of law. As stated in the latter provision:

> It shall lie on the grounds of lack of competence of the Court of First Instance, a breach of procedure before it which adversely affects the interests of the appellant as well as the infringement of Community law by the Court of First Instance.

The application of this provision to appeals against interim relief decisions may entail two kinds of difficulties. First, there are the difficulties inherent in the distinction between points of law and findings of fact. Second, the precise identification of the grounds of appeal is not always easy.

The first issue goes beyond the specific scope of Community law: I shall not therefore address it here.[106] As to the second issue, the relatively brief experience of application of Article 51 of the Statute to date offers a number of helpful indications.

[105] The issue which is addressed in this section should be distinguished from the question of appeals brought against final judgments of the CFI. As per Article 53 of the Statute of the Court of Justice, an appeal shall not have suspensory effect 'without prejudice to Articles 185 and 186 of this Treaty'. The Statute thus provides that the Court may 'if it considers that circumstances so require', order, in the context of an appeal, that the judgment of the CFI annulling the contested decision be suspended (see, for example, Order in C-345/90 P (R) *Hanning* [1991] ECR I-231, which upheld the application for suspension; C-35/92 P (R) *Frederikson* [1992] ECR I-2399, which dismissed the application for suspension). As noted by R Joliet (n 3) 254, fn 2: 'Il est, en revanche, difficile de concevoir une demande de sursis contre un arrêt du Tribunal qui rejette un recours: la demande de sursis doit alors être dirigée contre l'exécution de la décision qui était attaquée devant le Tribunal' ('It is however difficult to conceive of an application to suspend a judgment of the CFI that dismissed an action brought before it: the application for suspension should then be directed against execution of the decision that was previously challenged before the CFI'—my translation).

[106] I would just refer to the Order of the Court of 30 April 1997, C-89/97 P(R) *Moccia Irme v Commission* [1997] ECR I-2327, where it is held that 'the legal assessment of the facts' is included in the notion of error of law.

Seven appeals have thus far[107] been brought against interim orders of the President of the CFI. The first two were withdrawn by the applicants,[108] one of them[109] following an agreement reached during the hearing before the President of the Court.

In four cases, the President of the Court dismissed the appeals. In the first of those cases,[110] the appeal was rejected on grounds that the contested Order, contrary to the applicant's submission, had breached neither the right to effective judicial protection nor the principle of proportionality.

In another case, the President of the Court, after recalling that the Court does not review findings of fact, confirmed the broad discretionary power conferred on the judge hearing the application for interim relief at first instance.[111]

In a third case,[112] the appeal Court applied the well-established case-law according to which the applicant, as provided for in Article 12(1)(c) of the Rules of Procedure of the Court, must identify precisely which aspects of the order are being contested and state the legal arguments relied on in support of the application for it to be set aside.[113] Furthermore, it recalled that the judge hearing the application for interim relief at first instance is not required to rule explicitly on all the points of fact and law raised in the course of the interlocutory proceedings, it being sufficient that the reasons given justify that order in the light of the circumstances of the case and enable the Court to exercise its powers of review (para 25).

Lastly, by an Order of 30 April 1997,[114] the President of the Court dismissed the appeal brought against the Order of the President of the CFI in a State aid case under the ECSC Treaty.[115] The President of the Court observed, on the one hand, that 'the assessment of an applicant's interest in obtaining the measures which he seeks takes on particular importance in proceedings on an application for interim relief' and, on the other hand, that in the case at hand,

> the interest put forward by the appellant in benefiting from the positive indirect effects of the measures sought appears to be so remote and hypothetical that the judge hearing the application for interim relief cannot be criticised for not having expressly taken it into account in dismissing the application for suspension of operation of the decision at issue.[116]

[107] August 1997.

[108] I refer to the appeals brought against the Orders of the President of the CFI of 21 November 1990, T-39/90 R *SEP v Commission* [1990] ECR II-649, and of 16 July 1992, *SPO* (n 49). See Orders of the President of the Court ordering the removal of the cases from the registry, C-372/92 (R) *SEP v Commission* [1991] ECR II-2043 and C-369/92 P(R) *SPO v Commission* [1993] OJ C112/9.

[109] *SEP* (n 109).

[110] *Transacciones Marítimas* (n 42).

[111] *Atlantic Container* (n 16) above.

[112] Order of the President of the Court of 11 July 1996, C-148/96 P (R) *Goldstein v Commission* [1996] ECR I-3883.

[113] This requirement is not met by an appeal which confines itself to repeating or reproducing the pleas in law and arguments previously submitted to the CFI, including those based on facts expressly rejected by that Court. (*Goldstein* (n 112) para 24).

[114] *Moccia Irme* (n 106).

[115] *Moccia Irme* (n 14).

[116] At para 30 of its Order, the President of the CFI dismissed a second request for an interim measure seeking that the Commission call upon the Italian authorities to suspend the payment of the

Thus far, the President of the Court has overturned an interim order of the President of the CFI on just one occasion, in *Antonissen v Council and Commission.*[117]

The President of the CFI had dismissed an application for interim measures seeking an advance payment by the Community in order to avert the bankruptcy of the applicant before the CFI could render its judgment in the action for damages concerning the 'milk quota' disputes. The interim relief sought was dismissed on the ground that it 'would amount to a payment in advance of compensation for future and uncertain damage' and thus 'would anticipate the argument on the substance of the case since, when assessing whether there was a *prima facie* case, the President would have to rule whether there was *prima facie* non-contractual liability on the part of the Community and then grant in part the measures sought in the main application—an order against the Community to pay the amounts claimed—without the merits of that application in the light of the second paragraph of Article 215 of the Treaty having been examined. However, a finding of liability, with the effects that it entails, cannot be taken on the basis of a *prima facie* case; it must be based on a definitive assessment of the facts and pleas in law put forward, and therefore requires that a procedure be followed in which all the parties are guaranteed the right to a fair hearing'.[118]

The Order of the President of the Court offers an interesting analysis of the objectives and nature of the interim relief proceedings. The President of the Court overturned the Order of the President of the CFI on the grounds that '[n]either the importance of the prima facie case put forward by the applicant nor the degree of urgency which he alleged seem to have been taken into consideration in that reasoning',[119] and that the contested Order appeared to indicate that a measure such as that sought was 'inconsistent with the conditions for or nature of an interim application, irrespective of the factual and legal circumstances of the

aid at issue to the other applicant undertakings. He also rejected the possibility of holding in reserve the funds that had been granted to the applicant by the Italian Government but which had not been paid by reason of the Commission's refusal to authorise the aid. Without calling into question the reasonableness of the Decision of the President of the CFI, the reasoning used in the Order to show that the measures sought would be of no use to the applicant does not seem entirely convincing. Indeed, the judge hearing the application for interim relief could have used Article 39 of the ECSC Treaty as a legal basis for the adoption of measures preventing the termination of the payment of the aid. Concerning, in particular, the request to hold the funds in reserve, the President of the Court considered it an issue of 'decisive importance'. Nevertheless, since the applicant on appeal did not challenge this point, the appeal could not but be dismissed. It would however have been possible (preferable even) to base the rejection of the application for interim measures on the fact that only the Commission, pursuant to the *Boussac* (n 3) case-law, was competent to order this sort of measure addressed to a Member State.

[117] Orders of the President of the CFI of 29 November 1996, T-179/96 R *Antonissen v Council and Commission* [1996] ECR II-1641, of the President of the Court of 29 January 1997, C-393/96 P(R) *Antonissen v Council and Commission* [1997] ECR I-441, and of the President of the CFI of 21 March 1997, *Antonissen* (n 61).

[118] Order of the President of the CFI, *Antonissen* (n 117) para 30.

[119] *Antonissen* (n 117). The President of the Court notes in this regard, first, that 'it is expressly stated that there was no need to consider whether the pleas in law and arguments put forward by the applicant in justification of the measure sought were well founded' and, second, that, regarding urgency, the Order 'did not show clearly and unequivocally that the President's reasoning was based on an examination of the circumstances of the individual case' (ibid para 34).

individual case'.[120] The President of the Court further observed that 'an absolute prohibition on obtaining a measure of that kind, irrespective of the circumstances of the case, would not be compatible with the right of individuals to complete and effective judicial protection under Community law'.[121]

According to the President of the Court '[i]t is therefore not possible to rule out in advance, in a general and abstract manner, that payment, by way of an advance, even of an amount corresponding to that sought in the main application, may be necessary in order to ensure the practical effect of the judgment in the main action and may, in certain cases, appear justified with regard to the interests involved',[122] duly balanced by the judge hearing the application for interim relief. 'Such a measure, if granted, would not necessarily prejudge the decision on the substance of the case, since an interim measure lapses when final judgment is delivered'.[123]

Nevertheless, the President of the Court underlined that 'recourse to such a type of measure, which is more likely than others to give rise in fact to irreversible effects, in particular in the event of the applicant's subsequent insolvency, must be restricted, and should be confined to cases where the prima facie case appears particularly strong and the urgency of the measures sought undeniable',[124] accompanied, if necessary, by an adequate condition or guarantee.

The President of the Court then referred the case back to the CFI under Article 54(1) of the Statute of the Court.

In the Order adopted thereafter, the President of the CFI once again dismissed the application for interim relief, although relying on different grounds and after balancing the interests at stake. After re-examining the case, he concluded that in the absence of a *prima facie* direct causal link between the damage invoked and the Community regulation and a serious breach of a superior rule of law for the protection of individuals, the condition of a particularly solid *fumus boni juris* was not met and the application should therefore be dismissed without its being necessary to assess the condition of urgency.

F. Stay of Interim Relief Proceedings and Referral

The applications for interim relief in the so-called 'mad cow disease' cases, mentioned above, raised a novel procedural question. In the case brought before the CFI,[125] the Commission requested the latter, pursuant to Article 47(3) of the Statute of the Court and to Articles 77 and 78 of the Rules of Procedure of the CFI, to stay

[120] ibid para 35.
[121] ibid para 36.
[122] ibid para 37.
[123] ibid para 39.
[124] ibid para 41.
[125] T-76/96 R *The National Farmers' Union* (n 78) paras 28–35.

proceedings until the Court ruled on the request for interim relief brought before it by the United Kingdom in connection with an action for annulment of the same measure that was the subject matter of the applications before the CFI.[126] In the alternative, the Commission requested that the CFI decline jurisdiction pursuant to Article 47 of the Statute of the Court and to Article 80 of the Rules of Procedure of the CFI.

The President of the CFI dismissed both requests after recalling that

> the EC Statute of the Court of Justice and the Rules of Procedure of the Court of First Instance do not contain any specific provision under which the Court of First Instance may stay proceedings for interim relief or decline jurisdiction in respect of an application to suspend the operation of a measure, when a parallel application for suspension of the operation of the same measure is pending before the Court of Justice.[127]

Specifically as regards the application to stay proceedings, the President of the CFI observed that to order such a measure 'is, in principle, incompatible with the very nature and purpose of the legal remedy which proceedings for interim relief, an emergency procedure, represent',[128] and that, absent any specific justification, a stay of the proceedings would be inconsistent with the principle of proper administration of justice. Moreover, he recalled that the parties may appeal against the Order made by the President of the CFI in the proceedings for interim relief and noted that by delaying consideration of the applicants' request for interim measures, a stay of the proceedings could impair the protection of their procedural rights and legitimate interests.

Regarding the Commission's request to the effect that the CFI should decline jurisdiction with regard to the application for interim relief, the President of the CFI held that, '[b]y virtue of the principle that courts must exercise the jurisdiction conferred on them, the Court of First Instance cannot, save in the cases expressly provided for in the Statute, when it has jurisdiction to hear an action under the relevant provisions of Decision 88/591, as amended, decline such jurisdiction. The third paragraph of Article 47 of the Statute provides solely for the possibility of the Court of First Instance declining jurisdiction in regard to applications for annulment'[129] and does not refer to applications for interim measures.

It is my view that this approach is the most appropriate and reasonable one in light of the right to effective judicial protection and the principle of proper administration of justice.

[126] The Commission submitted a similar request for stay in the main proceedings before the CFI until the Court ruled on the substantive action brought by the United Kingdom.

[127] *The National Farmers' Union* (n 78) para 31.

[128] ibid para 32.

[129] ibid para 33.

9

Effective Judicial Protection with Regard to Community Funds—May One be Directly Concerned by a Decision Addressed to a Member State?[*]

ARTICLE 230 EC lays down the conditions under which an action for annulment may be brought before the Court of Justice (hereinafter the 'ECJ' or the 'Court') and the Court of First Instance (hereinafter the 'CFI') seeking review of the legality of acts adopted by the Community institutions. That provision is an important instrument for the protection of individual rights that may be affected by unlawful acts of those institutions.

As is well-known, Article 230 EC distinguishes between two main categories of applicants: while Member States and the main Community institutions enjoy unlimited *locus standi* for bringing an action for annulment before the ECJ, private parties may only challenge a Community act under certain circumstances.

Indeed, according to Article 230(4) any 'natural or legal person' may only 'institute proceedings against a decision addressed to that person or against a decision which, although in the form of a regulation or a decision addressed to another person, is of direct and individual concern to the former.'

The interpretation of those admissibility requirements has given rise to a large volume of case-law, which it is not always easy to reconcile, as well as to many learned commentaries in the legal literature.[1] In that regard, the Community

* First published as 'La protection juridictionnelle des particuliers en matière de fonds communautaire. Peut-on être 'directement concerné' par une décision adressée à un État membre?' in J-C Masclet et al (eds), *Mélanges en l'honneur de Philippe Manin—L'Union européenne: Union de droit, Union des droits* (Paris, Edns A Pedone, 2010).

The author acknowledges the assistance of Luís Pinto Monteiro, associate lawyer at PLMJ, for his assistance in preparing the original version of this chapter.

[1] On this topic, see, amongst others, K Lenaerts, D Arts and I Maselis, *Procedural Law of the European Union*, 2nd edn (London, Sweet and Maxwell, 2006) 250–55; HG Schermers and D Waelbroeck, *Judicial Protection in the European Communities*, 5th edn (Kluwer Law and Taxation Publishers, 1991) 241–44; E Biernat, *The 'Locus Standi' of Private Applicants under Article 230(4) EC and the Principle of Judicial Protection in the European Community* (New York, The Jean Monnet Program, Jean Monnet Working Paper 12/03, NYU School of Law, 2003); J-V Louis, G Vandersanden, D Waelbroeck and M Waelbroeck, 'La Cour de Justice, Les Actes des Institutions' *Commentaire Mégret*, vol 10, 2nd edn (Collection Études Européennes, Université de Bruxelles, 1993); J Boulouis, M Darmon and J-G Huglo, *Contentieux Communautaire*, 2nd edn (Paris, Dalloz, 2001) 175 ff.

case-law has undergone a number of modifications, either of a general scope or that are limited to specific areas of Community law. Consequently, in the current state of Community law, the outcome of actions brought by individuals for annulment of Community measures has become less predictable and thus the actual scope of the principle of effective judicial protection is less clear.

My intention in the remainder of this chapter is to review certain aspects of the current Community case-law with regard to the condition of direct concern in respect of decisions addressed to another person, notably a Member State, within the field of application of the rules governing the application of EC structural funds.

By means of this chapter, I wish to pay tribute to Professor Philippe Manin in recognition of his important contribution to the development of Community law.

I. THE EVOLUTION OF THE COMMUNITY CASE-LAW WITH RESPECT TO THE REQUIREMENT OF 'DIRECT CONCERN'

Plaumann[2] is generally considered to be the landmark case as regards the conditions of admissibility in actions for annulment brought by individuals.

The case had its origin in an action brought by an importer against a decision of the European Commission addressed to the Federal Republic of Germany, whereby the Commission refused to authorise the German authorities to suspend customs duties in relation to certain fruits imported from third countries.

In its judgment, the Court made a number of statements that are relevant to the determination of the scope of Article 173(2) of the EEC Treaty (now Article 230(4) EC),[3] in light of the principle of effective judicial protection.

The Commission contended in the course of the proceedings that the expression 'another person' in this provision did not refer to Member States in their capacity as sovereign authorities and that individuals could thus not bring an action for annulment against the decisions of the Commission or of the Council addressed to Member States.

The Court's response to this argument represents an expression of the old Latin rule '*ubi lex non distinguit nec nos distinguere debemus*', inasmuch as it made clear that the provision in question neither defined nor limited the scope of the words 'another person'.

Moreover, the Court pointed out that the wording and the natural meaning of this provision justify the broadest interpretation and that the provisions of the Treaty regarding the right of action of interested parties must not be interpreted restrictively. Therefore, the Treaty being silent on the point, a limitation in this respect may not be presumed.

[2] Case 25/62 *Plaumann & Co v Commission* [1963] ECR (English Special Edition) 95.

[3] The judgment is mostly notorious for its formula interpreting the requirement of individual concern, on the basis of which the action was dismissed as inadmissible.

Some years later, in *Commune de Differdange*,[4] the Court added that the purpose of Article 173(2) of the Treaty is to ensure that legal protection is also available to a person who, whilst not the person to whom the contested measure is addressed, is in fact affected by it in the same way as is the addressee.

However, considerable obstacles hindered the admissibility of actions brought by individuals against Community measures where the latter require national implementing provisions in order to produce effects on the legal situation of those individuals.

It is settled case-law that natural or legal persons may institute proceedings against Community acts which are sufficient in themselves and which require no such implementing provisions.[5] However, this is, in principle, not the case where the Community acts require national authorities to adopt implementing measures in order for legal effects to be produced.

In such event, the Community act will only be effective through the national implementing measures, which may then be challenged by their addressees before the competent national courts. In the context of proceedings before those courts, the applicant may indirectly challenge the validity of the relevant Community act constituting the legal basis for the contested national measure, by inviting the domestic court to refer a question for preliminary ruling to the ECJ.

As K Lenaerts put it,[6] this system of legal protection reflects the structure of the Community legal order and that of its legislative instruments.

Nevertheless, the case-law has also recognised that it is necessary to take into account the degree of autonomy and the margin of discretion granted to the national authorities responsible for implementing the contested Community act.

Since its judgment in *International Fruit*,[7] in 1971, the Court has made clear that, inasmuch as national authorities do not enjoy any discretionary powers as regards the issue of import licences and are limited to merely collecting the data necessary in order that the Commission may assess the underlying economic situation and take its decision on the matter, the issue of or refusal to issue import licenses must be regarded as flowing from the Commission's decision, even where Member States must subsequently adopt the national measures required to give effect to that decision.

Later, in several judgments of 29 March 1979,[8] the Court held that the fact that the implementation of a provision contained in a regulation calls for the adoption of implementing measures by the national authorities does not prevent that

[4] Case 222/83 *Commune de Differdange et al v Commission* [1984] ECR 2889 para 9.

[5] Case 294/83 *Parti écologiste 'Les Verts' v European Parliament* [1986] ECR 1339 para 31; Opinion of Advocate General K Roemer in *Plaumann* (n 2) paras 114–15.

[6] K Lenaerts, D Arts and I Maselis (n 1) 251.

[7] Case 44/70 *NV International Fruit Company v Commission* [1971] ECR 411 paras 23–28.

[8] Cases 113/77 *NTN Toyo Bearing Company Ltd and Others v Council* [1979] ECR 1185 para 11; 118/77 *Import Standard Oil (ISO) v Council* [1979] ECR 1277 para 26; 119/77 *Nippon Seiko et al v Council and Commission* [1979] ECR 1303 para 14; 120/77 *Koyo Seeiko Co and Others v Council* [1979] ECR 1337 para 25; 121/77 *Nachi Fujikoshi Corporation and Others v Council* [1979] ECR 1363 para 11.

provision from being of direct concern to the natural or legal persons to whom it applies where such implementation is purely automatic and is, moreover, carried out in pursuance not of intermediate national rules but of Community rules alone. Therefore, the proposition that interested persons should, where appropriate, bring the matter before the national courts having jurisdiction does not hold in such circumstances.

The Court also held in *Salerno*[9] that a regulation adopted for the sole purpose of recruiting certain persons under conditions derogating from the provisions of the Staff Regulations was of direct concern to them, to the extent that the appointing authority had no discretion with regard to its implementation, in particular for the purpose of determining the entry grades of the persons concerned.

In *Sofrimport*,[10] the Court held that a regulation adopted in the fruit and vegetable sector suspending the issue of import licences for products originating in a non-member country was of direct concern to importers whose goods were in transit to the Community at the time of its entry into force, inasmuch as it required national authorities to reject pending applications for import licences, leaving them no discretion in that regard.

Conversely, where national authorities enjoy a margin of discretion for the implementation of Community acts, the effects on the applicant's legal position cannot be attributed to the Community act in question, but rather to the national measures taken to determine its content and to ensure its implementation.

That is why the Court held, in *Alcan*,[11] that an authorisation granted by the Commission to open a tariff quota merely creates a power in favour of the Member State concerned, so that neither the grant nor the refusal of a tariff quota can be of direct concern to undertakings which might possibly have benefited from such a quota. Indeed, such benefit could only result from the opening of a tariff quota by national authorities following an authorisation granted by the Commission to the Member State.

In *Mannesmann-Roehrenwerke*[12] the Court stated that the fixing by a Community regulation, under an international arrangement between the Community and the United States, of the percentage of the Community quota for exports of steel pipes and tubes described as 'oil country tubular goods', or OCTG tubes, to the United States allocated by way of a sub-quota to the Federal Republic of Germany, did not directly affect the legal position of the undertakings that manufacture those tubes in Germany. Indeed, the issue of export licences to those undertakings was not based directly on that percentage but depended, firstly, on the manner in which the Commission had calculated and adjusted the Community export limit

[9] Joined Cases 87/77, 130/77, 22/83, 9/83 and 10/83 *Vittorio Salerno and Others v Commission* [1985] ECR 2523 paras 30, 31.

[10] C-152/88 *Sofrimport v Commission* [1990] ECR I-2477 para 9.

[11] Case 69/69 *SA Alcan Aluminium Raeren and Others v Commission* [1970] ECR 385 paras 13–15.

[12] Case 333/85 *Mannesmann-Roehrenwerke AG and Paderwerk v Council* [1987] ECR 1381 paras 13–14.

and fixed Germany's sub-quota on the basis of that limit and, secondly, on the apportionment of that sub-quota by the national authorities among the undertakings concerned, which was in no way an automatic process but was carried out on the basis of a number of criteria whose implementation involved the exercise of a discretion.

Nevertheless, before concluding that an individual is not directly concerned, a true discretionary power, as K Lenaerts has put it,[13] must be found to exist.

Having that in mind, the Court ruled in *Bock*[14] that a decision of the Commission authorising a Member State to prevent the import of certain products was of direct concern to an undertaking where, having requested the competent national authorities to grant it an import licence for those products, it was informed that its request was to be rejected as soon as the Commission had authorised the Member State to do so.

Then came *Piraiki-Patraiki*.[15] The Court there went further than in *Bock* by recognising that a Commission decision addressed to a Member State and authorising it to impose a system of quotas on imports from a third country may be of direct concern to the exporters, even in the absence of any declaration of intention to that effect by the national authorities, where there can be no doubt as to the intention of those authorities to which the authorisation has been granted to avail themselves of it.

Both the Commission and France had argued, in the course of the proceedings, that the applicants were not directly affected by the contested decision since it merely authorised the Member State in question to institute a quota system on imports of the products at issue (cotton yarn of Greek origin) and thus left the Member State that had requested the authorisation free to make use of it or not.[16]

The Court acknowledged, in that regard, that in the absence of implementing measures adopted at national level the Commission decision could not have affected the applicants. It added, however, that this fact did not in itself prevent the decision from being of direct concern to the applicants where other factors justified the conclusion that they had a direct interest in bringing the action.[17]

The Court pointed out, in that respect,[18] that even before being authorised to do so by the Commission, the French Republic had applied a very restrictive system of licences for imports of the relevant product. It observed, moreover, that the request for protective measures not only came from the French authorities, but sought to obtain the Commission's authorisation for a system of import quotas that was stricter than that which was finally granted.

[13] K Lenaerts, D Arts and I Maselis (n 1) 252.

[14] Case 62/70 *Werner A Bock v Commission* [1971] ECR 897 paras 6–8.

[15] Case 11/82 *SA Piraiki-Patraiki and Others v Commission* [1985] ECR 207 paras 6–10.

[16] ibid, para 6.

[17] ibid, para 7.

[18] ibid, para 8.

In those circumstances, the possibility that the French Republic might decide not to make use of the authorisation granted to it by the Commission decision was entirely theoretical, since there could be no doubt as to the intention of the French authorities to do so.[19]

Similarly, in *Toepfer*,[20] the Court held that a decision of the Commission to maintain protective measures that had already been adopted by a Member State was of direct concern to an interested party within the meaning of Article 173(4) of the Treaty. As the Court stated, since a decision of the Commission amending or abolishing protective measures was directly applicable and concerned interested parties subject to it as directly as the measures that it replaced, it would be illogical to say that a decision to retain protective measures could have a different effect, since the latter type of decision did not merely approve such measures, but actually conferred validity upon them.

The specific case of actions brought before the Court against the refusal to take measures against third persons, whether Member States or other undertakings, is also worth mentioning. In holding that the actions brought by complainants are admissible in such cases, the Court has placed particular emphasis on the legal effects that concern applicants and on the protection of the procedural guarantees that apply to them.

The action in *FEDIOL*[21] was brought against a decision of the Commission not to initiate an anti-subsidy proceeding against a third country in respect of alleged export subsidies following a complaint lodged with the Commission by the applicant. The complainant actively participated in the proceedings before the Commission, in the course of which it had been granted the opportunity to make known its views.

Without formally distinguishing the requirements of direct and individual concern, the Court held that complainants have the right to bring an action and may not be refused the right to put before the Court any matters which would facilitate a review of the question (i) whether the Commission observed the procedural guarantees granted to complainants by a Community regulation and (ii) whether that institution committed manifest errors in its assessment of the facts, omitted to take into consideration any essential matter that might indicate the existence of subsidies or based the reasons for its decision on considerations amounting to a misuse of power.[22]

That case-law of the Court is particularly relevant in the field of State aids. Indeed, it follows from this line of case-law that particular consideration must be given, on the one hand, to the role played by the applicant in the opening and

[19] ibid, para 9.

[20] Joined Cases 106 and 107-63 *Alfred Toepfer and Getreide-Import Gesellschaft v Commission* [1965] ECR 405 para 411.

[21] Case 191/82 *EEC Seed Crushers' and Oil Processors' Federation (FEDIOL) v Commission* [1983] ECR 2913 paras 29–30.

[22] The same approach was in substance taken by the Court in case 264/82 *Timex Corporation v Council and Commission* [1985] ECR 849 paras14–16.

during the course of the administrative procedure and, on the other hand, to the impact on the applicant's market position resulting from the aid which is the object of the contested decision.

Thus, in *Cofaz*,[23] the Court held that the undertakings that had lodged a complaint against a Member State pursuant to Article 93 of the EEC Treaty and further participated in the procedure subsequently opened by the Commission were not only individually but also directly concerned by the decision whereby the Commission terminated the said procedure. As regards the latter condition of admissibility, the Court considered that the Commission decision left intact all the effects of the pricing system that had been the subject of the complaint, whereas the applicants were seeking a decision abolishing or amending the aid in question.[24]

The case-law relating to the interpretation of the condition of direct concern in actions brought by a natural or legal person against a decision addressed to another person was 'codified' in *Glencore Grain*[25] and *Louis Dreyfus*,[26] both judgments of 5 May 1998.[27]

Relying on its existing case-law, the Court held that

> for a person to be directly concerned by a Community measure, the latter must directly affect the legal situation of the individual and leave no discretion to the addressees of that measure who are entrusted with the task of implementing it, such implementation being purely automatic and resulting from Community rules without the application of other intermediate rules.[28]

The Court further added[29] that the same applies 'where the possibility for addressees not to give effect to the Community measure is purely theoretical and their intention to act in conformity with it is not in doubt'.

Finally, reference must also be made to the case-law of the Community courts concerning the rules governing financial assistance granted by the European Social Fund (ESF).

[23] Case 169/84 *Compagnie française de l'azote (Cofaz) SA and Others v Commission* [1986] ECR 391 para 30.

[24] See also the judgment of the CFI in Joined Cases T-447/93, T-448/93 and T-449/93 *Associazione Italiana Tecnico Economica del Cemento (AITEC) and Others v Commission* [1995] ECR II-1971 paras 33 ff, 41, 59, 63.

[25] C-404/96 P *Glencore Grain Ltd v Commission* [1998] ECR I-2435 paras 41–42.

[26] C-386/96 *Societé Louis Dreyfus Cie v Commission* [1998] ECR I-2309 paras 43–44.

[27] The Court's findings in this regard have also been invoked, though with differing outcomes, in subsequent case-law in relation to Community acts of both individual and general application. The CFI's ruling of 3 May 2002 in Case T-177/01 *Jégo-Quéré et Cie SA v Commission* [2002] ECR II-2365 para 26, belongs to the latter category of actions challenging the legality of regulations, ie of measures of general application. This ruling of the CFI was annulled by the ECJ in Case C-263/02 P *Commission v Jégo-Quéré* [2004] ECR I-3443, on the grounds that the requirement of individual concern had not been met. See also C-486/01 P *Front National v European Parliament* [2004] ECR I-6309 paras 30 and 34.

[28] See *Glencore Grain* (n 25) para 41.

[29] ibid, para 42.

As the Court found in *Vlaams Fonds:*[30]

> It is equally settled case-law that a Commission decision reducing or cancelling financial assistance granted by the ESF is capable of directly and individually concerning the beneficiaries of such assistance and of adversely affecting them, even though the Member State concerned is the sole interlocutor of the ESF in the relevant administrative procedure. It is the beneficiaries of the aid who are adversely affected by the economic consequences of the decision to reduce or cancel the assistance since they have primary liability for repayment of the sums paid without warrant (see, to that effect, *Lisrestal at al v Commission*, paragraphs 43 to 48 and the case-law cited).

A number of conclusions may be drawn from the abovementioned case-law:

(i) The conditions for admissibility of actions brought by individuals are not to be interpreted restrictively.
(ii) This conclusion is a corollary of the right to effective judicial protection which is a general principle of Community law drawn from the common legal traditions of the Member States and from Articles 6 and 13 of the European Convention on Human Rights and which is now enshrined in Article 47 of the Charter of Fundamental Rights of the European Union.
(iii) The condition of direct concern requires that the Community measure in question produce effects on the individual's legal position directly and that no margin of discretion be left to the addressee of such measure, that is, the person or entity responsible for its implementation.
(iv) The condition of direct concern is also met where the possibility for the addressee of the Community act not to implement it is purely theoretical, thus leaving no genuine doubt as to its intention to give full effect to the act in question.

II. RECENT DEVELOPMENTS OF THE CASE-LAW ON THE REQUIREMENT OF DIRECT CONCERN

In its recent case-law, beginning with the judgments in the *Regione Siciliana I*[31] and *Regione Siciliana II* cases,[32] the Luxembourg courts seem to have followed a more restrictive approach as regards the possibility of bringing an action for annulment against a Commission decision that has an impact on the applicant's

[30] T-102/00 *Vlaams Fonds voor de Sociale Integratie van Personen met een Handicap v Commission* [2003] ECR II-2433. See also cases T-138/89 *NBV and NBV v Commission* [1992] ECR II-2181 para 33; T-212/00 *Nuove Industrie Molisane v Commission* [2002] ECR II-347 paras 33 and 47; T-310/00 *MCI Inc v Commission* [2004] ECR II-3253 para 44; T-271/94 *Eugénio Branco Lda v Commission* [1996] ECR II-749 paras 51 and 58; and T-351/05 *Provincia di Imperia v Commission* [2008] ECR II-241 paras 32–34.

[31] T-341/02 *Regione Siciliana v Commission* [2004] ECR II-2877; ECJ, C-417/04 P *Regione Siciliana v Commission (Regione Siciliana I)* [2006] ECR I-3881.

[32] T-60/03 *Regione Siciliana v Commission (Regione Siciliana II)* [2005] ECR II-4139; ECJ, C-15/06 P *Regione Siciliana v Commission* [2007] ECR I-2591.

legal position, within the context of financial assistance provided by Community structural funds.

The reasoning followed by the Community courts in these related cases illustrates the hesitations, doubts and uncertainties that characterise the judicial approach to this area of EU law.

Indeed, whilst in the former case[33] the CFI, by order of the third chamber (three judges), held the action brought by Regione Siciliana inadmissible, in the latter case[34] it rejected, by judgment of the first enlarged chamber (five judges), the claim of inadmissibility that had been raised by the Commission.

Both cases concerned the grant of financial assistance by the European Regional Development Fund (ERDF) for the realisation of infrastructure projects in Sicily (Italy).

In both cases the Commission had, by decisions addressed to the Italian Republic, withdrawn part of the financial assistance originally granted and ordered repayment of the amounts that it considered to have been unduly paid.

The Commission, without ever questioning whether the applicant was individually concerned by the contested decision, argued in both cases before the CFI that the action was inadmissible since the decision did not directly concern the applicant.

In Case T-341/02 (third chamber), the CFI[35] recalled the case-law[36] pursuant to which, within the institutional system of the Community and the rules that govern relations between the Community and the Member States, it is for the Member States, in the absence of any provision to the contrary in Community law and in light of the principle of subsidiarity, to ensure that Community regulations are implemented within their territory. Within that context, it is incumbent upon the Member States to take the necessary individual decisions regarding the undertakings concerned in accordance with national rules and procedures, subject to the limits imposed by Community law.[37]

The CFI dismissed the application as inadmissible on grounds that may be summarised as follows.[38]

The Court noted, in the first place, that the Community funds granted by way of ERDF financial assistance are to be paid by the Commission to the Member State concerned. It held that there is nothing to prevent the Member State in question from deciding to make good, out of its own funds, the portion of the Community financing that has been withdrawn and thus to finance itself the completion of the works relating to the project in question.

[33] *Regione Siciliana I* (n 31).

[34] *Regione Siciliana II* (n 32).

[35] *Regione Siciliana I* (n 31) paras 59–61.

[36] Joined Cases 205/82 to 215/82 *Deutsche Milchkontor et al v Germany* [1983] ECR 2633; Joined Cases 89/86 and 91/86 *Étoile Commerciale and CNTA v Commission* [1987] ECR 3005 para 11; and T-244/00 *Coillte Teoranta v Commission* [2001] ECR II-1275 para 42.

[37] *Coillte Teoranta* (n 36) paras 59–61.

[38] *Regione Siciliana I* (n 31) paras 64–79.

Secondly, the contested decision did not include any provision requiring the Italian Republic to recover, from the beneficiaries, the sums that had been unduly paid. In that connection, the obligation imposed on the Italian authorities merely to inform the final beneficiary of the contested decision's existence could not be regarded as giving rise to an obligation to recover from the latter the amounts unduly paid. The proper implementation of the contested decision therefore required only that the Member State refund to the ERDF the sums which were indicated therein. The Commission could only require the restitution of the sums illegally paid from the entity which had been granted the assistance, ie the Member State concerned.

That being so, reimbursement of the Community funds paid to the applicant was the direct consequence, not of the contested decision, but of the subsequent action taken by the Italian Republic according to its legislation in order to comply with its obligations under Community law. The possibility that particular circumstances might lead the Italian Republic to decide not to claim reimbursement of the assistance in dispute and to bear itself the burden of reimbursing to the ERDF the amounts which it had wrongly considered itself authorised to pay out could not therefore be excluded.

In that connection, the CFI also observed that the file did not show that the Italian Republic had expressed an intention to pass on to the applicant, or to the final beneficiaries, the financial consequences of any Commission decision reducing the assistance at issue.

Lastly, the applicant did not adduce any evidence in support of its assertion that the Italian Republic had no discretion as to whether to recover the sums unduly paid and did not establish that, even if the Italian Republic had such discretion, it was purely theoretical.

In the light of the foregoing considerations, the CFI concluded[39] that the contested decision did not directly affect the applicant's legal situation and that the applicant was not therefore directly concerned by that decision since the latter only produced legal effects as between the Commission and the Italian Republic.

Conversely, in case T-60/03, the CFI (first chamber, extended composition) followed a significantly different approach. Indeed, the Court considered the applicant to be directly concerned by the Commission's decision and thus rejected the plea of inadmissibility.[40]

First of all, the CFI held that by terminating the assistance received by the applicant, the contested decision had, firstly, rescinded the Commission's obligation to pay the remaining balance of the assistance and, secondly, given rise to a new obligation requiring the Italian Republic to repay the advances already paid to it and passed on to the applicant.

[39] ibid, paras 80–86.

[40] *Regione Siciliana II* (n 32) paras 44–68.

It noted, moreover, that the contested decision must necessarily have directly affected the applicant's legal situation in several respects. In addition, the decision left the Italian authorities no discretion, its implementation being purely automatic under Community rules alone without there being any need to make reference to other intermediate rules.

The CFI further observed that once the decision to grant assistance had been adopted and notified to the Italian Republic, the applicant could reasonably and legitimately believe, for the purposes of carrying out the project funded by the assistance, subject to compliance with the conditions attached to that decision to grant assistance and with the rules applicable to the ERDF, that the total amount of that assistance would be at its disposal. On that basis, the applicant could thus plan and budget for its expenses with a view to carrying out the works necessary for the project.

The CFI recalled, in particular, that neither Community law nor domestic law allowed the Italian authorities to deprive the applicant of the amounts of that assistance, or to use them for any other purpose. Thus, so long as the abovementioned conditions and rules were respected, the Italian authorities had no power to demand repayment, even in part, of those sums from the applicant.

With regard, first of all, to the alteration of the applicant's legal situation, the CFI found that the contested decision had the direct and immediate effect of changing the applicant's financial situation by depriving it of the balance of the assistance remaining to be paid by the Commission. Since the assistance had been cancelled, the unpaid balance of it would not be paid to the Italian Republic by the Commission and the Italian authorities would not, therefore, be able to pass it on to the applicant, which would force the latter to seek alternative financing.

Furthermore, the CFI stated that the contested decision also directly altered the applicant's legal situation in that it was liable to give rise to an obligation to repay the sums already paid as advances. In fact, the effect of the contested decision was directly to change the applicant's legal status from that of unarguably being a creditor in respect of those sums to that of being a debtor, potentially at least.[41]

As regards, next, the requirement that the contested decision be automatically applicable, the CFI observed that it was indeed automatically and without more that the contested decision produced the abovementioned twofold effect on the applicant. According to the CFI, that effect of the contested decision flowed from Community law alone. The national authorities had, in this connection, no discretion in their duty to implement the decision.

Furthermore, the CFI remained unconvinced by the Commission's argument that national authorities could, in theory, decide to relieve the applicant of the financial consequences that the contested decision directly entailed for it, by

[41] As the CFI put it (para 54), the contested decision meant that it was no longer impossible under both Community and domestic law for the national authorities to demand repayment from the applicant of the sums advanced, thus automatically changing the applicant's legal situation vis-à-vis those national authorities.

funding out of State resources the balance of the Community assistance withheld, on the one hand, and/or the repayment of the Community advances already received by the applicant, on the other. The CFI found, in that regard, that a national decision providing funding of that magnitude would not in fact mean that the Commission's decision would cease to apply automatically, since, legally speaking, the national decision would remain outside the sphere of application of the contested decision, as a matter of Community law.[42]

Following appeals against the rulings of the CFI that have just been described, the ECJ ruled against the admissibility of the application in both actions.

The appellant, *Regione Siciliana*, argued in one of the appeal cases[43] that finding its action inadmissible would constitute a denial of justice, since, as an infra-state entity, it could not bring an action against the Italian Republic before the national courts.

The Court responded to that argument[44] by pointing out that the judicial protection of natural or legal persons who are unable, by reason of the conditions for admissibility laid down in the fourth paragraph of Article 230 EC, to directly challenge Community measures of the kind of the contested decision, must be guaranteed by an effective right of action before national courts. Those courts are required, in accordance with the principle of cooperation in good faith laid down by Article 10 EC, so far as possible, to interpret and apply national procedural rules governing the exercise of rights of action in a way that enables such persons to challenge the legality of any decision or other national measure relating to the application to them of a Community act such as that at issue and to plead the invalidity of that latter act, asking the competent court to make, where necessary, a reference to the Court of Justice for a preliminary ruling on its validity.

The restrictive line of case-law described above was applied by the CFI in the orders made in the context of an action for annulment brought in 2006 by the Municipality of Gondomar (Portugal).[45]

[42] Pursuant to the CFI's reasoning in paras 59 and 60 of the judgment, a national decision providing alternative funding would have the effect of putting the applicant back in the situation it was in before the contested decision was adopted, thus bringing about a second alteration of the applicant's legal situation that had initially been changed by the contested decision. This second alteration of the applicant's legal situation is attributable to the national decision alone and not to the implementation of the contested decision. To put it another way, it would be necessary for a specific national funding decision to be adopted in order to counter the automatic effects of the contested decision.

[43] *Regione Siciliana II* (n 32) para 28.

[44] ibid, para 39.

[45] T-324/06 R *Município de Gondomar v Commission* [2007] ECR II-55 (summary); T-324/06 *Município de Gondomar v Commission* [2008] II-173 (summary). The latter order of the CFI was appealed before the ECJ, and that appeal was rejected by order of the Court on 24 September 2009 [C-501/08 P *Município de Gondomar v Commission* [2009] I-152 (summary)].

III. OBSERVATIONS ON THE CURRENT LINE OF CASE-LAW

The restrictive approach that was followed in the recent rulings of the Community courts gives rise to certain doubts, in particular as regards the conditions for the exercise of the right to effective judicial protection in the Community legal order.

First, I am not sure that simply referring to the nature of the Community institutional system and to the rules that govern the relationship between the Community and the Member States in this field is sufficient to resolve these issues.[46]

As a matter of fact, this reference may, in my view, simply explain the existence of the problem itself. Indeed, it is precisely because the Community institutional system makes Member States, to a large extent, the enforcers of Community policies (notably with regard to financial assistance by Community structural funds) that a considerable number of the Commission's decisions, which affect the interests of individuals, are not directly addressed to the latter, but to the Member States, which are subsequently required to give effect to them in respect of those individuals.

It is precisely for that reason that an examination of the requirement of direct (and individual) concern is necessary pursuant to Article 230(4) EC, in order to assess whether an action for annulment is admissible or not.

In fact, when a decision is directly addressed to an individual whose legal position is affected, an action for annulment brought by that individual is automatically admissible under Article 230(4) EC, first part, without it being necessary for the last part of that provision even to come into play.

In that regard, I believe that the case-law codified in *Glencore Grain* and *Louis Dreyfus*[47] is fully applicable regardless of the Community fund at issue—ESF, ERDF, EAGGF or Cohesion Fund—as I do not see any convincing reason to draw a distinction between those funds for the purposes of applying Article 230(4) EC.

[46] This position is not contradicted by my Opinion as Advocate General in *Étoile Commercial and CNTA* (n 36) above. Indeed, the specific situation at stake in that case was significantly different from the one examined here: the contested decision related to the clearance of the accounts presented by a Member State, in respect of the European Agricultural Guidance and Guarantee Fund (EAGGF), whose object was simply to verify and to certify whether the expenses paid by the national authorities were chargeable to the EAGGF, that is, whether they were in conformity with Community rules. As regards economic operators, such Commission decisions are merely declaratory in nature, since any binding effects will only flow from measures taken by national authorities in the exercise of their own powers, which is manifestly not the case as regards Commission decisions reducing or cancelling Community financial assistance for certain projects or ordering the reimbursement of sums unduly paid. Moreover, in *Étolie Commercial*, the relevant national authorities had made payment of the subsidies in question conditional upon the provision by the beneficiary of a guarantee for repayment on demand—a provision which was not required by Community law.

[47] Cases *Glencore Grain* and *Louis Dreyfus* (n 25 and n 26 respectively).

As the CFI recalled in *Regione Siciliana II*:[48]

> in order to ascertain whether the act of a Community institution is of direct concern to a person within the meaning of Article 230 EC it is necessary to look to its substance in order to establish whether, regardless of its form,[49] it has an immediate effect on that person's interests, so bringing about a distinct change in that person's legal situation.

This condition is met whenever the relevant Community regulation, Commission decision or domestic legislation explicitly imposes on national authorities the duty to pass on to those persons ultimately affected the financial consequences of that regulation or decision.

In light of the abovementioned case-law, I take the view that this is also the case whenever it becomes clear that the national authorities, while theoretically having a certain margin of appreciation, will not exercise it in practice or, in any event, did not actually make use of it in the case at hand. It is then clear that the Commission's decision will, in itself, directly produce effects on the legal position of the addressee. That is all the more true given that, when national authorities ultimately decide not to exercise the power to pass on the financial consequences of the decision to the recipient of the assistance that has been withdrawn, and suffer those consequences themselves, the action will be admissible not because of a lack of direct concern but by reason of a lack of legal interest in bringing an action.

That effect is particularly obvious where the national body's role consists in nothing more than communicating to the beneficiary of the Community aid a copy of the Commission's decision informing him that, by virtue of that decision and for the reasons stated therein, he is deprived of some of the aid and that he should therefore reimburse any amounts unduly received.

That being so, the fact that the individual is refused access to the Community courts might create an insurmountable obstacle to his or her exercise of the right to effective judicial protection, particularly in the context of national administrative law systems, which, as is the case in many Member States, do not allow, in principle,[50] for a mere implementing act to be subject to judicial review.[51]

In this context, the argument that it is for national courts to establish the necessary remedies in order to ensure appropriate legal protection for individual rights that may be affected by Commission decisions of this sort appears to involve an excessive degree of interference with Member States' procedural autonomy, in particular as regards the organisation of their judicial systems. In order to comply

[48] *Regione Siciliana II* (n 32) para 65.

[49] I would add: of any other factor not pertaining to its substance.

[50] Or whereby, confronted with the ambiguity of the applicable legislation, the case-law and the legal literature are divided as to whether and to what extent mere implementing acts may be subject to a judicial review of their legality, thus casting doubt on the possibility of such judicial control.

[51] According to Portuguese law (Article 151(2) and (3) of the Code of Administrative Procedure), implementing measures are only amenable to judicial review where they exceed the limits of the act being implemented or where they are tainted by their own inherent defects.

with the logic underpinning this reasoning, the national legislature may be forced to forgo a principle (that mere implementing acts are not, in general, subject to judicial review), which is widely accepted as an integral part of its national legal traditions in the field of administrative law.

In addition, in some Member States the courts are known to be reluctant to refer questions for preliminary ruling to the Court of Justice, and national authorities are often unwilling to challenge the legality of Commission decisions which, although addressed to them, actually affect the financial interests of the ultimate beneficiaries of Community assistance. In such circumstances, private persons run the risk of being deprived of effective judicial remedies for the enforcement and protection of their Community law rights.

10

Application of Article 6 of the European Convention on Human Rights to 'Posts in the Civil Service'[*]

I. INTRODUCTION

PURSUANT TO ARTICLE 6 of the Convention for the Protection of Human Rights and Fundamental Freedoms, generally known as the 'European Convention on Human Rights' (hereinafter, the 'Convention' or the 'European Convention'),

> 1. In the determination of his civil rights and obligations or of any criminal charge against him, everyone is entitled to a fair and public hearing within a reasonable time by an independent and impartial tribunal established by law.

The main aim of this chapter is to trace the evolution of the case-law of the European Court of Human Rights (hereinafter, the 'Court') regarding the determination of the scope of Article 6 of the Convention, in particular when it comes to the application of the notion of 'civil rights and obligations' in disputes arising in relation to a contractual or statutory employment relationship between, on the one hand, government officials or other civil servants and, on the other hand, the Contracting Member States. The analysis of that case-law will include a critical reflection on its starting points and on the main phases of its development.

My choice of topic may surprise those who know that this subject matter does not belong to my usual field of legal work. I made this choice for two main reasons. First, I was driven to explore this subject by the difficulties I faced in connection with the admissibility of a complaint filed with the Court against the Portuguese

[*] A French version of this article entitled 'L'article 6 de la Convention européenne des droits de l'Homme et son application aux "emplois dans la fonction publique"' was published in *Mélanges en homage à Georges Vandersanden—Promenades au sein du droit européen* (Brussels, Bruylant, 2008) 845–72.

The preparation of this chapter in its first (French) version owes much to the assistance of Sara Carvalho de Sousa, a young lawyer, former trainee at PLMJ and assistant lawyer at the European Court of Human Rights, in Strasbourg. In particular, Sara has assisted me in the updating of the case-law after *Pellegrin*. I am also indebted to Marisa Larguinho, another young trainee, for her research assistance into academic opinion and case-law.

Republic on behalf of Mr António Vitorino d'Almeida, former cultural attaché to the Portuguese Embassy in Vienna and both a renowned intellectual and a recognised musician, whose contract had suddenly been terminated. Mr Vitorino de Almeida was reinstated after an order by the competent administrative courts, dismissed again the day after that reinstatement and, finally, having run the gauntlet of bureaucratic red-tape and of interminable court proceedings, was denied any right to compensation.[1]

Second, I wish to honour my dear friend and colleague, Georges Vandersanden, who, throughout his career, has contributed to the development of the law and to the proper administration of justice in the field of European civil service law. We often came face to face in different, though complementary, capacities. The clarity and perceptiveness of his reasoning and his intellectual honesty and soundness of judgment have always been to me both a source of inspiration and a motive for great respect.

II. DIFFICULTIES OF INTERPRETATION AND THE DEVELOPMENT OF THE CASE-LAW

The uncertainties surrounding the scope of application of Article 6 of the Convention, in particular in the context of disputes arising out of employment relationships between Contracting Member States and government officials or other civil servants, have led the judges of the Court to reformulate the case-law with the aim of establishing an objective and fair, but at the same time sufficiently broad criterion for the application of that provision.

At the core of the difficulties of interpretation at issue lies one of the most enigmatic expressions contained in Article 6,[2] 'the determination of his civil rights and obligations'. Clearly, the authors of the Convention aimed to distinguish between private law and public law disputes, in order to avoid excessive intrusion by the Court in those areas that were considered as falling within the State's exclusive jurisdiction and, in particular, to prohibit interference in the exercise of public powers governed by administrative law.

In that context, the Court, acknowledging that the law in many Member States of the Council of Europe recognized a fundamental distinction between public servants and employees in the private sector, consistently accepted that 'disputes

[1] The procedure before the Court did not end with a decision on the admissibility since it was possible to reach an agreement with the Portuguese Government under the auspices of the Minister of Foreign Affairs, Mr Jaime Gama, who is currently the President of the Portuguese Parliament (*Assembleia da República*). Mr Gama understood the unfortunate position in which Mr Vitorino d'Almeida had been placed, for which I am grateful to him.

[2] Amongst other unclear and open-ended expressions used in Article 6, we may identify 'fair trial' and 'fair hearing', 'reasonable time', 'independent and impartial tribunal'.

relating to the recruitment, employment and retirement of public servants were as a general rule outside the scope of Article 6 § 1'.[3]

The expansion, since 1950, of the areas of activity and of the forms in which State intervention takes place in the supply of public goods and in the regulation of social and economic affairs, has rendered the frontier between public and private law 'in many areas, nebulous and fluid'.[4] That has inevitably led to a reassessment of the case-law concerning the scope of the protection provided for by Article 6 in the context of disputes concerning employment relationships between the State and individuals.

That reassessment took place gradually over a period of years.

First of all, the Court emphasised the autonomy, under the Convention,[5] of the concept of 'civil rights and obligations' with regard to the identity of the parties, the type of law applicable,[6] the status[7] of the competent authority[8] and the capacity in which that authority was acting (as a private employer or as a public authority).[9]

Next,[10] the Court sought to widen the scope of the concept of 'disputes concerning civil rights and obligations'. First, it held that particular importance should be attached to the 'purely or essentially pecuniary nature' of the claim as a criterion for applying Article 6 § 1;[11] second, it stressed that the civil character of rights and obligations should be displaced only when the core of the powers of *imperium* and the corresponding discretionary prerogatives of the administration were at stake. As the Court pointed out, notwithstanding the public law aspects involved, 'when the State is not using discretionary powers and may be compared, in this respect, with an employer who is a party to a contract of employment governed by private law', the right in issue may be held to have a civil character.[12]

[3] See, for instance, *Glasenapp and Kosiek v Germany*, 28 August 1986, A nº 104, 26, § 49 and nº105, 20, § 35; *Massa v Italy*, 24 August 1993, A nº 265-B, § 26. See also *Neigel v France*, 17 March 1997, *Reports* 1997-II, 411, § 44; *Fusco v Italy*, 2 September 1997, *Reports* 1997-V, 1732, § 20.

[4] See J-C Soyer and M De Salvia, 'Commentaire à l'Article 6' in L-E Petitti, E Degaux and P-H Imbert (eds), *La Convention européenne des droits de l'homme—Commentaire article par article* (Paris, Economica, 1995) 251. The original expression in French is 'en maintes zones, brumeuse et mobile'.

[5] *Konig v Federal Republic of Germany*, 28 June 1978, A nº 27, §§ 88, 89; *Deweer v Belgium*, 27 February 1970, A nº 35, § 42.

[6] Civil, commercial or administrative law.

[7] Either judicial or administrative.

[8] *Ringeisen v Austria*, 16 July 1971, A nº 13, § 94.

[9] *Konig* (n 5) A nº 27, § 90.

[10] In 1992–1993. cf J-C Soyer and M De Salvia (n 4) 251–52.

[11] This approach was applied in cases *Editions Périscope v France*, 26 March 1992, A nº 234-B, §§ 39, 40, and *Tomasi v France*, 27 August 1992, A nº 241-A, § 121. See also *De Santa v Italy*, *Lapalorcia v Italy*, *Abenavoli v Italy*, *Nicodemo v Italy*, 2 September 1997, 1997-V, 1663, § 18, 1677, § 21, 1690, § 16 and 1703, § 18, respectively.

[12] This was applied, for instance, to the pension rights of a '*carabiniere*' or a judge or to the payment of a disability allowance to another public servant. See the Court's judgments in cases *Francesco Lombardo v Italy*, 26 November 1992, A nº 249-B, § 17; *Giancarlo Lombardo v Italy*, 26 November 1992, A nº 249-C, § 16; *Salesi v Italy*, 26 February 1993, A nº 257-E, § 19. See also *Cazenave de la Roche v France*, 9 June 1998, *Reports* 1998-III, 1327, §§ 43, 44; *Le Calvez v France*, 29 July 1998, Reports 1998-V, 1900–01, § 58; *Benkessiouer v France*, 24 August 1998, *Reports* 1998-V, 2287, §§ 29–30; *Couez v*

However, notwithstanding the progressive enlargement of the notion of civil disputes within the meaning of Article 6, a wide margin of uncertainty remained concerning the determination of the scope of protection granted by that provision to those employed in the public service.[13]

As a matter of fact, a general distinction between public servants and employees in the private sector continued to appear in the Court's case-law, albeit nuanced by the specific characteristics of each case.

Similarly, the Court has applied Article 6 to disputes between tax authorities and individuals regarding the refusal of tax allowances but not to disputes relating to an allegedly unjustified tax increase. As Soyer and De Salvia wrote, '[d]isturbing questions, since they impinge upon the overall coherence of a system of protection whose development would be shocking if it were to take place irrationally'.[14]

III. THE *PELLEGRIN* CASE

The Court acknowledged, in *Pellegrin*,[15] that, as it stood, the case-law in this field 'contains a margin of uncertainty for Contracting States as to the scope of their obligations under Article 6 § 1'.

First and foremost, the Court noted that 'in the *Neigel* case, for example, the criterion of the absence of discretionary powers was not taken to be decisive for the applicability of Article 6 § 1'; it then pointed out that 'the criterion relating to the economic nature of a dispute, for its part, leaves scope for a degree of arbitrariness, since a decision concerning the "recruitment", "career" or "termination of service" of a civil servant nearly always has pecuniary consequences' and an impact on that civil servant's 'means of subsistence'.[16]

France, 24 August 1998, *Reports* 1998-V, 2265, § 25. It must nevertheless be stressed that, even under that approach, the essentially pecuniary nature of the right claimed (or, in other words, the impact of the dispute on the applicant's 'means of subsistence') remained one of the aspects to be taken into consideration by the Court when applying Article 6 § 1.

[13] P Tavernier, 'Faut-il réviser l'article 6 de la Convention européenne des droits de l'homme? (A propos du champ d'application de l'article 6)' in *Mélanges en hommage à Louis Edmond Petitti* (Brussels, Bruylant, 1998) 707–20, wrote rather vigorously in 1998: 'La jurisprudence relative à l'applicabilité de la Convention aux fonctionnaires et agents publics semble, pour le moment, manquer totalement de cohérence.' ('The case-law on the applicability of the Convention to public servants and agents seems, for the moment, to be completely devoid of coherence.') He also said that the picture regarding the field of application of this provision is 'peu satisfaisant et pour le moins cahotique' ('not very satisfactory and, at the very least, chaotic' (715).

[14] 'Questions troublantes, parce qu'elles concernent la cohérence globale d'un système protecteur, dont le développement irrationnel risquerait de choquer'. See J-C Soyer and M De Salvia (n 4) 253.

[15] *Pellegrin v France* (GC), 8 December 1999, nº 28541/95, *Reports* 1999-VIII, § 60.

[16] The Court used strong words in this regard: 'The Court can thus only confirm what it stated in its *Pierre-Bloch v France* judgment in relation to electoral disputes, when it held: "proceedings do not become 'civil' merely because they also raise an economic issue" (judgment of 21 October 1997, *Reports* 1997-VI, p. 2223, § 51).'

The Court then announced its intention 'to put an end to the uncertainty which surrounds application of the guarantees of Article 6 § 1 to disputes between States and their servants'.[17]

Nevertheless, the Court found that the distinction existing in France (as in other Contracting States), on which the parties in the procedure based their arguments, between two categories of staff in public service, namely 'officials under contract' (generally governed by private law) and 'established servants' (generally governed by public law), was not appropriate for that purpose. In fact, established servants and contractual officials frequently perform equivalent or similar tasks; therefore the nature, private or public, of the applicable national law could not be decisive in itself, as it would lead to inequality of treatment from one State to another and between State employees performing equivalent duties, even within the same Contracting State.[18]

In the light of the foregoing and in order to dissipate the ambiguity of the existing case-law, the Court decided to make an autonomous interpretation of the term 'civil service', which

> would make it possible to afford equal treatment to public servants performing equivalent or similar duties in the States Parties to the Convention, irrespective of the domestic system of employment and, in particular, whatever the nature of the legal relation between the official and the administrative authority (whether stipulated in a contract or governed by statutory and regulatory conditions of service).[19]

To that end, the Court considered that it should apply a 'functional criterion', based on the nature of the employee's duties and responsibilities, and in so doing

[17] *Pellegrin* (n 15) § 61.

[18] It must be recognised that, very often, the nature of the functions involved influences the type of legal relationship between the civil servant and the public Administration. The diplomatic service provides an example: servants belonging to the 'diplomatic corps' (ambassadors, consuls, counsellors) performing duties which correspond to the core function of representing the State in foreign relations are generally appointed by decree to posts subject to a specific regime which takes into account the special bond of trust and loyalty with the nation. All other posts in diplomatic representations (social, cultural, commercial or press attachés, administrative assistants, secretarial workers, butlers and porters, drivers, gardeners) are either subject to the general regime governing the civil service or are recruited under contracts that are governed by public or private law, limited in time and without any statutory link. The case of Mr António Victorino d'Almeida (*António Victorino D´Almeida v Portugal*, 21 February 2002, nº 43487/98—Section IV, struck out from the list decision), illustrates this reality. Mr Victorino d'Almeida was hired by decision of 22 March 1974 of the Minister of Foreign Affairs as a 'cultural attaché' to the Portuguese Embassy in Vienna (Austria). The legal relationship between the applicant and the ministry was established by contract of 22 March 1974, which did not bring the applicant into the 'diplomatic corps' or the 'diplomatic career'. At that time, the law in Portugal distinguished, in view of the tasks to be performed within the internal and external services of the ministry, between diplomatic staff, administrative staff and employees under contract charged with performing tasks of a technical nature. The department of justice also represents a striking example of such variation in the legal status of its civil servants, including, on the one hand, judges and public prosecutors, and, on the other hand, all other servants employed in the justice service. Again, the nature of the tasks performed and that of the juridical link often overlap. This only makes the application of such criteria more difficult.

[19] *Pellegrin* (n 15) § 63.

make a restrictive interpretation, in accordance with the object and purpose of the Convention, of the exceptions to the safeguards afforded by Article 6 § 1.[20]

The Court then established a distinction, within domestic administrations, between, on the one hand, posts involving the exercise of responsibilities in the general interest or participation in the exercise of powers conferred by public law and, on the other hand, all other public service posts.

As regards the first category, the State has a legitimate interest in requiring from those who hold such posts, to which is attached a portion of the State's sovereign power (typical examples are the armed forces and the police), a special bond of trust and loyalty, which is not the case in respect of other posts which do not involve that specific 'public administration' aspect.[21]

The Court's position is thus that it will determine on a case-by-case basis, 'whether the applicant's post entails—in the light of the nature of the duties and responsibilities appertaining to it—direct or indirect participation in the exercise of powers conferred by public law and duties designed to safeguard the general interests of the State or of other public authorities', in which case the disputes between the administrative authorities and that employee will be excluded from the scope of the application of Article 6 § 1 of the Convention.[22]

In the light of the foregoing, disputes concerning pension rights would necessarily fall within the scope of the application of Article 6 § 1, since the retired (or retiring) agent[23] has, by definition, ceased to maintain a special link with the administration and is, to that extent, in a position similar to that of a private law employee.

It must be stressed that, in the process of shaping this line of case-law, the Court has attached special importance to the case-law of the Court of Justice of the European Communities (hereinafter the 'Court of Justice') concerning the interpretation of the term 'employment in the public service', used in Article 48(4) of the EEC Treaty (Article 39(4) EC)[24] as an exception to the principle of freedom of movement of workers established by paragraph 1 of the same provision, as well as to the guidelines issued by the European Commission, in particular in its Communication of 18 March 1988.[25]

As regards the case-law of the Court of Justice, the Court made reference, in particular, to the judgments in cases *Commission v Belgium*, of 17 December 1980,[26] and *Commission v Luxembourg*, of 2 July 1996.[27] It appears from those

[20] ibid § 64.

[21] ibid § 65.

[22] ibid § 66.

[23] And *a fortiori* his/her heirs and successors.

[24] Hereinafter, the numbering introduced by the Treaty of Amsterdam will be used throughout, even where reference is made to the former Article 48.

[25] 'Freedom of movement of workers and access to employment in the public service of the Member States—Commission action in respect of the application of Article 48(4) of the EEC Treaty' (88/C/72/02) [1988] OJ C72/2.

[26] Case 149/79 *Commission v Belgium* [1980] ECR 3881.

[27] C-473/93 *Commission v Luxembourg* [1996] ECR I-3248.

judgments that the Court of Justice, in order to determine the scope of the derogation laid down in Article 39(4), also applied a functional criterion based on the nature of the duties and responsibilities pertaining to the post at issue. According to the Court of Justice, that derogation applies only to posts involving direct or indirect participation in the exercise of public powers and to functions whose purpose is to safeguard the general interests of the State or of other public authorities, thus requiring from the holders a particular bond of solidarity with the State and the peculiar reciprocity of rights and duties inherent in the relationship between a State and its nationals.

Similarly, the European Commission, in its Communication of 18 March 1988, building on the case-law of the Court of Justice, considered that the derogation in Article 39(4) 'covers specific functions of the State and similar bodies such as the armed forces, the police and other forces for the maintenance of order, the judiciary, the tax authorities and the diplomatic corps'.

IV. THE CASE-LAW OF THE COURT OF JUSTICE ON ARTICLE 39(4) EC

The position taken by the Court in *Pellegrin* represents a step forward on the road to imposing an 'objective' or 'functional' criterion, with the aim of clarifying the scope of Article 6 § 1 of the Convention and thus of reducing uncertainty in that regard.

Nevertheless, the Court, by relying on the case-law of the Court of Justice regarding Article 39(4) EC, left a certain number of questions unanswered.

First, it must be noted that the case-law in question was developed by the Court of Justice for the purpose of interpreting the Treaty provisions regarding the free movement of workers and the principle of non-discrimination on grounds of nationality, with a view to clarifying the scope of a specific exception to that freedom.

Thus, the context in which that case-law was developed and its particular characteristics are such that every precaution must be taken when transposing it, by analogy, to the very different area of law to which Article 6 of the Convention belongs, intended as that latter provision is to operate in the quite different field of human rights protection.

In that regard, the Court of Justice has held[28] that Article 39(4) EC, as a derogation from the fundamental principles of freedom of movement and non-discrimination, must be construed in such a way as to limit its scope to what is strictly necessary for safeguarding the interests which that provision allows the Member States to protect. The Court of Justice has observed that many posts in the public administration are remote from the specific activities of the public service because they do not involve direct or indirect participation in the exercise of powers conferred by public law

[28] See *Deborah Lawrie-Blum v Land Baden-Wurttemberg* 66/85 [1986] ECR 2121 para 26; *Commission v Italy* 225/85 [1987] ECR 2625 para 7.

or duties designed to safeguard the general interests of the State or of other public authorities; thus, they cannot benefit from the exception laid down in Article 39(4). That applies, in particular, to the majority of posts in the fields of research, health care, inland transport, post and telecommunications and in the water, gas and electricity supply sectors.[29]

Moreover, the Court of Justice has stated that access to certain posts may not be limited by reason of the fact that, in a given Member State, persons appointed to such posts have the status of civil servants. To make the application of Article 39(4) EC dependent on the legal nature of the relationship between a civil servant and the administration would, in fact, enable the Member States to determine at will the scope of application of that provision. Such an approach is all the more unacceptable at a time when the governments in a growing number of Member States are choosing to submit the relationship between them and their servants to a legal link similar to that prevailing in the private sector.[30]

Such arguments explain the choice made by the Court of Justice in favour of a 'functional criterion', under which a post's status depends on the nature of the tasks and responsibilities to be performed.[31]

The Court of Justice has firmly rejected a 'formal or institutional criterion', thus preventing recourse by EU Member States to provisions of their domestic legal systems in such a way as to impair the unity and effectiveness of the Treaty provisions on freedom of movement of workers and equality of treatment of nationals of all Member States.[32]

The approach of the Court of Justice was thus guided by the need to ensure that the provisions of Community law regarding a fundamental freedom should not be restricted in their scope by interpretations of the concept of public service based on domestic law alone, since any national definition of that concept might have widened the scope of the exception to that vital general principle of the Community legal order.

According to the case-law,[33] Member States may not generally exclude nationals of other Member States from all posts in an entire given area of State activity, solely because such posts depend on the State or have some link with the accomplishment

[29] *Commission v Luxembourg* (n 27) para 31. The Court of Justice found that the strict conditions required for the application of Article 39(4) were not fulfilled in many of the cases it examined. That finding was made with regard, for example, to hospital nurses and children's nurses, plumbers, carpenters, electricians and garden hands in the service of local authorities or public establishments (*Commission v Belgium* (n 26), and [1982] 1845; *Commission v France* 307/84 [1986] ECR 1725 para 13), trainee teachers (*Lawrie-Blum* (n 28) para 28), researchers (*Commission v Italy* (n 28) para 9), foreign language assistants (*Allué et Coonan* 33/88 [1989] ECR 1501 para 9), secondary school teachers (*Bleis* C-4/91 [1991] ECR I-5627 para 7), primary school teachers (*Commission v Luxembourg* (n 27) para 34), specialist doctors (*Kulliope* C-15/96 [1998] ECR I-47 para 13).

[30] In Portugal the 'individual employment contract' is increasingly replacing, as between civil servants and the authorities, the traditional public law model of a statutory link.

[31] *Commission v France* (n 29) paras 11–12.

[32] *Commission v Belgium* (n 26) point 19.

[33] ibid paras 11–12; *Commission v Luxembourg* (n 27) para 36; *Commission v Italy* (n 28) para 9.

of its tasks. Only those posts involving direct or indirect participation in the exercise of powers conferred by public law and duties designed to safeguard the general interests of the State or of other public authorities may be subject to a nationality condition.

A case-by-case analysis of the specific tasks carried out by each civil servant must therefore be conducted in order to ascertain whether or not the exercise of public powers is inherent in that individual's post. A distinction must be established within each career path, department or staff list between those tasks or posts which involve the exercise of public powers and those which do not, since only the former may be reserved to the nationals of a Member State.

The same approach has been followed in the case-law regarding equality of treatment between men and women in determining the scope of the exception on grounds of public safety. In cases concerning the employment of a police officer in Northern Ireland or of a chef in the British Royal Marines, the Court of Justice upheld the view that the principle of equal treatment for men and women is not subject to any general reservation as regards measures taken on grounds of the protection of public safety and that any derogations from that principle may only be permitted in exceptional circumstances.[34]

The Court of Justice also held that, in determining the scope of any derogation from a principle giving rise to individual rights, such as the equal treatment of men and women, another general principle of Community law, namely the principle of proportionality, must also be observed.[35]

V. *PELLEGRIN* REASSESSED

In *Pellegrin*, the Court attempted to put an end to the uncertainty and arbitrariness resulting from the use of the pecuniary nature of the dispute as a criterion whose application by the Court had, moreover, been somewhat erratic. The Court replaced that criterion with a functional criterion based on the nature of the tasks and responsibilities carried out by the civil servant concerned. To that end, the Court drew inspiration from the case-law of the Court of Justice on the concept of 'employment in the public service' used in Article 39(4) EC.

That being so, it is not easy to understand how the Court reached the conclusion that Article 6 § 1 was not applicable in that case. Mr Pellegrin, a French national, had been recruited under a contract with the Ministry of Cooperation and Development as a technical adviser to foreign governments within the framework of an overseas cooperation programme. Before signing the contract with the French Government, he had worked mainly as a management and accountancy consultant in the private sector. He applied for the public service job at issue on the basis of the professional experience he had thus acquired.

[34] See 222/84 *Johnston* [1986] ECR 1651 para 26; C-273/97 *Sirdar* [1999] ECR I-7403 para 16.

[35] See judgments *Johnston* and *Sirdar* (n 34), paras 38 and 26 respectively.

The Court nevertheless considered that the applicant, as 'one of the civilian cooperation staff in post in foreign States, was under specific obligations "inherent in the public-service nature" of his duties'.[36] The Court further considered that 'such an activity, which comes under the aegis of a government Ministry and partakes of the conduct of foreign relations, typifies the specific activities of the public service as defined above'.[37]

It is true that the Court acknowledged that it still needed 'to examine the particular nature of the applicant's duties and responsibilities in the course of his employment'.[38] However, after quickly dismissing the applicant's submission that, since it would have been possible to entrust his duties to a private consultant, they did not involve powers conferred under public law,[39] the Court held that 'the tasks assigned to the applicant gave him considerable responsibilities in the field of the State's public finances, which is, *par excellence*, a sphere in which States exercise sovereign power'.[40]

With respect, that conclusion could hardly be said to represent a faithful application of the criterion that the Court advocated in general terms in that very same judgment, based on the case-law of the Court of Justice. Indeed, the latter case-law requires that a distinction be made between, on the one hand, the general field of State activity at issue and, on the other hand, the nature of the specific tasks performed by the civil servant within that field of State activity.[41]

The Court's reasoning in the case at hand leads to the conclusion that the mere fact of exercising an activity in a sector linked to the general interests of the State is sufficient in itself to deprive a civil servant of the protection afforded to him or her by Article 6 § 1 of the Convention. It follows that the sovereign nature of a particular field of State activity would automatically be sufficient to turn any related post, even one of a purely technical nature, into an exercise of public power—like King Midas, who turned to gold everything he touched…

Furthermore, in today's complex world such an approach seems liable to entail an unjustified discrimination between posts of the same nature, depending on whether they happen to be filled by public servants or carried out by private entities. Police officers as compared to private security agents in charge of maintaining pubic order, warders in a prison run by the State as compared to guards in a prison under private management, public as compared to private notaries: each of these comparisons may be regarded as a relevant example of such ambivalence.

The specific political preferences of each State as regards the privatisation or maintenance under State control of the bodies that perform particular tasks that

36 See *Pellegrin* (n 15) § 68.

37 ibid.

38 ibid § 69.

39 ibid.

40 See *Pellegrin* (n 15) § 70.

41 These same considerations apply to the case of Mr António Victorino d'Almeida, on which the Court did not have to rule by means of a final judgment, since the case was settled by agreement between the applicant and the Portuguese Government.

were formerly the exclusive preserve of the public sector could therefore determine the scope of Article 6 § 1. The—in my view unacceptable—consequence of such an approach was that courts and tribunals in those Contracting States that favour privatisation were subject to stricter controls regarding the right to a fair trial than States whose policy is to give the State a bigger role in the provision of those same services of general interest; the guarantees secured to individuals by Article 6 § 1 thus varied accordingly.

The shortcomings inherent in such an approach were highlighted by the minority of judges who handed down a powerful Joint Dissenting Opinion in *Pellegrin*:[42]

> The main reason for the exclusion of civil service disputes from the scope of Article 6, which was to a large extent prompted by a State-centred outlook, was to preserve the public authorities' ius imperii, which was supposedly in danger of being undermined by judicialisation of related disputes. But that justification has now largely lost its significance. Of their own accord most member States have 'judicialised' civil service disputes, if not entirely then at least for the most part. To avoid discrimination between the subjects of law the procedural safeguards afforded on that account to civil servants must logically be the same as those applicable to other types of dispute, which incontestably fall within the scope of Article 6. Since the Convention acts as a benchmark, it would be surprising if the institutions charged with its supervision afforded fewer safeguards than the domestic courts (§6).

In that regard, it seems to me that the analogy drawn by the Court between Article 6 and the case-law of the Court of Justice applying Article 39(4) EC is neither convincing nor appropriate.

Indeed, when the Court rules on the scope of Article 6 of the Convention it is not deciding whether, in the field of free movement of workers and, more specifically, on the issue of access to particular posts, discrimination on grounds of nationality (or gender) may be objectively justified by reference to the public nature of the post or for reasons of public safety. Rather, the Court is called upon to determine whether an individual occupying a particular post is entitled to the guarantee of a fair trial enshrined in Article 6 of the Convention.[43]

In other words, the issue is whether, and to what extent, a national of a Contracting State may be deprived of the protection afforded by the Convention simply because he is an employee of the State.

It is, once again, worth referring, in this regard, to the above-quoted Joint Dissenting Opinion:

> Since Article 6 of the Convention expressly provides: 'In the determination of his civil rights and obligations ..., everyone is entitled to a fair ... hearing within a reasonable time by [a] ... tribunal ...', we consider that that provision applies to all disputes that are decisive for a person's legal position, even if he or she is a civil servant. We can see no

[42] See the Joint Dissenting Opinion of Judges Tulkens, Fischbach, Casadevall and Thomassen.

[43] See, in that respect, the Joint Dissenting Opinion, §2, third sentence.

> valid reason for depriving persons in the public service of the legal protection which is regarded for other workers as a safeguard so essential as to constitute a fundamental right. Salaries, dismissals or transfers are matters which may have a profound influence over people's lives, including persons working in the public service (§5).

I take the view that it is precisely in the context of civil service disputes that the right to effective judicial protection against arbitrariness is of the utmost importance, regardless of the nature of the particular functions performed. It is difficult to understand how, when a Member State has agreed to make civil service disputes 'justiciable', ie to submit them to judicial review, the Court may not intervene to enforce the guarantees inherent in the right to a fair trial.

It follows from the foregoing that it is not possible to transpose mechanically the principles underlying the case-law of the Court of Justice on Article 39(4) EC to the very different context of the scope of application of Article 6 of the Convention. In my view, such a transposition may only be justified as regards the general principle that individual rights and fundamental freedoms must be interpreted broadly, whereas the exception concerning employment in the public service must be subject to a strict interpretation.

VI. THE IMMEDIATE POST-*PELLEGRIN* PERIOD

I shall now examine how the *Pellegrin* criterion was applied by the Court in the aftermath of that judgment.

First, the Court applied the 'functional criterion' in such a way that it excluded from the scope of protection of Article 6 certain disputes between the public administration, on the one hand, and police officers or members of the armed forces, on the other hand.[44] The Court also rejected the application of that same provision to disputes concerning employment as a member of a local police force ('vigile urbano'),[45] as a senior academic teacher at a National Fire Academy,[46] as

[44] See *Linde Falero v Spain* (dec), 22 June 2000, nº 51535/99; *Batur v Turkey* (dec), 4 July 2000, nº 38604/97. These cases were about disputes regarding the dismissal on disciplinary grounds of a member of the *Guardia Civil* and a naval officer, respectively.

[45] *Rotondi v Italy* (dec), 26 September 2000, nº 45343/99.

[46] *Kepka v Poland* (dec), 11 July 2000, nº 31439/98 and 35123/97, Reports 2000 IX. The Court held that the fact that, during the entire period of his service, the applicant worked as a lecturer could not be assessed in isolation from his other duties and responsibilities. In fact, the applicant pursued his academic career not at a civilian university or academy, but at a quasi-military academy, whose activities were governed by the rules concerning higher military academies. Thus, the applicant held a military officer's rank and was considered to be a member of the armed forces. Consequently, he was required to obey orders from his superiors and to give orders to his subordinates, to comply with strict rules of discipline, and to accept the hierarchical relationships and other conditions inherent in the military environment. Moreover, his functions as a teacher in the fire fighters corps included scientific research related to matters considered crucially important for national defence.

an officer in the secret police,[47] as a lawyer serving in the police corps[48] and as a naval officer.[49]

Likewise, by applying the 'functional criterion' the Court excluded from the scope of Article 6 § 1 disputes involving qualified civil servants in the Ministry of Foreign Affairs and members of the diplomatic corps, given their participation in the conduct of international relations involving the exercise of public powers.[50]

In Article 6 disputes involving attachés to embassies (or permanent representations), the Court considered the characteristics and circumstances of the activities performed on a case-by-case basis.

In *Liontas v Greece*[51] and *Kolotkov v Russia*,[52] the Court recalled *Pellegrin* and ruled that the activities of the diplomatic corps entailed 'direct or indirect participation in the exercise of powers conferred by public law and duties designed to safeguard the general interests of the State', with the consequence that they were excluded from the scope of Article 6.

Conversely, in *Frydlender v France*[53] and *Gobry v France*,[54] the Court, taking into consideration the specific functions performed, held that the guarantees inherent in the right to a fair trial did apply.

[47] *Stanczuk v Poland* (dec), 14 June 2001, n° 45004/98.

[48] *Veresova v Slovakia* (dec), 1 February 2005, n° 70497/01. The Court considered that the proceedings at issue did not involve a determination of any of the applicant's 'civil rights and obligations' and thus excluded application of Article 6 § 1, simply because she was serving in the police and, because of the nature of the functions and responsibilities performed by that service, her employment could be regarded as a direct participation in the exercise of public authority. The Court's reasoning in this regard was thus exclusively based on the nature of the tasks generally carried out by the police service, irrespective of the individual role of the applicant in that organisation.

[49] *Kanaiev v Russia*, 27 July 2006, n° 43726/02, §18. The Court considered that the applicant, who was a captain of the third rank, 'wielded a portion of the state's sovereign power' and held that Article 6 § 1 did not apply, although the dispute concerned the non-execution of a judgment rendered in favour of the applicant regarding travel expenses.

[50] *Martinez-Caro de la Concha Castaneda and Others v Spain* (dec), 7 March 2000, n° 42646/98; *GK v Austria* (dec), 14 March 2000, n° 39564/98.

[51] *Liontas v Greece* (dec), 9 December 2004, n° 8628/02. The applicant had been 'conseiller économique' in a diplomatic representation and the dispute regarded the refusal to renew his contract.

[52] *Kolotkov v Russia* (dec), 9 March 2006, n° 41146/02. The Court considered that the post involved possible access to information comprising State secrets.

[53] *Frydlender v France*, 27 June 2000, n° 3079/96, Reports, 2000-VII, §38-41. The applicant, a graduate from the National Agronomic Institute in Paris, was first engaged as an official employed under an individual contract ('agent contractuel') by the Economic Development Department of the Ministry for Economic Affairs and posted to Athens as a technical adviser. He was later posted to the New York economic development office as head of an autonomous section, to handle more specifically the promotion of French wines, beers and spirits, working under the authority of the chief commercial adviser. His job was thus to facilitate and stimulate exports of certain categories of products and to advise and assist official and semi-official bodies and individual exporters or importers. In view of the nature of the duties performed by the applicant and the relatively low level of his responsibilities, the Court considered that he was not carrying out any task which could be said to entail, either directly or indirectly, duties designed to safeguard the general interests of the State.

[54] *Gobry v France*, 6 July 2004, n° 71367/01. The applicant, administrator at the INSEE, was posted to the French Embassy in Moscow as third attaché to the chief of the economic mission, in charge of assisting French companies wishing to set up for business in the region. Taking into consideration

In *Frydlender*,[55] the Court observed that *Pellegrin* was intended to restrict the situations in which public servants could be denied the practical and effective protection afforded by the Convention, and in particular by Article 6 thereof. Consequently, the Court should adopt a restrictive interpretation, in accordance with the object and purpose of the Convention, of the exceptions to the safeguards afforded by Article 6 § 1.[56] The Court further observed that this restrictive interpretation would be undermined[57] if the Court were to find, by analogy or by extension, that the activities of the staff of the economic development offices as a whole, whatever the nature of their duties and their level of responsibility, entailed the exercise of powers conferred by public law.

In other cases, the Court was called upon to review disputes regarding posts as judge, President of the Supreme Court, registrar and public prosecutor. It held that the applicants in all those cases had specific responsibilities in the administration of justice, thus belonging to a sphere in which States exercise their sovereign authority, and were therefore members of the 'public service' as defined in *Pellegrin*. Application of Article 6 of the Convention was thus ruled out in all those disputes.[58]

The Court has also dismissed as inadmissible complaints filed on the basis of alleged breaches of Article 6 by a head of department in the Ministry of Agriculture and Forestry,[59] a governor in the Department of Co-operative Development,[60] a tax inspector[61] and a deputy solicitor-general.[62]

Conversely, the Court has ruled in favour of the admissibility of Article 6 claims in the case of other categories of posts, on grounds that the latter, although closely related to the public service, did not involve the accomplishment of a task designed to safeguard the general interests of the State nor, directly or indirectly, the exercise of public powers: employees in public hospitals or State clinics (doctors, nurses, laboratory technicians, biologists, cooks, etc),[63] secondary school teachers and caretakers in State schools,[64] university lecturers,[65] auxiliary

the applicant's position within the hierarchy, the nature of his functions and the low degree of responsibility attached to his post, the Court held that Article 6 of the Convention was applicable.

55 *Frydlender* (n 53) § 40.

56 See *Pellegrin* (n 15) § 64, *in fine*.

57 As the French Government suggested in the instant case.

58 See *Pitkevich v Russia* (dec), 8 February 2001, nº 47936/99; *Kajanen and Tupmaala v Finland* (dec), 19 October 2000, nº 36401/97; *Harabin v Slovakia* (dec), 9 July 2002, nº 62384/00; *Laloyaux v Belgium* (dec), 14 November 2002, nº 73511/01; and *Sidabras and Dziaulas v Lituania* (dec), 1 July 2003, nº 55480 and nº 59330/00.

59 *Stadler v Austria* (dec), 6 January 2000, nº 27633/95.

60 *Azinas v Cyprus* (dec), 19/06/2001, nº 56679/00.

61 *Sidubras and Dziautus v Lithuania* (dec) 1 July 2003, nº 55480 and nº 59330/00.

62 *Mickovski v Republic of Macedonia* (dec), 10 November 2005, nº 68329/01.

63 *Musiani v Italy* (dec), nº 41813/98; *Alesiani and 500 others v Italy* (dec), 29 February 2000, nº 41806/98; *Centioni and Others v Italy* (dec), 29 February 2000, nº 41807/98.

64 *Volkmer v Germany* (dec), 22 November 2001, nº 39799/98; *Procaccini v Italy* (dec), 30 March 2000, nº 31631/96, §§ 13–14.

65 *Peterson v Germany* (dec), 22 November 2001, nº 39793/98.

justice officials,[66] researchers in a State-run scientific institute,[67] social workers and civil servants administering social security,[68] employees in national railway companies.[69]

With respect, the consistency of that case-law appears doubtful, to say the least. In two particular cases concerning strikingly similar activities, the Court followed opposite approaches.

In *Vainiokangas*,[70] the Court considered that the applicant's post as mayor entailed direct participation in the exercise of powers and duties conferred on the municipality by public law with the aim of safeguarding its general interests. The Court therefore declared that the right claimed was not of a 'civil' nature and considered Article 6 inapplicable.

By contrast, in *Richard-Dubarry*,[71] the application submitted by a former mayor of Noisy-Le-Grand in France in respect of court proceedings arising from alleged acts of mismanagement in her capacity as chairwoman of associations in receipt of public funds when she had been in office, was declared admissible by the Court, since the dispute was considered as concerning a 'civil' obligation. In its judgment, the Court referred extensively to the case-law of the French *Conseil d'État*.[72]

During this first phase after *Pellegrin*, the application made by the Court of the traditional criterion based on the 'pecuniary nature' of the claims and its attempts to combine that approach with the '*Pellegrin* criterion', are also open to criticism. A striking example of this is provided by the Court's rulings in the *Martinie* case.

The applicant in the case, a public accountant in a French school, was held liable to pay to the State certain sums of money received in the course of the exercise of his duties in the school and in an adjacent sports centre. A Chamber of the Second Section of the Court first decided[73] that Article 6 § 1 of the Convention was applicable since the private-law aspects of the case were predominant and the

[66] *Alvarez Dapena and Others v Spain* (dec), 17 October 2000, nº 47977/99; *Alberto Sanchez v Spain* (dec), 16 November 2004, nº 72773/01.

[67] *Donadze v Georgia* (dec), 24 May 2005, nº 74644/01.

[68] *SM v France* (dec), 18 July 2000, nº 41453/98; *Lambourdière v France* (dec), 2 August 2000, nº 37887/97.

[69] *Predota v Austria* (dec), 18 January 2000, nº 28962/95; *Pramov v Bulgaria* (dec), 30 September 2004, nº 42986/98; *Neshev v Bulgaria* (dec), 28 October 2004, nº 40897/98. However, in *Rabus v Germany* (dec), 9 February 2006, nº 43731/02, the Court refused to apply Article 6 to a technician employed in the German Telecoms Corporation based in particular on the following considerations: 'the status of German civil servants is founded on a special relationship of trust with the State and based on the officials' duty of allegiance (*Treuepflicht*) whose counterpart is the State's fiduciary duty (*Fürsorgepflicht*). Since permanent civil servants are appointed by a public authority by deed of appointment "for life" and accordingly enjoy particular protection against dismissal, disciplinary proceedings originating from this relationship have a different significance, purpose and procedure than those instituted against non-officials and typically belong to the realm of public law'.

[70] *Vainiokangas v Finland* (dec), 7 September 2000, nº 31766/96.

[71] *Richard-Dubarry v France* (dec), 1 June 2004, nº 53929/00, Reports, 2003 XI.

[72] See ibid paras 54, 70, 80. It is however worth recalling that the Court has consistently held that the legal notions used in the Convention should receive an autonomous interpretation.

[73] *Martinie v France* (dec), nº 58675/00, 13 January 20004, Reports, 2004 II.

pecuniary obligation at stake was 'civil' within the meaning of Article 6. The Court emphasized that the criterion of 'participation in the exercise of powers conferred by public law' established in *Pellegrin* only served the purpose of determining whether 'disputes relating to the recruitment, careers and termination of service of public servants fall outside the scope of Article 6 § 1 under its civil head'.[74] The Court thus considered the *Pellegrin* judgment irrelevant to the case at hand.

However, on referral from another Chamber of the Second Section, the Court, sitting in its Grand Chamber composition,[75] recalled that

> *Pellegrin* was [...] a departure from precedent, and [had] since been confirmed, regarding the principles it established and the criterion of applicability of Article 6 § 1 it laid down, by a large number of judgments and decisions of the Court.[76]

The Court therefore held, as had the Chamber in its admissibility decision, that Article 6 § 1 was applicable but it reached that conclusion by a different reasoning. In the Grand Chamber's view, in the light of the judgment in *Pellegrin*,

> [n]either the nature of the duties carried out by the applicant, nor the responsibilities attached to them, support the view that he participated 'in the exercise of powers conferred by public law and duties designed to safeguard the general interests of the State or of other public authorities' unless these concepts are to be construed broadly.[77]

As emphasised in *Pellegrin*,[78] the correct approach was, however, in accordance with the object and purpose of the Convention, to adopt a restrictive interpretation of the exceptions to the safeguards afforded by Article 6 § 1.

It is worth noting that, as in *Richard-Dubarry*, the Court gave extensive consideration to the case-law of the French *Conseil d'État*, but nevertheless defined its position regardless of that case-law according to which the French Court of Auditors, when auditing accounts submitted by public accountants, does not make a determination in respect of either a criminal charge or civil rights and obligations within the meaning of Article 6 § 1 of the Convention.[79]

All in all, despite the Court's commitment to putting an end to the uncertainty arising from the pre-*Pellegrin* case-law, it is respectfully submitted that it did not achieve that objective in the seven years following that judgment, since, at the end of that period, there was still no clear and unambiguous line of case-law.

As the Court later recognised,[80] the judgments handed down in the years following *Pellegrin* illustrate the fact that the nature of the applicant's duties and his status are not always easy to determine. In some situations, the applicant's precise role within the civil service cannot readily be ascertained on the basis of the

[74] ibid § 27.
[75] *Martinie v France* (GC), nº 58675/00, 12 April 2006, §§ 26–30.
[76] ibid § 28.
[77] ibid § 30.
[78] See *Pellegrin* (n 15) § 64.
[79] See *Martinie* (GC) (n 75) § 14.
[80] See the following part of this chapter on the *Vilho Eskelinen* judgment.

tasks actually performed. In certain cases, the level of an individual's involvement in the exercise of public functions, which might justify disapplying Article 6, irrespective of the nature of the tasks assigned to him or her, is difficult to establish.

VII. THE HAPPY ENDING: *VILHO ESKELINEN*

The time may have come to change course, as the Court acknowledged in *Vilho Eskelinen*, a judgment of 19 April 2007.[81]

The applicants in that case were members of the police service in Finland (or their heirs) and respectively occupied the posts of senior constable, sergeant and office assistant; one applicant was a retired police officer. Their dispute with the authorities concerned the loss of a 'remote-area' allowance to which they claimed to be entitled and an increase in the distance that they had to travel to work following a change in their duty station as a result of an internal reorganisation. The applicants alleged violations of Article 6 § 1, complaining, *inter alia*, about the excessive length of the proceedings and the lack of any oral hearing before the domestic courts.

The parties expressed opposing views regarding the applicability *ratione materiae* of Article 6 § 1.

The applicants contended (i) that their service and salaries were not related to the exercise of powers conferred by public law, (ii) that the dispute was neither about the exercise of public powers (the individuals concerned were not complaining about the decision to change the location of their place of work as such), nor about issues of recruitment, career development or termination of service, (iii) on the contrary, the dispute concerned their right to their remuneration which was, they argued, of a private law character, being a contractual matter regulated by the collective agreement between employees and their employer and which also had an impact on the level of their pensions.[82]

For its part, the Finnish Government contested the applicability of Article 6 of the Convention on the grounds that the applicants' duties entailed direct participation in the exercise of public authority and duties designed to safeguard the general interests of the State, as defined in *Pellegrin*.[83] In the Government's view, the fact that the applicants' pecuniary interests were allegedly at stake did not change that assessment since, according to the judgment in *Pierre-Bloch*,[84] 'proceedings do not become "civil" merely because they also raise an economic issue'.[85]

In order to reach a decision on the applicability of Article 6 § 1, the Court proceeded to carry out a thorough examination of the case-law before *Pellegrin*

[81] *Vilho Eskelinen and Others v Finland* (GC), nº 63235/00, 19 April 2007.

[82] ibid § 32.

[83] Based on the Court's reasoning in *Veresova* (n 48), the same conclusion should apply to the post of office assistant.

[84] *Pierre-Bloch* (n 16) § 51.

[85] *Vilho Eskelinen* (n 81) § 35.

and of the review of that case-law carried out in *Pellegrin* itself,[86] followed by an examination of the cases decided subsequently.[87]

The Court concluded from that analysis that the functional criterion applied had not simplified the analysis of the applicability of Article 6 to disputes to which a civil servant is a party. On the contrary, it even indicated that the new criterion had brought about a greater degree of uncertainty in this area.[88] The Court deduced from that analysis that the functional criterion adopted in *Pellegrin* required further development.[89]

In that respect, the Court stressed that the application of the functional criterion could lead to anomalous results. In fact, on a strict application of the *Pellegrin* approach it would appear that the office assistant should enjoy the guarantees of Article 6 § 1, whereas the police officers would certainly not, irrespective of the fact that the substantive dispute was identical in respect of all the applicants.[90]

The Court held, in that context, that it was

> particularly striking that, taken literally, the 'functional approach' requires that Article 6 be excluded from application to disputes where the position of the applicant as a State official does not differ from the position of any other litigant or, in other words, where the dispute between the employee and the employer is not especially marked by a 'special bond of trust and loyalty'.[91]

Whilst acknowledging that, 'in the interests of legal certainty, foreseeability and equality before the law', it 'should not depart, without good reason, from precedents laid down in previous cases', the Court held that 'a failure [...] to maintain a dynamic and evolutive approach would risk rendering it a bar to reform or improvement'.[92] *Pellegrin* should thus be understood simply as a first step away from the previously applicable principle of inapplicability of Article 6 to disputes involving members of the civil service, towards a more balanced partial applicability approach.[93]

The Court pointed out that in many Contracting States civil servants have access to the courts in respect of claims relating to salary and allowances, dismissal or recruitment, on a similar basis to employees in the private sector, no conflict between the vital interests of the State and the right of those individuals to judicial protection being perceived by the domestic legal system. The basic premise that certain servants, because of their functions, are bound by a special bond of trust

[86] ibid §§ 43–51.

[87] ibid §§52–55.

[88] ibid § 55. The Court also referred, *mutatis mutandis*, in this context, to *Perez v France* (GC), nº 47287/99, § 55, Reports, 2004-I.

[89] *Vilho Eskelinen* (n 81) § 56.

[90] ibid § 51.

[91] ibid § 53.

[92] ibid § 56.

[93] ibid § 57.

and loyalty towards their employer is not then appropriate as a distinguishing criterion.[94]

As the Court pointed out,[95] 'Articles 1 and 14 of the Convention stipulate that "everyone within [the] jurisdiction" of the Contracting States must enjoy the rights and freedoms in Section I "without discrimination on any ground"', and the guarantees thus established in the Convention thus extend, in principle, to civil servants.[96]

Only convincing reasons relating to the effective functioning of the State or to some other public necessity might ultimately justify that certain categories of applicant be denied the protection provided for by the Convention against unfair or lengthy proceedings, in circumstances where the applicants have, under the applicable national legislation, the right to have their claims examined by a tribunal.[97]

It is worth noting that the Court turned once again to European Community law, which it considered to be a source of 'useful guidance' and drew more rigorously and extensively upon it in *Vilho Eskelinen* than it had done in *Pellegrin*.

The Court first referred to Article 47 of the Charter of Fundamental Rights of the European Union (proclaimed on 7 December 2000) concerning the right to an effective remedy and to a fair trial, and to the Explanations relating to the Charter, originally prepared under the authority of the Praesidium of the Convention and finally integrated in the Final Act of the Treaty establishing a Constitution for Europe. Although they do not have equal authority to the Charter, these Explanations have been considered by the Court as constituting a 'valuable tool of interpretation intended to clarify the provisions of the Charter'.[98]

The Court quoted, in particular, the Explanations relating to Article 47(2) of the Charter, according to which (extract):

> In Union law, the right to a fair hearing is not confined to disputes relating to civil law rights and obligations. That is one of the consequences of the fact that the Union is a community based on the rule of law as stated by the Court in Case 294/83, *Les Verts v European Parliament* (judgment of 23 April 1986, [1988] ECR 1339). Nevertheless, in all respects other than their scope, the guarantees afforded by the ECHR apply in a similar way to the Union.

The Court went on to deduce from that passage of the Explanations that, in the context of European Community law, the guarantees prescribed by Article 47 of the Charter are not confined to civil rights and obligations or to criminal matters within the meaning of Article 6 of the Convention.

The Court also observed that the Court of Justice applies a broader approach in favour of judicial control, as illustrated by its judgment in *Johnston v Chief*

[94] ibid.

[95] *Vilho Eskelinen* (n 81) § 58.

[96] See, *mutatis mutandis*, *Schmidt and Dahlstrom v Sweden*, 6 February 1976, A nº 21, 15, § 33; *Engel and others v The Netherlands*, 8 June 1976, A nº 22, 23, § 54; *Glasenapp v Germany* (n 3) 26, § 49; *Ahmed and others v United Kingdom*, 2 September 1998, Reports, 1998-VI, 2378, § 56.

[97] *Vilho Eskelinen* (n 81) § 59.

[98] ibid § 30.

Constable of the Royal Ulster Constabulary,[99] a case brought by a female police officer on the basis of the 'Equal Treatment Directive' of 1976.[100] The Court of Justice held that:

> The requirement of judicial control stipulated [in Article 6 of Council Directive 76/207] reflects a general principle of law which underlies the constitutional traditions common to the Member States. That principle is also laid down in Articles 6 and 13 of the European Convention for the Protection of Human Rights and Fundamental Freedoms of 4 November 1950. As the European Parliament, Council and Commission recognized in their Joint Declaration of 5 April 1977 (...) and as the Court has recognised in its decisions, the principles on which that Convention is based must be taken into consideration in Community law.

As the Court has recognised, this and other Court of Justice case-law[101] shows that judicial control in Community law has a wide scope. If an individual can rely on a substantive right guaranteed by that law, then his or her status as a person involved in the exercise of State power does not render the requirements of judicial control inapplicable.[102] Moreover, the role of the Charter in this regard was largely to codify the existing case-law of the Court of Justice.

Nevertheless, the Court recognises the legitimate interest that the State may have in curtailing access to the courts when it comes to certain categories of staff. That said, it is primarily for the Contracting States, not the Court, to expressly identify those specific areas of public service involving the exercise of discretionary powers inherent in State sovereignty where the interest of the individual in comprehensive judicial protection must give way.[103]

As the Court has recalled,[104] two conditions must be fulfilled in order for the respondent State to be able to rely, before the Court, on the applicant's status as a civil servant in order to displace the protection enshrined in Article 6. Firstly, domestic law must have expressly excluded access to a court for the post or category of staff in question. Secondly, the exclusion must be justified on objective grounds in the public interest. The mere fact that the applicant works in a sector or department which participates in the exercise of public powers is not in itself decisive. Contrary to what the Court said in *Pellegrin*, it is not therefore sufficient for the State to establish that the civil servant in question participates in the exercise of public power or that there exists a 'special bond of trust and

[99] *Johnston* (n 34) para 18.

[100] Council Directive 76/207/EEC of 9 February 1976 on the implementation of the principle of equal treatment for men and women as regards access to employment, vocational training and promotion, and working conditions [1976] OJ L39, 40–42.

[101] See in particular *Panayotova and Others v Minister voor Vreemdelingenzaken en Integratie* C-327/02 [2004] ECR I-11055 para 27.

[102] *Vilho Eskelinen* (n 81) § 60.

[103] The Court exerts its supervisory role subject to the principle of subsidiarity (*Z and Others v United Kingdom* (GC), nº 29392/95, § 103, Reports, 2001-V). If a domestic system bars access to a court, it is for the Court to verify that the dispute is indeed such as to justify application of the exception to the guarantees provided for by Article 6. If it does not, then there is no issue and Article 6 § 1 will apply (*Vilho Eskelinen* (n 81) § 61).

[104] *Vilho Eskelinen* (n 81) § 62.

loyalty' between the servant and the State. The State must also show that the subject-matter of the dispute is related to the exercise of State power or that it has called that special bond into question.

VIII. CONCLUSION

Bearing in mind the approach I proposed that the Court follow in the case of Mr Victorino d'Almeida, I am naturally gratified by these recent developments in the case-law, which prioritises the right to a fair trial regardless of the nature of the legal relationship existing between the individual and the State.[105]

The Court has applied this new line of case-law in a number of subsequent cases: *Dovguchits*,[106] *Pridatchenko*,[107] *Rizhamadze*,[108] *Tratar*,[109] *Nedelcho Popov*,[110] *Josephides*,[111] and *Micallef*.[112]

There is now a presumption in favour of the applicability of Article 6 § 1 to disputes between public servants and a Contracting State. That presumption means that the Court has finally managed to overcome the arguments, based on the text of the Convention, opposing recognition of the right to a fair trial to individuals employed in the public service.

Admittedly, recourse to the Convention will only be available where Contracting States agree to grant their civil servants some degree of judicial protection by allowing them access to the courts in respect of disputes arising from relationships of a 'public' nature in the first place. Once that right is enshrined in the laws of the Contracting States, which should indeed be the norm in States governed by the rule of law, there will be no possible justification for excluding the application of the guarantees established in Article 6 § 1 to cases brought by public servants.

I am not convinced by the argument raised by the dissenting judges in the *Vilho Eskelinen* case, according to which, since legal systems vary from one State to another, the reasoning followed in the judgment is likely to have the effect of making the applicability of Article 6 § 1 to disputes between the State and its agents dependent on domestic law. In the view of the dissenting judges, far from providing an 'autonomous interpretation' of that provision, the judgment is a cause of additional uncertainty and arbitrariness and represents 'an inappropriate step back'.

[105] Five judges in the Grand Chamber issued a dissenting opinion (see Joint Dissenting Opinion of Judges Costa, Wildhaber, Türmen, Borrego Borrego and Jočienė, as well as the partly Dissenting Opinion of Judge Jočienė). The reasoning put forward by the dissenting judges was based on the *Pellegrin* case-law in that it had been applied by the Court for seven years with no particular difficulty and should not therefore be abandoned.

[106] *Dovguchits v Russia*, 7 June 2007, nº 2999/03.

[107] *Pridatchenko and Others v Russia*, 21 June 2007, nº 2191/03, 3104/03, 16094/03, 24486/03.

[108] *Rizhamadze v Georgia*, 31 July 2007, nº 2745/03.

[109] *Tratar v Slovenia*, 4 October 2007, nº 76141/01, 25387/02, 5925/05.

[110] *Nedelcho Popov v Bulgaria*, 22 November 2007, nº 61360/00.

[111] *Josephides v Cyprus*, 6 December 2007, nº 33761/02.

[112] *Micallef v Malta*, 15 January 2008, nº 17056/06.

Admittedly, the approach taken by the Court, in conjunction with the principle of subsidiarity, does not establish an absolute right to effective judicial protection and to a fair trial, to which all individuals are entitled irrespective of the legal status of their relationship with the State and the nature of the matter in dispute. However, given the current text of the Convention and, more specifically, in view of the precise wording of Article 6 § 1 and the reference therein to 'the determination of [...] civil rights and obligations', the current interpretation is probably the farthest the Court could have gone in the direction of broadening the scope of that provision's protection.[113] It is thus fair to conclude that European Community law currently affords those fundamental rights a wider protection than that provided by the Convention.

In any case, the evolution of the case-law shows that the Court wishes to extend the scope of application of the right of access to the courts, even as regards disputes raised by civil servants, as far as it can. In *Nedelcho Popov*,[114] the Court emphasised that, although that right is not absolute and may be subject to limitations, such limitations must not restrict or reduce the individual's access to justice in such a way or to such an extent that the very essence of that right is impaired.[115] In view of the principle of subsidiarity, the Court then found that there was no justification in the case for restricting the applicant's right of access to a court.

Such an approach is consistent with other precedents from the case-law,[116] in which the Court has stated that the right to a fair hearing before a tribunal, as guaranteed by Article 6 § 1 of the Convention, must be interpreted in the light of its Preamble, which declares the rule of law to be part of the common heritage of the Contracting States.

In *Vilho Eskelinen* and the subsequent cases, the Court has managed to reverse the previous rule under which civil servants were presumptively excluded from the protection of Article 6 and has replaced it with a general rule under which such protection is presumed to be available in the context of disputes between civil servants and the State. It is now therefore the respondent State that bears the burden of proving, first, that pursuant to the domestic law the applicant has no right of access to a court and, second, that the exclusion of the guarantees provided for in Article 6 is reasonable and objectively justified.

The present state of the case-law represents a significant improvement in the protection of the right to a fair trial for public servants, but it remains to be seen whether further progress is still possible within the framework of the Convention, as currently worded.

[113] Only an amendment to the Convention would make it possible to further clarify (or extend) the scope of Article 6 § 1. This was unsuccessfully attempted by adding an Article 6 *bis* in a new Protocol. See, eg, P Tavernier (n 13) 715 ff.

[114] *Nedelcho Popov* (n 110) § 37.

[115] See also *Golder v the United Kingdom*, judgment of 21 February 1975, Series A nº 18, 18, § 36 and *Ashingdane v the United Kingdom*, judgment of 28 May 1985, Series A nº 93, 24, § 57, on which the Court relied upon in *Nedelcho Popov* (n 110).

[116] *Dovguchits v Russia* (n 106) § 26.

Part IV

Competition and State Aid

11

*How Far Should National Courts Go in Drawing All the Necessary Inferences from the Last Sentence of Article 88(3) EC?**

I. INTRODUCTION

Pursuant to Article 88(3) EC,

> [t]he Commission shall be informed in sufficient time to enable it to submit its comments, of any plans to grant or alter aid. If it considers that any such plan is not compatible with the common market having regard to Article 87, it shall without delay initiate the procedure provided for in paragraph 2. The Member State concerned shall not put its proposed measures into effect until this procedure has resulted in a final decision.

The last sentence of the said provision lays down a prohibition, or standstill obligation, addressed to Member States, which was held to have direct effect. Consequently, in order to safeguard the rights and interests of third parties, national courts are bound to enforce it.

The present chapter addresses the key issue of determining how far national courts may go in the enforcement of the last sentence of Article 88(3) EC when Member States fail to comply with the standstill obligation provided for therein.

II. DIRECT EFFECT OF THE LAST SENTENCE OF ARTICLE 88(3) EC

The ECJ acknowledged at an early stage the principle of direct effect as central to the development of EC law.

* First published in 'New Developments in European State Aid Law 2005', Proceedings of the 3rd Experts' Forum held in Brussels on 26 and 27 May 2005, *European State Aid Law Quarterly* (Brussels, European State Aid Law Institute and Lexxion Verlagsgesellshaft mbH, 2006) 45–52. The author acknowledges the assistance given by João Martins, of PLMJ, in the preparation of the original version of this chapter.

In *Van Gend & Loos*[1] the Court held that 'Community law not only imposes obligations on individuals but is also intended to confer upon them rights which became part of their legal heritage' and that

> the fact that Articles 169 and 170 of the EEC Treaty enable the Commission and the Member States to bring before the Court a State which has not fulfilled its obligations does not deprive individuals of the right to plead the same obligations, should the occasion arise, before a national court.

One year after this general statement, in *Costa v ENEL*,[2] the Court again had the opportunity to deal with the issue of direct effect, this time in connection with the last sentence of Article 88(3) EC (then Article 93(3) EC). Although in somewhat unclear wording, the ECJ held that, 'by accepting the procedures laid down in Article [88], the States have entered into an obligation with the Community, which binds them as States but creates no individual rights except in the case of final provision of Article [88](3)'. In other words, the last sentence of Article 88(3) EC creates rights in favour of individuals which they can enforce at the appropriate level.

In *Lorenz*,[3] the Court later clarified the main implications of the direct effect of the abovementioned provision. As per the judgment in that case, '[t]he prohibition of implementation referred to in the last sentence of Article [88](3) [...] gives rise to rights in favour of individuals, which national courts are bound to safeguard'.[4] As to the scope of the direct effect, the Court stated that '[t]he immediately applicable nature of this provision extends to the whole of the period to which it applies'.[5]

> Thus the direct effect[6] of the prohibition extends to all aid which has been implemented without being notified and, in the event of notification, operates during the preliminary period, and where the Commission sets in motion the contentious procedure, up to the final decision.[7]

The Court's judgment in *Lorenz* thus made clear that the scope of protection of the last sentence of Article 88(3) EC covers *(i)* the period prior to notification

[1] Case 26/62 *NV Algemene Transport—en Expeditie Onderneming van Gend & Loos v Netherlands Inland Revenue Administration* [1963] ECR 1.

[2] Case 6/64 *Flaminio Costa v ENEL* [1964] ECR 585.

[3] Case 120/73 *Lorenz GmbH v Federal Republic of Germany* [1973] ECR 1471.

[4] ibid, para 8. As the Court underlined in Case 33/76 *Rewe Zentralfinanz* [1976] ECR 1989 and Case 45/76 *Comet* [1976] ECR 2043, the role of national courts in ensuring legal protection which citizens derive from the direct effect of provisions of Community law stems directly from the principle of cooperation laid down in Article 5 of the Treaty (now Article 10 EC).

[5] By using indifferently the expressions 'direct effect' and 'immediately applicable', the Court maintains the ambiguity that arises from the wording of former Article 189 (now Article 249 EC).

[6] As will be seen below, in C-354/90 *Fédération Nationale du Commerce Extérieur des Produits Alimentaires (FNCE) and Syndicat National des Négociants et Transformateurs de Saumon v French Republic* [1991] ECR I-5505, the Court preferred to speak of 'immediate enforceability' instead of 'direct effect'.

[7] *Lorenz* (n 3) para 6.

of the aid, *(ii)* after notification, the period of preliminary examination by the Commission[8] and *(iii)* until a final decision is taken, where the Commission initiates the contentious procedure laid down in Article 88(2) EC.

III. PROCEDURAL RULES

In *Lorenz* the Court shed further light on the procedural rules which national courts should apply for safeguarding the direct effect of Article 88(3) EC, last sentence. As a matter of principle, 'it is for the internal legal system of every Member State to determine the legal procedure leading to this result'.[9]

This principle was consistently reaffirmed by the Court in its subsequent case-law, notably in *Rewe Zentralfinanz*[10] and in *Comet*,[11] where the ECJ stated that

> [...] in the absence of community rules on this subject, it is for the domestic legal system of each member state to designate the courts having jurisdiction and to determine the procedural conditions governing actions at law intended to ensure the protection of the rights which citizens have from the direct effect of Community law.

However, as follows from both the principle of equivalence and the principle of effectiveness, '[...] the direct effect of the prohibition in question requires national courts to apply it without any possibility of its being excluded by rules of national law and of any kind whatsoever.'

Pursuant to the principle of equivalence, the national procedural rules applicable cannot be less favourable than those relating to similar actions of a domestic nature.[12] According to the principle of effectiveness, national procedural rules cannot be such as to render practically impossible or excessively difficult the exercise of those rights that individuals derive from Community law.[13]

Such approach lies at the heart of the fundamental principle of effective judicial protection of individuals. Hence, as the Court stated in *Johnston*[14] and *Borelli*,[15]

> the requirement of judicial control of any decision of a national authority reflects a general principle of Community law stemming from the constitutional traditions common to the Member States and has been enshrined in Articles 6 and 13 of the European Convention for the Protection of Human Rights and Fundamental Freedoms.

[8] According to Article 4(5) of Council Regulation (EC) No 659/1999 of 22 March 1999 laying down detailed rules for the application of Article 93 of the EC Treaty [1999] OJ L83/1, which codified the guidance provided in *Lorenz*, the duration of the preliminary period of examination by the Commission is set, in principle, in two months.

[9] *Lorenz* (n 3) para 9.

[10] See *Rewe Zentralfinanz* (n 4).

[11] *Comet* (n 4).

[12] See in this respect, *Rewe Zentralfinanz* (n 4). See also Case 158/80 *Rewe-Handelsgesellschaft Nord* [1981] ECR 1805.

[13] C-261/95 *Palmisani* [1997] ECR-I-4025.

[14] Case 222/84 *Johnston* [1986] ECR 1651.

[15] C-97/91 *Borelli* [1992] ECR I-6313.

It is against this background that the developments that are mentioned below are to be read.

IV. THE RESPECTIVE ROLES OF NATIONAL COURTS AND OF THE COMMISSION

The roles of national courts and of the Commission in ensuring that Member States comply with their obligations under Articles 87 and 88 of the EC Treaty, although complementary, are perfectly distinct.

The ECJ held in *FNCE*[16] that

> [...] the principal and exclusive role conferred on the Commission by Articles [87] and [88] of the Treaty, which is to hold aid to be incompatible with the common market where this is appropriate, is fundamentally different from the role of national courts in safeguarding rights which individuals enjoy as a result of the direct effect of the prohibition laid down in the last sentence of Article [88](3) of the Treaty.

A. Role of the Commission

As the ECJ has emphasised,[17] Article 88 EC provides for a special procedure whereby the Commission keeps aid under constant review and supervision, implying the examination and appraisal of complex economic factors subject to rapid change.

It is to enable the Commission to set in motion the adequate procedure and to monitor aid schemes that the first sentence of Article 88(3) EC provides for an obligation on Member States to notify any plans to grant or alter aid before they are put into effect.

The Commission has an exclusive competence, after conducting an initial review under Article 88(3) EC and at the end of the contentious or consultative procedure[18] under Article 88(2) EC, to rule on the compatibility of an aid with the common market.

The Commission is empowered to order interim measures requiring the Member State to suspend ('suspension injunction') or provisionally to recover ('recovery injunction') the payment of any unlawful aid pending the outcome of the procedure, under the conditions laid down in Article 11(1) and (2) of Council Regulation No 659/1999.[19] The Commission is also entitled to request a Member

[16] *FNCE* (n 6), para 14.

[17] Case 78-76 *Steinike & Weinlig v Federal Republic of Germany* [1977] ECR I-595 and C-39/94 *Syndicat français de l'Express international (SFEI) et al v La Poste et al* [1996] ECR I-3547.

[18] Both expressions have been used by the Court.

[19] See n 8 above.

State, by decision ('information injunction'), to provide all necessary information (Article 10(3) of Council Regulation No 659/1999).[20]

At the end of the procedure, and having examined the compatibility of the aid with the common market, the Commission may, if appropriate, order the recovery of the amount of aid that has already been paid.[21]

However, the Commission cannot order State aid to be repaid solely on the ground that it has not been notified in accordance with Article 88(3) EC.[22]

B. Role of National Courts

As the ECJ recalled in *FNCE*,[23] '[t]he involvement of national courts is the result of the direct effect which the last sentence of Article [88] of the Treaty has been held to have.'

Since the lawfulness of measures giving effect to aid is affected if national authorities act in breach of that sentence '[n]ational courts must offer to individuals in a position to rely on such breach the certain prospect that all the necessary inferences will be drawn, in accordance with their national law'. In the Court's own words, such inferences regard 'the validity of measures giving effect to the aid, the recovery of financial support granted in disregard of that provision and possible interim measures'.[24]

With regard to interim measures, the ECJ explained that:

> Where it is likely that some time will elapse before it gives its final judgment, it is for the national court to decide whether it is necessary to order interim relief such as the suspension of the measures at issue in order to safeguard the interests of the parties.[25]

In performing their task, national courts 'do no more than preserve, until the final decision of the Commission, the rights of individuals faced with a possible breach by State authorities of the prohibition laid down by the last sentence of Article [88](3) of the Treaty'.[26]

However, when national courts rule on such matters, 'they do not thereby decide on the compatibility of the aid with the common market, the final determination

[20] In this respect, Council Regulation No 659/1999 codifies the findings of the ECJ in C-301/87 *French Republic v Commission (Boussac)* [1990] ECR I-307 para 18–20, where the Court held that 'in order for [the system of control of State aid laid down in Article 88 EC] to be effective, that system presupposes that conservatory measures may be taken to counteract any infringements of the rules laid down in Article [83](3).'

[21] *Boussac* (n 20) para 22. See also Article 14 of Council Regulation No 659/1999 (n 8).

[22] *SFEI* (n 17) para 43. See below, as regards the role of national courts.

[23] *FNCE* (n 6) para 11.

[24] ibid, para 12. See also C-17/91 *Lornoy a o v Belgium* [1992] ECR I-6523 paras 30 and 31, however, without reference to interim measures.

[25] *SFEI* (n 17) para 52.

[26] *FNCE* (n 6) para 14.

on that matter being the exclusive responsibility of the Commission, subject to the supervision of the Court of Justice'.[27]

Nevertheless, the ECJ had the opportunity to clarify that

> national courts may have cause to interpret the concept of aid contained in Article 87 to determine whether a State measure introduced without observance of the preliminary examination procedure provided for in Article 88(3) ought to have been subject to that procedure.[28]

In case of doubt as to whether the measure at issue should be qualified as State aid, national courts may seek clarification from the Commission[29] or request that the Court gives a preliminary ruling under Article 234 of the EC Treaty.

Moreover, national courts may be called upon to rule directly on the compatibility of an aid measure with the common market when such aid is covered by a block exemption, such as Council Regulation (EC) No 994/98 of 7 May 1998 on the application of Articles 92 and 93 of the Treaty establishing the European Community to certain categories of horizontal State aid.[30] As stated in its preamble, block exemption regulations can be directly applied by national courts, without prejudice to Article 177 (now Article 234) of the Treaty.[31]

In addition, in response to doubts raised by the national court, the ECJ made clear in *SFEI*[32] that, when a national court and the Commission are concurrently seized of the matter, the initiation by the Commission of a (preliminary or consultative) procedure under Article 88 'cannot release national courts from their duty to safeguard the rights of individuals in the event of a breach of the requirement to give prior notification'.[33]

The sections below aim at addressing the core question mentioned in the title of this chapter.

[27] ibid, para 14; *SFEI* (n 17) para 42. As AG Jacobs held in his Opinion delivered in *SFEI*, para 9: 'The role of the national courts in applying the Treaty rules on aid is an important but subsidiary one.'

[28] *Steinike & Weinlig* (n 17) para 14; *SFEI* (n 17) para 49.

[29] Cooperation between national courts and the Commission in the field of State aid is governed by Commission Notice (95/C 312/07), [1995] OJ C312/8. Assistance from the Commission or the Court in this field is of paramount importance to a national judge, who, most likely, rarely deals with such situation.

[30] [1998] OJ L142/1.

[31] In *Steinike & Weinlig* (n 17) para 10, the Court had already acknowledged that if the parties concerned cannot simply, on the basis of Article 87 EC alone, challenge the compatibility of an aid with EC law before national courts, 'there is this right however where the provisions of Article [87] have been applied by the general provisions provided for in Article [89] or by specific decisions under Article [88](2)'.

[32] *SFEI* (n 17) para 44.

[33] ibid. The Court held, at para 45, the following: 'Any other interpretation would have the effect of encouraging the Member States to disregard the prohibition on implementation of planned aid. Since the Commission can do no more than order further payments to be suspended so long as it has not adopted its final decision on the substance of the matter, the effectiveness of Article [88](3) would be weakened if the fact that the Commission was seized of the matter were to prevent the national courts from drawing all the appropriate conclusions from the infringement of that provision.'

V. MUST NATIONAL COURTS ORDER REPAYMENT OF AID THAT HAS NOT BEEN NOTIFIED TO THE COMMISSION?

This question was raised by the Tribunal de Commerce of Paris in the *SFEI* case.

The Spanish Government, which intervened in the proceedings before the Court, proposed a negative answer. In its opinion, failure to comply with the obligation of prior notification to the Commission, set forth in Article 93(3) EC (now Article 88(3) EC), could only trigger interim measures, which include, in their most severe form, the suspension of payment of the aid. Hence, prior to a decision finding the aid incompatible with the common market, it would not be possible to order repayment. A different solution would imply anticipating a decision on substantive issues.

The French and German Governments, as well as one of the parties to the main proceedings, also submitted that national courts were never required to order repayment in such circumstances.

The ECJ was clear as to the powers of national courts in this respect.[34]

The Court held that the role of a national court seized of an application based on the last sentence of Article 88(3) EC goes beyond that of a judge ruling on an application for interim relief. In fact, the national court is under a duty to provide protection in the final judgment it gives in such a case against the consequences of unlawful implementation of aid.

Moreover, according to the ECJ, the decision of the national court cannot be challenged by the Commission and, in any case, the latter's final decision does not have the effect of regularising ex post facto the measures unlawfully implementing aid.[35] This means that the Commission does not have competence to decide that an aid scheme put into effect contrary to Article 88(3) EC is legal.

Lastly, the ECJ held that a national court requested to order the repayment of aid must grant that application if it finds that the aid was not notified to the Commission, unless, by reason of exceptional circumstances, repayment is inappropriate.

VI. REIMBURSEMENT OF CHARGES LEVIED TO FINANCE UNLAWFUL STATE AID

In *Lornoy*,[36] the Court was asked whether a compulsory contribution constituting a parafiscal charge, levied under the same conditions on both domestic and

[34] *SFEI* (n 17) para 67–71.

[35] Otherwise, the direct effect of that prohibition would be impaired and the interest of individuals, which are to be protected by national courts, would be disregarded (see *FNCE* (n 6) para 16). Indeed, any other interpretation would encourage Member States to disregard the prohibition laid down in Article 88(3) EC. Thus, if national courts could only order suspension of any new payment, aid already granted would subsist until the Commission's final decision finding aid incompatible with the common market and ordering its repayment.

[36] *Lornoy* (n 24).

imported products alike and paid to a fund which operated solely for the benefit of domestic products, was compatible with the Treaty provisions on State aid.

The Court found that a parafiscal charge of this kind might indeed constitute State aid incompatible with the common market if the conditions for the application of Article 87 EC were met. In that respect, the Court also held that it was for the national courts to uphold the rights of those concerned, by drawing all the inferences, in accordance with their national law, as regards the validity of measures implementing the aid in question and the recovery of the financial support granted. However, the Court did not specifically address the question of whether such charges should be refunded to those who had paid them.[37]

The Court also avoided dealing with this issue in *GEMO*.[38] This case concerned the setting up by a French law of a mandatory public service system which provided farmers and slaughterhouses with the free collection and disposal of animal carcasses and dangerous slaughterhouse waste which they produced. This service was carried out by private undertakings financed through State resources, namely by a meat purchase tax imposed mainly on meat retailing supermarkets, but not on small meat retailers.

The purpose of the question thus referred by the *Cour administrative d'appel de Lyon* for preliminary ruling was essentially to determine whether a system such as that at issue in the main proceedings could be regarded as State aid, within the meaning of Article 92(1) of the Treaty (now Article 87 EC).

The French Government, referring to the Court's judgments in *EKW*,[39] *Idéal Tourisme*[40] and *Banks*,[41] claimed that the national court was not entitled to order reimbursement of the tax unduly levied.

Once again, the Court limited its reply to the 'positive' side of the question, by considering that the statutory scheme at issue favoured certain undertakings[42] over others.

[37] Partly because the question was not explicitly raised by the referring court and partly because the ECJ also considered that such compulsory contribution could constitute either a charge having an equivalent effect to custom duties prohibited by Article 12 of the Treaty (now Article 25 EC) or a discriminatory taxation prohibited under Article 95 of the Treaty (now Article 90 EC).

[38] C-126/01 *Ministère de l'Économie, des Finances et de l'Industrie v GEMO* [2003] ECR I-13769.

[39] C-437/97 *Evangelischer Krankenhausverein Wien (EKW)* [2000] ECR I-1157 paras 51–54. The Court considered the question submitted to be wholly irrelevant to the resolution of the disputes in the main proceedings. For that reason, it held that is was unnecessary to reply to it.

[40] C-36/99 *Idéal Tourisme SA v Belgian State* [2000] ECR I-6049 paras 26–29. The Court considered the question put by the referring court manifestly irrelevant to the outcome of the case in the main proceedings and thus did not answer it.

[41] C-390/98 *HJ Banks & Co Ltd v The Coal Authority and Secretary of State for Trade and Industry* [2001] ECR I-6117 paras 77–79, 94 and operative part 2.

[42] These could be the farmers and slaughterhouses that received a free service, the carcass disposal undertakings paid by the State for the operation of the service in question and the small meat retailers which were not required to pay the meat purchase tax.

It should be pointed out that, in *Banks*,[43] the Court went to the point of considering, within the context of the European Coal and Steel Community Treaty, that

> [i]n a situation such as that in the main proceedings, the finding of the existence of unlawful aid, on the ground that it was not authorised by the Commission at the time it was granted, and, as the case may be, of discrimination between producers within the meaning of Article 4(b) of the Treaty, in that some producers were subject to the payment of royalties whereas others were exempted, cannot lead to producers who have been made subject to those royalties being retrospectively exonerated from them.

Therefore, '[p]ersons liable to pay an obligatory contribution cannot rely on the argument that the exemption enjoyed by other persons constitutes State aid in order to avoid payment of that contribution'.

Nevertheless, it is noteworthy that, in a judgment rendered in 1970,[44] the ECJ had already held that, Article 93(2) of the Treaty [now Article 88 (2) EC], by taking into account the connection which may exist between the aid granted by a Member State and the method by which it is financed through State resources,

> does not allow the Commission to isolate the aid as such from the method by which it is financed and to disregard this method if, in conjunction with the aid in its narrow sense, it renders the whole incompatible with the common market.

Consequently, it ruled that 'the aid cannot be considered separately from the effects of its method of financing.'

However, it took more than 30 years for the Court to draw the most important inferences from this early intuition.

It was the Advocates Generals' (hereinafter referred to as 'AG') insistence that finally became the driving force behind the change in the Court's approach.

VII. THE ADVOCATES GENERALS' OPINIONS—PUSHING FORWARD

First, in *FNCE*, AG Jacobs submitted that

> national courts [...] must [...] take any steps which appear necessary in the circumstances to nullify the effects of the breach of the last sentence of Article 93 (3). [...] Where the aid has been financed by charges imposed on undertakings, the national courts may be required to order that those charges be refunded.[45]

Later on, in *Lornoy*, AG Tesauro expressed the view that 'persons liable to parafiscal charges intended to finance State aid may contest the collection thereof, and if appropriate, seek recovery of such charges, where [...] the national authorities

[43] *Banks* (n 41).
[44] Case 47/69 *France v Commission* [1970] ECR 487 paras 4, 8.
[45] Opinion of AG Jacobs in *FNCE* (n 6) para 27.

have applied such charges in breach of the obligations to notify and not to give effect to State aid laid down by Article 93(3) of the Treaty'.[46]

In his Opinion in *GEMO*,[47] AG Jacobs highlighted the fundamental difference between the case at issue and the three cases which had been invoked by the French Government in support of the argument that the referring court should be precluded from granting a refund. Indeed, as the AG submitted, GEMO's main argument was not that the exemption of small meat retailers from the payment of the tax constituted aid, but that the tax at issue was the financing side of a broader State aid scheme in favour of French farmers and slaughterhouses and in favour of carcass disposal undertakings.

The AG added that it follows from *Lorenz* and *FNCE* that there is no basis in Community law for prohibiting a national legal order from granting the right to a refund of the tax in a case where both the notification and the standstill requirement have been infringed:

> It follows, on the contrary, from several leading judgments of the Court that that remedy is not only permissible, but may sometimes even be required by Community law to ensure the effectiveness of the prohibition in the last sentence of Article 68(3) EC.[48]

In the AG's view, under the principle of procedural autonomy,[49] it is for the national legal order to determine precisely which national measures are affected by the invalidity of the measures giving effect to the aid and what consequences that invalidity has for the refund of charges collected on the basis of the measures concerned.[50]

Jacobs therefore concluded[51] that a national court which intends to order the refund of charges collected on the basis of a law adopted in breach of Article 88(3) EC does not violate any of those principles but rather furthers the effectiveness of Community law.

Jacobs' Opinion in *GEMO* constituted, at the time, the most clear invitation to the ECJ to pave the way for accepting the principle that charges collected in breach of State aid rules should be refunded, as a natural consequence of the national courts' obligation to draw, for the protection of individuals' rights, all necessary inferences from a breach by a Member State of the last sentence of Article 88(3) EC.

Nevertheless, it was clear that the AG's main purpose was to criticise the Court's judgment in *Banks* and to support the admissibility of the reference for preliminary ruling in question, despite the French Government's contention to the contrary. For that reason, he did not go further than admitting the possibility, under national law, for a domestic court to order the refund of illegal charges.

46 Opinion of AG Tesauro in *Lornoy* (n 24) Conclusion, ECR I-6544-6545.
47 Opinion of AG Jacobs in *GEMO* (n 38) paras 35–45.
48 ibid, para 39.
49 Limited only by the principles of effectiveness and equivalence.
50 Opinion of AG Jacobs in *GEMO* (n 38) para 44.
51 ibid, para 45.

Therefore, the question of whether (and if yes, under what conditions) Community law itself requires Member States to refund charges levied for the unlawful purpose of financing illegal aid was still left open.

However, in his Opinion in the *Van Calster* case,[52] AG Jacobs was given the opportunity to take a step further.

This case raised precisely the question of the compatibility with Article 88(3) EC of parafiscal charges levied to finance a system of aid that had not been notified to or authorised by the Commission. The case concerned a Belgian law providing for a Fund to be set up with the aim of financing compensation, allowances and other benefits connected with combating animal diseases and improving the hygiene, health and quality of animals and animal products.

The Fund was financed in part through compulsory charges imposed on natural and legal persons who rose, processed, transported, handled, sold or traded animals.

The system was not notified to the Commission and was found to be incompatible with Article 92(2) EC [now Article 87(2) EC], insofar as the compulsory charges were also imposed on animals and products from other Member States.

A new law amended the national regime, in particular in that it no longer provided for a charge in respect of imported animals. The new system of compulsory charges applied retroactively with effect from the date of the entry into force of the old system. After notification, the new legislation was declared compatible with the common market.

Mr Van Calster and others, who were required to pay charges to the 'animal fund', as they bought, slaughtered and sold cattle or marketed meat, sought reimbursement of part of those charges.

In his Opinion, AG Jacobs pointed out to the contrary indications stemming from the Court's decisions and to the need to establish whether Community law requires the repayment of charges levied to finance aid, which has not been notified to, and authorised by the Commission.[53] Indeed, it was not clear from the case law 'what effect the State aid rules have on charges specifically levied to finance aid illegally granted before the aid is authorised'.[54]

After recalling the *FNCE* judgment,[55] AG Jacobs held that national provisions introducing charges specifically levied for the purpose of financing aid fall within those 'measures giving effect to the aid,' the legality of which must be assessed by national courts pursuant to the last sentence of Article 88(3). In broad terms, those charges must be regarded as forming part of the aid regime they serve, as their sole justification is to be found in the regime.[56]

[52] Opinion of AG Jacobs in Joined Cases C-261/01 and C-262/01 *Belgische Staat v Eugène van Calster and Felix Cleeren and Openbaar Slachthuis NV* [2003] ECR I-12249 para 54.

[53] ibid, para 28.

[54] ibid, para 29.

[55] *FNCE* (n 6). AG Jacobs considered *FNCE* to be the closest case to *Van Calster* and a ruling that still seemed in principle correct.

[56] Opinion of AG Jacobs in *Van Calster* (n 52) para 35.

As the AG suggested, this approach might help to explain the conflicting dicta in the case-law on the point of whether the State aid rules apply to charges levied to finance aid illegally granted, and therefore whether such charges are recoverable. In the AG's Opinion,

> the answer may depend on the nature of the link between the charges and the aid. Where the aid is financed out of general taxation, it would seem clearly inappropriate to require the tax to be recoverable. Where however the tax is levied specifically for the purpose of financing the aid, recovery will be appropriate.[57]

He thus concluded that in the latter case, national courts must order reimbursement of the tax or charge. In Jacobs' view, such a conclusion was also justified by the principle of effectiveness: in fact, it may be only the taxpayer who has an incentive to challenge the aid; certainly the State, and the recipient of the aid, will normally have no incentive to do so.[58]

Moreover, the AG was of the opinion that

> the recovery of charges financing an aid scheme is particularly important if the charges may themselves create distortions of competition and trade which would add to and reinforce the distortion produced by the aid itself. That may occur if they are imposed on competitors of the beneficiaries of the aid or if the charges are such as to produce a protective effect and give some form of advantage to the domestic market.[59]

In that case, a double distortion effect may occur when the disturbance to competition resulting from the aid itself is increased by the way such aid is financed.

In the following section, we will assess how the ECJ reacted to the proposals put forward by its AG.

VIII. THE NEW CASE-LAW

In *Van Calster*,[60] the ECJ, drawing inspiration from its 1970 judgment in *France v Commission*,[61] endorsed its AG's Opinion by finding that the method by which an aid is financed may render the entire aid scheme incompatible with the common market. Therefore, an aid cannot be considered separately from the effects of its method of financing, where that method forms an integral part of the measure.[62]

By way of consequence, notification of the aid must also cover the method of financing, inasmuch as that method is an integral part of the planned measure.[63] In that case, the consequences of a failure by the national authorities to comply

[57] ibid, para 36.
[58] ibid, para 38–39.
[59] ibid, para 40.
[60] *Van Calster* (n 52).
[61] *France v Commission* (n 44).
[62] *Van Calster* (n 52) para 49.
[63] ibid, paras 50–51.

with the last sentence of Article 88(3) EC must apply also to that aspect of the aid.[64]

In view of that, the ECJ concluded that

> where an aid measure of which the method of financing is an integral part has been implemented in breach of the obligation to notify, national courts must in principle order reimbursement of charges or contributions levied specifically for the purpose of financing that aid.[65]

Another question referred to the ECJ by the Belgium court in *Van Calster* was whether the Treaty precluded a new State aid scheme from being retroactive in such a way that charges were levied on transactions that took place several years before notification.

On that point, the Court replied that a legislative method consisting in applying retroactively a scheme of aid and charges in order to remedy the consequences of the breach of the obligation to make prior notification of the former aid system is incompatible with Article 88(3) EC.

If such a method were upheld, the Member States could immediately put a plan for State aid into effect without notifying it to the Commission and the consequences of a failure to notify could be avoided by abolishing the measure and reintroducing it simultaneously with retroactive effect.[66]

However, the *Van Calster* judgment left unanswered the question concerning the conditions under which taxes can be regarded as forming an integral part of an aid measure.

That question was first approached in the recent judgments in *Streekgewest Westelijk Noord-Brabant (SWNB)*[67] and *Pape*,[68] whereby the ECJ held that:

> For a tax, or part of a tax, to be regarded as forming an integral part of an aid measure, it must be hypothecated to the aid measure under the relevant national rules, in the sense that the revenue from the tax is necessarily allocated for the financing of the aid. In the event of such hypothecation, the revenue from the tax has a direct impact on the amount of the aid and, consequently, on the assessment of the compatibility of the aid with the common market.[69]

[64] ibid, para 52.

[65] ibid, para 54.

[66] ibid, para 60. The Court also took the opportunity to confirm the position it had adopted in *FNCE* (n 6) and *Lornoy* (n 24), in that the illegality of an aid measure, or a part of it, owing to infringement of the obligation to notify prior to its implementation, is not affected by the fact that the measure has been held to be compatible with the common market by a final decision of the Commission. Such a decision could not have the effect of regularising ex post facto implementing measures which were invalid because they had been taken in breach of the prohibition laid down by the last sentence of Article 88(3) EC (ibid, paras 62–63).

[67] C-174/02 *Streekgewest Westelijk Noord-Brabant (SWNB)* [2005] ECR I-85.

[68] C-175/02 *F J Pape v Minister van Landbouw, Natuurbeheer en Visserij* [2005] ECR I-127.

[69] ibid, para 15 and *SWNB* (n 67) para 26.

In *SWNB,* the Court also addressed the question of whether the last sentence of Article 88(3) EC might be relied on by a litigant who is not necessarily affected by the distortion of cross-border competition arising from the grant of an aid.

To this effect, the ECJ first stated that, where a possible breach by the national authorities of the prohibition of putting aid into effect is invoked by individuals who may rely on it and is established by the national courts, the latter must take all the consequential measures under national law.[70]

It then held that, as regards the national rules relating to the determination of an individual's standing and legal interest in bringing proceedings, 'Community law requires that such rules do not undermine the right to effective judicial protection when exercising the rights conferred by Community law.'[71]

Finally, the Court made clear that an individual may have an interest in relying before the national court on the direct effect of the prohibition on implementation referred to in the last sentence of Article 88(3) EC, not only in order to erase the negative effects of the distortion of competition created by the grant of unlawful aid, but also in order to obtain a refund of a tax levied in breach of that provision. In the latter case, the question of whether an individual has been affected by the distortion of competition arising from the aid measure is irrelevant; the only fact to be taken into consideration is that the individual is subject to a tax which is an integral part of a measure implemented in breach of the abovementioned prohibition.[72]

IX. CONCLUSION

More than 40 years after *Costa v ENEL*,[73] the problems and doubts arising from the direct effect of the last sentence of Article 88(3) EC and from the resulting role of national courts in enforcing individual rights affected by unlawful aid continued to receive a number of answers from the ECJ, which contributed to clarify the scope of intervention of national courts in ensuring that effect.

However, as for one of the most recent topics addressed by the Court—namely whether and under what conditions charges levied specifically to finance unlawful aid should be refunded—some questions still remain unclear.

Indeed, it is to be assessed on a case by case basis if a tax or a parafiscal charge (or part of it) can be considered as 'hypothecated' to an aid measure in such a way that the illegality of the aid which has been granted entails the illegality of the tax or charge and the obligation to refund it.

The possible discrepancies between the different linguistic versions of the ECJ's rulings do not help to clarify the legal situation in this regard. For instance,

[70] *SWNB* (n 67) para 17.
[71] ibid, para 18.
[72] ibid, para 19.
[73] *Costa* (n 2).

the French version of the *SWNB* and *Pape* judgments use the expression 'lien d'affectation contraignant', whose meaning is no less ambiguous than the corresponding 'hypothecated' in the English version.

Moreover, the Court takes the precaution of adding that its pronouncements apply 'in principle', which leaves to the practice of application to determine how the rule and the exceptions will work.

The ECJ judgment in *Pearle*[74] illustrates how important the sources of legal uncertainty in this field may be.

In that case, the questions for preliminary ruling referred to the ECJ by the Netherlands Supreme Court were raised in the context of proceedings concerning the lawfulness of charges imposed on its members by a public body (the Central Industry Board for Skilled Trades—the 'Board'), with a view to funding a collective advertising campaign for the benefit of undertakings in the optical services sector.

In its ruling, the Court recalled that for the advantages conferred on the recipients to be capable of being categorised as aid within the meaning of Article 87(2) EC, they must, on the one hand, be granted directly or indirectly through State resources and, on the other hand, be imputable to the State. The Court considered that the first of these conditions was not met in the circumstances of the case, for the following two main reasons.

First, the monies used for the purpose of funding the advertising campaign were collected by the Board from its members who benefited from the campaign by means of compulsory levies earmarked for the organisation of that campaign. Since the costs incurred by the public body for the purpose of that campaign were offset in full by the levies imposed on the undertakings benefiting therefrom, the Board's action did not tend to create an 'advantage', which would constitute an additional burden for the State.

Second, the advertising campaign was not the initiative of the Board, but of a private association of opticians, and was put into effect for a purely commercial purpose determined by the trade and which had nothing to do with a policy determined by the national authority.

As regards the first reason, it must be recognised that the extent to which the burden and the advantage are offset is sometimes extremely difficult to assess.

Concerning the second reason, it may be asked whether the existence of State aid always requires the presence of a policy determined by public authorities.

It follows from the foregoing that national courts are called upon to play an increasingly important role in reviewing the legality of aid granted by Member States and in upholding the individual rights of those concerned. However, such a complex task may become even more intricate by legal uncertainty as shown

[74] C-345/02 *Pearle BV, Hans Prijs Optiek Franchise BV and Rinck Opticiëns BV v Hoofdbedrijfschap Ambachten* [2004] ECR I-7139.

above. National courts will therefore need guidance from the Commission and enlightenment from the Court.

In this respect, one might ask whether the setting up, in the field of State aid, of a network bringing closer national courts, national competition authorities and the Commission would allow for a more effective and homogeneous enforcement of Community law.

Depending on the success of the modernisation of EC antitrust policy, a Community legislative framework for decentralisation under the aegis of the Commission in the area of State aid (similar to Regulation No 1/2003 for State aid) could contribute to increasing efficiency in the enforcement of Articles 87 and 88 EC. Or is this mere science fiction?

12

Regional Selectivity and State Aid—the Azores *Case*[*]

I. INTRODUCTION

THE RECENT JUDGMENT of the European Court of Justice (hereinafter the 'ECJ' or the 'Court') in *Portuguese Republic v Commission (Azores)*[1] highlighted the conditions under which tax measures adopted by a regional authority should be considered as State aid.

The importance of this judgment is that it made clear, contrary to the Commission's practice, that not all advantages granted to undertakings by a regional authority are to be considered as State aid. Moreover, the Court laid down the principles that may guide the Member States and the Commission in deciding whether a particular measure taken by a regional authority must be considered a State aid and assessed as such.

II. THE GENERAL CRITERIA IN ARTICLE 87(1) EC FOR RECOGNISING STATE AID

Article 87(1) EC considers in principle any aid granted by a Member State which distorts or threatens to distort competition to be incompatible with the common market, 'save as otherwise provided in this Treaty'. The Treaty provision does not precisely define the notion of State aid; it nevertheless provides some of the elements that contribute to such a definition. The case-law of the ECJ filled the existing gap.

It follows from both the Treaty and the jurisprudence that a State aid measure can be deemed to exist where the following cumulative criteria are met:

a. The measure in question confers on the recipients a financial advantage, relieving them of charges normally borne by their own budgets. This can be made, eg, through the granting of subsidies or of a guarantee that makes it

[*] First published in 'New Developments in European State Aid Law 2006', Proceedings of the 4th Experts' Forum held in Brussels on 18 and 19 May 2006, *European State Aid Law Quarterly* (Brussels, European State Aid Law Institute and Lexxion Verlagsgesellshaft mbH, 2006) 15–23.

[1] C-88/03 *Portuguese Republic v Commission (Azores)* [2006] ECR I-7115.

possible for the beneficiaries to have access to credit in better conditions than the current ones, or through tax or other State charges' reductions.[2]

b. This advantage is granted by a Member State or through public resources. Tax reductions granted by regional authorities, leading to lower State revenue, might satisfy this criterion.[3]
c. The measure in question must be selective in that it favours certain undertakings or the production of certain goods. If the measure can be justified by the nature or the general scheme of the tax system, it cannot be considered selective.[4]
d. The measure distorts or threatens to distort competition and affects trade between Member States.

III. THE ISSUE OF REGIONAL SELECTIVITY IN THE CONTEXT OF STATE AID

The notion of regional or geographic selectivity should be clearly distinguished from that of material selectivity. The latter applies when a State measure favours certain undertakings, or undertakings in a certain industry or sector of the economy. By contrast, regional selectivity refers to a situation where a regime more favourable than the one prevailing in the rest of the country applies to undertakings operating within a certain limited area of the territory.

Since selectivity is a core issue in State aid cases, it is crucial to determine, for the purpose of establishing whether the rules on State aids apply, under what conditions a measure, eg a fiscal measure, taken by an autonomous and constitutionally competent region of a Member State, can be considered selective, and therefore a State aid measure.

Tax systems are, in general, not uniform: different rates of taxation can apply to different sources of income or in different regions of the country. Within this context, one can then ask, as Advocate General Geelhoed did in his Opinion in the *Azores* case,[5] 'in what circumstances do variations in the national tax rate adopted solely for a designated geographical area of a member State fall under the definition of State aid'.

In order to avoid any contamination of the question of regional selectivity by the issue of material selectivity, the question should be formulated with more precision:

> Can a non-selective tax measure [i.e. that applies to all the undertakings operating in the geographical area in question irrespective of the sector of the economy] taken by an autonomous regional authority become selective when compared with similar measures

[2] Eg C-143/99 *Adria Wien* [2001] ECR I-8365 paras 38–39. As regards tax reductions, the Commission, in its Notice on the application of the State aid rules to measures relating to direct business taxation (Official Journal C 384, 10.12.1998, 3–9), emphasised that a loss of tax revenue is equivalent to the consumption of State resources in the form of fiscal expenditure (para 10).

[3] Case 248/84 *Germany v Commission* [1987] ECR 4013.

[4] See case 173/73 *Italy v Commission* [1974] ECR 709.

[5] *Azores* (n 1); Opinion delivered on 20 October 2005.

taken by the central authorities of the same Member State and thus be considered as State aid?

IV. THE OVERALL CONTEXT OF THE PROBLEM

A. The Emergence of Regions in the Constitutional Framework of the EU

The issue of regional selectivity for the purpose of application of the rules on State aid gains momentum at a time when devolution of powers, including in taxation, to decentralised bodies and Member States' regions becomes a kind of general movement characterising the constitutional evolution of several Member States. Recognising the legitimacy and the importance of such movement, the successive amendments of the Treaty have expressed the emergence of Regions in the constitutional framework of the EU.

First of all, the Maastricht Treaty proclaimed the subsidiarity principle as one of the basic principles of institutional organisation of the European Community, implying that 'decisions are taken [...] as closely as possible to the citizen' (see Article 5 EC and Article 1 TEU). It also established the Committee of the Regions, representing regional and local bodies of Member States, and included it among the institutions and organs of the Community (now Article 7 EC). Articles 263 to 265 EC, as amended by the Treaty of Nice, establish that the members of the Committee are representatives of regional and local bodies who either hold a regional or local electoral mandate, or are politically accountable to an elected assembly. Those Treaty provisions entrust this body with important advisory status.

Thirdly, the Maastricht Treaty amended Article 146 EEC (now Article 203 EC) in order to allow a national government to be represented by a regional minister at the Council meetings. Lastly, the case-law expressly admitted a regional body to challenge Commission decisions addressed to the respective Member State, insofar as such decisions affect the way that the regional body exercises its own powers.[6]

B. The Allocation of Powers in Tax Matters

The issue of application of State aid rules to tax measures adopted by regional authorities within a Member State is also influenced by the question of the distribution of fiscal powers between the Community and Member States.

[6] See T-214/95 *Het Vlaamse Gewest v Commission* [1998] ECR II-717; cases T-32/98 and T-41/98 *Nederlandse Antillen v Commission* [2000] ECR II-201. See also MS Prieto, *Las Comunidades Autónomas ante el Tribunal de Justicia y el Tribunal de Primera Instancia de las Comunidades Europeas* (La Coruña, Tirant lo Blanch, 2003).

As is generally recognised, direct taxation is, in principle, a competence of Member States. The organisation of national systems of direct taxation is considered as an inherent attribute of national sovereignty, and the EC legislator does not have, in principle, to intervene in such matters.

Of course, the competences of Member States in the field of economics must be exercised in compliance with Community law. The question is then whether the use of fiscal powers by the Member States, namely in what concerns the devolution of powers on tax matters to regionally competent authorities, may deprive the rules of the Treaty on State aids of their effectiveness.

C. The Commission Notice on Direct Taxation

The Commission Notice on the application of the State aid rules to measures relating to direct business taxation[7] (hereinafter the 'Notice', the 'Commission Notice' or the 'Notice on Direct Taxation') set guidelines for clarifying the application of State aid rules to tax measures adopted by Member States. It sought, in particular, to provide clarification to the question whether a tax measure can be qualified as aid under Article 92(1) of the EC Treaty (now Article 87(1) EC).[8]

According to the Commission Notice, the main criterion in applying Article [87(1)] to a tax measure is that the measure confers to certain undertakings in the Member State an exception to the application of the tax system. The common system applicable should thus first be determined. Only then should we examine whether the exception to the system or differentiations within that system are justified 'by the nature or general scheme' of the tax system. If this is not the case, then State aid is involved (paragraph 16).

In the Commission's view, only measures the scope of which extends to the entire territory of the State, escape the abovementioned specificity criterion. As the Commission held, measures which are regional or local in scope may favour certain undertakings (paragraph 17). However, the Notice did not go further than that in assessing the very nature of the problem of regional selectivity and the conditions in which non selective regional tax measures can escape being characterised as State aid.

D. The Case-Law of the Community Courts

On several occasions, the ECJ dealt with the question of the application of State aid rules to measures taken by regional authorities in Member States. However, the previous judgments of the Court or the Advocates General's Opinions did not, in

[7] See n 2 above.

[8] See the Notice (n 2) para 2.

fact, address the issue of whether a specific tax measure adopted by an autonomous regional authority should necessarily be held to constitute a State aid.

It is true that in *Germany v Commission*,[9] the ECJ, referring to 'any aid granted by a member state or through state resources in any form whatsoever', set out the principle that Article 87(1) applies to all aid financed by public resources, including aid granted by regional or local bodies of the Member States. However, such statement is not helpful for the purpose of establishing whether a tax measure adopted by a regional authority of a Member State is or is not an aid under Article 87(1). On the contrary, it assumes that the question has already received a positive answer, implying that the relevant conditions laid down in Article 87(1) were satisfied. In that case, the aid granted by the Land North Rhine-Westphalia applied only in *some* assisted areas of its territory. The situation is completely different when the measure in question applies without discrimination to *all the undertakings* in the *entire territory* under the jurisdiction of a regional authority.

A later case, *Germany v Commission*,[10] for its part, concerned a national legislation granting tax deductions to *certain* undertakings (comprising new capital companies with no more than 250 employees), which had both their registered office and their central administration in one of the new *Länder*, or in Berlin. Once again, no inference could be drawn from this judgment to a case where a tax reduction is applied, without selectivity, to all the undertakings in the entire territory under the jurisdiction of a regional authority.

Other cases, such as *Commission v Italy*[11] and *Exécutif Regional Wallon v Commission*,[12] also concerned aid granted by a regional authority to *certain* undertakings in *certain* sectors of the economy within the region. Therefore, the element of selectivity was clearly present.

In Joined Cases *Administración del Estado v Juntas Generales de Guipúzcoa*,[13] the ECJ was asked to rule on the compatibility with former Article 92 EC of the provincial laws ('normas forales') adopted by three authorities belonging to the Autonomous Community of the Basque Country. Those laws contained urgent fiscal measures intended to aid investment and stimulate economic activity, thus giving certain undertakings and natural persons subject to the tax system of the Basque territories a number of advantages, which the undertakings and natural persons subject to the common system did not have.

In his Opinion, Advocate General A Saggio considered that the laws adopted by the Juntas Forales should be characterised as 'aid' within the meaning of Article 92 of the Treaty, since they were selective in nature. However, the case was withdrawn before the Court had to issue its ruling.

[9] C-248/84 *Germany v Commission* [1987] ECR 4013.
[10] C-156/98 *Germany v Commission* [2000] ECR I-6857.
[11] C-130/83 *Commission v Italy* [1984] ECR 2849.
[12] C-62/87 *Exécutif Regional Wallon v Commission* [1988] ECR 1573.
[13] Joined Cases C-400/97, C-401/97 and C-402/97 *Administración del Estado v Juntas Generales de Guipúzcoa.*

In any case, one should bear in mind that the situation under consideration in that case was far from the same than the one in question in the *Azores* case. Indeed, the tax concessions granted by the Spanish autonomous regions were, in fact, selective in that they were granted only to undertakings meeting certain requirements set out in the applicable legislation, concerning the residence for tax purposes, or a considerable percentage of the total volume of transactions in the Basque territory. Moreover, the Advocate General underlined that the reasons given by the Basque Authorities for the adoption of the measures at issue showed that they were short-term measures which aimed at improving the competitiveness of the companies to which they applied, so as to meet the challenges of the market; they did not reflect any specificity of the territory in question which would require fiscal treatment different from that in force in the rest of the Spanish territory. The scheme which resulted from the provisions in question in fact satisfied only the desire to favour investment in the 'Historic Territories' (see paragraph 38 of the Opinion).

Nothing of this corresponds to the situation of the Azores region, which, as will be developed hereunder, cannot be considered as 'merely a matter of form' (paragraph 37 of the Opinion).

V. THE *AZORES* CASE: THE SPECIFIC CONTEXT

Data helps us understand why the Azores are a specific case deserving the appropriate special treatment. The Azores are an archipelago consisting of nine islands scattered along more than 600 kilometres of the Atlantic Ocean, 1500 kilometres away from the nearest mainland territory, with a total area slightly exceeding 2.300 km^2. The islands were formed by the action of numerous volcanoes that erupted in the region. Seismic activity is frequent, and the last volcanic eruption occurred in the late 1960s. The climate is rigorous; most of the year the islands are under dense fog, heavy rains and strong winds.

The economic indicators characterise a situation which is clearly one of the most depressed in the EU: 15 per cent of the working population is directly employed in agriculture and fisheries; 30 per cent works for the Government. The GDP per inhabitant being 55 per cent of the EU-15 average, the Azores were, in 1999, the fifth poorest region in Europe.

Taking into consideration all these factors, the Portuguese Constitution of 2 April 1976 considered the archipelagos of Azores and Madeira as autonomous regions, with their own political and administrative statutes, and self-governing institutions directly elected by the people within the region: a regional government and a regional parliament, with ample legislative, regulatory, political, administrative, financial and fiscal powers.

On the fiscal and financial side, the regions are empowered to create and collect their own local taxes and to adapt the national tax system to the regional specificities. The regional budget is thus financed by the regions' own tax revenues and, as required by a principle of active national solidarity, by transfers of funds from the State budget, calculated according to a formula set out in Article 30 of the framework law on the finances of the autonomous regions (Law No 13/98 of 24 February 1998).[14] This law lays down the general principles and objectives of regional fiscal and financial autonomy. According to Article 37 thereof, the Legislative Assemblies of the Autonomous Regions (Azores and Madeira) are entitled to reduce national income and corporation tax (and VAT) rates by up to 30 per cent. The regional legislature of Azores exercised this competence by Regional Legislative Decree No 2/99/A of 30 December 1999, approving a reduction of 15 per cent (later 20 per cent) to the national rate of income tax and of 30 per cent to the rate corporation tax.

It is important to note that Article 299(2) EC expressly recognised the peculiarity of the situation of some EU outermost regions and established a special regime for them. As a matter of fact, Article 299(2) sets out the principle that the provisions of the Treaty apply to those regions. However, taking into account the structural social and economic situation of the French overseas departments, the Azores, Madeira and the Canary Islands, which is compounded by their remoteness, insularity, small size, difficult topography and climate, economic dependence on a few products, the permanence and combination of which severely restrain their development, it empowered the EC institutions to adopt specific measures aimed, in particular, at laying down the conditions of application of the Treaty to those regions, including common policies. Among the areas that are to be taken into account when adopting those specific measures, the Treaty specially mentions State aids.

VI. THE COMMISSION'S APPROACH

On December 11, 2002 the Commission adopted its Decision 2003/442/EC, on the part of the scheme adapting the national tax system to the specific characteristics of the Autonomous Region of the Azores which concerns reductions in the rates of income and corporate tax[15] (hereinafter the 'Decision' or the 'Commission Decision'). It took the view that the reductions in the tax rates concerned constituted, for firms situated in that particular region in Portugal, an advantage which other undertakings wishing to carry out similar economic operations in other areas of Portugal could not enjoy. Therefore, those reductions constituted State aid within the meaning of Article 87(1) EC.

The Commission cites its decision-making practice as recalled in its Notice on Direct Taxation (paragraph 17), according to which only measures whose scope extends to the entire territory of the State escape the specificity

[14] Diário da República I, series A, No 46, 24.2.1998, 746.

[15] [2003] OJ L150/52.

criterion laid down in Article 87(1) EC. According to the Commission Decision (paragraph 26),

> it follows both from the general scheme of the Treaty, which concerns aid granted by the State or through State resources, and from the fundamental role the central authorities of the Member States play in defining the political and economic environment in which firms operate, thanks to the measures they adopt, the services they provide and possibly the financial transfers they make, that the framework in which such a comparison should be made is the economy of the Member State.

The Commission also took the view that, in defining aid, a distinction based solely on the body that decides the measure—ie, whether the authority is regional or central—would be unsatisfactory, since such a distinction would compromise the objective nature of the concept of aid (Decision, paragraph 27).

As regards the Autonomous Region of Azores, the Commission pointed out the fact that this case did not concern 'a mechanism that would allow all local authorities of a particular level (regions, districts or others) to introduce and levy local taxes with no reference at all to national taxation' (Decision, paragraph 31). The Commission seems hence to take the view that only when the devolution of powers to decentralised authorities is perfectly symmetrical across the country is it possible to escape considering the exercise of such powers in the fiscal field as constituting derogation from the national tax system. Indeed, since the Commission appeared to believe that 'the reference framework' for the purpose of establishing the existence of a fiscal advantage is, in any case, the national context within the Member State, it would not be possible, in the circumstances of the case, to define a 'normal taxation' by reference to which 'the very existence of an advantage can [...] be established' (Decision, paragraph 26).

In the Commission's view, the reductions in the rate of income tax applicable in the Azores could also not be justified by the nature or the general scheme of the Portuguese tax system, since they did not derive from the application of principles such as proportionality or progressive taxation, and the objectives of regional development attributed to them could not be considered inherent to the Portuguese tax system (Decision, paragraph 33).

The Commission therefore considered that the measures in question constituted operating aid (Decision, paragraphs 34–35). Nevertheless, referring to its Guidelines on national regional aid,[16] it stated that, insofar as the reductions in the rates of income and corporation tax were applicable to firms that operated outside the financial sector, such aid could be regarded as compatible with the common market under the derogation in Article 87(3)(a) EC. In regard to undertakings operating in the financial sector, those reduced rates were, however, not considered justified by their proportionality and contribution to regional development (Decision, paragraphs 38–40).

[16] [1998] OJ C74/9, as amended on 9 September 2000 ([2000] OJ C258/5).

VII. THE PROPOSED CRITERIA FOR DECISION-MAKING

A. The Arguments Underlying the Position of the Portuguese Republic

The main line of argumentation of the Portuguese Republic against the Commission Decision was based on the consideration that the fiscal regime of Azores did not constitute State aid in that it was not selective, since it applied to all undertakings in the region without distinction; and, in any event, the reductions in the charges borne by those undertakings were justified by the nature or the structure of the Portuguese tax system.

The Portuguese Government submitted, first of all, that the Commission was wrong to take the whole of Portuguese territory as the reference framework. Member States are free to decide, according to their constitutions, how to allocate fiscal powers between central authorities and decentralised bodies, either federal or regional. In this context, the rationale for fiscal autonomy is the same as for political autonomy; therefore to go against this basic evidence would be to oppose constitutional sovereignty of Member States. According to the Portuguese Constitution, Azores and Madeira are the only autonomous regions, bearing similar characteristics as outermost European insular regions, which justifies that they are granted such ample legislative, political and administrative powers.

As Nicolaides put it,[17] a

> measure is selective or discriminatory [only] if, without objective justification, it does not apply uniformly to all the firms it can potentially apply to. Since a measure adopted by a regional authority has, by definition, limited regional scope, it can be selective only if it applies partially to firms within the region in question.

In this context, the relevant benchmark should be the uniformity or not of the tax measure within the region, not the level of the national tax rate.

Contrary to the Commission's position, the particular tax regime of Azores (and Madeira) did not constitute derogation or an exception to the national tax regime, but rather the exercise of the constitutional sovereignty of the competent authorities. In those conditions, it should be irrelevant whether this constitutional sovereignty is exercised by way of 'regional taxes' or through a modulation of 'national taxes'.

As regards the argument inferred by the Commission from the existence of financial transfers and other advantages, eg investments in infrastructures, granted to the region by the central authorities, the Portuguese Government argued, first, that there is no link or any kind of correlation between such transfers or infrastructural investments, on the one side, and the tax reductions in the region, on the other side. In fact, the former are the expression of the global economic, financial and budget policy of the State, and do not constitute any kind

[17] P Nicolaides, 'Fiscal State Aid in the EU: The Limits of Tax Autonomy' (2004) 27 (3) *World Competition* 365, 393.

of compensation for the tax reductions. Moreover, any financial transfers to the Autonomous Regions are made according to a pre-established formula set in the framework law on the finances of the Autonomous Regions, and the region is, in any event, responsible for the financial consequences of its tax policy within the applicable general legal framework.

In this context, the recent case-law of the ECJ concerning the relationship between an aid scheme and the way it is financed is of the utmost importance. Indeed, in a line of case-law ranging from *Van Carlsten*[18] and *Pearle*[19] to *SWNB*[20] and *Pape*,[21] the Court made clear that an aid cannot be considered separately from the effects of its method of financing, where that method forms an integral part of the measure.[22] In *SWNB* and *Pape*, the Court clarified that

> [f]or a tax, or part of a tax, to be regarded as forming an integral part of an aid measure, it must be hypothecated to the aid measure under the relevant national rules, in the sense that the revenue from the tax is necessarily allocated for the financing of the aid.[23]

None of these circumstances was present in the *Azores* case.

Finally, the Portuguese Republic submitted that, apart from the question of selectivity, the tax reductions in question resulted directly from the founding principles of the Portuguese tax system, in particular the principles of redistribution and national solidarity. They also satisfied the conditions for application of Article 299(2) EC and, moreover, were justified by the nature, structure and objectives of the Portuguese tax system in that they contributed to the allocation of the tax burden in accordance with the ability to pay, with the aim of redistribution. In this regard, and contrary to the Commission's position,[24] the Portuguese Republic took the view that there is no reason to distinguish between internal and external objectives of the tax system and, moreover, to identify the former with the sole purpose of collecting revenues.[25]

[18] Joined Cases C-261/01 and C-262/01 *Van Carlsten and Cleeren* [2003] ECR I-12249.

[19] C-345/02 *Pearle* [2004] ECR I-7139.

[20] C-174/02 *Streekgewest Westlijk Noord-Braban (SWNB)* [2005] ECR I-85.

[21] C-175/02 *Pape* [2005] ECR I-127.

[22] On this issue, see JL da Cruz Vilaça, 'How far Should National Courts Go in Drawing all the Necessary Inferences from the Last Sentence of Article 88(3) EC?', *New Developments in European State Aid Law* 2005, Proceedings of the 3rd Experts' Forum held in Brussels on 26 and 27 May 2005, *EstAL Quarterly* (Brussels, European State Aid Law Institute and Lexxion Verlagsgesellshaft mbH, 2005) 45, 51.

[23] *SWNB* (n 20) para 26; *Pape* (n 21) para 15.

[24] In its Notice on the application of State aid rules to measures relating to direct business taxation (n 2), the Commission held that '[a] distinction must be made between, on the one hand, the external objectives assigned to a particular tax scheme (in particular social or regional objectives) and, on the other, the objectives that are inherent in the tax system itself. The whole purpose of the tax system is to collect revenue to finance State expenditure' (paragraph 26). This approach seems to be based on a too narrow conception of the objectives of a tax system.

[25] The same opinion is shared by P Rossi-Maccanico, 'State Aid Review of Member States' Measures Relating to Direct Business Taxation' (2004) 2 *Eur State Aid Law* 229. The Author suggests that '[t]he external objectives have been consistently taken as reference by the Court to expand the notion of

B. The Criteria Proposed by the United Kingdom

In support of the Portuguese Republic, the United Kingdom Government argued in its submissions before the Court that where, as in the *Azores* case, the legislature of an autonomous region sets tax rates which apply uniformly across the region concerned, but which are lower than those applied by decision of the national legislature to other parts of the Member States, the selectivity of the measure cannot be inferred simply from the fact that the other regions are subject to a different level of taxation, on the basis of an asymmetric devolution of fiscal powers.

In this context, the United Kingdom submitted that, before considering regional tax rates which are lower than national tax rates as selective and therefore qualifying them as State aid, the Commission should have regard to the following factors or criteria:

— The degree of constitutional autonomy, including jurisdiction in tax matters, of the infra-State authority that established the reduced tax rate.
— The fact that the decision on the reduced tax rate is taken by a body which is elected by, or otherwise democratically accountable before the people of the region.
— The fact that the financial consequences of the decision are borne by the region, without being offset by subsidies or contributions from other regions or from the central government.

C. The Advocate General's Opinion

In his Opinion delivered on the 20th October 2005, Advocate General Geelhoed rightly recognised that the *Azores* case raised an important question, which went beyond the circumstances of the case: what principles apply in assessing whether variations in national tax rates adopted solely for a designated geographical area of a Member State fall within the scope of the Community State aid rules? Since the question had never received an answer from the Court, the formulation of a test or principles of assessment were thus indispensable.[26]

According to the Advocate General,[27] the crucial question to be answered concerned the point of reference that should be used to assess the selectivity of a geographically limited national tax rate variation and hence its nature as State aid. If, as was the Commission's position, one should in all cases take as a framework of reference the entire territory of the Member State, then *prima facie* all national

inherent objective of a tax system to include external objectives that are absorbed by the tax system as guiding principles, even when they are not necessary to the existence of a tax system' (243).

[26] *Azores* (n 1); Opinion of AG Geelhoed, paras 42–43.

[27] ibid, paras 45–47.

tax variations limited to a geographic area of a Member State would qualify as geographically selective and the State aid rules would apply.[28]

If, however, in certain cases the geographic area in which the variations apply is taken as reference point, such variations will not be selective if they apply to all undertakings operating within that area. In that case, the only Treaty instruments available to reduce distortions of competition within the common market resulting from different national legislations will be Article 94 EC and Articles 96 and 97 EC.

In tackling this question, the Advocate General distinguished three scenarios when reductions in national tax rates for a geographic area within a Member State are at stake:[29]

— In the first scenario, the central government unilaterally decides that the national tax rate should be reduced within a defined geographic area: the measure is selective.
— In the second scenario, all local authorities at a particular level (regions, districts or others) have the autonomous power to set the tax rate for their territorial jurisdiction: in the absence of any nation-wide rule, there is no exception or derogation to the general tax system, and thus no selectivity.
— The third scenario is somewhat more sophisticated: a tax rate lower than the national tax rate is decided upon by a local authority and applicable only within the territory of that local authority.

In the third scenario, which applies to Azores, the crucial question, according to the Advocate General, is whether the lower tax rate results from a decision taken by a local authority that is 'truly autonomous' from the central government of the Member State. By 'truly autonomous', the Advocate General meant institutionally, procedurally and economically autonomous:

— *Institutionally autonomous*: the decision is taken by a local authority with its own constitutional, political and administrative status separate from that of the central government.
— *Procedurally autonomous*: the decision is taken without direct intervention of the central government in the procedure of setting the tax rate and without any obligation on the part of the local authority to take into consideration the interests of the central State.

[28] P Nicolaides, 'State Aid and Taxation by Sub-National Authorities' (2005) *New Developments in European State Aid Law*, Proceedings of the 3rd Expert's Forum held in Brussels on 26 and 27 May 2005, *EStAL Quarterly* (Brussels, European State Aid Law Institute and Lexxion Verlagsgesellshaft mbH, 2005) 19, 24, expressed the same in the following way: 'the Decision concerning taxation in the Azores reveals that *[in the Commission's opinion]* if a regional measure is a deviation from a national measure, it will be found to be inter-regionally selective, even if it is not intra-regionally selective'.

[29] *Azores* (n 1); Opinion of AG Geelhoed, paras 50–56.

— *Economically autonomous*: the lower tax rate applicable within the region is not cross-subsidised or financed by central government, so the economic consequences of these reductions are borne by the region itself.

If all of these types of autonomy are present, the decision of the local or regional authority cannot be classified as 'selective' for Article 87(1) EC purposes. In the Advocate General's view, whenever 'true autonomy' exists, there is no reason, on either logical or doctrinal grounds, to distinguish between 'symmetrical' and 'asymmetrical' devolution of tax powers. As he rightly pointed out, the choice of which, if any, regions within a Member State should have devolved tax powers 'is evidently one of constitutional policy heavily dependent on the unique historical and economic circumstances of that region'.[30]

At the same time, the Advocate General held that there is no reason to fear the rules on State aid being circumvented by Member States' choosing to alter the internal organisation of competence for taxation within their territories. Indeed, a merely formal empowerment of regional authorities to act in the taxation sphere, subject to conditions defined by the central government and without true autonomous decision-making, would not be enough to remove a measure from the scope of Article 87(1) EC. Finally, the Advocate General considered that the argument taken by the Commission from the need of legal certainty for Member States did not justify extending the scope of Article 87(1) beyond its purpose.

Applying the guidelines exposed so far to the instant case, the Advocate General found that the tax reductions applied within the Azores region satisfied the selectivity criterion and thus constituted State aid. The Advocate General first acknowledged that the decision resulting in the contested tax reductions was taken in an institutionally autonomous manner. However, as regards procedural autonomy, he emphasised that those reductions had been taken on the basis of the constitutional principles of national solidarity, cooperation between the State and the autonomous regions, redistribution and reciprocity extending to the whole national territory, thus contradicting, in his view, the principle of true procedural autonomy.

The Advocate General also contested that the Autonomous Region of the Azores made its tax decisions in a manner truly economically autonomous, given the existence of financial transfers from the State budget that act as countervailing funding to correct inequalities in economic conditions, within the framework of cooperation between national and regional authorities to achieve a balanced economic development.[31] Finally, and basing his considerations on the Commission Notice on Direct Taxation[32] and on the judgment of the Court of

[30] *Azores* (n 1); Opinion of AG Geelhoed, para 60.
[31] *Azores* (n 1); Opinion of AG Geelhoed, paras 71–72.
[32] Commission Notice (n 2) paras 16, 23, 26.

First Instance in *Diputación Foral de Álava*,[33] he found that the tax reductions at issue were not justified by the nature and the general scheme of the tax system.

VIII. THE JUDGMENT OF THE COURT IN THE *AZORES* CASE

In its judgment in the *Azores* case, the ECJ, although dismissing the action, made a number of important pronouncements, which ran counter to the apparently established decision practice of the Commission in this field and laid the ground for a new approach towards the question of regional selectivity.

The Court started its assessment by recalling its judgment in *Adria-Wien Pipeline*, where it stated that, as regards selectivity, 'which is a constituent factor in the concept of State aid',[34] the

> question to be determined is whether, under a particular statutory scheme, a State measure is such as to favour certain undertakings or the production of certain goods [...] in comparison with other undertakings which are in a legal and factual situation that is comparable in the light of the objective pursued by the measure in question.[35]

This also constituted the starting point to the Portuguese Republic's reasoning.

According to the Court,[36] such an analysis is also required in respect of a measure adopted not by the national legislature but by an infra-State authority, in order to determine whether, within the context of a particular legal system, that measure constitutes an advantage for certain undertakings in comparison with others which are in a comparable situation. In this respect, the ECJ confirmed that the reference framework has a particular importance in the case of tax measures, since the very existence of an advantage may be established only when compared with 'normal' taxation. In that context, the 'normal' tax rate is the rate in force in the geographical area constituting the reference framework.

In that connection, the Court held that the reference framework need not necessarily be defined as coinciding with the limits of the Member State concerned, so that a measure applicable only in a limited geographical area of that Member State and conferring an advantage in only one part of the national territory is not selective on that ground alone for the purposes of Article 87(1) EC. In order to establish the conditions under which the area of jurisdiction of an infra-State body, and not the country as whole, constitutes the relevant context for the assessment of selectivity of the tax measures, the Court used the notion of 'sufficient autonomy', as one corresponding to the concept of 'true autonomy' used by the Advocate General.

[33] Joined Cases T-346/99, T-347/99 and T-348/99 *Diputación Foral de Álava* [2002] ECR II-4259.

[34] *Azores* (n 1) para 54.

[35] C-143/99 *Adria-Wien Pipeline* [2001] ECR I-8365 para 41. See also C-308/01 *GIL Insurance and Others* [2004] ECR I-4777 para 68, and C-172/03 *Heiser* [2005] ECR I-1627 para 40.

[36] *Azores* (n 1) paras 55 ff.

The ECJ then explicitly recognised[37] that, when a regional or local authority adopts, in the exercise of sufficiently autonomous powers in relation to the central power, a tax rate lower than the national rate, one which is applicable only to undertakings present in the territory within its competence, the legal framework appropriate to determine the selectivity of a tax measure may be limited to the geographical area where the infra-State body, in particular on account of its status and powers, plays a fundamental role in the definition of the political and economic environment in which those undertakings operate.

As regards the case under examination, the Court applied the reasoning proposed by the Advocate General to the tax reductions decided by the Autonomous Region of the Azores and concluded that, in spite of having a political and administrative autonomous status, it lacked sufficient economic and financial autonomy, given the existence of compensatory financial transfers from the central State on account of the principle of national solidarity and the reduction of inequalities.

Finally, the Court also decided that the mere fact that the regional tax system is conceived in such a way as to ensure the correction of inequalities does not allow the conclusion to be drawn that every tax advantage granted by the authorities of the autonomous region concerned is justified by the nature and overall structure of the national tax system.

IX. CONCLUSION

The *Azores* case constitutes a landmark decision as regards the assessment of the notion of selectivity on geographical grounds for the purpose of application of Article 87(1). Indeed, it sets new limits to the application of State aid rules to tax measures adopted by regionally autonomous bodies within the context of a Member State.[38]

It made clear that the national territory or the country as a whole does not constitute the only reference framework for assessing the selectivity of a tax measure. In doing so, the Court opposed a clear rebuttal to the Commission's persistent assertion that the national framework for assessment was the only admissible

[37] ibid paras 65–66.

[38] This judgment can be held to follow a line of case-law—*Preussen Electra* (Case C-379/98 *Preussen Elektra AG v Schhleswag AG, in the presence of Windpark Reußenköge III GmbH and Land Schleswig-Holstein* [2001] ECR I-2099) *Stardust Marine* (Case C-482/99 *French Republic v Commission* I-4397), *Pearle* (n 19)—by which the ECJ is attempting to clarify the scope of Article 87(1). That case-law already led to a narrowing of the scope of that provision, thus contributing, in the view of President Vesterdorf, 'A Further Comment on the New State Aid Concept as this Concept Continues to be Reshaped—Pearle: A Further Piece of State aid puzzle?' (2005) 26 *New Developments in European State Aid Law* 1, 7, to increase 'legal certainty by seeking to provide a clear cut test for measures which fall outside the remit of Article 87(1)' and to bring about 'a decrease of what may be regarded as excessive red tape, which places an unwelcome burden on undertakings, national authorities and national courts as well as the Commission and the Community Courts'.

one,[39] and called a halt to any attempt to promote a kind of creeping harmonisation in the field of direct taxation without following the procedures laid down in Articles 94, 96 and 97 EC.

Provided that the constitution of a Member State empowers decentralised authorities with 'sufficiently autonomous powers' in the field of taxation, the assessment of selectivity to be made on tax measures adopted by those authorities moves from the national to the regional or local level, so that the measures in question cannot be considered as selective when they apply without discrimination to all the undertakings in the same situation within the region. The ECJ also made clear that there is no reason at all to distinguish, from this point a view, between 'symmetrical' and 'asymmetrical' devolution of fiscal powers to decentralised authorities.

The Court therefore set an appropriate balance between the correct application and the effectiveness of State aid rules, for one part, and the respect that should be paid to national sovereignty on direct tax matters and to the constitutional autonomy of Member States to decide on the allocation of tax powers between central and regional authorities within the country, for the other.

One can only regret that the Court (a) still placed emphasis, without a critical analysis, on the distinction between, on the one hand, the objectives attributed to a particular tax scheme which are extrinsic to it and, on the other hand, the mechanisms inherent to the tax system itself, which are necessary to achieve such objectives, and (b) did not pay due attention to the possible application of the *Van Carlsten* and *Pape* case-law as concerns the link between the State measure and its method of financing, as suggested by the applicant.

[39] See in this respect the blunt statement of the Court in *Azores* (n 1) para 59.

13

Selectivity and Distortion of Competition in State Aid—an Unorthodox Analysis[*]

I. INTRODUCTION

ALTHOUGH BOTH THE European Court of Justice (hereinafter the 'ECJ') and the Court of First Instance (hereinafter the 'CFI') have endeavoured to set out generally applicable criteria in order to define and identify State aid measures, it still remains difficult to acknowledge that there is a coherent and consistent line of case-law which would allow one to recognise, in each concrete case, which measures should be considered State aid. The notion of 'specificity' or 'selectivity', either *material* or *geographical*, is at the core of ambiguity and explains why undertakings, governments and individuals cannot rely on a clear set of guidelines in assessing the existence of State aid.

As regards the so-called 'material selectivity', the recent judgments of the CFI (13 September 2006) and the ECJ (22 December 2008), as well as the Opinion of Advocate General Mengozzi (17 July 2008) in the *British Aggregates* cases,[1] illustrate the difficulties inherent in such a notion, in particular as regards its relationship with the criterion of 'distortion of competition'. Nevertheless, the root of the problem must be sought throughout the traditional decisional practice and case-law in this respect.

[*] First published in EStAL, (2009) *European State Aid Law Quarterly* 8, 4, 443–51, under the title 'Material and Geographic Selectivity in State Aid—Recent Developments (A Personal View)'.

[1] T-210/02 *British Aggregates Association (BAA) v European Commission* [2006] ECR II-2789; C-487/06 P *European Commission v BAA* [2008] ECR I-10515.

As far as the notion of 'geographical' or 'regional selectivity' is concerned, the question was the object of important, yet contradictory rulings in the *Azores*,[2] the *Basque Country*[3] and *Gibraltar* cases.[4]

II. MATERIAL SELECTIVITY

A. The Current Case-Law

Article 87(1) EC applies to aid 'which distorts or threatens to distort competition by favouring certain undertakings or the production of certain goods'.

In their judgments, it is the latter aspect that the EC courts emphasise. As the CFI stated in *BAA*,[5] in order to constitute State aid for the purpose of Article 87(1) EC, a measure must, in particular, be capable of conferring a selective advantage,[6] to the exclusive benefit of certain undertakings or certain sectors of activity.

As a matter of fact, the EC courts usually carry out their examination in respect of the characterisation of a measure as State aid on the sole basis of the criterion

[2] C-88/03 *Portugal v Commission (Azores)* [2006] ECR I-7115.

[3] Joined Cases C-428/06 to C-434/06 *Unión General de Trabajadores de La Rioja (UGT–Rioja)* (C-428/06), *Comunidad Autónoma de la Rioja* (C-429/06) *v Juntas Generales del Territorio Histórico de Vizcaya, Diputación Foral de Vizcaya, Cámara de Comercio, Industria y Navegación de Bilbao, Confederación Empresarial Vasca (Confebask)* and *Comunidad Autónoma de la Rioja* (C-430/06), *Comunidad Autónoma de Castilla y León* (C-433/06) *v Diputación Foral de Álava, Juntas Generales de Álava, Confederación Empresarial Vasca (Confebask)* and *Comunidad Autónoma de la Rioja* (C-431/06), *Comunidad Autónoma de Castilla y León* (C-432/06) *v Diputación Foral de Guipúzcoa, Juntas Generales de Guipúzcoa, Confederación Empresarial Vasca (Confebask)* and *Comunidad Autónoma de Castilla y León* (C-434/06) *v Diputación Foral de Vizcaya, Juntas Generales del Territorio Histórico de Vizcaya, Cámara de Comercio, Industria y Navegación de Bilbao, Confederación Empresarial Vasca (Confebask)* [2008] I-6747.

[4] T-211/04 *Government of Gibraltar v Commission* and T-215/04 *United Kingdom v Commission* [2008] ECR II-3745. On appeal against the CFI's judgment, the ECJ (Case C-106/09 P *Commission v Government of Gibraltar and United Kingdom* and C-107/09 P *Spain v Government of Gibraltar and United Kingdom* [2011] ECR I-11113) upheld the legality of the Commission decision on grounds that the proposed tax reform was materially selective, so that the plea raised by Gibraltar and the United Kingdom, relating to the absence of regional selectivity, was held to be ineffective and therefore not examined.

[5] See *BAA* (n 1) para 105.

[6] Such selective advantage may be the intrinsic consequence of the measure itself as it was intended to be from the outset or instead the result of its application in the complex circumstances of each case. As the CFI made clear in T-55/99 *Confederación Española de Transporte de Mercancías (CETM) v Commission* [2000] ECR II-3207 para 40, '[t]he applicant's argument that there was no prior identification [...] of the individual addressees of the measure contained therein, must be rejected. The fact that the aid is not aimed at one or more specific recipients defined in advance, but that it is subject to a series of objective criteria pursuant to which it may be granted, within the framework of a predetermined overall budget allocation, to an indefinite number of beneficiaries who are not initially individually identified, cannot suffice to call in question the selective nature of the measure and, accordingly, its classification as State aid within the meaning of Article [87](1) EC. At the very most, that circumstance means that the measure in question is not an individual aid. It does not, however, preclude that public measure from having to be regarded as a system of aid constituting a selective, and therefore specific, measure if, owing to the criteria governing its application, it procures an advantage for certain undertakings or the production of certain goods, to the exclusion of others.'

of selectivity, leaving aside, at this stage of reasoning, the issue of distortion of competition. Some of the statements of both courts seem to be representative of such an approach.

In *Adria-Wien Pipeline*,[7] the ECJ held that:

> The only question to be determined is whether, under a particular statutory scheme, a State measure is such as to favour 'certain undertakings or the production of certain goods' within the meaning of Article [87](1) EC in comparison with other undertakings which are in a legal and factual situation that is comparable in the light of the objective pursued by the measure in question.

In *Spain v Commission*,[8] a similar statement was introduced by the rather strong expression: 'the application of Article [87](1) EC only requires it to be determined…', thus leading to the conclusion that '[i]f so, the measure satisfies the condition of selectivity which defines State aid as laid down by that provision'.

Similarly, in *Ladbroke Racing*,[9] the CFI considered aid as an objective concept, 'the test being whether a State measure confers an advantage on one or more particular undertakings'.

A particularly clear statement in this regard can be found in *Italy v Commission*,[10] where the Court held that Article 87(1) 'prohibits State aid which "[favours] certain undertakings or the production of certain goods", that is to say aid which is selective'.

In short, the courts appear, in general, to take the view that when 'selectivity' is present then distortion of competition follows as a consequence, thus triggering the application of Article 87(1) EC.

Following such line of case-law, selectivity is to be considered as a stand-alone requisite, the presence of which is not only *necessary* but also *sufficient* to conclude on the existence of State aid.

The case-law and the Commission's decisional practice have, in fact, paid, in general, little attention to the other two conditions for an aid granted by a Member State to fall under the scope of Article 87(1) EC: 'distortion of competition' and 'effect on intra-Community trade'.

In its decisions on State aid, the Commission traditionally contented itself with rough indications relating to the conditions of affecting trade between Member States and distorting competition.[11] It must, however, be said that this approach has not always been upheld by the Court.

Indeed, in *Leeuwarder v Commission*,[12] the Court of Justice criticised the Commission for not having included in its decision a statement of reasons with

[7] C-143/99 *Adria-Wien Pipeline* [2001] ECR I-8365, para 41.

[8] C-409/00 *Spain v Commission* [2003] ECR I-1487, para 47.

[9] T-67/94 *Ladbroke Racing v Commission* [1998] ECR II-1, para 52.

[10] C-172/03 *Italy v Commission* [2005] ECR I-10901, para 94. See also the judgment of the CFI in *Gibraltar* (n 4) para 77.

[11] See eg Commission Decision 2002/142/EC of 18 July 2001, relative to an aid granted by Netherlands to Valmont Nederland BV [2002] OJ L48, 20 February 2002, 20, paras 19–22.

[12] Joined Cases 296-318/82 *Leeuwarder v Commission* [1985] ECR 809, paras 22–24.

regard to the assessment of the requirement that the aid in question affected trade between Member States and distorted or threatened to distort competition by favouring certain undertakings or the production of certain goods. After pointing out that the Commission had merely repeated the wording of the Treaty provision without any factual indications, the Court held that even if, in certain cases, the very circumstances in which the aid is granted are sufficient to show that the aid is capable of affecting trade and distorting or threatening to distort competition, the Commission must, at least, set out those circumstances in its decision. In this respect, the Court stressed the importance of considering the situation of the relevant market, the position of the undertaking receiving the aid in that market, the pattern of trade between Member States in the products in question and the undertaking's exports.

Nonetheless, as suggested by Advocate General Capotorti in his Opinion in the *Philip Morris* case,[13] regarding the impact on competition, Article 87(1) EC may be read as establishing a simple criterion according to which the condition of distortion of competition would not be fulfilled only when no product similar or substitutable to those manufactured by the beneficiary of the aid existed in the common market. As this seldom occurs, it was held in the legal literature[14] that the condition of distortion of competition is always met and can thus, in principle, be presumed to be fulfilled.[15]

The condition of 'affecting trade between Member States' has also been subject to a wide interpretation. In the *Philip Morris* case,[16] the Court admitted that '[w]hen State financial aid strengthens the position of an undertaking compared with other undertakings competing in intra-Community trade, the latter must be regarded as affected by that aid'.[17] From that statement, Advocate General Jacobs in his Opinion of 1994 in the *Spain v Commission*[18] cases concluded that it was 'clear from the Court's case-law that the requirement of an effect on trade between Member States is easily satisfied'.

I would like to express the view that this test may not always be adequate or sufficient.

[13] Case 730/79 *Philip Morris Holland* [1980] ECR 2671; Opinion of AG Capotorti, 2698.

[14] See JF Bellis, *Les critères de la distorsion de concurrence et de l'effet sur le commerce interétatique* in M Dony and C Smits (eds), 'Aides d'État' (Brussels, IEE-ULB, 2005) 97–106, in particular 99.

[15] The CFI appears to take a similar view in Case T-214/95 *Vlaams Gewest* [1998] ECR II-717 para 46, when assessing the impact of small amounts of aid on the application of Article 87. The Court held that: 'Where a public authority favours an undertaking operating in a sector which is characterised by intense competition by granting it a benefit, there is a distortion of competition or a risk of such distortion. Where the benefit is limited, competition is distorted to a lesser extent, but it is still distorted. The prohibition in Article [87](1) EC applies to any aid which distorts or threatens to distort competition, irrespective of its amount, in so far as it affects trade between Member States.'

[16] See *Phillip Morris* (n 13) para 11.

[17] See also C-148/04 *Unicredito Italiano* [2005] ECR I-11137 para 56.

[18] Opinion delivered on 23 March 1994 in Joined Cases C-278-280/92 *Spain v Commission* [1994] ECR I-4103 para 33.

B. Refining the Approach

Although, in many cases, the mere existence of selectivity may indeed be liable to distort or to threaten to distort competition, I believe that the wording, the objective and the context of Article 87(1) EC require a somewhat more complex approach, suitable for application in the complex circumstances which generally characterise measures of selective aid.

As recalled earlier, for the purpose of application of Article 87(1) EC, a State aid measure is defined by reference to any aid granted by a Member State 'which distorts or threatens to distort competition by favouring certain undertakings or the production of certain goods'. This provision should be read as regarding selectivity as a constituent element of the notion of distortion of competition, which is inherent to the very notion of State aid as defined in Article 87(1) EC.

If it is so, it does not seem possible to infer simply from the fact that a measure is selective that it is to be classified as aid within the meaning of Article 87(1) EC when the measure in question, in itself and within the legal and economic context in which it is applied, is not liable to distort or to threaten to distort competition. It is by distorting or threatening to distort competition that selective measures shall be deemed to be 'incompatible with the common market'.

It is true that distinguished commentators[19] consider that Article 87 EC comes within a policy of 'fair' or 'loyal' competition, therefore pertaining to a context different from Article 81 EC.

Moreover, the Treaty, by including the expression 'favouring certain undertakings or the production of certain goods', may allow for an interpretation according to which protection of competitors, not protection of competition as a process, is the real objective of Articles 87 and 88 EC.[20]

This, however, is not the only possible interpretation. Firstly, the Treaty rules on competition applying either to undertakings or to Member States should be interpreted according to the same standard. Secondly, favour to an undertaking or a production should be irrelevant when there are no competitors that may be harmed and competition on the market cannot be affected.

This is consistent not only with the wording of Article 87(1) EC but also with its position in the system of the Treaty under the heading 'rules on competition', applying to Member States. The slightly different way in which Articles 81(1) EC and 87(1) EC are phrased—'which have as their object or effect the prevention, restriction or distortion of competition' versus 'which distorts or threatens to distort competition'—do not appear to imply anything relevant from the point of view of their respective interpretation.

[19] See JF Bellis (n 14) 98.

[20] See also JF Bellis (n 14).

A measure may, therefore, favour certain undertakings or products without being considered State aid when it does not affect the competitive position of other undertakings or products or the structure of competition on the market.[21]

As shown in *BAA*, this consideration may even play a role in deciding on the admissibility of an action brought by a competitor whose market position is significantly affected by a State measure, granting an advantage to some undertakings or categories of undertaking. Indeed, as Advocate General Mengozzi emphasised in his Opinion in that case,[22] 'the effect on the applicant's competitive position [is] the primary criterion for the purposes of assessing whether the action [is] admissible'.[23] Such assertion was upheld by the ECJ in its judgment in that same case.[24]

Moreover, as both the CFI and the Advocate General in the subsequent appeal to the ECJ pointed out,[25] the purpose of the levy at issue was to transfer some of the demand for virgin aggregates to alternative products, in order to encourage the use of such products and to reduce the extraction of virgin aggregates, thus being a measure intended to have a direct effect on the structure of the market and hence on the competitive position of undertakings active on that market.

Case C-409/00 *Spain v Commission*[26] provides a good example which serves to elucidate this question. Indeed, when a given regime of aid covers different categories of vehicles—big tractors and lorries, small lorries and vans, buses and coaches, trailers and semi-trailers—it is clear that competition is not affected in the same way as regards all those categories. It then becomes crucial to define the relevant markets on which the aid measure may have an impact and to examine the market characteristics as a pre-condition for Article 87(1) EC to apply.

In the abovementioned case, the Court did perform a perfunctory examination of the 'relevant markets' at issue and distinguished aid granted to 'non-professional transport companies' from 'aid granted to professional transport

[21] Conversely, even general measures, which are not limited either to a particular sector or to a particular territory and do not apply to a limited category of undertakings, 'may be caught by the prohibition laid down in Article 87(1) EC if their implementation is left to the discretion of the national authorities as regards, in particular, the choice of recipients, the amount and the conditions of the financial assistance' (Opinion of AG Mengozzi in Case C-487/06 P, *BAA* (n 1) para 81). This is so because such general measures may threaten to distort competition between undertakings.

[22] *BAA* (n 1); Opinion of AG Mengozzi, paras 30–50, especially para 32.

[23] As the Advocate General underlined, 'the harm of which BAA complains does not derive from the fact that its members are required to pay the AGL [a levy imposed, for environmental reasons, on virgin aggregates used in construction but of which were exempt alternative materials and aggregates exported from the UK], but from the competitive disadvantage they allegedly suffer by reason of the fact that some competing producers are exempt from the AGL' (*BAA* (n 1); Opinion of AG Mengozzi, para 47).

[24] As the Court stressed in para 35 of its judgment, 'irrespective of whether the aid measure in question is individual or general in nature, an applicant must, when bringing into question the soundness of the decision assessing the aid as such, demonstrate that [...] the position of the applicant on the market in question is substantially affected by the aid which is the subject of the decision in question'.

[25] See *BAA* (n 1) paras 55–56; Opinion of AG Mengozzi, para 65.

[26] *Spain v Commission* (n 8).

companies'. The conclusion[27] was that 'those two categories of beneficiaries [...] do not belong to the same sector and do not operate in the same market'.

The Court also acknowledged[28] that the contested decision contained an assessment of the effect of the aid at issue on the transport sector, namely that the aid was likely to help the beneficiaries compete with large undertakings established in Spain. It also recalled[29] that when a sector, such as the transport sector in conditions of overcapacity, is characterised by strong competition, aid of relatively little importance can affect competition and trade between Member States.

However the Court failed to consider distortion of competition as an integral part of the notion of aid for the purposes of application of Article 87(1) EC. On the contrary, it considered it necessary to establish, first, that the aid at issue fell within the scope of Article 87(1) EC and, second, that it distorted or threatened to distort competition, as if they were two different steps in the analysis.[30]

In *Netherlands v Commission*,[31] however, the CFI rightly pointed out that 'classification as aid requires that all the [*four*] conditions set out in Article 87(1) EC are fulfilled'. However, having concluded that the measure in question was not selective, within the meaning of *Adria-Wien*, the Court did not need to address the issue of 'distortion of competition'.[32]

Conversely, when a measure is deemed to be selective, it is still necessary to assess whether, as an integral part of the notion of aid, it distorts competition, including in the analysis the effects on competition both on the same market and on the upstream, downstream or other related markets.[33]

In brief, I propose an approach which mirrors the one that is characteristic to Article 81. On the one hand, Article 81(1) EC prohibits agreements, decisions by associations of undertakings and concerted practices that have as their object or

[27] ibid, para 67.

[28] ibid, para 75.

[29] ibid, paras 76–77.

[30] ibid, para 77.

[31] T-233/04 *Netherlands v Commission* [2008] ECR II-591, para 63. See also C-126/01 *Gemo* [2003] ECR I-13769 paras 21–22. However, in *Gemo*, once again, the Court considered the measure in question to be a State aid because it was selective, without assessing whether it distorted competition in the common market. The Court limited itself to consider, in para 42 of the judgment, that 'the fact that, in France, the costs of carcass disposal are borne neither by farmers nor by slaughterhouses necessarily has a positive impact on meat prices, thus making that product more competitive on the markets of the Member States where such costs are normally paid out of the budget of competing traders'. Moreover, the Court made this assessment in connection with the analysis of the condition of 'affecting trade between Member States' and not in connection with the condition of 'distorting competition'.

[32] When a measure is not selective and does not constitute State aid, distortions of competition within the common market may be tackled by other instruments: Article 94 EC, Articles 96 and 97 EC (see, in this regard, Opinion of Advocate General Geelhoed in *Azores* (n 2), para 46).

[33] On the other hand, in *Azores*, the Commission raised the argument that the fact that a regional tax reduction has or may have the effect of distorting competition within the common market is, in principle, sufficient for it to satisfy the selectivity criterion (see Opinion of Advocate General Geelhoed in the same case, ibid, para 58. However, in the absence of regional selectivity, owing to the sufficiently autonomous powers of a given regional authority, the issue of (material) selectivity and distortion of competition is to be assessed within the limits of the region.

effect to (significantly) prevent, restrict or distort competition, whereas Article 87(1) EC prohibits State aid that, by being selective, (significantly) distorts or threatens to distort competition.

On the other hand, while Article 81(3) EC provides a 'legal exception' to the prohibition contained in Article 81(1) EC with respect to agreements or practices that satisfy certain conditions, Article 87(3) EC is similarly an exempting provision from the prohibition laid down in Article 87(1) EC.

To consider that a State aid falls within the scope of application of Article 87(1) EC for the simple reason that it is 'selective' would be tantamount to considering that an agreement falls within Article 81(1) EC simply because it constrains 'conduct' or restricts the 'economic freedom' of the parties to that agreement.

This is why I am supportive of the guidelines issued by the Commission in its State aid Action Plan of 2005, favouring a more 'refined economic approach' when dealing with State aids. According to the Action Plan, 'State aid control comes from the need to maintain a level playing field for all undertakings active in the Single European Market' and from the concern 'with those State aid measures, which provide unwarranted selective advantages to some firms, preventing or delaying the market forces from rewarding the most competitive firms, thereby decreasing overall European competitiveness'.[34]

I am, therefore, in favour of an approach that puts competition, and not just selectivity, the consumer, and not just the competitors, at the heart of State aid policy.[35]

As underlined by Ahlborn and Berg,[36] the current policy under the State aid provisions and the approach still prevailing in judicial review bear resemblance to the early period of legal formalism in the application of Article 81 EC.

By contrast, the adoption of a clear 'effects-based approach' in the application of State aid rules aimed at safeguarding the competitive process in the internal market (and not simply at protecting competitors) is coherent with the approach taken for the application of Article 81 EC after *Delimitis*[37] and proposed in the Commission's Discussion Paper and in its Communication on 'Guidance on the Commission's enforcement priorities' as concerns the application of Article 82.[38]

[34] The Commission's approach since 2004 represented an attempt to implement a more flexible view, focused on measures which produce significant economic effects at the Community level but neither of the two draft Communications for the definition of a new framework for the assessment, respectively, of lesser amounts of State aid and of State aid which has limited effect on intra-Community trade has been followed by a final communication (see JF Bellis (n 14) 98).

[35] That is why, in a case like the one concerning Ryanair and Charleroi airport, I would support the Directorate General for Competition (DG COMP) and its concern with the consumers' interest against the Directorate General for Energy and Transport (DG TREN) and its sensitivity to the competitors' claims.

[36] C Ahlborn and C Berg, 'Can State Aid Control Learn from Antitrust? The Need for a Greater Role for Competition Analysis under the State aid Rules' in Biondi, Eeckout and Flynn (eds), *The Law of State Aid in the EU* (Oxford, Oxford University Press, 2004).

[37] Case C-234/89 *Stergios Delimitis v Henninger Bräu AG* [1991] ECR I-935.

[38] The Court of Justice itself pointed out in several instances that Article 87(1) does not distinguish between measures of State intervention by reference to their causes or their aims—environmental,

This should not involve any kind of 'carbon copy' approach since the type of competitive analysis suitable for all those fields is not necessarily the same.[39] However, I do not share the view that the interest of the consumers should not be taken into account in this context. In fact, the impact of the measure on the consumers should be considered, however complex the task may be, by balancing the gains for consumers in a given geographical market against the losses in other markets.

III. REGIONAL OR GEOGRAPHICAL SELECTIVITY

As regards 'geographical (or regional) selectivity', after years of hesitation and questioning, a new journey in the jurisprudence started some three or four years ago. The '*coup d'envoi*' was given by the judgment of the ECJ in the *Azores* case,[40] which set the tone for a shift in the traditional path.

First, it stated, in reply to the Commission's submission, that the reference framework for the determination of a tax advantage need not necessarily be defined within the limits of the whole territory of the Member State concerned, so that a measure conferring an advantage in only a part of the national territory is not selective on that ground alone for the purposes of Article 87(1) EC.[41] When an autonomous infra-State body plays a fundamental role in the definition of the political and economic environment in which undertakings operate, it is the area in which that body exercises its powers, and not the country as a whole, that

economic, social or otherwise—but defines them in relation to their effects (C-75/97 *Belgium v Commission (Maribel bis/ter)* [1999] ECR I-3671, para 25; *Spain v Commission* (n 8) para 46). In *Maribel* (para 51) the Court therefore took the right approach when it stated that the Belgian social security scheme for wage earners was a scheme of sectoral aid that improved the competitive position of the undertakings concerned, both on the Belgian market and on the export market, in relation to undertakings established in other Member States by relieving them of part of their social costs, and that consequently it was liable to affect trade between Member States and to distort or to threaten to distort competition. Reference should also be made to the ECJ judgment in *BAA* (n 1), paras 84–92, where the Court upheld the criticism made by Advocate General Mengozzi (Opinion, paras 98, 102) of the first instance ruling, namely to the extent that the CFI held that 'the Member States are free, in balancing the various interests involved, to set their priorities as regards the protection of the environment and, as a result, to determine which goods or services they are to decide to subject to an environmental levy' (para 115). However, I will not enter into the intricate discussion about, on the one hand, the relevance of the specific objectives (environmental or other) pursued by the State measure or of the nature and the general scheme of the tax system in question or, on the other hand, their connection with the notion of selectivity. These issues, together with the discussion about the scope of Member States' jurisdiction on tax matters and the interplay between paras (1) and (3) of Article 87 EC, were at the core of the *BAA* cases, but fall outside the scope of my reflection, which concerns the relationship, with regard to the notion of State aid, between selectivity and distortion of competition.

39 In this respect, see C Ahlborn and C Berg (n 36) 48–50.

40 Judgment of 6 September 2006, *Azores* (n 2). See JL da Cruz Vilaça, 'Regional Selectivity and State Aid: The Azores Case' in 'New Developments in European State Aid Law' (2006) *European State Aid Law Quarterly* 15.

41 *Azores* (n 2) para 57.

constitutes the relevant context for the assessment of whether a measure adopted by such a body favours certain undertakings in comparison with others in a comparable legal and factual situation.[42]

Next, it must be recalled that the Court did not take a position in regards to the question of whether such conclusion would still be valid in the case of an asymmetrical devolution of powers in fiscal matters to local or regional bodies within a Member State.

However, Advocate General Geelhoed was clear in submitting[43] that when a local authority takes its decision with 'true autonomy', 'there is no logical or doctrinal ground for distinguishing between "symmetrical" [...] and "asymmetrical" devolution of tax powers', the choice being 'one of constitutional policy heavily dependent on the unique historical and economic circumstances of that region'.

Finally, the Court established a set of criteria that would permit to examine whether a given measure was adopted by an infra-State body in the exercise of powers '*sufficiently autonomous*'[44] vis-à-vis the central power.

For a given measure to be regarded as having been adopted in the exercise of sufficiently autonomous powers, the Court, following its Advocate General, considered that such a measure must fulfil the following conditions: *(i)* be taken by a regional or local authority with a political and administrative status separate from that of the central government ('*institutional autonomy*'); *(ii)* be adopted without the central government being able to directly intervene in the determination of its content ('*procedural autonomy*'); *(iii)* the financial consequences of the measure (in that case, a reduction of the national tax rate for undertakings in the region) must not be offset by aid or subsidies from other regions or central government ('*economic autonomy*').[45]

Applying these criteria to the case under appeal, the Court considered that the Azores region could not be considered sufficiently autonomous since the reduction in tax revenue for the region was offset by the existence of financial transfers from the central government, in light of the principles of national solidarity and of correction of inequalities.

On this point, the Court disregarded the fact that such financial transfers to the constitutionally autonomous regions of Azores and Madeira are made according to a pre-established formula set out in the framework law on the finances of the autonomous regions. It also did not consider the arguments drawn by the

[42] ibid para 58.
[43] *Azores* (n 2); Opinion of AG Geelhoed, para 60.
[44] Or 'truly autonomous', as Advocate General Geelhoed preferred to call it.
[45] *Azores* (n 2) para 67. The expressions between round brackets were used by Advocate General Geelhoed in his Opinion.

Portuguese Republic from the *Pape*[46], *Van Calster*[47] and *Pearle*[48] case-law[49] and from the fact that there is no link or any kind of correlation between such transfers and infra-structural investments, on the one hand, and the tax reductions in the region, on the other hand, the former being the expression of the global economic, financial and budgetary policies of the State.

On the contrary, the Court considered[50] that

> the two aspects of the fiscal policy of the regional government, namely the decision to reduce the regional tax burden [...] and the fulfilment of its task of correcting inequalities derived from insularity, [were] inextricably linked and [depended], from the financial point of view, on budgetary transfers managed by central government.

The judgment in the *Azores case* raises doubts that must be carefully examined. Indeed, it is doubtful whether the concept of 'sufficient autonomy' can be deemed a useful tool to ascertain in every case the 'selectivity' of a regional tax measure. This was shown two years later by the Court's judgment in the *Basque Country* cases.[51]

First of all, the notions used to appraise the nature as State aid of a given regional tax measure are ambiguous enough to have given rise to such contradictory understandings as those expressed in the *Basque Country* cases by UGT-Rioja, on the one hand, and by Confebask, on the other hand. Whereas the former claimed that there was 'absolutely no doubt that the tax measures at issue in the main proceedings constitute State aid', Confebask claimed, for its part, that 'since the judgment in *Portugal v Commission* is very clear [...] there can be no doubt that the tax measures at issue in the main proceedings do not constitute State aid'.[52]

Secondly, the Court, confronted with the Commission's contention that the assessment whether the regional body played a fundamental role in the definition of the political and economic environment in which undertakings operate constituted a precondition for the operation of the three criteria set out in paragraph 67 of the *Azores* judgment, had to clarify the meaning of this judgment. It clearly stated (as had been done by Advocate General Kokott in her Opinion) that no such precondition is laid down in that judgment.

[46] C-175/02 *F J Pape v Minister van Landbouw, Natuurbeheer en Visserij* [2005] ECR I-127.

[47] Joined Cases C-261/01 and C-262/01 *Belgische Staat v Eugène van Calster and Felix Cleeren and Openbaar Slachthuis NV* [2003] ECR I-12249.

[48] C-345/02 *Pearle BV, Hans Prijs Optiek Franchise BV and Rinck Opticiëns BV v Hoofdbedrijfschap Ambachten* [2004] ECR I-7139.

[49] On this line of case-law, see JL da Cruz Vilaça, 'How Far Should National Courts Go in Drawing all the Necessary Inferences from the Last Sentence of Article 88(3) EC?' in 'New Developments in European State Aid Law' (2005) *European State Aid Law Quarterly* 45.

[50] *Azores* (n 2) para 76.

[51] *Basque Country* (n 3).

[52] See *Basque Country* (n 3) paras 37 and 38.

Thirdly, as regards procedural autonomy, the Court,[53] implicitly diverging from the opinion of Advocate General Geelhoed in the *Azores* case, considered that

> an infra-State body's obligation to take into consideration the State interest in order to respect the limits of the areas of competence which are accorded to it does not, generally, constitute an element calling into question the procedural autonomy of that body where it adopts a decision within those limits.

Finally, regarding economic and financial autonomy, the Court, in its judgment in the *Basque Country* cases[54] and apparently contradicting its own findings in *Azores*, found that

> the mere fact that it appears from a general examination of the financial relations between the central State and its infra-State bodies that there are financial transfers between the former and the latter, cannot, in itself, suffice to demonstrate that those bodies do not assume the financial consequences of the tax measures which they adopt and, accordingly, that they do not enjoy financial autonomy, since such transfers may take place for reasons unconnected with the tax measures.

It is worth mentioning in this respect that in the case of the Basque autonomous territories, financial transfers may also take place from the regions to the State budget or to other autonomous territories through a compensation fund, according to a principle of national solidarity. It would be odd to think that this factor should play any role in deciding on the existence of 'sufficient autonomy', since the criterion for assessment cannot depend on the region in question being richer or poorer than the national average.

Differences in the kind of judicial relief sought in each case may provide an explanation for such apparent double standards in the judicial review of tax measures coming within the competence of regional autonomous bodies. Indeed, whereas the *Azores* case related to a direct action for annulment of a Commission's decision, the *Basque* case concerned a reference for a preliminary ruling originating in a national court. In the latter case, the Court finally considered that it was for the national court to determine whether the criteria of autonomy laid down in paragraph 67 of the *Azores* judgment were satisfied.

However, it does not seem appropriate that the answer to such fundamental questions depends on the form of process that was followed in each circumstance. Moreover, as is apparent from the *Basque* decision, the national courts may be granted such a wide margin of discretion that runs counter to the principles of equality and legal security.

Three months after the *Basque* ruling, the CFI delivered its judgment in the *Gibraltar* cases.[55] The judgment, concerning a reform of corporate tax adopted by the Government of Gibraltar, is of great importance in several respects.

[53] ibid, para 108.
[54] ibid, para 135.
[55] *Gibraltar* (n 4).

First of all, the CFI held that 'the determination of the reference framework has a particular importance in the case of tax measures, since the very existence of an advantage may be established only when compared with "normal" taxation', the 'normal' tax rate being 'the rate in force in the geographical area constituting the reference framework'.[56]

Having concluded that the reference framework corresponded, in that case, exclusively to the geographical limits of the territory of Gibraltar, the CFI held that 'no comparison can be made between the tax regime applicable to companies established in Gibraltar and that applicable to companies established in the United Kingdom for the purpose of establishing a selective advantage favouring the former'.[57]

It follows from this assessment that there is no selectivity when the measure in question applies without distinction to all the companies in similar circumstances within the region.

Secondly, with regard to the condition of 'financial autonomy', the CFI, 'interpreting' the use of the verb 'offset' in the *Azores* judgment, observed that it meant that 'a causal link must exist between the tax measure at issue adopted by the infra-State body and the financial support from other regions of the central government of the Member State concerned'. The CFI rightly pointed out that the interpretation proposed by the Commission[58] would make the third condition set out in the judgment on the tax regime in the Azores a dead letter, since it would be very difficult to conceive of an intra-State body which does not receive any financial support, in whatever form, from central government.[59]

Thirdly and concerning the abovementioned condition, the CFI made clear that, in its view and as it had been submitted by the Portuguese Republic in the *Azores* case, the burden of proving the causal link lies upon the Commission.[60]

Furthermore, with regard to material selectivity, the CFI clarified and brought to the Commission's attention the road map to follow in order for it to classify a tax measure as selective.[61]

[56] ibid, para 80.

[57] ibid, para 115.

[58] According to which the condition of 'financial autonomy' implies that no assistance is even potentially available to the infra-State body to offset the effects of the body's decisions about its tax measures (*Gibraltar* (n 4) para 102).

[59] ibid, para 106.

[60] ibid, paras 112–13: 'in the absence of evidence to the contrary adduced by the Commission, it must be found that none of the abovementioned financing serves to offset any financial consequences that the tax reform would entail for Gibraltar'. 'Since therefore there is nothing that can cast doubt on the applicant's assertions that Gibraltar does not receive any financial support from the United Kingdom that offsets the financial consequences of the tax reform, it must be held that the third condition set out in the judgment on the tax regime in the Azores is met in the present instance'.

[61] ibid, paras 141–45.

Finally, it is worth noting that the CFI found it necessary to underline[62] that with regard to the determination of the tax system,

> as Community law currently stands, direct taxation falls within the competence of the Member States. Thus, it is solely the latter, and infra-State bodies which have sufficient autonomy [...] in relation to central government, that have competence to devise systems of corporate taxation which they consider the best suited to the needs of their economies. Furthermore, [...] application of the Community rules on State aid is without prejudice to the power of the Member States to decide on their economic policy and, therefore, on the tax system—and the common or 'normal' regime under it—which they consider the most appropriate and, in particular, to spread the tax burden as they see fit across the different factors of production and economic sectors.

It is my view that this approach strikes an adequate balance between the requirements of State aid rules and the powers retained by the Member States.

From the evolution of the case-law described above, it is therefore possible to conclude that obscurity as regards the notion of selectivity is being progressively dissipated; however it remains to be seen how the jurisprudence in this regard will consolidate.

[62] ibid, para 146.

14

The Duration of Non-Compete Obligations in Full-Function Joint Ventures[*]

THE FIRST FEATURE that strikes one when embarking upon research into 'ancillary restraints' in the context of EU competition and merger control law is the scarcity of works specifically devoted to this subject and the scant attention paid to it by academics.[1]

Yet the inclusion of such clauses, either in merger agreements or in cooperation agreements between otherwise independent undertakings, has become increasingly frequent and the related litigation, whether before courts of law or arbitral tribunals, has raised issues of ever greater legal and economic significance.

That is why I have chosen this topic for the present chapter which I am dedicating to Professor Panayotis Soldatos, to pay tribute to his important contribution to the development of the European Union's constitutional law and to recall a memorable meeting in Montréal, many years ago, in a context related to European competition law.

[*] A French version of this chapter has been published under the title 'La durée des clauses de non-concurrence en cas de création d'entreprises communes à caractère concentratif' in Réalisations et défis de l'Union européenne, Droit-Politique-Économique, *Mélanges en hommage à Panayotis Soldatos* (Brussels, Bruylant, 2012) 249–266.

[1] However, a number of works on different aspects of ancillary restraints are worth mentioning: DL Holley, 'Ancillary Restrictions in Mergers and Joint Ventures' *Fordham Corporation Law Institute* 423 (Barry Hawk ed) 423–59; JR Modrall, 'Ancillary Restrictions in the Commission's Decisions under the Merger Regulation: Non-Competition Clauses' (1995) 1 *European Competition Law Review* 40–48; FE González Díaz, 'The Notion of Ancillary Restraints under EC Competition law' (1995) 19 *Fordham International Law Journal* 3 951–98; G Conte, 'Ancillary Restraints' in G Drautz and C Jones (eds), *EU Competition Law* II (Deventer/Heverlee, Claeyes & Casteels, 2006) 66–468; H Lesguillons, 'Les clauses de non-concurrence en droit européen de la concurrence, Les grandes clauses des contrats internationaux' (2006) 4 *Revue de Droit des Affaires Internationales/International Business Law Journal*, 495–533. Regarding, specifically, a review of Spanish law and of the practice of the competition authorities in Spain, see M Muñoz Juan, 'Las restricciones accesorias a operaciones de concentración en la Ley 15/2007' (2010) 17 *Gaceta Jurídica de la Unión Europea y de la Competencia* 33–53.

I. NON-COMPETE OBLIGATIONS AS ANCILLARY RESTRAINTS

It is common practice to include in concentration agreements different types of what are known as 'ancillary clauses' that are not an integral part of the proposed operation itself but that limit the freedom of action of the parties on the market, thus entailing restrictions on competition, of greater or lesser importance, that the parties consider indispensable to the successful implementation of the transaction.[2]

Council Regulation (EC) No 139/2004 of 20 January 2004 on the control of concentrations between undertakings (hereinafter 'Regulation 139/2004'),[3] refers to 'ancillary restraints' as those 'restrictions directly related and necessary to the implementation of the concentration'.[4]

Those concepts, which are based on criteria that are 'objective in nature', are currently explained in the 'Commission Notice on restrictions directly related and necessary to concentrations', of 2005 (hereinafter the '2005 Notice').[5]

For a restriction to be regarded as 'directly related to the implementation of the concentration', it is not enough for it to have been agreed at the same time or in the same context as the concentration: such restrictions must actually be closely linked to the concentration itself.[6] That is, their imposition must be subordinated to the implementation of the concentration and must bear a strong economic link to the main transaction[7] in order to ensure a smooth transition to the new company structure in place after the transaction.[8]

[2] It seems that the first formulation of the ancillary restraints doctrine was made in Judge William Taft's Decision in *United States v Addyston Pipe & Steel Co* [85 F. 271 (6th Cir 1898), *aff'd as modified*, 175 U.S. 211 (1899). (See FE González Díaz (n 1) 954). However, several cases concerning non-compete clauses in the context of the sale of businesses are referred to in the English case-law dating back to the seventeenth and eighteenth centuries (see JR Modrall (n 1) 428). As will be seen below, in the European Community/Union legal system, the concept of ancillary restrictions was first developed by the Commission, under the supervision of the Court of Justice, within the field of application of Article 85(1) EEC, but it gained a new significance and impact with the entry into force of the first Merger Regulation.

[3] [2004] OJ L24/1.

[4] See Article 6(1)(b), second subparagraph, Article 8(2), third subparagraph, as well as recital 21 of Regulation 139/2004.

[5] Commission Notice on restrictions directly related and necessary to concentrations [2005] OJ C56/24.

[6] ibid, para 12.

[7] In the words of D Berlin, 'Contrôle des concentrations' in L Idot (ed), *Commentaire J. Mégret—Droit communautaire de la concurrence* 3rd edn (Institut d'études européennes/Éditions de l'Université de Bruxelles) 301, it consists in an 'economic link and not a mere coincidence in time or in form with the concentration' (in the original: 'un lien économique et non [...] une coïncidence temporelle ou formelle avec l'opération de concentration').

[8] See the 2005 Notice (n 5) para 12. As the Commission stresses, 'a restriction could, if all other requirements are fulfilled, be "directly related" even if it has not been entered into at the same time as the agreement carrying out the main object of the concentration' (2005 Notice, ibid, para 12, fn 1).

In a certain way those restrictions may be seen as 'the inevitable consequence of the concentration itself',[9] which is why they must be assessed together with the concentration, in line with the objectives of Regulation No 139/2004 and taking into consideration the criteria laid down in Article 2 thereof.[10]

Such restrictions must, moreover, be 'necessary to the implementation of the concentration'.

As the Court of First Instance (hereinafter the 'CFI') pointed out in the *Métropole Télévision (M6) et al v Commission* case,[11] the condition that a restriction be 'necessary' requires a twofold examination: it is necessary to establish, first, whether the restriction is objectively necessary for the implementation of the main operation and, second, whether it is proportionate to it. In that regard, the CFI endorsed, in substance, the Commission's understanding as outlined in the 'Notice regarding restrictions ancillary to concentrations', of 1990 (hereinafter the '1990 Notice').[12]

As the CFI put it, in order to appraise the objective necessity of a restriction it is necessary first to determine whether, in its absence, the main operation would be

[9] E Navarro, A Font, J Folguera and J Briones, *Merger Control in the EU*, 2nd edn (Oxford, Oxford University Press, 2005) 309. As the authors note (ibid, 308), the terms 'ancillary restraint' stress the subordinated importance of the restriction in relation to the main object of the concentration, whereas the expression 'directly related' underlines the necessary causal link between the two.

[10] Otherwise, the effects of the restrictions will be severable from the concentration itself and must be assessed according to Articles 101 and 102 TFEU (which 'remain potentially applicable') and other related regulatory texts and notices (2005 Notice (n 5) para 7).

[11] Case T-112/99, *Métropole Télévision (M6) et al v Commission* [2001] ECR II-2459. See also case 42/84 *Remia et al v Commission* [1985] ECR 2545, para 20.

[12] Commission Notice regarding restrictions ancillary to concentrations [1990] OJ C203/5. The *M6* case dealt with the application of Article 85 of the Treaty to a cooperative joint venture. The *Remia* case concerned the transfer of an undertaking encompassing non-compete obligations and falling within the field of application of Article 85 of the Treaty at a time when the first Merger Regulation had not yet been adopted. As the Court observed in paragraph 17 of this judgment, 'the fact that non-compete clauses are included in an agreement for the sale of an undertaking is not of itself sufficient to remove such clauses from the scope of Article 85(1) of the Treaty'. It must be said, in this respect, that Regulation 1310/97 (below) largely deprived of interest (and thus put an end to the related difficulties) the distinction between concentrative and cooperative joint ventures inasmuch as every joint venture of a lasting and structural nature ('full-function joint venture') must from then on be examined in the light of the rules on merger control. The criteria laid down by the case-law are nevertheless similar regardless of the factual and legal context of the transaction (see *M6*, above, paragraphs 115–17, and the Commission Notice concerning the assessment of cooperative joint ventures (93/C 43/02) [1993] OJ C43/2, paras 65–69. In any case, as JR Modrall notes (n 1 above, 46), the distinction established in the initial version of the Merger Regulation between concentrative and cooperative joint ventures favoured a more flexible approach from the Commission as regards the former type of joint venture, since, by definition, they do not give rise to coordination among the parent companies or between them and the joint venture, since they involve the lasting withdrawal of those companies from the joint venture's market. See also, in this respect: Commission Decision of 21 December 1992 (IV/33.03, *Fiat/Hitachi*) [2003] OJ L20/10; Commission Decision of 12 December 1994 (IV/34.891, *Fujitsu AMD Semiconductor*) [1994] OJ L341/66; Commission Decision of 27 July 1994 (IV/34.857, *BT-MCI*) [1994] OJ L223/36; Commission Decision of 21 December 1994 (IV/34.252, *Philips-Osram*) [1994] OJ L378/37; Commission Decision of 17 July 1996 (IV/35.337, *Atlas*) [1996] OJ L239/23; Commission Decision of 17 July 1996 (IV/35.617, *Phoenix/GlobalOne*) [1996] OJ L239/57).

difficult or even impossible to implement.[13] Using rather more precise language, the Commission explains the 'objective necessity' requirement as meaning that, in the absence of the restrictive clauses, the main transaction could not be implemented or could only be implemented under more uncertain conditions, at substantially higher cost, over an appreciably longer period or with considerably greater difficulty.[14, 15]

Where a restriction is objectively necessary to implement the main operation, it is still necessary, however, to check that its duration and its material and geographical scope do not exceed what the implementation of that operation reasonably requires.[16]

It is not necessary, however, to carry out a full economic analysis of such restrictions or an autonomous assessment of their impact on the market. The consequence, in terms of legal assessment, implied by the fact that a restriction is ancillary to the main transaction, is that the legality of those restraints depends solely on their connection to that transaction.[17]

The procedural rules under which the Commission applies those principles have also changed with time.

As amended by Regulation No 1310/97 of 30 June 1997,[18] Council Regulation (EEC) No 4064/89 of 21 December 1989, on the control of concentrations

[13] *M6* (n 11) paras 107, 109. As the CFI observed, examination of the objective necessity of a restriction in relation to the main operation cannot but be relatively abstract. It would not therefore be a question of analysing whether, in the light of the competitive situation on the relevant market, the restriction was indispensable to the commercial success of the main operation. As a matter of fact, in the absence of a rule of reason in Community competition law it would be wrong to interpret the requirement for objective necessity as implying a need to weigh the pro and anti-competitive effects of an agreement. Such an analysis could only take place within the specific framework of Article 85(3) of the Treaty, now Article 101(3) TFEU (see paragraphs 107 and 109 of the judgment). In this respect, it should be noted that the adoption of Regulation 1/2003 (Council Regulation (EC) No 1/2003 of 16 December 2002 on the implementation of the rules on competition laid down in Articles 81 and 82 of the Treaty [2003] OJ L1), bringing to an end the old system of mandatory notification in order to obtain an individual exemption and replacing it with a system of 'legal exception', rendered obsolete the procedural question whether the Commission should consider a notification under the Merger Regulation as a request for an exemption under Regulation No 17 with respect to ancillary restraints (see, in this regard, DL Holley (n 1) 425–26).

[14] See the 1990 Notice (n 12) II.5, the 2001 Notice (n 21) para 8, and the 2005 Notice (n 5) para 13. The expression 'with considerably greater difficulty' replaced in the two Notices of 2001 and 2005 the words 'with considerable less probability of success', used in the 1990 Notice.

[15] In its practice the Commission has considered a great number of restrictions to be 'objectively necessary' to the implementation of the main transaction. However, in its Decision of 18 December 2000 (COMP/M.1863, *Vodafone/BT/Airtel JV* [2001] OJ C42/11, paras 19–20), it held that a non-compete clause agreed between the parties was not 'directly related and necessary for the implementation of the concentration since Airtel is a well established company and its absence does not imply that the concentration could not be implemented or could only be implemented under more uncertain conditions, at substantially higher cost, over an appreciable longer period or with considerably higher difficulty'.

[16] See *M6* (n 11) para 113. See also the 1990 Notice (n 12) para 6, the 2001 Notice (n 21) para 9, and the 2005 Notice (n 5) para 13.

[17] See FE González Díaz (n 1) 963.

[18] Council Regulation (EC) No 1310/97 of 30 June 1997 amending Regulation (EEC) No 4064/89 on the control of concentrations between undertakings [1997] OJ L180/1.

between undertakings[19] (hereinafter 'Regulation 4064/89' or the 'first Merger Regulation') provided, in Article 6(1)(b), second subparagraph, and in Article 8(2), second subparagraph, second sentence, that any decision declaring the concentration compatible with the common market *shall also cover* restrictions directly related and necessary to the implementation of the concentration.[20]

In its 'Notice on restrictions directly related and necessary to concentrations', of 2001[21] (hereinafter the '2001 Notice'), that replaced the 1990 Notice, the Commission outlined, in light of its experience and administrative practice, its interpretation of the two provisions of Regulation 4064/89, cited above.

In the Commission's position,[22] the legal framework in force at the time did not impose on it an obligation to assess and formally address ancillary restrictions. According to the Commission, any such assessment was of a merely declaratory nature, as all restrictions meeting the criteria set out in Regulation 4064/89 were already cleared by operation of law, whether or not they were explicitly examined in the Commission's decision. As a result, the Commission would no longer make such assessments in its merger decisions.[23]

The Commission's position was struck down by the Court of First Instance in its judgment of 20 November 2002 in *Lagardère et Canal+ v Commission*.[24, 25] Relying on the wording of Article 6(1)(b), second subparagraph, of Regulation 4064/89, read in the light of its objective and legal context, the CFI found that the legislature had intended not only to confer on the Commission an exclusive competence to adopt binding decisions in this domain but also to afford the benefit of legal certainty to the parties in relation to ancillary restrictions.[26]

[19] Council Regulation (EEC) No 4064/89 of 21 December 1989, on the control of concentrations between undertakings [1989] OJ L395/1. Version pursuant to the corrigendum published in 1990, OJ L257/13. Regulation last amended by Regulation 1310/97, above. Corrigendum published in 1998, OJ L40/17.

[20] See also recital (25) of Regulation 4064/89 and recital (7) of Regulation 1310/97. The French version of the regulation reads as follows: '... couvre également ...'.

[21] Commission Notice on restrictions directly related and necessary to concentrations (2001/C 188/03) [2001] OJ C188/5. This Notice has been replaced by the 2005 Notice, which was adopted after the entry into force of Regulation 139/2004 (n 3).

[22] 2001 Notice (n 21) para 2.

[23] The Commission considered this approach compatible with its practice in respect of cases qualifying for simplified treatment since 1 September 2000. See Commission Notice on a simplified procedure for treatment of certain concentrations under Council Regulation (EEC) No 4064/89 [2000] OJ C217/32, para 14.

[24] Case T-251/00 *Lagardère SCA and Canal+ SA v Commission* [2002] ECR II-4825.

[25] The Commission acknowledged in its pleadings before the CFI that since the adoption of Regulation 4064/89 its merger control decisions included reasoning relating to ancillary restrictions. However, it submitted that the sole purpose of this practice was to give undertakings the benefit of its experience in the field, to make a contribution to the development of a legal theory of ancillary restrictions and to amplify the guidance given on the interpretation of that concept in its 1990 Notice (para 52 of the judgment).

[26] *Lagardère* (n 24) para 103.

The CFI came to the conclusion[27] that where the parties to a concentration notify the Commission of contractual clauses as restrictions directly related and necessary to the implementation of the concentration, they must be deemed to form an integral part of the notification and, in the case of a clear and precise request, the Commission is bound to provide an adequate reply, which is in the nature of a decision, in the same way as it is for the approval of a concentration.[28]

The new wording of Articles 6 and 8 of Regulation 139/2004 has taken into account the CFI's remarks. Those provisions read as follows:[29] 'A decision declaring a concentration compatible *shall be deemed*[30] to cover restrictions directly related and necessary to the implementation of the concentration.'

The Commission was thus able to carry on with the practice that had been overturned by the CFI under the first Merger Regulation. That is explained in the 2005 Notice by the following sentence: 'The amendment of the rules governing the assessment of restrictions directly related and necessary to the implementation of the concentration (…) introduces a principle of self-assessment of such restrictions.'[31]

Given the system of self-assessment adopted by the legislature in relation to ancillary restraints, the guidance provided by the Commission in its notices became increasingly important in order to ensure the necessary legal certainty for undertakings.

The successive applicable sets of rules may raise a number of delicate issues where a procedure starts under the application of a given legal framework and comes to an end or is subject to judicial review after the law has been amended. The 'rules of conflict' to observe differ according to whether the issues at stake are of a procedural or of a substantive nature. Changes in the Commission's practice, which are not always clearly and consistently outlined in the multiple notices it has published, give rise to further difficulties of application.

The remainder of my analysis of ancillary restraints will be focused on the issue of the duration of non-compete obligations.

[27] As to the CFI's reasoning on the powers and obligations of the Commission, see paras 73 to 103 of the judgment in the *Lagardère* case.

[28] *Lagardère* (n 24) para 90. The CFI recalled in this regard that 'form CO', a model of which was annexed to Regulation (EC) 447/98 of 1 March 1998 on the notifications, time-limits and hearings provided for in Regulation 4064/89 [1998] OJ L 61/1 stated, at para 11.1, that 'if the parties to the concentration, and/or other involved parties [...] enter into ancillary restrictions directly related and necessary to the implementation of the concentration, these restrictions may be assessed in conjunction with the concentration itself'. In that context, the parties to the concentration were 'asked to identify each ancillary restriction in the agreements provided with the notification for which [they requested] an assessment in conjunction with the concentration' and 'to explain why these [restrictions were] directly related and necessary to the implementation of the concentration'. See in this respect *Lagardère* (n 24) para 89.

[29] See Article 6(1)(b), second subparagraph, and Article 8(1), second subparagraph and (2), third subparagraph, as well as recital (21) of Regulation 139/2004 (n 4).

[30] Our emphasis. The French version reads: '… est reputée couvrir …'.

[31] See 2005 Notice (n 5).

II. EVOLUTION OF THE COMMISSION'S PRACTICE AS REGARDS THE DURATION OF NON-COMPETE OBLIGATIONS

As of the 1990 Notice, the Commission[32] seems to have adopted an increasingly strict approach to the duration of non-compete obligations, regardless of whether the transaction at hand concerns the transfer of an undertaking (or of a part thereof)[33] or the creation of a joint venture.

With regard to the transfer of an undertaking, the 1990 Notice[34] considered appropriate, as a rule, a period of up to five years where the transfer of the undertaking included the goodwill and know-how, and a period of two years where it included only the goodwill.

The Commission nonetheless pointed out that these were not absolute rules and that they would not preclude a prohibition on competition of longer duration in particular circumstances where, for example, the parties could demonstrate that customer loyalty would persist for a period longer than two years or that the economic life cycle of the products concerned was longer than five years.

Moreover, in relation to full-function joint ventures, the 1990 Notice[35] acknowledged that, to the extent that the obligation on the parent undertakings not to compete with the joint venture was essentially aimed at achieving the lasting withdrawal of the parents from the market assigned to the joint venture and, as a result, their disappearance as actual or potential competitors of that new entity,

[32] In the period prior to the adoption of the first Merger Regulation, the Commission applied the doctrine of ancillary restraints in the light of Article 85(1) to the assessment of non-compete clauses and other restrictions in relation both to the sale of a business (Commission decisions *Nicholas/Vitrapo* [1964] OJ L2287/64; 76/743/EEC, *Reuter/BASF* [1976] OJ L254/40; 83/670/EEC, *Nutricia* [1983] OJ L376/22; 85/78/EEC, *Mecaniver/PPG* [1985] OJ L35/54; 84/387/EEC, *BPCL/ICI* [1984] OJ L212/1; 87/3/EEC, *ENI/Montedison* [1988] OJ L5/13) and to joint ventures (Commission decisions 75/95/EEC *SHV/Chevron* [1975] OJ L38/14—the non-compete clause notified to the Commission had the same duration as the joint venture agreements, ie 50 years; 87/100/EEC; *Mitchell Cotts/Sofiltra* [1987] OJ L41/31; 90/410/EEC *Elopak/Metal Box-Odin* [1990] OJ L209/15). The Commission undertook to codify its former administrative practice in the 1990 Notice (n 12). For a review of the Commission's practice prior to the entry into force of the first Merger Regulation, see FE González Díaz (n 1) 958–82.

[33] In the 2001 Notice (n 21) (paras 12–13) and the 2005 Notice (n 5) (paras 17–18), the Commission explains, in relation to the acquisition of an undertaking, that although the restrictions agreed between the parties to the transaction may be to the benefit of the purchaser or of the vendor, the need for the purchaser to benefit from a certain level of protection is generally more compelling than the corresponding need for the vendor. Indeed, in order genuinely to obtain the full value of the assets transferred, the purchaser must be able to benefit from some protection against competition from the vendor, allowing him time to gain the loyalty of customers and to assimilate and exploit the know-how transferred.

[34] 1990 Notice (n 12) III-A.2.

[35] ibid V and V-A.

the prohibition may be regarded not merely as ancillary to the concentration but as an integral part of it.[36, 37]

Conversely, in the 2001 Notice,[38] the Commission, in view of its past experience and practice,[39] reduced from five to three years the normally admissible duration of non-compete obligations where the transfer of the undertaking includes elements of both goodwill and know-how.[40]

At the same time, the flexibility clause that had been accepted by the Commission in the 1990 Notice became stricter:

> Longer durations can only be justified in a limited range of circumstances, for example where it can be shown that customer loyalty to the seller will persist for more than two years, or for more than three years where the scope or nature of the know-how transferred justifies an additional period of protection.[41]

The Commission also hardened its approach in relation to non-compete obligations in the case of joint ventures within the meaning of Article 3(2) of Regulation 4064/89. The 2001 Notice indicated that such clauses could only be justified during the period necessary for setting up the joint venture and to enable it to enter the market, which the Commission considered to be, as a general rule, a period of up to five years. Non-compete clauses of a duration exceeding three years would need to be duly justified by the particular circumstances of the case at hand.[42]

That new practice had, in fact, been foreshadowed by certain decisions adopted by the Commission when the 1990 Notice was still in force, notably in

[36] This obviously implied that the non-compete obligations be limited to the duration of the activities of the joint venture, so long as the parent companies enjoyed a controlling stake in it, and to cover only products sold in the same markets (either those markets where both the joint venture and the parent companies were active or those where the parent companies sold their products before the transaction). See, in this respect, decisions of 19 May 1998 (IV/M.1132, *BT/ESB* [1998] OJ C307/5), para 20; of 22 June 1998 (IV/JV 2, *ENEL/FT/DT*, [1999] OJ C178/15), para 42; of 6 July 1998 (IV/M.1124, *Maersk Air/LFV Holdings* [1998] OJ C253/4), para 36; of 13 July 1998 (IV/M.1199, *UTA Telekom AG/Swisscom* [1998] OJ C288/4), para 24; of 17 November 1998 (IV/M.1334, *Volvo Aero/ABB/Turbogen* [1999] OJ C24/25), para 18–19; of 26 November 1998 (IV/JV.14, *Panagora/DG Bank* [1999] OJ C68/10), para 38; of 1 June 1999 (IV/JV.18, *Chronopost/Correos* [1999] OJ C302/6), para 43; of 1 December 1999 (IV/M.26, *Freecom Dangaard* [1999] OJ C365/2), para 30; of 13 December 1999 (IV/M.1675, *Ducros/Hero France* [2000] OJ C53/15), para 38; of 11 May 2000 (IV/M. 1745, *EADS* [2000] OJ C307/4), para 213; of 10 July 2000 (IV/M.1964, *Planet Internet/Fortis Bank/Mine JV* [2000] OJ C374/10), para 16; of 29 August 2000 (IV/M.1913, *Lufthansa/Menzies/LGS/JV*) [2001] OJ C127/11), paras 17–18. In some of the abovementioned decisions, in particular the earliest ones, the Commission appears to have confused the condition of being an integral part of the concentration and the condition of being ancillary (directly related and necessary) to it. As seen above, that distinction stems from the 1990 Notice (n 12) itself (see paras V and V-A). The Commission sometimes also refers to the need for a controlling stake either in the joint venture or in its competitors or both.

[37] On the ambiguities inherent in the expression 'lasting withdrawal from the market assigned to the joint venture', as used by the Commission in the 1990 Notice (n 12), see DL Holley (n 1) 453.

[38] 2001 Notice (n 21) para 15.

[39] See ibid, n 14, and the Commission's decisions mentioned therein.

[40] At the same time, the Commission retained, as a rule, the two-year period for cases of transfer including only goodwill (see the Commission Decisions mentioned in fn 15 of the Notice).

[41] 2001 Notice (n 21) para 15, and the Commission Decision cited in fn 16.

[42] 2001 Notice (n 21) para 36.

Bertelsmann[43] and in *Stora Enso*.[44] Longer periods were nonetheless accepted in exceptional circumstances.[45]

The Commission also strongly asserted that non-compete obligations between parent undertakings and their joint ventures extending beyond the lifetime of the joint venture ('post-termination non-compete clauses') could *never* be regarded as directly related and necessary to the implementation of the concentration.[46]

As a matter of fact, the Commission's administrative practice in the years prior to the adoption of the 2001 Notice[47] had already pointed in this direction, subject to various caveats.[48]

[43] See Commission Decision of 1 September 2000 (IV/M.51 *Bertelsmann/Mondadori/Bol Italia* [2000] OJ C290/03), paras 28–31. The parties had included in their Shareholders' Agreement a non-compete clause binding them and all undertakings under their control not to engage in the type of business undertaken by the joint venture during the (unlimited) period of validity of the joint venture agreement and for a period of one year after a shareholder's exit. The parties explained that the non-compete clause served the purpose of concentrating the parties' efforts in the joint venture and giving the joint venture an unimpeded opportunity for market entry. The Commission, however, considered that the non-compete clause was indeed directly related to and necessary for the market entry of the joint venture and could therefore only be justified for a period of five years.

[44] Commission Decision of 22 December 2000 (IV/M.2243 *Stora Enso/Assidomän/JV* [2001] OJ C49/5), paras 46–49. The non-compete clause notified to the Commission was envisaged by the parties for the entire duration of the joint venture agreement and for 12 months thereafter. The Commission considered that the obligation was justified for a period of only five years.

[45] In its Decision of 6 December 2000, *Framatome/Siemens/Cogéma/JV* (COMP/M.1940 [2001] OJ L289/8), paras 147–48, the Commission agreed to consider a non-compete clause of 30 years duration as ancillary to a concentration in the nuclear sector. The Commission took into account the fact that the nuclear industry is an industry with unusually long economic life cycles, justifying a long period of protection in order to enable the joint venture to assimilate the nuclear know-how which was transferred to it by both parent companies and to safeguard the considerable value of the investments made by the parent companies from any free-riding behaviour on the part of the other parent company in respect of the know-how and goodwill generated by the joint venture. It should, however, be noted that the parties had initially envisaged a non-compete clause for the entire duration of the agreement. Also, in *Pfizer/Aventis* (COMP/M.37.590 *Pfizer/Aventis*, 'XXXIst Report on Competition Policy 2001'—SEC (2002) 462 Final, para 242), the Commission agreed to qualify as an ancillary restraint a non-compete obligation for a period of 20 years after the parties gave a commitment to reduce it from the proposed duration of 30 years and in view of the relatively weak market positions of the parties involved and the lack of any appreciable foreclosure effects stemming from the exclusive dealing arrangements between those parties.

[46] 2001 Notice (n 21) para 36.

[47] In a considerable number of decisions adopted during the period of application of the 1990 Notice (n 12), the Commission indeed refused to qualify as ancillary restrictions non-compete clauses going beyond the lifetime of the joint venture, even for a short period. See in this respect, the *Bertelsmann* and *Stora Enso* decisions, n 43 and n 44 above, n 39 and n 40, and the Commission's decisions cited in n 36 above. The same hostility towards non-compete clauses exceeding the duration of the joint venture could be found in the decisions concerning the application of ex-Article 85 of the Treaty to cooperative joint ventures. See, for example, Decision of 18 October 1991 (IV/32.737 *Eirpage* [1991] OJ L306/22), para 7(5) (the parties agreed, at the request of the Commission, to delete from agency agreements a non-compete clause envisaged for a period of three years after the agreements had terminated), as well as the decision in the *Alenia-Honeywell* case, mentioned in the 'XXIIIrd Report on competition policy', 1993, para 226 (the parties had to renounce a very strict post-termination non-compete clause).

[48] In the case of a cooperative joint venture entered into by Fujitsu and AMD (Decision of 12 December 1994, IV/34.891, *Fujitsu/AMD Semiconductor* [1994] OJ L341/66, paras 33 and 35), the Commission found that a clause precluding each party from manufacturing competing products for

Following the adoption of Regulation 139/2004, the Commission once again changed, in the 2005 Notice, its attitude as to the permissible duration of non-compete obligations.

Concerning the transfer of an undertaking, the Commission[49] took the view that non-compete obligations imposed on the vendor are justified for periods of up to two or three years, depending on whether the transfer of the undertaking includes the transfer of customer loyalty in the form of both goodwill and know-how or only of goodwill, respectively.[50]

However, it must be noted that, unlike the previous Notices, the 2005 Notice does not contain any flexibility clause that could allow a longer period of protection even in a limited set of circumstances.[51]

As regards the duration of non-compete obligations as between parent undertakings and joint ventures, two main points must be highlighted.

a period of two years after it sold its shares in the joint venture was directly related and necessary to the implementation of the joint venture. It should, however, be noted that this Decision took into consideration the special circumstances of the case at hand: the clause applied only if either party sold its shares in the joint venture within the first 10 years of the life of the joint venture, a period which started to run from the date of the agreement, that is at least two years before the first commercial sale of the joint venture's products. The Commission has, in fact, considered it justified that an effective protection from competition be secured for the setting up and proper development of the joint venture (maximum of seven to eight years) in order to compensate for the very significant investment of financial and technological resources, and to offset the risks involved in successfully developing the products of the joint venture, particularly in view of the parent companies' complementary areas of expertise. In *BIB* (Decision of 15 September 1999, IV/36.539 *British Interactive Broadcasting/Open ('BiB')* [1999] OJ L312/1, para 148), the Commission cleared a non-compete clause applicable for a period of 12 months after a shareholder lost joint control over the company provided that the loss of control occurred within three years of the date on which the Commission Decision took effect. The reason for that restriction was the need to protect a joint venture and the investors against a parent company withdrawing from the joint venture and taking unfair advantage of the know-how acquired during its participation in the joint venture. In *Pfizer/Aventis*, the Commission, for the reasons cited above in n 45, justified as an ancillary restraint a three-year post-termination non-compete obligation after the parties gave a commitment to reduce the prohibition period from five years after termination. Similarly, in its Decision of 7 November 2000 (IV/M.2066 *Dana/Getrag* [2001] OJ C51/9), para 11, the Commission qualified as an ancillary restraint a post-contractual non-compete covenant during a limited period following withdrawal of one of the partners as the remaining partner had a legitimate interest in ensuring that its continued involvement in the joint venture was not undermined by competition from the departing partner, who would have received a considerable amount of information with regard to the joint venture's competitive strategy, its products, its costs and prices as well as its customers, and who would be able to exploit this knowledge to its competitive advantage.

[49] See the 2005 Notice (n 5) para 20.

[50] By contrast, the Commission considers that when the transfer is limited to physical assets (such as land, buildings or machinery) or to exclusive industrial and commercial property rights (the holders of which could immediately take action against infringements by the transferor of such rights), non-compete clauses cannot be considered necessary (2005 Notice ibid, para 21). That approach was criticised during the public consultation on the draft notice. It was recalled, for instance, that the transfer of physical assets may implicitly include the transfer of immaterial assets that are necessary to allow the acquirer to fully undertake an economic activity (see Comments submitted by the Association française des entreprises privées (AFEP)).

[51] That approach was also criticised during the public consultation (see, for example, the Comments submitted by Wind Telecomunicazioni, Linklaters and Simmons & Simmons). D Berlin (n 7) 305, considers, however, that those periods are merely indicative and that the parties to the concentration are free to show that a longer period is necessary.

First, the Commission has now clarified that those obligations[52] 'can be regarded as directly related and necessary to the implementation of the concentration for the lifetime of the joint venture'.[53] Although that conclusion as to the duration of non-compete obligations was never explicitly drawn in the 2001 Notice where, as a general rule, such a clause was considered justified for a period of up to five years,[54] the reasoning in paragraph 36 of the 2005 Notice is basically the same as that in paragraph 35 of the 2001 Notice, ie, that non-compete clauses reflect, *inter alia*, the need to ensure good faith during negotiations, the need to fully utilise the joint venture's assets and to enable the joint venture to assimilate the know-how and goodwill provided by its parents, and also the need to protect the parents' interests in the joint venture against competition, particularly competition facilitated by the parents' privileged access to the know-how and goodwill transferred to or developed by the joint venture. That the very same reasoning can lead to such different conclusions is, it is submitted, a legitimate cause for bemusement.

Second, the express refusal by the Commission to qualify as 'ancillary' non-compete obligations going beyond the duration of the joint venture agreement was removed from the text of the Notices. It remains to be seen whether that textual change will have any material impact on the Commission's approach to joint ventures in future. In any event, the guidance provided in that regard has certainly been weakened.

III. SOME FINAL NON-ANCILLARY REMARKS

In my view, a number of observations may be made in relation to the Commission's understanding of non-compete obligations.

First of all, the administrative practice of the Commission and the guidance it has provided have developed in a somewhat erratic way. This may, of course, be explained by the need to address practical problems arising from the application of the law and to adapt policy to the evolution of the surrounding factual and legal circumstances. That state of affairs nevertheless represents a source of **legal uncertainty** for undertakings.

The situation described above is particularly unfortunate in view of the introduction by Regulation 139/2004 of a system of self-assessment as regards ancillary clauses.

Next, some further comments may be made as concerns the expression 'can be regarded as directly related and necessary to the implementation of the concentration for the **lifetime of the joint venture**', used in the 2005 Notice.

[52] Provided that the non-compete clauses are limited to the products, services and territories covered by the joint venture agreement.

[53] 2005 Notice (n 5) para 36.

[54] 2001 Notice (n 21) para 36.

The Commission illustrates its approach in that regard by reference to certain Decisions made during the period between 1996 and 2000. In those Decisions,[55] the Commission followed the line set out in its 1990 Notice, from which it departed in the 2001 Notice.[56]

The question then arises whether, in its 2005 Notice, the Commission has reverted to its original understanding so that any non-compete clause would *ipso facto* be considered as justified throughout the entire lifetime of the joint venture, even when unlimited in duration.

Although this conclusion appears consistent with the underlying idea that the parent undertakings should withdraw from the market assigned to the joint venture, a different reading is also possible. A less stringent interpretation, taking into account the specific circumstances of each case, may actually be preferred in practice, as the use of the expression '*can be regarded*' instead of '*shall be regarded*' indeed suggests. However, if that approach is the one that the Commission intends to take, then the value of the Notice from the standpoint of legal certainty will be diminished.

Thirdly, the elimination of any specific guidance on how non-compete obligations extending **beyond the lifetime of the joint venture** will be dealt with, may give rise to complex questions of interpretation.

Should it be inferred from this omission that the situation is not covered by the 2005 Notice? We might then be faced with 'a novel or unresolved question giving rise to genuine uncertainty' within the meaning of recital 21 of Regulation 139/2004,[57] which enables the parties to ask the Commission to assess, expressly and individually, whether or not the restriction is directly related to, and necessary for, the implementation of the concentration.

The main problem is that the administrative practice of the Commission in that regard, as it may be deduced from the Decisions published prior to the adoption of Regulation 139/2004, does not provide the parties with clear guidelines on the basis of which they might carry out their own assessment of the non-compete obligations they envisage entering into for the period post-termination of the joint venture.

[55] See decisions of 15 January 1998 (IV/M.1052, *Eastman Kodak/Sun Chemical* [1998] OJ C32/5), para 40, of 7 August 1996 (IV/M.727, *BP/Mobil* [1996] OJ C381/8), paras 51–52, of 3 July 1996 (IV/M.751, *Bayer/Hüls* [1996] OJ C271/16), para 31, and of 6 April 2000 (IV/M.1832, *Ahold/ICA Förbundet/Canica* [2000] OJ C362/6), paras 25–26. However, what appears from the non-confidential text of the Decision is that in *Ahold*, the non-compete clause was notified (and cleared) only for a certain limited period of time, not for the entire duration of the joint venture. In any case, the Commission has not always been faithful to this line of practice. Indeed, in the Decision of 28 February 2000 (IV/M.39—*Bertelsmann/Planeta/NEB*), para 30, the Commission refused to clear a non-compete obligation aligned with the unlimited duration of the joint venture and limited it to a period of five years. The same taxonomic confusion between ancillary restraints and restrictions that may be considered an integral part of the concentration, which I noted above (see n 33), may also be observed here.

[56] See para 36 of the 2001 Notice (n 21). See also E Navarro et al (n 9) 320.

[57] See also paras 3 to 6 of the 2005 Notice (n 5).

I do not think it is possible to infer that, as they are no longer expressly prevented from being qualified as ancillary restrictions, post-termination non-compete clauses will necessarily be accepted in any case. Their *a priori* restrictive effect does not allow for such a conclusion.

Neither would it be appropriate to infer, *a contrario*, from the last sentence of paragraph 36 of the 2005 Notice, that any non-compete obligation between the parent companies and a joint venture going beyond the duration of the agreement should necessarily and automatically be appraised under Article 101 TFEU. The past practice of the Commission shows that, in certain specific circumstances, such non-compete clauses may be considered directly related and indeed necessary to the implementation, or the termination, of the joint venture.

That said, no guidance is given on the boundaries that must be placed on such clauses in accordance with the *proportionality principle*, or on *whether they should be assessed as clauses directly related and necessary to the creation or, conversely, to the termination of the joint venture*.

In fact, such obligation may be agreed upon the exit of one (or more) parent undertakings from the joint venture, while the latter still remains on the market under the sole control of one parent company. That situation may be treated as an acquisition of an undertaking with transfer of control and the imposition of a non-compete obligation on the vendor.[58]

A particularly delicate issue arises when the post termination non-compete clause was agreed at the time when the joint venture was set up rather than when the agreement comes to an end.[59]

[58] It should however be acknowledged that the two situations are not necessarily identical. In fact, while the acquirer of a company, in which it has never had a stake and of whose business it does not have a detailed knowledge, should, as a rule, benefit from appropriate protection against undue competition from the vendor in order to be able to gain market access, a parent company, which acquires sole control over a joint venture on the exit of the other partner, has inevitably had the opportunity to learn, during the lifetime of the joint venture, the main aspects of the business and to acquire the necessary know-how and goodwill. It is not therefore in the same position as a purchaser that becomes involved in a new activity from scratch.

[59] The Commission's decisions that may be relevant in this regard do not seem conclusive. The Decision of 24 February 1993 (IV/M.304—*Volkswagen AG/VAG/ (UK) Ltd*) [1993] OJ 38, concerns an agreement entered into at the time of the dissolution of a joint venture, which had been set up prior to the enactment of the first Merger Regulation. In the Decision of 18 March 1998 (IV/M.1113, *Nortel/Norweb*) [1998] OJ C123/3, the Commission considered that the extension of a non-compete clause for two years following termination of the joint venture related to a possible future operation, which was not part of the notified transaction and not therefore covered by the Decision. Similarly, in its Decisions of 21 December 1998 (IV/M.1368, *FORD/ZF*) [1999] OJ C32/5, and of 2 February 2000 (IV/M.1786, *General Electric Company/Thomson CSF/JV*) [2000] OJ C61/6, the Commission considered that the extended period of prohibition on competition following the withdrawal of one of the parents was neither an integral part of the notified transaction nor ancillary to it and that the justification of the clause would have to be assessed in relation to future transactions upon termination of the joint venture, without clarifying whether such clauses could or could not be included in agreements relating to future transactions. By contrast, in a number of other Decisions adopted in 1998—of 26 February 1998 (IV/M.1014, *British Steel/Europipe*), [1998] OJ C181/3; of 2 July 1998 (IV/M.1211, *Magnetti Marelli/Telespazio*), [1998] OJ C286/5; of 24 August 1998 (IV/M.1260, *Edon/Rova/Reco*), [1998] OJ C369/9—the Commission agreed to assess both the non-compete clauses for the lifetime of the latter and those applicable after termination together with the agreements creating the joint venture; indeed, it considered them to be ancillary for certain periods. In turn, in the

Since disputes as to whether restrictions are directly related and necessary to the implementation of a concentration, thus being automatically covered by the Commission's clearance decision, are now under the jurisdiction of national courts,[60] if the Commission does not intervene in the exercise of its 'residual function',[61] the resulting legal uncertainty risks harming undertakings by affecting the proper conduct of their business.

Moreover, legal uncertainty increases in a situation where the Commission, by virtue of its economic approach, calls for the application of similar criteria to the assessment of **clauses other than non-compete obligations** but which may, in certain circumstances, produce comparable, albeit not strictly identical, effects (*non-solicitation* and *confidentiality* clauses; *exclusivity* and *preference* clauses; *priority rights*; *rights of first refusal*; obligations of *prior consultation* or *notification*; restrictions to the *conduct of directors*; restrictions on the *use of trade marks*).[62]

Lastly, I would like to make some remarks on the appropriate framework for the assessment of clauses limiting the right to hold or acquire **minority shareholdings** in a company competing with the business transferred or the joint venture. The key issue is to determine under what conditions such restrictions may be treated as non-compete obligations.

The 2005 Notice addresses this question in paragraph 25, inserted in title III, under the heading: 'Principles applicable to commonly encountered restrictions in cases of acquisition of an undertaking'.[63]

According to that Notice, such clauses shall be considered ancillary restraints, unless they prevent the vendor from purchasing or holding shares *purely for financial investment purposes*, without granting him or her, directly or indirectly, management functions or any material influence in the competing company.

A number of issues arise in this context.

First of all, one may question whether, and under what conditions, such guidelines, though developed to deal with the transfer of an undertaking, also apply

Decision of 2 February 2000 (COMP/M.1820, *BP/JV Dissolution*), [2000] OJ C98/9, the non-compete clauses were only agreed at the time of the joint venture's dissolution and when sole control over its assets was acquired.

[60] 2005 Notice (n 5) para 2.

[61] ibid paras 2 and 3.

[62] In this respect, we may compare paragraphs 41 of the 2001 and 2005 Notices (n 21 and n 5). In the 2001 Notice the Commission explained that, 'since the scope of these clauses may be narrower than that of non-compete clauses, they may be considered directly related and necessary to the implementation of the concentration in a larger number of circumstances'. Such a reference was removed from para 41 of the 2005 Notice. This may be explained, as regards the duration of the obligations, by the Commission's new approach consisting in regarding non-compete obligations between the parent undertakings and a joint venture as directly related and necessary to the implementation of the concentration for the lifetime of the joint venture (para 36 of the 2005 Notice, last sentence). Paragraph 20 of the 2001 Notice should also be compared to para 26 of the 2005 Notice, both concerning the acquisition of an undertaking; the latter paragraph should also be read in conjunction with para 41 of the same Notice: whereas in the latter the Commission refers to the 'same principles as for non-compete clauses', in para 26 the Commission employs the less stringent expression 'have a comparable effect and are therefore evaluated in a similar way to non-compete clauses'.

[63] See also the 2001 Notice (n 21) para 19.

to the relationship between parent undertakings and their joint venture, either during the lifetime of the joint venture or the acquisition of minority stakes after the parent's exit or, *a fortiori*, after termination of the joint venture. In fact, the Notice does not explicitly deal with this issue, merely stating in paragraph 40, that 'non-compete obligations between non-controlling parents and a joint venture are not directly related and necessary to the implementation of the concentration'.

That statement is most likely rooted in the idea that what matters when it comes to non-compete obligations is the undertaking's ability to effectively control different businesses that compete against each other. That being so, a clause under which a parent company is precluded from acquiring a minority stake in an undertaking competing with the joint venture 'purely for financial investment purposes' is not to be regarded as an ancillary restriction.[64]

Yet the issue is not entirely settled. It is still necessary to assess the meaning of the expression '*material influence in the competing company*', as mentioned in paragraph 25 of the 2005 Notice. Indeed, the acquisition of a minority interest where the purchaser obtains, directly or indirectly, material influence over the competing undertaking cannot generally be seen as an investment made for purely financial purposes.

On the one hand, the meaning of the terms '*directly or indirectly*' needs to be determined. In particular, it must be decided whether it bears the same meaning as the expression 'of fact or law' contained in Article 3(2) of Regulation 139/2004.

On the other hand, and more importantly, it should be determined whether the expression 'material influence' has the same or rather a different, less strict, meaning as compared to the words 'decisive influence', which Article 3(2) of Regulation 139/2004 uses in order to define the concept of 'control'. In the latter case, the acquisition of a minority shareholding in a competing undertaking where the acquirer, without obtaining formal control, may nevertheless exercise material influence in view of its strategic interests should not be regarded as purely for financial investment purposes.[65]

[64] The Commission applied this principle in its *BiB* Decision (n 48). In this case the joint venture agreement prohibited the shareholders or any affiliate from holding more than a 20% interest in a competitor. The Commission held that such a restriction could not be considered directly related and necessary to the operation of the joint venture as the clause was not limited to the acquisition of material influence but also included the purchase of shares for investment purposes only. The Commission therefore examined whether the clause fulfilled the criteria set out in Article 81(3) of the Treaty.

[65] In a Decision of 11 June 2001 (COMP/M.2441, *Amcor/Danisco/Ahlstrom*), [2001] OJ C273/6 paras 26–31, the Commission found that a non-compete clause, a non-acquisition of minority shareholding stakes clause insofar as it conferred the possibility to exercise material influence in a competing undertaking and, *mutatis mutandis*, non-solicitation provisions, all agreed between the parties, could be considered ancillary to the operation for a period of three years from completion of the transaction. The Commission further considered that this reasoning also applied to the minority shareholder in the joint venture, Ahlstrom, in order to avoid conflicts of interest since it had contributed a substantial part of its business to the joint venture company. In its judgment in Cases 142 and 156/84 *British American Tobacco (BAT) and RJ Reynolds v Commission* [1987] ECR-4487 paras 37–38, the Court of Justice held that, although the acquisition by one company of an equity interest in a competitor does not in itself constitute conduct restricting competition, it may nevertheless serve as an instrument for influencing the commercial conduct of the companies in question so as to restrict

Whether a share capital threshold should be laid down, which would enable a finding of material influence whenever it was exceeded, is one of several unresolved questions in this field.[66]

In light of the ambiguity that remains surrounding the questions raised above, the undertakings concerned should be entitled, in my view, to request the Commission, in the silence of the relevant Notice currently in force and in the absence of a published Commission Decision on the relevant issue,[67] to expressly assess whether or not any restriction is directly related to, and necessary for, the implementation of the concentration, as envisaged in recital 21 of Regulation 139/2004 for 'novel or unresolved questions giving rise to genuine uncertainty'.

The obstacles frequently encountered in searching out and accessing the relevant Commission Decisions, together with a 'maximalistic' approach to the protection of *confidential information* which sometimes renders largely useless the publication of Decisions from which relevant indications as to the administrative practice of the competent authority might otherwise be gleaned,[68] increases the importance of the guidance that may be found in those Commission Decisions that are duly publicised.

or distort competition on the market on which they carry out business. According to the Court, that would be true in particular where, by the acquisition of a shareholding or through subsidiary clauses in the agreement, the investing company obtained legal or de facto control over the commercial conduct of the other company. See also the Commission Decision of 10 November 1992 relating to a proceeding pursuant to Articles 85 and 86 of the EEC Treaty (IV/33.440, *Warner- Lambert/Gillette et al* and IV/33.486 *BIC/Gillette et al*) [1993] OJ L116/21, where the Commission found that an agreement granting Gillette, the strongest operator on the market, significant pre-emption and conversion rights and options in Eemland, its main competitor, in a situation where Gillette held 22% of Eemland's equity, enabled Gillette to influence Eemland's commercial conduct even in the absence of voting rights or other habitual shareholders' rights (paras 25–26). On the implications that the acquisition of minority shareholding stakes may have from the standpoint of the powers of the Commission to order interim measures under Regulation 139/2004, see the Order of the President of the Court of First Instance of 18 March 2008 in Case T-411/07 R *Aer Lingus v Commission* [2008] ECR II-411. See also H Leupold and J Haans, 'Minority Shareholdings and Merger Control after Ryanair/Aer Lingus—"No worries, mate?"' (2008) *European Competition Law Review* 624–28.

[66] See in this respect A MacGregor, 'Mind the Gap: Reviewing Dangerous Minority Shareholding Cases in Brussels' (2011) 10 5 *Competition Law Insight* 18.

[67] In its Decision of 22 December 2009 (COMP/M.5728, *Crédit Agricole/Société Générale Asset Management*), [2010] OJ C107/1, paras 13–25, the Commission refused to qualify as ancillary to the concentration, under Regulation 139/2004, certain notified distribution agreements, in view of their wide scope and long duration.

[68] A number of Decisions adopted by national competition authorities may serve as an example. See, for instance, the Decision of the Portuguese Competition Authority (AdC) of 1 July 2010, Ccent 21/2010 *Newrest/Servirail*, para 6; see also the Decisions from the same Authority of 30 October 2009, Ccent 39/2009, *Unicer/NewCoffee II*, para 5.3, of 2 September 2010; Ccent 35/2010, *Fujirebio/Innogenetics*, para 5.2; and of 7 April 2011, Ccent 44/2011, *Essilor/Shamir*, para 6. In those Decisions, the Competition Authority makes numerous references to the Commission's 2005 Notice. However, in the published non-confidential versions of those Decisions, the nature, content, and duration of the ancillary clauses examined remain largely undisclosed. The information partly disclosed to which it is possible to attach some significance pertains to the duration of two ancillary restraints scrutinised in the *Unicer/NewCoffee II* case: one of them (non-compete or non-solicitation clause?) was cleared for a maximum period of two years; as regards another, non-compete clause, the reader is informed that 'by virtue of the exceptional characteristics of this case' that clause is cleared for a period 'of more than three years', without even indicating an approximate maximum duration.

Part V

Studies on EU Law and Economic Integration

15

The European Union and the Transformation of the Andean Pact into the Andean Community: From the Trujillo Protocol to the Sucre Act[*]

WITH JOSÉ MANUEL SOBRINO HEREDIA[**]

I. INTRODUCTION: THE REASONS FOR REFORM AND THE CONTEXT OF THE EU-ANDEAN GROUP RELATIONSHIP

THE PROCESS OF Andean integration, unquestionably mature after 30 years,[1] has recently been institutionally rejuvenated by the amendments introduced in the Sub-Regional Andean Agreement (Cartagena Agreement) by the Trujillo Protocol of 10 March 1996, which created the

[*] Different versions of this text were published in Spanish: 'Del Pacto a la Comunidad Andina: el Protocolo de Trujillo de 10 de Marzo de 1996. Simple Reforma Institucional o Profundización en la Integración Subregional?' in D-26 (Madrid, 1996) *Gaceta Jurídica de la C.E. y de la Competencia,* 83-138; in Portuguese: 'A União Europeia e a Transformação do Pacto Andino na Comunidade Andina: do Protocolo de Trujillo à Acta de Sucre: tentativa de reanimar um moribundo ou oportunidade para relançar a cooperação intercontinental?', in 2 (Coimbra, 1997) *Temas de Integração* 5–51; and finally in English under the same title in (1998) *European Foreign Affairs Review* 3 13–52. In February 1996 and March 1997 in Lima (Peru) the authors undertook, as independent advisers to the European Commission, a support mission to the institutional reform of the Andean Pact. The opinions contained in this chapter are of their exclusive responsibility, and do not necessarily reflect the position of the Community institutions or the Andean authorities. Miguel Filipe Cruz Silvestre, then a PhD Researcher at the Law Department of the European University Institute Fiesole Florence, Italy, undertook the 1998 English translation of this article, which was revised by the first author for the current publication.

[**] José Manuel Sobrino Heredia, Professor Catedrático of Public International Law at the Universidad de La Coruña; head of the Jean Monnet Chair of Community Law; former Legal Secretary at the Court of Justice of the European Communities.

[1] For a brief overview of the historical evolution of the Andean Pact, see section II.

Andean Community.[2] In the comparative panorama of integration processes, this Protocol is one of the most ambitious institutional reforms of recent years. Its adoption illustrates the advances of the sub-region towards interdependence[3] and highlights a consensus on the historical importance of Andean integration as an instrument supporting the development of the member countries of the Cartagena Agreement.

In general, it can be said that on the American continent integration processes are now in a period of renewed vitality,[4] in the context of what has been called 'open regionalism', along the lines recommended by the Economic Commission to Latin America and the Caribbean (CEPAL).[5] This has taken place in a social and economic context more propitious to economic growth and development, with a slight decrease in the external debt burden, an improvement in public finances and a return of foreign investment.[6] This may allow the sub region to become an 'emerging zone' in the world economy, after the past 'lost decade'.

[2] The text of the Protocol appears as an appendix to the Trujillo Act, Seventh Andean Presidential Council, Trujillo, Peru, 9–10 March 1996.

[3] It can be observed that while the Andean exports to the rest of the world have increased by an average of 2% per year over the last decade, trade inside the bloc increased as much as 26% per year: thus, in 1970, intra-Andean trade was valued at US$112 million, while in 1995 it had reached US$3.428 billion. For more complete statistics, see JUNAC, *El futuro ha comenzado. Grupo Andino: Logros y desafios* (Lima, 1995). Simultaneously, steps were taken towards the consolidation of the free trade area (between Bolivia, Colombia and Venezuela since 1992, and with Ecuador since 1993), as well as the negotiation of the Andean common customs tariff (*Arancel Exterior Comun*—AEC), approved in November 1994 (Decision 370 of the Commission of the Cartagena Agreement), after more than two years of negotiations. The AEC, which entered into force in January 1995, applied from February of that year to Bolivia, Colombia, Ecuador and Venezuela, with four levels of customs duties, depending on the degree of elaboration of the product. As for Peru, it has temporarily retained, by agreement with its partners, a special treatment. However (as will be shown below), as a result of the failure of the negotiations for its complete integration into the AEC, Peru decided to leave the Andean Community. Finally, the creation, in the short term, of a common market was precisely one of the reasons why the Andean group initiated the process of institutional reform analysed here. On the main stages of the commercial integration of the Andean Group, see JUNAC, 'La integración Comercial', 2 *Documentos Andinos* (Lima, 1994).

[4] There is currently a spectacular increase, in this area of the world, in the number of initiatives institutionalising regional cooperation: the North America Free Trade Area (NAFTA), signed by Canada, the United States of America and Mexico, on 17 December 1992; the Association of Caribbean States (ACS), created by the Covenant signed on 24 July 1994, by 24 Caribbean and Latin American States and by a representative of the French Republic on behalf of Guadeloupe, Martinique and Guyana; the Group of Three (Mexico, Colombia and Venezuela); the Asia and Pacific Economic Cooperation Agreement; MERCOSUR, created by the Treaty of Asuncion of 26 March 1991, between Argentina, Brazil, Paraguay and Uruguay, with the purpose of creating a customs union from 1 January 1995; the Initiative of the Americas, which aims to create a free trade area within the whole of the Americas by the year 2005, etc.

[5] CEPAL uses the expression 'open regionalism' to describe the movement which combines special preferential trade agreements with market forces and commercial liberalisation. What open regionalism aims to achieve is the compatibility and the complementarity of integration policies with policies aiming to increase international competitiveness. See CEPAL, 'Open Regionalism in Latin America and the Caribbean: Economic integration as a Contribution to Changing Production Patterns with Social Equity' (Cartagena de Indias, 1994).

[6] On the improvement of the economic framework, see the Communication of the Commission to the Council and the European Parliament of 23 November 1995, 'Unión Europea-America Latina.

On the other hand, the Andean integration process has been hampered by a series of endogenous problems[7] and marred by the absence of clearly defined objectives. These have prevented a clear and decisive advance toward regional integration, thus bringing about a somewhat 'schizophrenic' process. Interregional cooperation has been considerably enhanced and the Andean Group seems to be working well. However, some Member States, attracted by emerging regional interest centres[8] and eager to improve their positions in a future free trade area that may embrace both North and South America, freely opt out to negotiate individually with third countries or with other American groups. Lastly, the main actors involved (states, and social and economic organisations) have a negative opinion of the existing institutional structure. The loss of importance of the Junta del Acuerdo de Cartagena (JUNAC) and the scarce activity of the Andean Court have certainly played a part in creating this negative opinion. Criticism of the institutional structure of the Cartagena Agreement had thus begun to multiply, as if the structure itself were responsible for the slow pace of the Andean integration.

The lowest point was reached with the decision of Peru, after signing the Trujillo Protocol, to leave the Cartagena Agreement when it proved impossible to reach an agreement on the pace and the terms of commercial liberalisation and on the approximation to the common external tariff. The withdrawal was announced by Peru a few days before the Sucre Summit of 22–23 April 1997. The objective of that Summit was to consolidate the advances brought about by the institutional reforms approved in Trujillo and also to adopt the complementary documents necessary to implement the reform. Peru's announcement created some

Actualidad y perspectivas del fortalecimiento de la associación, 1996–2000', COM (95) 495 final, Brussels, 1995. On the main macroeconomic data of the Andean Group, see JUNAC, 'Grupo Andino: 25 años de integración y desarrollo', 1 *Documentos Andinos* (Lima, 1994).

[7] This refers to the controversy over the frontiers between Ecuador and Peru, the deteriorating relationship between Peru and Venezuela, the shortcomings of the State authority in Colombia, the difficulties of economic policy in Venezuela, the political peculiarities of Peru and Ecuador, and even the landlocked geography of Bolivia. However, the participation of Peru in the integration process has always been marked, until the withdrawal announced before the Sucre Summit in April 1997, by a considerable ambiguity: sometimes partner, sometimes associated, beneficiary of countless mechanisms to evade the system and of many exceptions to the general rules. In addition, the Chilean withdrawal, in 1976, for reasons linked to the nature of the regime set up by General Pinochet, constituted, in the short term, a blow to the consistency of the Andean process, which lost a dedicated partner and a dynamic economy.

[8] Mexico, Central America, the Caribbean, Venezuela, Colombia and Ecuador, for instance, are inclined to shape a regional process oriented towards North and inspired by NAFTA, while Peru and Bolivia lean towards the South, thus reinforcing relations with Brazil, Argentina and MERCOSUR. These tendencies are illustrated by the setting up of the Group of Three between Venezuela, Colombia and Mexico (Ecuador has announced its intention of joining the Group), the association of Bolivia with MERCOSUR and the negotiations for the Chilean association. In addition, Mexico has signed a free trade agreement with Costa Rica and Venezuela, and established free trade areas with CARICOM (the Caribbean Community) and the MCCA (the Central American Common Market). We should finally note the attraction exerted over countries such as Chile and Peru by cooperation in the *Cuenca del Pacífico*.

turmoil and an unexpected scepticism about the consistency and strength of the integration process. Behind the scenes, negotiations averted the withdrawal by granting Peru further tariff concessions, agreed on during the meeting of the High Level Group which took place in Quito on 23 and 24 June 1997.[9]

It must also be remembered that the Andean Pact was a pioneer in relations between the European Community and Latin America: cooperation between the two regional blocs dates from 1976, the year in which an institutional relationship between the EC Commission and the Junta of the Cartagena Agreement was established. A political dialogue was subsequently launched between the Andean Council and the Council of Ministers of the European Community, paving the way for the signature in 1983 of the first General Agreement on Cooperation between the EEC and the Andean Pact. Some years later, in 1990, as a result of the convergence of interests of both organisations in the fight against drugs, the European Community unilaterally granted to four Andean countries (Bolivia, Colombia, Ecuador and Peru) a privileged access regime to the Community market in the framework of the Generalized System of Preferences (GSP). In 1994, this privileged regime was extended to Venezuela.

It is well known that in applying Article 130-U of the Treaty on European Union (TEU), the EU favours a regional focus in its development policy and in its external economic relationships. In this context, support for regional cooperation and integration is perceived as one of the most important components of the EU development policy, capable of contributing to the harmonious and progressive incorporation of the developing countries into the world economy, and to a durable growth.

The relations between the European Union and the Andean Group are based on a General Agreement on Cooperation of the so-called third generation, concluded in April 1993. By increasing their cooperation in anti-drugs policy, the Andean countries gain advantages from special treatment within the GSP, on condition that those countries maintain their efforts in the fight against drug trafficking. In addition, the European Union has adopted a new agricultural scheme of generalised preferences in which special advantages are granted to the Andean countries, in the framework of a policy to replace coca cultivation.[10] At the end of

[9] The High LevelGroup was set up by the Sucre Presidential Council to negotiate with Peru the terms of its withdrawal or its continuation in the Cartagena Agreement. The fifth meeting of this group, held in Quito, on the abovementioned date, resulted—quite surprisingly—in the reversal of the Peruvian decision to abandon the Community, in exchange for a timetable for a gradual integration in the free trade area and the adoption of the AEC until 31 December 2005. It has therefore been agreed that Peru will participate as a full member of the Andean Community in all the organs and institutions of the Andean Integration System, and as an observer at those meetings of the Commission which discuss issues related to the AEC.

[10] See Council Regulation (EC) No 3281/94 of 19 December 1994 applying a four-year scheme of generalized tariff preferences (1995 to 1998) in respect of certain industrial products originating in developing countries, especially Article 3(2) and Annex V (OJ [1994] L348/1); Council Regulation No 2820/1998, applying a multiannual scheme for the period 1 July 1999 to 31 December 2001 (OJ [1998] L357/1), especially Article 7 and Annexes V and VII.

1995 an agreement was also signed to control certain chemical substances which are used in the processing of narcotics.

As the commercial ties between the two regions developed and strengthened, the EC and its Member States became the main source of investment for the Andean Region. Community aid has covered a wide range of activities, including health care and agricultural improvement, education and professional training, the reform of the legal, judicial and prison systems, and also support for the strengthening and deepening of the integration process and its institutions.[11]

The signature on 30 June 1996 of a European Union–Andean Community Joint Declaration was a concrete example of the EU's interest in the region. This initiative was intended to promote exchanges of information and consultation on international issues of common interest, at the appropriate levels.[12]

This dialogue may eventually lead to the signature of an Andean Community–European Community Political, Economic and Commercial Interregional General Agreement, similar to those which the Community has signed with MERCOSUR (*Mercado Común del Sur*) and Chile. This could be an agreement based on three pillars: the strengthening and institutionalisation of the political dialogue; increased cooperation; gradual and reciprocal trade liberalisation, which might in the future include the possibility of establishing a free trade area.

The vagaries of integration on the American continent, and in the Andean sub-region in particular, made the countries of the Andean Group aware of the inadequacy of their institutions to cope with the challenges of the new times. This contributes to explaining why those countries decided to adopt a new institutional charter which, in taking account of the new situation, would improve their integration into the world economic system and, at the same time, put them in a better position to attract the attention of the European Union, which had hitherto been focused on other regional initiatives.

It was in this context that the Eighth Andean Presidential Summit[13] was held, in the Peruvian city of Trujillo, on 9 and 10 March 1996, and the Protocol modifying

[11] See the guidelines adopted in the Commission Communication 'Unión Europea-América Latina' (n 6) above. It should also be stressed in this context that, a long time before the missions on the Andean institutional reform which originated this article, the European Community has previously been associated with the institutionalisation process of the Andean Pact, through the assistance given by the Court of Justice to the preparation of the Statutes of the Court of Justice of the Cartagena Agreement, when the latter was created.

[12] The meetings contemplated in the Joint Declaration will take place as follows: (a) in Europe, between the President of the Andean Presidential Council, the Presidency of the Council of the EU and the President of the European Commission, whenever it is considered appropriate; (b) at the level of the Foreign Affairs Ministers, periodically, according to procedures to be approved by both sides, and alongside other ongoing political dialogues (for instance, with MERCOSUR or the Group of Rio); (c) at the appropriate levels, whenever the circumstances so justify, in order to pursue the analysis of questions of common interest.

[13] The Presidents of Bolivia, Colombia, Ecuador and Peru attended this Summit, as did the Foreign Affairs Minister of Venezuela in the capacity of personal representative of the President, and the President of Panama in the capacity of observer.

the Andean Sub-Regional Integration Agreement (Cartagena Agreement) was signed. This document, also known as the Trujillo Protocol, was the fruit of a long period of political maturation; it not only contained the blueprint for the new Andean institutional structure, but also transformed the Andean Pact into the Andean Community. The Andean Community is thus an expression of the will to move towards real political and economic integration.

However, an over-emphasis on institutional improvement can sometimes—perhaps intentionally—distract the attention from other conditions which are also necessary to a process of integration. This is precisely the issue we shall deal with in this chapter. Indeed, we shall attempt to answer the question whether the institutional reform devised by the Trujillo Protocol is suitable for responding to the challenges posed by the new general context.

We will start in section II by summarising the development of the Andean integration and the antecedents to institutional reform. In section III we will present the new institutional structure set up by the Trujillo Protocol. Section IV will examine the extent to which this new structure, reflecting the tensions which are inherent in the current phase of Andean integration, strengthens the capacity of the new institutions to respond to the requirements of advancing integration. In section V we shall make some observations on the development of the Andean Community and its relationship with the EU, taking into account the results and the context of the Sucre Summit, and we shall finally draw some conclusions in section VI.

II. THE PROCESS OF ANDEAN INTEGRATION FROM AN HISTORICAL PERSPECTIVE AND THE ANTECEDENTS OF THE TRUJILLO REFORM

A. The Original Institutional Structure and its Later Development

In 1969, the Declaration of Bogota laid the basis for the future Cartagena Agreement, the name by which the Sub-Regional Integration Agreement is more commonly known. It was signed in Cartagena de Indias on 26 May 1969 by the Plenipotentiary Representatives of Bolivia, Colombia, Chile, Ecuador and Peru, with the purpose of promoting the balanced and harmonious development of those countries, and of accelerating their growth through economic integration in order to improve the living standards of their citizens.[14] The Agreement entered into force on 16 October 1969, and underwent two later changes in membership: in February 1973 the accession of Venezuela was

[14] In the abundant bibliography dedicated to the subject of the origin and evolution of the Cartagena Agreement see, among others, M Perez Gonzalez, 'Las organizaciones intemacionales en América (III)' in M Diez de Velasco (ed), *Las Organizaciones internacionales*, 9th edn (Madrid, Tecnos 1995) 601 ff; M Carraud, *L'intégration des pays andins* (Paris, Economica, 1981); G Salgado, *El Grupo Andino. Un concepto nuevo en la integración económica* (Austin, Institute of Latin American Studies, The University of Texas at Austin, 1972); H Maldonado Lira, *El Pacto Andino: Perspectivas en la integración latino americana* (Quito, Universidad Andina Simón Bolivar, 1997).

formalised, and on 5 October 1976 Chile withdrew.[15] Finally, in 1997, Peru came close to withdrawing, but the danger was averted. Panama has also been accorded observer status, and participated in this capacity at the Eighth Andean Presidential Council of Trujillo.

The original institutional structure of the Agreement soon had to be reinforced to face the changes arising from the process of integration. This process has passed through successive phases of activity, of inertia and of revitalisation, it being in the last of these phases that the need for a fundamental institutional reform originated.

The Andean Pact, another name for the Cartagena Agreement, was established with two main organs, a Commission and a Junta; the setting up of an Advisory Committee and of a Social and Economic Assessor Committee as auxiliary bodies was also anticipated. During this first period other complementary organs were added, the most notable being the Andean Foment Corporation (**CAF—*Corporación Andina de Fomento***), an important financial institution founded in 1970.[16]

This institutional framework was later enriched with new organs. On 28 May 1979, the Court of Justice was created by a Treaty signed in Cartagena de Indias, which entered into force on 19 May 1983; the Court started functioning at the beginning of 1984. On 25 October 1979, a Treaty creating the Andean Parliament was signed in La Paz, to enter into force on 17 January 1984; the Parliament was included among the main organs of the system by Article 5 of the Quito Protocol of 12 May 1987, in force from 25 May 1988. Subsequently an agreement signed in Lima on 13 November 1979 established a Council of Chancellors and, finally, in the Machu Picchu Summit of 23 May 1990, the decision was taken to create an Andean Presidential Council.

We will describe now the composition and functions ascribed to the different organs and institutions within the system set up by the Andean Pact, which continued to function until the Trujillo Protocol entered into force. These will then be compared with the institutional structure set up by the Trujillo Protocol.

The ***Commission***, of intergovernmental composition, was made up of representatives from each of the Member States (Article 6). It was headed by a President, appointed by rotation for a period of one year (Article 9). As the highest organ of the Agreement, the Commission had exclusive legislative power in matters of its own competence. It issued Decisions (Article 6) which had binding legal force on the member countries. Ordinary meetings were held three times a year and

[15] Additional Protocol to the Cartagena Agreement, of 5 October 1976, Lima. Decision 102, 'Cese para Chile de los derechos y obligaciones derivados del Acuerdo de Cartagena', adopted on 4 August and 30 October 1976, Lima.

[16] Other organs were: the Andrés Bello Convention, whose purpose was to develop programmes in the areas of education, science and culture, the Hipólito Unanue Convention, to act in the field of health care and the Simón Rodriguez Convention, aimed at dealing with labour matters. Specifically on the CAF, see R Fesard, 'El tratado que creó la Corporación Andina de Fomento' (1968) 3 *Derecho de la Integración* 28–35, and FJ Vendrell, 'La Corporación Andina de Fomento como sujeto de Derecho internacional público' (1976) 22–23 *Derecho de la Integración* 43–65.

extraordinary meetings were held when called by the President of the Commission at the request of any of the member countries or of the Junta (Article 10). The Commission was empowered to formulate the general policy of the Agreement, to ensure respect for it, and to approve the rules necessary to fulfil its objectives; it also created the conditions necessary to coordinate development plans and to harmonise the economic policies of the Andean countries.

The ***Junta*** **(JUNAC)** was the technical and administrative organ of the Agreement. It was composed of three members appointed by the Commission and acted 'only in view of the interests of the sub region as a whole' (Article 13 of the Agreement). Its members had to 'be nationals of any Latin American country (…) and shall not ask for nor accept instructions of any Government, or national or international entity' (Article 14). The Junta issued Resolutions, a denomination introduced by the Quito Protocol (Article 12), and its function was, in general, to prepare and present to the Commission proposals to implement the Agreement and the decisions of the Commission. To carry out these duties the Junta had a permanent administration.

The ***Court of Justice*** was created[17] in the image of the Court of Justice of the European Communities.[18] Its five members were independent of their respective states when performing their judicial functions. Three types of remedy were available before the Court: action for failure to fulfil an obligation under the Agreement, action for annulment and reference for a preliminary ruling. The object of these remedies, as well as the legal capacity to sue and to be sued, was defined in conformity with the criteria adopted by the Court of Justice of the European Communities. In the Treaty creating the Andean Court, the uniform application, direct effect and primacy of Andean community law was expressly mentioned, including as regards primary and secondary law.[19] As pointed out by its former President, Fernando Uribe Restrepo, this reflected the recognition that the process of integration necessitated an autonomous legal order, which would not survive without an independent and dedicated judicial organ.[20]

The ***Andean Parliament***, composed of five representatives from each of the national Parliaments of the member countries, was a political forum that

[17] By the Treaty signed in Cartagena de Indias on 28 May 1979 (see above). See also Decision 184, 'Statutes of the Court of Justice of the Cartagena Agreement', adopted on 19 August 1983, and the 'Internal Regulation of the Court of Justice of the Cartagena Agreement', adopted by the Court on 9 May 1984.

[18] A comparative study of both judicial institutions can be seen in M Diez de Velasco, 'Nuevas perspectivas de la justicia interncional. El Tribunal de Justicia de las Comunidades Europeas y el Tribunal de Justicia del Acuerdo de Cartagena' R Vinuesa (ed) *Temas de Derecho Internacional en homenaje a Frida M Pfirter de Armas Barea* (Buenos Aires, Fundación del Centro de Estudios Internacionales de Buenos Aires, 1989) 257–69.

[19] On the legal order of the Cartagena Agreement, see, among others, G Pico Mantilla, 'El Derecho andino' (Quito, Tribunal de Justicia del Acuerdo de Cartagena, 1992).

[20] F Uribe Restrepo, 'El Derecho de la integración en el Grupo Andino', (Quito, Tribunal de Justicia del acuerdo de Cartagena, 1990) 1.

examined the evolution of the integration process, proposed measures for the harmonisation of legislation and acted through recommendations to foster the integration dynamics, although it did not have any legislative powers.[21]

The ***Council of Andean Chancellors*** comprised the Ministers of Foreign Affairs of the Member States and was responsible for determining the joint external policy of the Andean countries. By coordinating the external actions of the institutions of the Andean System, it contributed to working out and implementing the general policy of the sub-regional integration process. It also determined the means of carrying out the actions of the joint external policy, deciding on the most appropriate coordination and consultation levels to ensure their efficacy (Article 3 of the 1979 Treaty). The acts of the Council, adopted by consensus, could take the form of Declarations, Agreements, Resolutions or Recommendations (Article 7 of the 1979 Treaty). Ordinary meetings were held twice a year.

To give the integration process a wider political dimension, it was decided at the Machu Picchu Summit on 23 May 1990 to institute an ***Andean Presidential Council***, composed of the Presidents of the Andean countries. This was intended to be the supreme organ of the Andean integration system, in charge of determining the general policy which would guide the integration process and of evaluating, fostering and directing the integration and the implementation of actions in the common interest. The Presidential Council met every six months and its Directives were incorporated by the Commission into the Andean legal order.

B. The Ups and Downs of the Andean Project: The Development of Sub-Regional Integration

During its 30 years of existence, the Andean Group has developed from a closed model based on a scheme of import substitution, investment planning and narrow preference margins into an open model, based on community mechanisms, governed by market principles, receptive to foreign investments and imbued with pragmatism.[22]

In this process of change, Andean integration has clearly passed through several phases. It would be impossible, given the scope of this chapter, to examine all of these in detail. Therefore, and merely as an illustration of the ups and downs of

[21] R Barros, 'Atribuiciones del Parlamento Andino como órgano principal del Acuerdo de Cartagena y orientador del proceso de integración subregional' (1989) 146–147 *Integración Latina americana* 16–28. In fact, the designation as 'common deliberative organ' in Article 10 of the Treaty creating the Andean Parliament therefore did not imply that the Parliament was endowed with legislative powers (see below).

[22] JUNAC, 'Grupo Andino: 25 años de integración y desarrollo' (n 6) 1.

the integration process, we will briefly enumerate them, since they help to explain the reasons behind the reforms of the Trujillo Protocol.[23]

The *first stage*—which extended from the entry into force of the Cartagena Agreement ·in 1969 to the integration of Venezuela in the Andean Group in 1973—was characterised by the setting up of the institutional mechanisms and the first decisions in the fields of action defined in the Agreement (harmonisation of policies, industrial programmes, a liberalisation programme, the common customs tariff, the agricultural and cattle-breeding system, commercial competition, physical integration, special arrangements for Bolivia and Ecuador, negotiations with Venezuela).

The second *period* extended from the Venezuelan accession in 1973 to the withdrawal by Chile in 1976. At this stage, efforts centred on the means to deal with these two important changes in the composition of the Andean Pact.

The *third phase* comprised the period from the Chilean withdrawal in 1976 to the signature of the Arequipa Protocol in 1978. During this period, the Lima Protocol of October 1976 was adopted, modifying the timetable for the liberalisation programme and the adoption of the common customs tariff.

The *fourth stage* extended from the signing of the Arequipa Protocol to the beginning of the crisis of the system at the end of 1983. The Arequipa Protocol attempted pragmatically at adapting the integration process to the economic and political reality of the region, characterised as it was by external debt and political problems in almost all member countries. During this phase, special emphasis was also put on the establishment of all the sectoral programmes of industrial development.

It was during the *fifth phase*, from 1984 (when the Commission of the Cartagena Agreement failed to approve any substantive decision) until May 1987 (when the Quito Protocol was adopted) that the process entered a period of lethargy and generalised non-enforcement of Andean law.

The Quito Protocol of 1987 initiated the *sixth phase*, characterised by a revived interest in the process of integration which accelerated until it ran out of steam at the end of 1991. During this period, the most fruitful for sub-regional cooperation, the Galapagos Act in 1989, the La Paz Act in 1990 and the Barahona Act of 1991 were adopted, in addition to the Quito Protocol. These documents gave the integration process a political dimension, and facilitated the direct intervention of the Andean Presidents through the Andean Presidential Council, which began to issue Directives encouraging the process. During this period, the legislative activity of the Pact multiplied, and an important number of Decisions were adopted to make it technically and politically feasible to fulfil the objectives proposed in the Presidential Decisions. With the change in the general direction of

[23] A comprehensive study of this evolution and of its key phases can be found in H Maldonado Lira (n 14).

the process, the policy of import substitution, characteristic of a so-called 'inward integration', was replaced by a much more open, dynamic and flexible policy. The Galapagos Act (December 1989) thus contained a strategic outline for the direction of the group, its objective being to consolidate the Andean economic area, to improve its insertion in the international environment, and to reinforce its contribution to Latin American unity.

Finally, during this phase, specific programmes were also adopted for the establishment of a free trade area and for the institution of the AEC (*Arancel Exterior Comun* or common customs tariff). The year of the signature of the La Paz Act, 1991, was extremely important for the Andean integration, characterised as it was by an ambitious production of laws and by the growing convergence of the economic policies of the Andean countries.

The period from the beginning of 1992 to the early months of 1994—the *seventh stage*—was another critical phase. There was confrontation between Member States in several areas. Some were related to the Pact and its functioning, and were connected in particular with the difficulty of reaching agreement on the common customs tariff or on the criteria for harmonisation of macroeconomic policies. Others were territorial, linked with border issues, like the military confrontation between Peru and Ecuador arising from the escalation of the border conflict, or the suspension of relations between Venezuela and Peru, which led President Fujimori to dissolve the Parliament and the Supreme Court of Justice on 5 April 1992. This situation led the Commission of the Cartagena Agreement to adopt Decision 321 on the 'temporary suspension of Peru', which temporarily relegated Peru to the role of observer.

The *eighth and last period* ran from May 1994 to the end of that year. During this phase, the dispute over the participation of Peru in the Andean Pact was settled and the common customs tariff was adopted. On the first issue, in April 1994, the Commission of the Cartagena Agreement issued Decision 353 on the Participation of Peru in the Andean Group, where it was stated that Peru resumed full participation in the Group, with certain derogations in relation to tariff levels and the free trade area (Decision 377). Decision 370, 'Arancel Exterior Comun', approved the structure of the common customs tariff, opening the gates to an Andean Customs Union.[24]

C. The Work Preceding Institutional Reform

As mentioned, at the Galapagos Summit in December 1989, the Andean Presidents adopted a so-called Strategic Outline for the Guidance of the Andean Group in order to strengthen Andean integration and influence its development

[24] An analysis of these questions can be found in JUNAC, *La integración comercial* (n 3) above.

during the 1990s. In general, this attempted to reverse the tendency for Andean integration to be marginalised within the context of the economic development of its Member States.[25] This strategic outline was streamlined at the La Paz Summit, in November 1990, and was spelled out in detail at the Barahona Summit in December 1981. The Strategic Outline thus became a very important political instrument for re-launching the integration process and for defining a model that was readily adaptable to the new global environment characterised by the opening up of economies, trade globalisation, and the pursuit of competitive development. In the Declarations of the Andean Presidential Council, the need to re-examine the Andean institutional structure was repeatedly stated.

As already discussed, trust and mutual understanding between the countries of the region suffered a serious setback from the events that occurred between 1991 and 1994. Before a plan for thorough-going institutional reform could again be put on the agenda, the political environment had to be improved. At the same time, economic integration needed to be revitalised by the creation of a free trade area, the setting up of a common customs tariff and the harmonisation of the macroeconomic policies (Decision 304). The participation of the Andean Presidents in the integration process was a key component of this strategy.

The new plan should provide the Andean countries with an institutional framework which was technically and politically capable of promoting, directing, coordinating and regulating the development of the Andean integration,[26] and would meet the needs of their social, economic and political development. It was further believed that it would not only strengthen the Andean organs, but also improve the coordination of their activities.

[25] As specifically mentioned in the Galapagos Declaration: 'Nowadays, sub-regional integration is marginal to the social and economic evolution of the Andean countries, and this is expressed in several ways: intra-sub-regional trade represents a very small proportion of the total external trade of the sub-region; the integration has little weight in development plans and in economic national policies; the countries use the community instances in their relationships with third countries in an incipient way only; the main enterprises and productive activities are not significantly integrated in the common programmes and joint projects; the participation of the social players in the process is meagre; and, finally, the integrationist conscience, is not, in fact, sufficiently rooted.'

[26] This opinion, globally shared by the Andean political class, finds a clear expression in the voice of a qualified observer, Ambassador Hector Maldonado Lira, who stated that: 'the direction of the integration process requires the organisational strengthening and the functional renewal of the organs which perform commercial activities linked to the accomplishment of the strategic purposes of the Cartagena Agreement. The Presidential Council, the Andean Council of Chancellors, the Commission, the Junta, the Court of Justice and the Andean Parliament, as essential organs of the institutional structure shall be renewed, and shall re-define not only the links among themselves but also with the integrationist dynamics, in order to efficiently exert their condition of community entities. Likewise, the remaining organs which compose the Andean integration system: the Conventions (Andrés Belo, Hipólito Unanue and Simion Rodriguez), the Andean Foment Corporation and the Latin American Reserve Fund, must be organically synchronized with the integration scheme, in such a way that they shall be converted from relatively isolated entities into structural components, through which shall be performed the complementary activities to those outlined and executed by the community organs'. H Maldonaldo Lira, *La reforma institutional del Pacto andino, apuntes para una posición venezolana* (Brussels, 1995) 10.

These initiatives were given a more precise shape at the Quito Summit of 5 September 1995, which, after a four-year intermission, succeeded in summoning the Seventh Andean Presidential Council. In the subsequent Quito Act, the necessary guidelines for the restructuring of the Andean Pact and for the deepening of sub-regional integration were established, through the drafting of an Andean Integration System, which paved the way for the thorough political and institutional reforms of the integration process. Significantly, the upgrading of the Council of Ministers of Foreign Affairs[27] as an intergovernmental political body was announced at the same time as JUNAC was converted into a General Secretariat. The community character of the Junta was thus diminished by transforming it into a mere administrative secretariat.[28] A 'New Strategic Outline', was also adopted, containing the guidelines for Andean integration, based on an open model which reinforced the political, economic, commercial and cooperation external relations of the Group,[29] and increased the importance of the so-called social agenda.

Within this process of intergovernmental reflection, a High Level Group, composed of government representatives, was charged from November 1995 to February 1996 with the task of re-examining and redrafting the Quito Act in preparation for the Trujillo Presidential Summit. This preliminary work was coordinated by a *pro tempore* Secretariat, of which Peru was by then in charge, with the collaboration of JUNAC.

These meetings issued three working documents (on 6 December 1995, on 12 December 1995 and on 9 February 1996) containing a draft for a future protocol modifying the Cartagena Agreement, which inspired the Trujillo Protocol, to which we will now turn.

[27] It should be remembered that, initially, after the signing of the Cartagena Agreement, in 1968, the Ministers of Foreign Affairs were placed in charge of the integration process. Afterwards, during the 1970s and the 1980s, this supervisory role passed to the Ministers of Industry, Trade and Integration, who made up the Commission of the Cartagena Agreement. The Quito Act established that this function should again be performed by the Foreign Affairs Ministers.

[28] According to the Quito Act, the Andean Integration System was to comprise the following institutions and organs: the Andean Presidential Council, the Andean Council of Ministers of Foreign Affairs, the Enlarged Council of Ministers of Foreign Affairs, the Commission of the Cartagena Agreement, the Enlarged Commission of the Cartagena Agreement, the Andean Parliament, the Court of Justice of the Cartagena Agreement, the General Secretariat of the Cartagena Agreement, the Entrepreneurial Advisory Council, the Advisory Council for Labour Affairs, the Andean Foment Corporation, the Latin American Reserve Fund, Conventions and Agreements.

[29] The priorities for external relations set by the Quito Act are: the establishment of a common strategy for the deepening of the integration with Latin America and Caribbean, in particular with Panama and MERCOSUR; cooperation with the Caribbean, in particular the Association of the Caribbean States; participation in the integration process of the hemisphere; the strengthening of the relationships between the European Union and the Asian and Pacific countries; and the adoption of positions corresponding to strategic goals in international negotiations in the different fora, particularly in the World Trade Organisation.

III. THE NEW INSTITUTIONAL STRUCTURE SET UP BY THE TRUJILLO PROTOCOL

A. The Organs of the Andean Integration System

The Trujillo Protocol replaced Chapter II of the Cartagena Agreement (called 'Organs of the Agreement') with another Chapter II called 'Of the Andean Community and the Andean Integration System'. Article 5 creates the '***Andean Community***', integrating the sovereign states of Bolivia, Colombia, Ecuador, Peru and Venezuela, together with the organs and institutions of the '***Andean Integration System***'. In Article 48 it is specified that this Community is a sub-regional organisation with an international legal personality.

The organs and institutions that constitute the Andean Integration System are, according to Article 6, as follows: the Andean Presidential Council; the Andean Council of Ministers of Foreign Affairs; the Commission of the Andean Community; the General Secretariat of the Andean Community; the Court of Justice of the Andean Community; the Andean Parliament; the Entrepreneurial Advisory Council; the Labour Affairs Advisory Council; the Andean Corporation of Foment (*Corporación Andina de Fomento*); the Latin American Reserve Fund; the Simon Rodriguez Convention; the Social Conventions (*Convénios Sociales*) to be included in the Andean Integration System and any other *convénios* that may be set up in this context; the Andean University Simon Bolivar; the Advisory Councils established by the Commission; and the further organs and institutions to be created in the framework of the Andean sub-regional integration.

B. The Coordination Mechanism

The goal pursued by the ***Andean Integration System*** is, as referred to in Article 7, that of allowing an effective coordination of the organs and institutions that comprise it in order to strengthen the Andean subregional integration, to promote it externally and to consolidate and reinforce actions related to the integration process.

The coordination of the activities of the different organs and institutions, obviously necessary on account of their large number, is to be achieved by the coordination mechanism which Article 9 designates as the 'Meeting of the Representatives of the Institutions' which constitute the System. The provisions relating to their competences and functioning are contained in Articles 9 and 10.[30]

[30] The tasks of the Meeting of Representatives of the Institutions constituting the System are as follows (Article 9): (a) to exchange information on the actions accomplished by the respective institutions in order to execute the guidelines issued by the Andean Presidential Council; (b) to examine the possibility and the opportunity of adopting, by agreement between all or some of the institutions, coordinated actions, with the purpose of cooperating in fulfilling the objectives of the Andean Integration System; and (c) to take to the Andean Council of Ministers of Foreign Affairs, in an enlarged meeting, information on the actions developed in enforcing the guidelines issued.

This mechanism shall be presided over by the President of the Andean Council of Ministers of Foreign Affairs and the newly created General Secretariat of the Andean Community shall act as its Secretariat. Its regular meetings are to be called by the President at least once a year, and extraordinary meetings are to be held whenever one of its component institutions so request. The meetings are to be held in the place designated before the meeting.

C. The Andean Presidential Council

Section A of Chapter II (Articles 11 to 14) is devoted to the ***Andean Presidential Council***, described as the supreme organ of the Andean Integration System. Created in 1990 by the Act of Machu Picchu as a way of formalising the summit meetings that the Andean Presidents had been holding, this political organ has now become part of the Cartagena Agreement, and consequently belongs to its fundamental or primary law.

The Andean Presidential Council comprises (Article 11) the Heads of State of the countries which are members of the Cartagena Agreement. According to Article 13, this Council must meet regularly once a year, preferably in the country which holds the Presidency, and hold extraordinary meetings whenever it is considered desirable, in a place designated before its summoning. The members of the Andean Council of Ministers of Foreign Affairs and of the Commission, as well as the representatives of the organs and institutions of the System, can attend the Council meetings as observers.

The Presidential Council has a President, who is the supreme political representative of the Andean Community. The Presidency is held, successively, for one year and by alphabetical order, by each of the member countries (Article 14). In the exercise of its duties,[31] the Andean Presidential Council may adopt Directives. These Directives and the political guidelines contained therein are implemented by the organs and institutions of the system (Article 11).

D. The Andean Council of Ministers of Foreign Affairs

The ***Andean Council of Ministers of Foreign Affairs*** ('Andean Council') is governed by Section B, Articles 15 to 20. This organ, which was first created by the Treaty signed in Lima, on 13 November 1979, is also now incorporated into

[31] The duties of the Andean Presidential Council are as follows (Article 12): (a) to define Andean sub-regional integration policy; (b) to direct and strengthen actions to be taken in issues of interest to the sub-region, as well as those relating to coordination between the organs and institutions of the Andean Integration System; (c) to evaluate the development and the results of the Andean sub-regional integration process; (d) to examine and take positions on the opinions, initiatives and recommendations issued by the organs and institutions of the Andean Integration System; (e) to examine all the questions and issues related to the development of the Andean sub-regional integration process and to its external projection.

the Cartagena Agreement. The Andean Council, composed of the Ministers of Foreign Affairs of the member countries of the Cartagena Agreement (Article 15), functions in a fairly complex manner since it can meet either in simple or in enlarged formation.

In *simple formation* it is composed only of the Ministers of Foreign Affairs. In this form it meets regularly twice a year, preferably in the country which holds the Presidency; it may also hold extraordinary meetings at the request of any of its members, to be held wherever it is called upon to do so (Article 18).[32]

The Protocol also established the socalled *enlarged formation* of the Andean Council, composed of the members of the simple formation plus the representatives to the Commission, who shall meet at least once a year. It may also meet at the level of deputies whenever it is considered necessary, to deal with matters related to the Cartagena Agreement which are of common interest to both organs (Article 20).[33]

The Andean Council is presided over by the Minister of Foreign Affairs of the country holding the Presidency of the Andean Presidential Council in any particular year. It is also provided that the functions of coordinating the Andean Integration System, which fall to the President of the Andean Council, may likewise be performed by the Minister of Foreign Affairs of the country holding the Presidency of the Andean Presidential Council, in the capacity of *pro tempore* Secretariat of both organs, with the technical support of the General Secretariat of the Andean Community.

[32] The tasks of the Andean Council, when acting in its simple formation, are defined by Article 16 as follows: (a) to determine the foreign policy of the member countries in the issues which are of sub-regional interest, as well as to direct and coordinate the external action of the various organs and institutions of the Andean Integration System; (b) to determine, implement and evaluate, in coordination with the Commission, the general policy of the Andean sub-regional integration process; (c) to implement the Directives addressed to it by the Andean Presidential Council and to supervise the implementation of the Directives addressed to other organs and institutions of the Andean Integration System; (d) to sign Conventions and Agreements with third countries, or groups of countries, or international organisations on general issues of external policy and cooperation; (e) to coordinate the common position of the member countries at international fora and negotiations, within the limits of its competence; (f) to represent the Andean Community on the questions and acts of common interest, within its fields of competence, in conformity with the norms and objectives of the Agreement; (g) to recommend or to take measures aimed at achieving the objectives of the Cartagena Agreement, within the its limits of competence; (h) to supervise the harmonious accomplishment of the obligations derived from the Cartagena Agreement and from the Treaty of Montevideo of 1980; (i) and (j) to approve and modify its internal regulation as well as, on the proposal of the Commission, the Regulation of the General-Secretariat; and (k) to keep informed about and decide on all the other issues of common interest belonging to the fields of its competence.

[33] In enlarged formation, the Andean Council will deal with issues such as: (a) preparing the meetings of the Andean Presidential Council; (b) electing and, when necessary, replacing the Secretary General of the Andean Community; (c) putting forward to the Andean Presidential Council any amendments to the Cartagena Agreement; (e) evaluating the management of the General Secretariat; (e) examining the initiatives and proposals submitted to it by the member countries or by the General Secretariat; and (f) dealing with any other issues which the Council or the Commission, in common agreement, consider necessary.

Finally, it has been established that the Andean Council may issue Declarations and Decisions adopted unanimously. The latter form part of the legal order of the Andean Community (Article 17).

Section C, Articles 21 to 28, of the Agreement is dedicated to the ***Commission of the Andean Community***. According to those provisions, the Commission, in its *simple formation*, is composed of a plenipotentiary representative from each of the governments of the Member States. Each government may appoint a permanent representative and a deputy (Article 21). When meeting in *enlarged formation* of a sectorial character, the Commission of the Andean Community is comprised jointly of the permanent representative and the ministers and secretaries of State of the policy area under discussion at the meeting (Article 25).

In its simple formation, the Commission meets regularly three times a year, and, on an extraordinary basis, when called by the President at the request of any of the member countries or of the General Secretariat. Its sessions take place at the seat of the General Secretariat[34] but they may also be held in other locations (Article 24).[35]

The meetings of the enlarged Commission are convened by the President, on the initiative of one or more member countries or of the General Secretariat (Article 25).[36] The Office of President is held for one year by the representative of the country holding the Presidency of the Andean Presidential Council (Article 23).

[34] According to the Trujillo Protocol, the General Secretariat was to have its seat in Lima, Peru, where the Junta of the Cartagena Agreement already had its seat. The withdrawal of Peru from the Community would have led to the designation of a new seat (and, in fact, a new seat was chosen by the Sucre Summit—Santa Fé de Bogota). However, since Peru did not withdraw from the *Comunidad*, the General Secretariat remains in Lima.

[35] The following tasks are carried out by the Commission, in its simple formation: (a) to determine, implement and evaluate the Andean sub-regional integration policy in trade and investment matters, in coordination, when necessary, with the Council of Ministers of Foreign Affairs; (b) to adopt the necessary measures to fulfil the objectives of the Cartagena Agreement, as well as to implement the Directives issued by the Andean Presidential Council; (c) to coordinate the common positions of the member countries at international fora and negotiations, within the limits of their respective competences; (d) to supervise the harmonious accomplishment of the obligations deriving from the present Agreement and from the Montevideo Treaty of 1980; (e) to approve and modify its own regulation; (f) to approve, reject or amend proposals which the member countries, individually or collectively, or the General Secretariat submit for its consideration; (g) to maintain a permanent liaison with the organs and institutions composing the Andean Integration System, in order to ensure that the coordination of programmes and actions are directed to the accomplishment of their common objectives; (h) to represent the Andean Community in the issues and acts of common interest, within its fields of competence, in conformity with the norms and objectives of the Agreement; (i) to approve the annual budgets and evaluate the implementation of the budget of the General Secretariat and of the Court of Justice of the Andean Community, as well as to set the amount of the contribution of each member country; and (j) to submit a proposal for the internal regulation of the General Secretariat to the Andean Council of Ministers of Foreign Affairs.

[36] The Commission meets in its enlarged formation to deal with issues of a sectorial character, establish norms to ensure the coordination of development plans, and the harmonisation of the economic policies of the member countries, and, also, to be informed and decide on all matters of common interest (of a sectorial nature, it can be assumed) (see Article 25).

Contrary to what was stipulated in the former version of the Cartagena Agreement (Article 6), the Commission of the Andean Community is no longer the supreme organ of the Agreement, and no longer has a monopoly on legislation. Nevertheless, it retains some legislative powers, in that it may adopt Decisions that are part of the Andean Community legal order[37] and tends to constitute the core of Andean secondary legislation.

The initiative for issuing Decisions now belongs to the General Secretariat and the member countries;[38] proposals must, except in particular and duly justified cases, be put forward at least 15 days before the date of the Commission's meetings (Article 27). Each country has a vote, and decisions are approved by the (absolute) majority of the member countries (Articles 25, *in fine*, and 26).

However, for a decision to be validly adopted by the (absolute) majority of the member countries, there must be no dissenting votes (Article 26, paragraphs (a), (b) and (d)) and, on matters related to the special regime established for Bolivia and Ecuador (Article 26, paragraph (c)), the proposals must attract the votes of at least one of the two countries concerned. Proposals receiving the approval of the (absolute) majority of the member countries but which are the object of any votes against are devolved, for consideration, to the country which made the proposal. That country has between one and three months to bring an amended proposal back to the Commission[39] with the changes it considers necessary. The modified proposal will be considered approved if it attracts the votes of the (absolute) majority of the member countries (cf Articles 26, paragraph (b),[40] and 27).

E. The General Secretariat of the Andean Community

The ***General Secretariat of the Andean Community***, with which Section D, Articles 29 to 39, of the Protocol is concerned, is clearly the main innovation in the new Andean institutional scheme. Its creation was accompanied by the disappearance of JUNAC, the Junta of the Cartagena Agreement, the organ which had by far the greatest community character in the Andean Integration System. Like JUNAC, the General Secretariat is a permanent body with an essentially technical function, even though the Trujillo Protocol describes it, more precisely, as the executive

[37] However, contrary to what happens with the Decisions of the Andean Council (Article 17), it should be noted that Article 21 of the Protocol does not specify whether the Decisions of the Commission are part of the same legal order. It must however be read in conjunction with Article 1 of the Treaty Creating the Court of Justice.

[38] Thus, the General Secretariat, successor to JUNAC, has lost its monopoly of legislative initiative, and now exercises it jointly with the Member States.

[39] Or the Andean Council, since, according to the text of Article 27, the same mechanism applies to the respective deliberations.

[40] In the cases provided for in this provision, for which the initiative belongs to the General Secretariat, it is further required for the definitive approval of the proposal, that there be no negative votes. However, if a country has voted against on a prior occasion, this is not taken into account.

organ of the Andean Community. Its importance in the context of the Andean integration derives from the fact that it acts 'exclusively in view of the interests of the Subregion' (Article 29).[41]

As to its composition, the Trujillo Protocol establishes that the General Secretariat will be directed by a ***Secretary General***, assisted by Director-Generals, whose number and competences are to be established by Regulation. The Secretary General will be chosen unanimously by the Andean Council of Ministers of Foreign Affairs, in enlarged formation, from a selection of highly representative persons of recognised prestige who are nationals of the member countries, for a period of five years that may be renewed only once (Article 32).[42] The Director-Generals will be appointed by the Secretary General after prior consultation with the member countries and in conformity with the structure of the General Secretariat. The Director-Generals, to whom responsibility will be

[41] The tasks of the General Secretariat are as follows (Article 30): (a) to supervise the application of the Agreement and to ensure that the norms integrating the Andean Community legal order are respected; (b) to accomplish what is required by the Andean Council of Foreign Affairs Ministers and by the Commission; (c) to present to the Andean Council of Ministers of Foreign Affairs or to the Commission proposals for Decisions, in conformity with its respective competences, as well as to put forward initiatives and suggestions at the meeting of the Andean Council of Ministers of Foreign Affairs, to facilitate or accelerate the achievement of the Agreement and the realisation of its objectives with the least delay possible; (d) to carry out the required studies and propose the necessary measures concerning the special treatment applied to Bolivia and Ecuador and, in general, relative to the participation of these two countries in the Agreement; (e) to annually evaluate and inform the Andean Council of Ministers of Foreign Affairs and the Commission of the results of the application of the Agreement and the fulfillment of its objectives, paying special attention to the achievement of the principle of fair distribution of the benefits of integration, and to propose any corrective measures; (f) to perform the technical studies and the coordination tasks which are requested by the other organs of the Andean Integration System, and others that, in its opinion, are necessary; (g) to maintain permanent working relations with the member countries, in coordination with the national integration organ designated for this purpose in each country; (h) to set out its annual working programme, which shall include, preferentially, the works requested by the organs of the System; (i) to promote periodic meetings of the national organs in charge of determining and pursuing the economic policy and, especially, of those responsible for planning; (j) to maintain work relations with the executive organs of other regional integration and cooperation organisations in order to intensify their mutual relations of cooperation; (k) to draft the minutes of the meetings of the Andean Council of Ministers of Foreign Affairs and of the Commission, and to make proposals for the agenda of their meetings, in coordination with the Presidents of the referred organs; (l) to be the trustee of the minutes of the meetings and other documents of the organs of the Andean System of Integration and to guarantee their authenticity; (m) to publish the *Gaceta Oficial del Acuerdo de Cartagena* (Official Journal of the Cartagena Agreement); (n) to discharge the functions of secretary of the Meeting of Representatives of the institutions constituting the Andean System of Integration; and (o) to carry out other tasks which the law of the Andean Community expressly requests.

[42] The tasks of the Secretary General are described as follows (Article 34): (a) to act as the legal representative of the General Secretariat; (b) to propose to the Commission or to the Andean Council of Ministers of Foreign Affairs initiatives related to the internal regulation of the General Secretariat; (c) to hire and fire technical and administrative staff, according to the regulation of the General Secretariat; (d) to participate, with the right to intervene, at the sessions of the Andean Council of Ministers of Foreign Affairs, of the Commission and of their respective enlarged sessions, and, when invited, at the meetings of the other organs of the System; (e) to present to the Commission the draft annual budget for approval; and (f) to present to the Andean Council of Ministers of Foreign Affairs, meeting in enlarged composition, an annual report of the activities of the General Secretariat.

entrusted for certain technical areas, will be high-level professionals appointed strictly as a result of their academic achievements, high reputation, good character and experience; they must be nationals of one of the Member States and, in appointing them, account will be taken of the need to create a balanced subregional geographical distribution (Article 35).

The General Secretariat has the technical and administrative personnel necessary to fulfil its functions; even though a balanced subregional geographic distribution of its staff is desirable, the personnel may be of any nationality whatsoever (Article 37).[43]

Perhaps the most original provision regarding the composition and exercise of the functions of the General Secretariat is that enshrined in Article 36, according to which, for the resolution of the disputes in which interests of two or more Member States appear to be in conflict, the Secretary General is entitled to call upon the technical collaboration of Special Experts, whose appointment and duties will be governed by the internal regulation of the General Secretariat. This is the result of a last-minute compromise between the Heads of State at the Trujillo Summit.

According to Article 29, the General Secretariat adopts Resolutions, but it is not clear from the text of the Protocol whether these Resolutions are part of the Andean legal order. As happens with the Commission's Decisions, it is Article 1, paragraph (d), of the Treaty Creating the Court of Justice of the Cartagena Agreement, as amended by the Modifying Protocol of Cochabamba (see below) that permits to answer that question affirmatively.

F. The Court of Justice of the Andean Community

The Protocol establishes, in its Section E, Articles 40 and 41, that the ***Court of Justice*** is the judicial body of the Andean Community, has its seat in Quito and is governed by the Treaty which instituted it, by its modifying Protocols and by the Cartagena Agreement. The monopoly of judicial control held by the Court of Justice appears to be reinforced in Section I, Article 47, when, referring to the solution of disputes arising in relation to the application of the legal order of the Andean Community, it is made clear that this Community is subject to the rules of the Treaty which creates the Court.

In general terms, it can be said that, like the Court of Justice of the European Communities, the Court of Justice of the Andean Community ensures respect for the Andean legal order and its uniform interpretation; it also has jurisdiction in disputes stemming from its application, with complete independence of the governments and the organs of the System. The Treaty instituting the Court of Justice

[43] It is expected that these personnel will be, totally or partially, provided for by the JUNAC.

has recently been revised by the so-called Cochabamba Protocol,[44] with the aim of achieving an efficient system of judicial review of the sub-regional integration process. As a result of this Protocol, new types of action have been instituted and existing ones have been strengthened.

It is not our aim to explain the structure of the Court and the way in which it functions. Nevertheless, it is worth mentioning that some of the innovations introduced by the Cochabamba Protocol tend to make it easier for private parties to bring an action for annulment, by extending the time limit for such actions[45] and softening the admissibility conditions of actions brought by individuals against acts of a normative character.[46]

The Protocol (Article 21, second indent) expressly empowers the Court to order the suspension of operation of the contested act, as well as other interim measures, when they are necessary to preserve the full effectiveness of the final decision in the pending case. As provided for in Article 20, indents 2 and 3, an objection of illegality may also be raised before a national judge, leading to a declaration that the contested act is inapplicable, even when such an act cannot, or no longer, be challenged by the applicant, provided that a question for preliminary ruling on the validity of the Andean act is referred to the Court of Justice.

In addition, private parties, which were already admitted, when their rights were affected, to apply to national courts in the case of a breach of an obligation imposed on Member States by the Treaties,[47] may now bring infringement proceedings through the General Secretariat against a Member State, in the case of a failure to fulfil an obligation under the Andean law, under the same conditions as any member country can bring proceedings (Article 25, new). The combined use of the two methods of appeal is however excluded.

Finally, an action for failure to act, or for inactivity, has been created. This new judicial route, non-existent up to now in the Andean legal order, can be used, under certain conditions, by Member States and by private parties (Article 37).

G. The Andean Parliament

Section F, Articles 42 and 43, deals with the ***Andean Parliament***. This is described as the deliberative organ of the System, of a Community nature and with a

[44] Protocol Amending the Treaty Creating the Court of Justice of the Cartagena Agreement, signed in the city of Cochabamba, Bolivia, on 28 May 1996.

[45] From one to two years, after the contested provision entered into force (Article 20).

[46] Natural and legal persons can lodge an action for annulment against Decisions of the Andean Council and of the Commission, as well as against Resolutions of the General Secretariat and the *Convénios* 'which affect their individual rights or legitimate interests' (Article 19). As can be seen, the admissibility conditions are, at least on paper, more generous than those set out in Article 173 of the EC Treaty. Moreover, these conditions were already larger in the previous wording of the same provision, which referred to Commission Decisions and Resolutions of the Junta 'which are addressed to them and cause them harm'.

[47] See ex-Article 27, now Article 31.

mission to represent the peoples of the Andean Community. In accordance with this mission, it is established that, in the future, the Parliament, having its permanent seat in Santa Fé de Bogota, shall comprise members elected by universal and direct suffrage, following a procedure to be adopted through an Additional Protocol which will include the necessary criteria for national representation.

This is undoubtedly an innovation of the greatest importance to the future configuration of the Community, its democratic nature and its proximity to the Andean peoples and their aspirations. In transitional provisions (Article 7), it is specified that elections will be held within five years after the Protocol enters into force. Meanwhile, the Andean Parliament will be composed of representatives of the National Congresses, in conformity with their own internal regulations and the general regulation of the Andean Parliament (Article 42, second indent).[48]

H. The Advisory Bodies

As established in Section G (Article 44), the advisory institutions of the Andean System are the ***Entrepreneurial Advisory Council*** and the ***Advisory Council for Labour Affairs***, composed of delegates directly elected by the organisations representing businesses and trade unions in each of the member countries. These Councils can issue opinions, addressed to the Council of Ministers, to the Commission or to the General Secretariat, upon request or on their own initiative, on issues of regional integration, insofar as their interests are concerned.

The advisory councils may also be called to the meetings of the working groups or of the groups of governmental experts drawing up draft decisions, and may also participate, with right of intervention, in the meetings of the Commission.

Finally, Section H (Articles 45 and 46) refers to the financial institutions of the System: the ***Andean Foment Corporation*** and the ***Latin American Reserve Fund***, whose activities must also be coordinated with those of the General Secretariat.

[48] The competences conferred to the Andean Parliament (Article 43) are as follows: (a) to participate in the promotion and direction of the Andean sub-regional integration process, in order to consolidate Latin American integration; (b) to examine the advance of the Andean sub-regional integration process and the fulfilment of its objectives, requiring from the organs and institutions of the System the necessary periodic information; (c) to address recommendations on the draft annual budgets of the organs and institutions of the System, which are funded by direct contributions of the member countries; (d) to suggest to the organs and institutions of the System the actions or decisions having as their object or effect any modifications, improvements or new general guidelines in relation with the policy objectives and the institutional structure of the System; (e) to participate in the legislative process by proposing to the organs of the System the adoption of rules on issues of common interest and its incorporation into the legal order of the Andean Community; (f) to promote the harmonisation of the legislation of the member countries; and (g) to promote relationships of cooperation and coordination with the national Parliaments of the member countries, the organs and the institutions of the System, as well as with the parliamentary organs of integration or cooperation of third countries.

IV. THE RANGE OF INSTITUTIONAL RESPONSES GIVEN IN THE TRUJILLO PROTOCOL TO THE DEMANDS OF REGIONAL INTEGRATION

A. A Complex Institutional Machinery

The new institutional structure set out in the **Trujillo Protocol** reflects, in our view, the tensions existing within the Andean Group and even within the individual Member States with regard to the integration process. Indeed, the various ministries involved in each country often disagree as to which procedure should be followed, depending on the specific level of influence that is given to each of them, even though they may all share the same integrationist ideal. This tension, which was already perceptible in the different working documents containing the drafts for reform, is now expressed in the text of the Trujillo Protocol itself.

This has been done in such a way that it is no longer possible to clearly infer from the Protocol whether it is intended to move towards a closer integration of the States involved (by their giving up parts of their sovereignty in favour of more efficient institutions that involve the highest Andean political officials) or whether the institutional profusion simply disguises a lack of clear political will, making the institutions scapegoats for the obstacles put in the way of sub-regional integration.

B. The Preparatory Documents

The preparatory documents of the Trujillo Protocol were the result of complex and prolonged political negotiations. It is thus not surprising that they contain ambiguities and inconsistencies. Some of these were corrected while the first draft was being improved; others still remain in the text of the Trujillo Protocol.

Those preparatory documents[49] revealed in particular a persistent problem concerning the formal connection of the Andean Integration System with the institutional structure of the Cartagena Agreement, showing a series of repetitions and overlapping of the different parts. Indeed, in those documents it was proposed that a new Part A be added to the text of the Agreement, enumerating the different 'organs and institutions of the Andean Integration System', with reference to their tasks and competences. A Part B was to follow, indicating the 'objectives and mechanisms of the Cartagena Agreement' with a new enumeration

[49] The working documents all have the same title: 'Draft for a future Protocol modifying the Cartagena Agreement, prepared by the Junta of the Cartagena Agreement, in coordination with the pro tempore Secretariat of the Andean Council of Ministers of Foreign Affairs' (Lima). They are dated 5 December 1995, 12 January 1996 and 9 February 1996.

of bodies, this time of the Agreement, accompanied by the corresponding mention of their modes of operation, tasks and competences.[50]

C. The Trujillo Protocol: Improving the System

These ambiguities were corrected, to some extent, by the Trujillo Protocol, which, unlike the previous working documents, merely amends Chapter II of the Cartagena Agreement, ie the institutional structure of the Agreement, without altering its objectives and mechanisms (Chapter I).

Notwithstanding, certain difficulties persist. Indeed, the Andean Community and the Andean Integration System are referred to as if they were two different realities. First, Article 5 sets up that the 'Andean Community' and proceeds to integrate the organs and institutions of the 'Andean Integration System' into it. Secondly, Article 48 states that the Andean Community is a sub-regional organisation having international legal personality but, at the same time (Article 6), the Andean Integration System is configured as a set of Andean organs and institutions which, among other objectives, must promote (Article 7) the external projection of the integration process.

As a result, it is difficult to clearly define the legal profile of each of the entities involved. In addition, the text of the Protocol itself maintains the ambiguity by referring at some points to the Andean Community and at others to the Andean Integration System. It would be better if the Protocol had simply referred to the Andean Community and its organs and institutions, since a different legal content cannot be perceived for the notion of an Andean Integration System.

D. Institutional Problems

The system of 'organs and institutions' as it appears in the Protocol, have some problems. First, there are an excessive number. A certain institutional inflation is evident, in direct contrast with the much simpler institutional scheme of the Cartagena Agreement. It should be noted that more than 12 organs and institutions are listed, some of which may take more than one form (simple or enlarged).[51] Nor are their competences clearly determined, and there is a strong likelihood that this will lead to malfunctioning and conflict of jurisdiction, and

[50] This peculiar institutional structure is similar, in some ways, to the three pillar scheme of the Treaty on European Union, with the ambiguity (or lack of clarity) that this implies, aggravated by the absence of any provision, similar to Article C TEU, guaranteeing institutional unity. The reader therefore did not know if he/she was in the presence of two different international organisations, each with its own organs, or of the same organs with distinct functions, depending on the international organisation in question or the framework within which the functions were exercised.

[51] Such a high number of organs imply that certain bodies, such as the Simon Rodriguez Convention and the Andean University Simon Bolivar, even though qualified by Article 6 as organs or

therefore to institutional paralysis. The situation is aggravated by the absence of a truly effective judicial body capable of adjudicating on interinstitutional disputes.

The second problem which affects the consistency of the Andean institutional system is the lack of a clear differentiation, as regards both the nature and the hierarchy, between an organ and an institution or even among the organs themselves (Article 6).[52] Confusion then may arise, since on some occasions the term institution appears to be reserved for auxiliary bodies ('advisory institutions' and 'financial institutions'—Articles 44 and 45) while, under other circumstances, the term seems to be synonymous with 'organ'.[53]

Another potential source of controversy regarding the Andean institutional system is the ambiguous relationship existing between the Council of Ministers of Foreign Affairs and the Commission, mainly as regards their respective tasks and competences. In this context, it is not always possible to say which of the two bodies has, and under what circumstances, a higher hierarchical position and how, in practical terms, their operative relationships are to be carried on.

On the one hand, the Andean Council of Ministers of Foreign Affairs is responsible for 'implementing the directives addressed to it by the Andean Presidential Council and supervising the enforcement of those addressed to the other organs and institutions' (Article 16, paragraph (c)). This seems to give the Council of Foreign Affairs a key position within the System. On the other hand, the Commission is entrusted, among other tasks, with the mission to 'take the necessary measures for the achievement of the objectives of the Cartagena Agreement' (Article 22), which seems to confer on it a general competence in integration matters.

At the same time, both institutions are entrusted with a mission to directing and coordinating the Andean external action and with Community representation, a1ways within the boundaries of their respective competences. Moreover, it is provided that both organs shall act in a coordinated way, when dealing with the definition, execution and evaluation of sub-regional integration policy. Given the many areas of interface and the insufficient delimitation of the boundaries of their respective competences, this heralds future interinstitutional conflict.

Ill-defined typology of acts and hierarchy of laws may also bring about institutional tensions. As an example, both the Council and the Commission can adopt legally binding Decisions. However, while Article 17 states that Council

institutions of the Andean Integration System, are the object neither of development in the text of the Protocol nor of a reference to the Treaties establishing the Community or the System.

52 Former Article 5 of the Cartagena Agreement distinguished between the main organs of the Agreement (Commission, Junta, Court of Justice and Andean Parliament), auxiliary organs (Advisory Councils) and subsidiary organs (Councils which the Commission may establish).

53 For example, when it comes to define the composition and the tasks of the mechanism of coordination of the System, this mechanism is qualified as a 'Meeting of the Representatives of the Institutions which constitute the System' (Arts 9 and 10), when, in reality, these latter are called organs in other provisions. This contradiction also occurs in other parts of the text.

Decisions are part of the Andean legal order,[54] the same is not said, in Article 21, of Commission Decisions, it being necessary to resort to Article 1 of the Treaty Creating the Court of Justice, as amended by the Cochabamba Modifying Protocol, to clarify the issue.[55]

Moreover, adoption of the two kinds of Decision follow different rules: Council Decisions are taken by consensus while Commission Decisions are, in general, approved by absolute majority after a complex voting procedure to which reference has already been made (Articles 26 and 27).

Furthermore, it is not explained how and to what extent can the powers to initiate legislation, which are granted to the General Secretariat and to the Member States, be exercised. Nor is the right of 'legislative suggestion' which seems to result for the Andean Parliament from Article 43, paragraph (e), clearly defined.

This state of legislative confusion increases if one takes into account the profusion of acts which, according to the Protocol, the different bodies may adopt, whose legal scope is not clear.[56] Even though the nature of some of those acts is referred to in Articles 2 and 3 of the Treaty Creating the Court of Justice, the typology there is not complete.

The replacement of JUNAC with a General Secretariat, which will function, according to Article 29, as the executive and technical organ of the Agreement, will also give rise to a number of questions, linked either with its structure and composition or with its functions.

As regards the former, a complex structure is set up, comprising a Secretary-General, the Director-Generals, the technical and administrative staff, and the mysterious 'Special Experts'. As regards the role of the Secretary-General, this is to direct the executive organ of the Community, but the extension of his/her competences and the prominent role assigned to him/her transform him/her, in fact, into a kind of a single organ. The Director-Generals are attached to the Secretary-General, but neither their number nor their competences are defined in the Protocol, and are relegated to the internal regulation of the General Secretariat, which appears to underline the importance of the Secretary-General. In any case, such an organ is far from the structure of JUNAC, which was a collegial organ made up of three members appointed by the Commission.

[54] In this context, one may wonder whether the Declarations, which constitute the other type of act of the competence of the Andean Council, do not have binding legal force.

[55] The same can be said, as mentioned above, about the Resolutions of the General Secretariat.

[56] The Meeting of the Representatives of the Institutions makes 'Reports' (*Informes*) (Article 9, paragraph (c)); the Andean Presidential Council issues 'Directives' (Article 11); the Andean Council signs 'Agreements' and 'Conventions' (*Convenios*) with third countries (Article 16, para. (d)) and makes 'Declarations' and 'Decisions' (Article 17); the Commission issues 'Decisions' (Article 21); the General Secretariat expresses itself through 'Resolutions' (Article 29), even though it may also give 'Advices' (*Dictámenes*) (Article 39); the Andean Parliament issues 'Recommendations' (Article 43, paragraph (c)), and the Advisory Councils issue 'Opinions' (*Opiniones*) (Article 44).

The second group of questions concern the extent of the functions, tasks and competences ascribed, at least in theory, to the General Secretariat. These contrast with the technical role which is claimed for that organ. In practice, that may lead to the General Secretariat being limited to a purely technical executive role, thus losing the Community dimension which characterised JUNAC. Therefore, in order to see whether it becomes in practice a mere technical organ similar to those existing in international intergovernmental organisations (ALADI for instance), or a real integration institution, we have not only to examine the Regulation of the General Secretariat, approved in the meantime,[57] but also to take into account how the General Secretariat will function in practice.

The foregoing shows how difficult it is to identify, in the institutional structure set up by the Protocol, the intergovernmental and the integration aspects of the Andean regional process. In reality, the power of the intergovernmental bodies to appoint and dismiss the Community organ and to give it instructions[58] threatens to deprive of purpose or to considerably limit the essential task of the General Secretariat, of promoting the general interest of the Andean Group.[59] Nevertheless, the Trujillo Protocol marks a certain progress in comparison with its drafts and with the Cartagena Agreement (Article 7, paragraph (d)), in that the right of the Council and of the Commission to give instructions to the General Secretariat provided for in those documents is softened and replaced with a duty of the General Secretariat to perform the tasks entrusted to it by the Council and the Commission.

However, the situation may worsen if, in practice, the independence of the Secretary-General is not guaranteed, which would be particularly harmful as to the appointment of the Director-Generals (Article 35).[60] Concerning the latter, as said before, the Protocol does not specify their number. Should they be in the number of two, the design of the organ will make of it something close to JUNAC, ie, of a Community nature. If, conversely, the number of Director-Generals is set at four plus a Chairman, it will be composed of a representative from each Member State, thus having an intergovernmental composition. The Regulation of the General Secretariat will provide an answer to this question.

The lack of clarity of the mechanisms set up in the Protocol to ensure the coordination of the integration process is also cause for concern. First of all, the coordination function ascribed to the *pro tempore* Secretariat, in practice to the Ministry of Foreign Affairs of the country holding the Presidency of the Andean Presidential Council, does not permit to solve the complex questions

[57] See below.

[58] Article 30, paragraph (b): the General Secretariat shall 'accomplish the tasks which it will be charged by the Andean Council of Ministers of Foreign Affairs and by the Commission'.

[59] According to Article 30, paragraph (a), it is the task of the General Secretariat to 'supervise the application of this Agreement and to ensure respect for the legal order of the Andean Community'.

[60] This was to be done by the Secretary-General in consultation with the Member States.

arising from the large number of institutional bodies, given the temporary character of the Secretariat and its attachment to the Presidency (Article 19).

Secondly, it is not clear how the so-called 'Meeting of the Representatives of the Institutions composing the System', which could, nevertheless, constitute an interesting innovation from the point of view of the general coordination of the System, will develop, ie whether it will have a permanent structure or simply confine itself to sporadic meetings,[61] without any clear guidelines as to the choice of its members. It is to be presumed that these will be the heads of the organs and institutions. There is, however, a serious problem with this since, in the majority of the cases, the organs and institutions of the System are presided over by people of the same nationality, in their capacity as citizens of the State holding the annual Presidency of the Andean Presidential Council. Moreover, these representatives will change every year, which raises doubts as to the effectiveness of the coordination procedures, unless a permanent mechanism similar to the European COREPER is envisaged.

Adding to these difficulties, it is not made clear in the Protocol how the work of the *pro tempore* Secretariat, of the Meeting of Representatives and of the General Secretariat will be coordinated.

Although the Trujillo Protocol, read in the light of the Quito Act, makes it possible to conclude where the political initiative lies in the integration process (ie, the Andean Presidential Council and the Council of Ministers of Foreign Affairs), it does not enable one to determine which body (or bodies) has the legislative initiative. The role of the General Secretariat in this area, as the future integration organ, will have to be clarified and strengthened, even though the Protocol moves in a different direction, depriving the General Secretariat of its legislative monopoly.

Although this is a crucial point on which the progress of the whole procedure depends, the Protocol offers no guarantees as to the mechanisms which must ensure the effective application of the Andean legal rules. Even though references are made to the functions of the Court of Justice, the General Secretariat and the Commission in this area, it is not clear that those functions may be exercised with the independence and the effectiveness necessary to revitalise Andean integration. In this regard, the improvements which have been introduced in the competences of the Court of Justice by the Cochabamba Protocol require that a number of 'extra-legal' conditions (political, social, institutional and psychological) are met to work in practice.

Another serious problem does not find a clear answer either in the preparatory documents or in the Trujillo Protocol: it concerns the *democratic control* of the institutions and the participation and mobilisation of *citizens* in the process of Andean integration. The reference in Article 15 to the Andean Parliament as

[61] According to Article 19, regular meetings do not have to be held more than once a year.

the deliberative body of the System does not reflect its real powers, which are, in general, merely those of advice, promotion and guidance, and at the limit of 'legislative suggestion'.

Both the Protocol and its preparatory documents are the results of an arduous negotiating process between the different stakeholders at the national and sub-regional levels, in which the heart of the debate lies in the question of where the political and technical direction of the integration process should be located.

Traditionally, this direction was exercised by the 'plenipotentiary representatives at ministerial level' in the Commission, in practice the Ministers of Commerce and Industry of the member countries. With the relaunching of the integration process, the most senior Andean political figures have become more interested in intervening in the direction and the shaping of the process. An expression of that interest is the incorporation of the Andean Presidential Council and of the Andean Council of Ministers of Foreign Affairs into the institutional structure of the Community.

However desirable the presence of these organs in the institutional scheme may be, it can but cause severe tensions, as shown by the proposal to create such complex mechanisms as the Council of Ministers of Foreign Affairs in an enlarged formation.

These political tensions may also be found in the definition, structure and composition of the General Secretariat, in particular as to the question of whether it will be a real integration organ vested with important decision-making competences and powers of initiative, or a simple technical body in charge of carrying out instructions. On the one hand, it follows from the Quito Act (as well as from Article 32 of the Protocol) that the General Secretariat shall be headed by a highly representative person of recognised prestige in the sub-region. But, on the other hand, the Protocol reveals a clear intention of surrounding the Secretary General with a number of high ranking civil servants, closely linked to national decision-making levels, thus restraining his/her powers. Such ambiguities can undermine and paralyse the functioning of the whole system. The manner in which the internal regulation of the General Secretariat may resolve these ambiguities will be decisive.

V. THE EVOLUTION OF THE ANDEAN COMMUNITY AND THE RELATIONS WITH THE EU AFTER THE SIGNATURE OF THE TRUJILLO PROTOCOL: THE SUCRE SUMMIT

A. Relaunching the Andean Process

On 22 and 23 April 1997, the Eleventh Andean Presidential Council was held in the city of Sucre, constitutional capital of Bolivia. Its agenda was largely inspired by the idea of relaunching the Andean integration process.

The announcement by Peru, a few days earlier, of its decision to withdraw from the Cartagena Agreement not only introduced a new complication into the preparations for the Summit,[62] but also cast an unexpected and unwanted shadow over the development perspectives of the integration movement.

Although deploring the decision of the Peruvian Government, and expressing their hope for a reversal, the Presidents of the four remaining countries[63] reaffirmed 'their unbending commitment to continuing to advance in the Andean integration process' and took the joint decision to promote the establishment of the common market between them, with special emphasis on the liberalisation and the expansion of trade in services.

Two months later, Peru succeeded in getting an agreement that allowed it to reverse the decision to withdraw.

At the same time as the will to deepen the Andean integration process was being reaffirmed through the establishment of the new Andean institutional structure set up by the Trujillo Protocol, the four States restated 'their commitment to open regionalism, that privileges Latin American integration, in which context the ongoing negotiations with MERCOSUR are considered of primary importance'. These were the main decisions which were taken in Sucre.

Two further points must be highlighted: the first regards the *institutions*, whereas the second concerns *relations with the EU.*

B. The Draft Regulations

At the *institutional level*, the meeting of the Sucre Presidential Council was preceded by the preparation, undertaken by JUNAC,[64] of the draft Decisions regarding the internal Regulations of the Andean Council of Ministers of Foreign Affairs, the Commission and the General Secretariat, as well as the Rules of Administrative Procedure of the Andean Community, all to be approved by the respective competent bodies. The draft Decision regarding the internal regulation of the General Secretariat deserves further consideration.

The draft covers the nature, composition, tasks and competences of the General Secretariat (Chapter I), its internal organisation (Chapter II), the staff (Chapter III), the budget (Chapter IV), the seat of the Secretariat, and its immunities and privileges (Chapter V).

[62] All the more since other member countries, like Colombia and Venezuela, had made ratification of the Trujillo Protocol conditional upon the effective and complete reincorporation of Peru into the Andean free trade area.

[63] Bolivia, Colombia, Ecuador and Venezuela. The President of Panama was also present at the Summit as an observer. In his capacity of pro tempore President of MERCOSUR, the President of Paraguay also attended the Summit as a special guest. This shows the importance which is attached by the Andean group to the rapprochement with the bloc represented by MERCOSUR.

[64] And object of debate with the authors of this chapter.

It reasserts the nature of the General Secretariat as an 'executive organ', in charge of promoting the common interests of the sub-region. This may be seen as progress in comparison with the character of a 'technical organ' ascribed to JUNAC. The draft gives important powers to the Secretary-General (Article 11, paragraphs (a) to (s)) and specifies how he/she is appointed (by consensus among the members of the Andean Council, enlarged to the members of the Commission, for a period of five years, with a single possibility of re-appointment—Article 5). It also sets the number of Director-Generals at a maximum of two, each having under his/her supervision a Directorate-General by thematic area (Article 16), and establishes the manner of their appointment (by the Secretary-General, after consultation with the member countries, through the national integration bodies, for a three-year period, renewable only once—Article 17) and their competences (Article 18). It provides for the 'Special Experts', identifying these as 'two civil servants of the General Secretariat', appointed by the Secretary-General, for a non-renewable period of four years (Article 19), competent to give 'advice' and 'opinions' in disputes between two or more Member States, which are non-binding on the Secretary-General, but which he/she must take into consideration, as well as advice on the procedures for reconsideration of Resolutions which affect the interests of a Member State[65] (Article 20), if asked by the Secretary-General.

The draft Regulation empowers the Secretary-General to establish the internal organisation of the General Secretariat (Article 25). It adopts the general rules concerning the policy to be followed in hiring the personnel; this should take strictly into consideration the good reputation and competence of the candidates, as well as the institutional requirements and the need for a balanced sub-regional geographical distribution, in respect of the principles of equality and non-discrimination—Articles 26 and 27). It also contains provisions on incompatibilities (Articles 28 to 31), the rights and duties of the civil servants (to be developed in by internal regulations—Article 32), discipline (Article 34), and the system of remedies (by referring to other documents—Article 36). Finally, it defines the general principles of the annual budget of the General Secretariat, to be approved by the Commission and to be financed mainly by the contributions of the member countries (Articles 37 to 40).

Regarding privileges and immunities, it is stressed that the General Secretariat, its personnel and assets enjoy immunity of jurisdiction, except where expressly renounced (Article 42). Also the principle, common to international organisations law, that the privileges, immunities and other prerogatives are granted to civil servants only in the interest of facilitating the exercise of their functions, and do not constitute a way of exempting them either from their obligations or from abiding by the law, is restated (Article 46). As to the seat of the General

[65] The relationship between this procedure and the action for infringement provided for in the Treaty Creating the Court of Justice is not clear, in particular as concerns the action referred to in Article 24 of the Treaty.

Secretariat, this was likely to be in Lima, as JUNAC's seat (Article 41). However, the Andean Presidential Council, in view of the previously announced withdrawal of Peru from the Agreement, was obliged to temporarily establish it in the city of Santa Fé de Bogota. Since Peru did not in the end abandon the Community, the seat of the General Secretariat was permanently installed in Lima.

C. Ambiguities in the Draft Regulation

Some points are unclear in the draft Regulation. That is, first, the case of the institutional position of the General Secretariat. Its characterisation as an 'executive organ' does not make it the 'government' of the Andean Community. More accurately, it bears the characteristics of a technical organ which has to implement the decisions of the political organs, and to develop the general rules adopted by the competent bodies of the Agreement.

Secondly, the Regulation expresses the doubts and controversies regarding the role and the importance of the Secretary-General. Endowed with large powers within the General Secretariat, he/she largely merges into the latter, to such an extent that it becomes almost impossible to clearly distinguish one from the other, and to correctly separate their powers. In certain cases, for instance, the General Secretariat is granted powers that in fact belong to the Secretary-General.[66] On the other hand, the powers to organise, direct and represent the General Secretariat, as well as to appoint and dismiss the Director-Generals, Special Experts and remaining personnel give the Secretary-General a position of supremacy; but in practical terms it is necessary to see how the relationships will be established and developed between them, and what their respective degrees of autonomy will be. In this regard, much will depend on the personality holding the Office of Secretary-General and, in particular, on who takes up the job for the first time.[67]

Thirdly, as far as the Director-Generals and the Special Experts are concerned, it must be said that neither the nature of these bodies nor the relationship between them or with the Secretary-General is defined precisely in the draft Regulation. Indeed, a proper reading of the events shows that, to overcome any deadlock in the negotiations between the Member States claiming equal representation in the

[66] An example is Article 3, paragraph (p), according to which the General Secretariat must 'settle disputes between private parties through arbitration, as provided for in the Treaty Creating the Court of Justice of the Cartagena Agreement'. However, even if the dispute is indeed brought before the General Secretariat, the arbitrator is in fact the Secretary-General, who assures the legal representation of the General Secretariat.

[67] Surprisingly for those who expected a lengthy and tortuous negotiation process, the Sucre Presidential Council appointed the Venezuelan Ambassador Sebastian Alegrett, as the first Secretary-General, 'bearing in mind his great experience in the field of regional integration and the professional prestige which is recognised to him'.

structure of the General Secretariat, it was initially expected that four[68] 'Director-Generals' would be appointed, two of whom would be requested—but it was not clear under what terms and conditions[69]—to exercise the functions of Special Experts.

In any case, it will always be necessary to set up mechanisms of designation which, on the one hand, preserve the cohesion of the team and the authority of the Secretary-General and, on the other, guarantee the independence of the Special Experts in the exercise of their mission, particularly when they have to express opinions that differ from those of the Secretary-General. Doubts and concerns in this respect are accentuated by the possibility, also envisaged by Andean politicians, to offer the Member States the option for a panel of external experts to settle the disputes between them. Such a possibility, if it ever comes into effect, would bring disruptive elements or, at least, some degree of incoherence into the Andean legal order and into the dispute-resolution system. Such a possibility should therefore be handled with great care, in particular by allowing an appeal to the Andean Court.[70]

D. The Relations Andean Community-European Union

The second aspect to emphasise concerns the *Andean Community-European Union relationships*. It is useful to quote, in this regard, the conclusions of the Sucre Presidential Council, according to which the Presidents of the four member countries:

> Express their firm political will to strengthen the relationships with the European Union on the four pillars which support them: political dialogue; access to the European Single Market; the Framework Cooperation Agreement of 1993; and the Specialized Dialogue on the fight against drugs.
>
> Take note, with satisfaction, of the substantial increase in the commercial relations and in the investment flows between the Andean Community and the European Union through the Andean Generalized System of Preferences (SGPA), and urge the economic agents of both regions to maximize the opportunities offered by the interregional links.

[68] Eventually three (one Director-General and two Special Experts, or vice versa), if Peru had withdrawn, bringing the number of 'senior members' of the General Secretariat (including the Secretary-General) into line with the number of Member States.

[69] Different options may be envisaged, namely the appointment of one or two 'permanent' Special Experts, for a certain period of time, concurrently or not with the functions of Director-General, the appointment of the Director-Generals as ad hoc Special Experts, according to the matters at stake or by an adequate rotation criterion. In addition, the nationality of the Expert is taken into account when the dispute involves his/her country of origin.

[70] Other aspects not covered by the Regulation should also be clarified, such as that regarding the duty of Special Experts to issue an opinion and the time span for doing it, in order to avoid a logjam in the decision-making and conflict-solving process.

> Welcome with satisfaction the results of the Seventh Institutionalized Ministerial Meeting Rio Group—European Union and of the European Union—Andean Community Meeting, which were held in Noordwijk, The Netherlands, on 7 and 8 April 1997. They stress, in particular, the availability of the European Union to proceed with its technical support for the Andean region construction process.
>
> Agree that, once the new Andean institutional organization has entered into force, the President of the Andean Presidential Council and the Secretary-General shall give continuity to the political dialogue defined in Rome, in order to establish with the different European instances an agenda leading to a bi-regional association process that takes into account the new realities.

The presidential declaration on the relationship with the EU constitutes, together with similar reference concerning the relations with MERCOSUR, the expression of a clear priority regarding the external relations of the Andean Community, to which high importance is attributed.

Such a priority is matched, on the EU side, by the intensification of the contacts promoted by the Community mainly in the aftermath of the European Council held in Florence in July 1996, as well as following the signature, in Rome, on 30 July 1996, of the Joint Declaration between the two blocs. A new balance may thus be re-established between the Andean Community and MERCOSUR, in place of the clear dominance taken by the latter in the context of EU policy towards Latin America in 1995. The results of the Fourth Joint Commission EU-Andean Community, which met in Brussels on 13 November 1996, bear witness to that re-equilibrium.[71]

VI. FINAL REMARKS

Some final conclusions may be drawn from the foregoing. The first refers to the *structure* of the Trujillo Protocol. It must be recognised that the ambiguity which still persists regarding the difficult coordination between the Andean Community, the Andean Integration System and the Cartagena Agreement does not contribute to clarifying the functioning of the integration process. Further advances in this process therefore make it necessary to clarify the nature and the relationships between those realities, whatever they mean, in theory and in practice, as legal and political entities.

A second reflection stems from the idea that, notwithstanding the difficulties of the task, it is essential to promote an adequate *balance* between the different stakeholders, through mechanisms capable of safeguarding the effectiveness and the coherence of the system. Some of these mechanisms concern the *institutional system* and others the Andean *legal order*.

As far as the *institutional system* is concerned, the reform should have preserved three major interconnecting principles: the *simplicity* of the whole scheme, *clarity*

[71] See, in this respect, the Annual Report of Activities for 1996 of the Latin America Directory of DG-IB of the European Commission, February 1997 (internal document).

in interinstitutional relationships and *equilibrium* between the different actors within the institutional structure. Alongside these it would have been desirable to strengthen the coordination and liaison mechanisms, both at the Andean and the national level.

Even if an interinstitutional coordination organ exists in the Protocol, experience shows that an organisation of integration cannot fulfill its mission without a permanent coordinating body, functioning in close connection with the intergovernmental organ, to prepare its meetings and curtail the possible friction between the different ministries. Likewise, it would be appropriate to set up adequate coordination mechanisms at the national level[72] to ensure coordination between the different ministries participating in the process.

On the other hand, it should not be forgotten the need for a balanced but dynamic relationship between the organs and institutions representing national interests and those which pursue the common interest of the Andean Group, thus implying the strengthening of the role of the General Secretariat in pursuing the objectives of integration.

Concerning the Andean *legal order*, the questions raised by the Trujillo Protocol as to the typology of 'laws' and the hierarchy among them have already been referred to. Chapter 1 of the Treaty of 1979, which created the Court of Justice of the Andean Community, modified by the Cochabamba Protocol, certainly fills in some of the gaps left by the Cartagena Agreement in the version of the Trujillo Protocol. Indeed, Chapter 1, entitled 'On the Legal Order of the Cartagena Agreement', contains an enumeration of the Andean rules and their hierarchy, as well as an express mention of its effects: *direct applicability* and *primacy*. However, for reasons of transparency, it would have been preferable that said Chapter 1 be included in the Trujillo Protocol.[73]

From both a legal and a political[74] perspective, the Protocol would have gained in intelligibility if it had included a provision expressly stating that each of the Andean organs and institutions shall act only within the limits of the powers conferred on them in the Treaties (*principle of conferral*).

The clarity would also have been fostered by the inclusion in the Protocol of provisions spelling out the scope of the international legal personality of the Andean Community (Article 48),[75] particularly as regards the capacity to conclude international agreements. Since the Andean Community has international *ius contraendi*, it would have been particularly useful if a sub-section outlining

[72] Of the 'inter-ministerial committee or 'national integration body' kind.

[73] Or, at least, if the Trujillo Protocol had included express reference to Chapter 1 of the Treaty Creating the Court of Justice of the Andean Community.

[74] From this viewpoint, the objective would be to soothe any possible fears of certain states jealous of their sovereignty.

[75] This constitutes nevertheless a step forward in the law of international organizations. In fact, Treaties establishing those organizations do not usually expressly refer to the granting of international legal personality. An example is the vague reference (contained in Article 210 of the EC Treaty) to a legal personality which only later was characterized as 'international', thanks to development of the case-law.

the Andean treaty-making process had been included in Section J of the Protocol ('On the International Legal Personality and the Privileges and Immunities'). At the same time, the Court of Justice could have been given the capacity to issue *ex ante* opinions on the legality of the international agreements which the Andean Community was considering signing.

Next, the nature of the *Andean Parliament*, defined in Article 42 of the Protocol as the deliberative body of the System, having a Community character and representing the peoples of the Andean Community, deserves some critical reflection. Indeed, in the current state of affairs the Andean Parliament neither is the deliberative organ of the System, on the political or the legislative side, nor does it directly represent the peoples of the sub-region but instead 'the peoples of the States which constitute the Andean Community'. The Andean Parliament will definitely come closer to the description made of it in the Protocol when, as expected, it will be composed of representatives directly elected by the Andean citizens, and its intervention in the legislative process becomes a reality.

From the point of view of the *financial resources* of the Andean Community, it would obviously be difficult, in the present stage of the integration process, to give the organisation its own resources, even though the establishment of the common customs tariff could open up that possibility. However, the economic independence of the Community is of vital importance to the achievement of the whole Andean construction.

Article 28 of the Protocol, by establishing that 'the member country which exceeds a delay of one year for the payment of its current contributions to the General Secretariat or to the Court of Justice of the Andean Community, cannot exercise its right to vote in the Commission, in so far as the situation is not regularized' constitutes a step in the right direction. Nevertheless, the member countries' financial obligations would be strengthened if the Andean Court of Justice was empowered to declare that Member States which do not pay the quotas are infringing the Agreement, and furthermore to devise some other type of sanction (such as blocking CAF funds to the State(s) concerned).

This is essentially a political question. Nevertheless, the serious and well-known budgetary problems of the Andean Community weigh heavily on the integration project.

Finally, the need to bring the integration process closer to the Andean *citizens* has to be stressed. From that point of view, it would have been appropriate if the Trujillo Protocol had included a Preamble mentioning, among the objectives pursued, those of strengthening democracy, promoting social cohesion, as well as closer relations between the Andean peoples and their participation in the Andean project, taking decisions as closely as possible to the citizens in conformity with a principle of subsidiarity, and reinforcing the presence and the influence in the integration process of institutions representative of the Andean peoples.

The new institutional architecture introduced by the Trujillo Protocol in the integration process regrettably shows a decrease in the level of influence of

Community organs, since it focuses instead on the political will of the States as the 'driving force' of this process. This carries the risk that this attempt at regional integration, which was once a good example of integration in Latin America, will become a mere mechanism for intergovernmental cooperation. This possibility also worries the Andean partners, who cannot afford to witness the bypassing of the Community *acquis* or the weakening of the 'common front' *vis-à-vis* the outside world, thus causing them to stay in isolation and marginalised in ongoing continental and intercontinental negotiations.

The recent overcoming of the institutional crisis created by Peru's threat to withdraw, as well as the ratification of the Trujillo Protocol and of the Cooperation Agreement with the European Union by all the member countries of the Andean Community, is expected to give a new impetus to the integration process, thus strengthening the hand of those who support it.

16

On the Application of Keck *in the Field of Free Provision of Services**

I. INTRODUCTION

THE JUDGMENTS OF the Court of Justice (hereinafter 'ECJ' or 'the Court') in *Alpine Investments*[1] (hereinafter '*Alpine Investments*' or '*Alpine*') and *De Agostini*[2] raised the controversial issue of the applicability of the principles laid down in *Keck and Mithouard*[3] (hereinafter '*Keck*') to the field of free provision of services.

Numerous articles and commentaries have already been devoted to those judgments, many of which are based on the idea that such judgments are to be interpreted as meaning that the ECJ refused, once and for all, to transpose the Keck doctrine to the field of application of Article 59 of the EC Treaty (now Article 49 EC).

In that context, the purpose of this chapter is twofold. First, to put that line of case-law in perspective and try to ascertain what might be its real scope. Second, to explore possible ways of clarification in this field which, without hampering the functioning of the internal market and the ability of the Treaty to ensure achievement of the freedom to provide intra-Community services, might allow a coherent approach in the interpretation of the provisions of the Treaty concerning, on the one hand, free movement of goods and, on the other hand, free provision of services.

* Published in M Andenas and W-H Roth (eds), *Services and Free Movement in EU Law* (Oxford, Oxford University Press, 2003). A first version of this chapter, entitled 'An Exercise on the Application of Keck and Mithouard in the Field of Free Provision of Services', was published in *Mélanges en Hommage à Michel Waelbroeck* (Brussels, Bruylant, 1999). The author acknowledges the assistance of Mr Ricardo Oliveira, of PLMJ, and Mr Christian Kohler, head of the Library Division of the EC Court of Justice, in the preparation of the first version.

1 Case C-384/93 *Alpine Investments BV v Minister van Financiën* [1995] ECR I-1141.

2 Joined Cases C-34, 35 and 36/95 *Konsumentombudsmannen (KO) v De Agostini (Svenska) Förlag AB*, and *KO v TV-Shop i Sverige AB* [1997] ECR I-3843.

3 Joined Cases C-267 and 268/91 *Keck and Mithouard* [1993] ECR I-6047.

II. *ALPINE INVESTMENTS*

In *Alpine Investments*, the Court was asked by a Dutch court to examine a national legislation prohibiting undertakings established in the Netherlands from contacting individuals by telephone, without their prior consent in writing, in order to offer them various financial services (a practice known as 'cold calling'). Alpine Investments BV, the applicant in the main proceedings, was a company incorporated under Dutch law and established in the Netherlands, specialised in commodities futures.[4] It offered three types of services in relation to commodities futures contracts: portfolio management, investment advice and the transmission of clients' offers to brokers operating on commodities futures markets both within and outside the Community. Despite being established only in the Netherlands, Alpine Investments BV had clients also in Belgium, France and the United Kingdom.[5]

The governments of the Netherlands and the United Kingdom, intervening in the proceedings, submitted that, since the prohibition in question was a generally applicable measure, it was not discriminatory and had neither as its object nor as its effect to put the national market at an advantage over providers of services from other Member States. Furthermore, as it affected only the way in which the services were offered, it was analogous to the non-discriminatory measures governing 'selling arrangements' which, according to *Keck*, fell outside the scope of Article 30 of the EC Treaty (now Article 28 EC). In their view, ex Article 59 was thus not applicable to the case under analysis.

The Court did not uphold such arguments and held that, since the prohibition in question deprived the operators concerned of a rapid and direct technique for marketing and for contacting potential clients in other Member States, it could constitute a restriction on the freedom to provide cross-border services.[6]

The Court's ruling has been examined by commentators in the light of the Keck doctrine. Indeed, some authors believe that the judgment expresses the rejection, by the Court, of any transposition of that doctrine to the field of free provision of services.

Laurence Idot[7] took the view that 'insofar as the application of Article 59 EC presupposes in any case an intra-Community transaction, any attempt to extend

[4] As the Court explained, 'the parties to a commodities futures contract undertake to buy or sell a specified quantity of a commodity of a given quality at a price and date fixed at the time the contract is concluded. They do not, however, intend actually to take delivery of or to deliver the commodity but contract solely in the hope of profiting from price fluctuations between the time the contract is concluded and the month of delivery. This can be done by entering into a mirror-image transaction on the futures market before the beginning of the month of delivery' (*Alpine Investments* (n 1) para 4).

[5] See *Alpine Investments* (n 1) para 5.

[6] See *Alpine Investments* (n 1) para 28.

[7] L Idot, (1995) 11 *Europe* 264. My translation. In the original: 'Dans la mesure où l'application de l'article 59 CE suppose en toute hypothèse une prestation intracommunautaire, toute tentative d'extension de la jurisprudence *Keck* paraît condamnée'.

the Keck case-law does not seem possible'. Hatzopoulos[8] considered that the judgment could give rise to, at least, three different interpretations, which he labelled as 'distinguishing *Keck*', 'limiting the scope of *Keck*' and 'ignoring *Keck*'. In the author's opinion, the Court 'completely ignored' the *Keck* judgment and merely stuck to 'the traditional pre-*Keck* approach to such an extent that *Keck* seems to be a remote nightmare'.

In J-G Huglo's opinion,[9] the Court in *Alpine* clearly signalled to be willing to avoid 'any contamination of the matter of free provision of services with the *Keck and Mithouard* case-law [...] as regards free movement of goods'.[10] The author went on to state that

> it is indeed difficult to understand how the latter case-law could be transposed into the field of free provision of services where the concept of restriction is narrower and, in any case, more linked with the conduct of the economic operator than the formulation used in *Dassonville*.[11]

Some criticised the Court for using in *Alpine* a 'defective reasoning' and for not applying the *Keck* case-law by analogy. Moreover, the Court was censured for not stating clearly whether this attitude represented a 'total ban' or simply a decision specifically limited to the case at stake.[12]

By contrast, others expressed the opinion that, even if the Court did not uphold the submissions of the two intervening governments as regards the concept of 'selling arrangements' developed in *Keck*, it nevertheless did not set aside the latter case-law.[13] Poiares Maduro[14] went so far as to state that the Court upheld, in *Alpine*, 'the potential application of Keck to the freedom to provide services'.

I would not draw from the Court's ruling in *Alpine* any definitive or decisive inference as to the possibility of transposing the *Keck* case-law into the field of free provision of services. As any other judgment of the Court, *Alpine Investments* has to be read in the light of the precise circumstances of the case. Indeed, as the Court acknowledged in paragraph 36 of its judgment, the prohibition of 'cold calling' laid down in the Dutch legislation is not analogous to the legislation

[8] V Hatzopoulos, 'Annotation to Case C-384/93, *Alpine Investments v Minister van Financiën*' (1995) 35 *Common Market Law Review* 1427, 1438.

[9] J-G Huglo, 'Commentaire' (1995) *Revue trimestrielle de Droit européen* 827–834.

[10] My translation. In the original: 'toute pollution de la matière de la libre prestation des services par la jurisprudence *Keck et Mithouard* inaugurée récemment pour les marchandises'.

[11] My translation. In the original: 'on discerne mal comment, en effet, transposer cette jurisprudence en matière de libre prestation des services où la notion d'entrave est plus étroite, et en tout cas, moins détachée du comportement de l'opérateur économique que la formule de l'arrêt *Dassonville*'.

[12] See C Gimeno Verdejo, 'La noción de servicios y la eventual traslación de la jurisprudencia *Keck* al ámbito de la libre prestación de servicios en la sentencia *Alpine Investments*' (1996) 14 *Cuadernos Europeos de Deusto* 186. See also F Berrod (1995) 3 *Revue du Marché unique européen* 305. The doubts raised by the Court's ruling are carefully underlined by the latter author in the following terms: 'il semble que la Cour refuse l'application de la jurisprudence Keck et Mithouard aux services' ('it appears that the Court refuses application of the Keck case-law to services'—my translation).

[13] M Luby, 'Chronique de jurisprudence' (1997) 2 *Journal du Droit international* 564.

[14] M Poiares Maduro, 'The Saga of Article 30 EC Treaty: To Be Continued' (1998) 5 *Maastricht Journal of European and Comparative Law* 298.

concerning selling arrangements, held in *Keck* to fall outside the scope of Article 30 of the EC Treaty.

There the Court takes on its own account the point made by Advocate General Jacobs in his Opinion.[15] According to the Advocate General,

> there is a significant difference between *Keck* and the present case. In *Keck*, the Court was concerned with rules of the importing State relating to selling arrangements for the sale of goods in the territory of that State. In the present case, the exporting State requires compliance with its own rules of marketing not only for the provision of services in its territory but also in the territory of other Member States.

Should both cases be similar, would the Court have proceeded to apply the *Keck* solution? It is not certain. But what, in my view, the judgment in *Alpine* does not permit to infer is the opposite conclusion, ie that the Court ruled out the possibility of extending *Keck* to the intra-Community provision of services. The fact is that the Court's ruling in *Alpine* corresponds to the nature, subject matter and effects of the national rules which applied in that case, as well as to the scope of Article 49 EC (ex Article 59 of the EC Treaty) as compared with Articles 28 and 29 EC (ex Articles 30 and 34 of the EC Treaty).

Let us consider, first, the nature and effects of the national provisions at issue. As Advocate General Jacobs rightly pointed out,[16] those rules constituted a restriction on the freedom to provide intra-Community services, as they directly and significantly restricted the ability of operators established in the Netherlands to market their services in the territory of other Member States.[17] The Court upheld such understanding in paragraph 38 of the judgment. Of course, a Member State is free to regulate the marketing, in its own territory, of services provided by persons established in that State. However, it does not have unlimited freedom to regulate the marketing of such services in the territory of other Member States.[18] Being a restriction on marketing services in another Member State, the rules under analysis in *Alpine* thus constituted a restriction to provide intra-Community services, which fall within the scope of ex Article 59.

[15] *Alpine Investments* (n 1); Opinion of AG Jacobs, para 60.

[16] ibid, paras 47–48 and 51–56.

[17] That is why the judgment in Case C-379/92 *Peralta* [1994] ECR I-3453 is irrelevant as regards an *Alpine*-like situation. Not only did the rules examined by the Court in *Peralta* not apply to the provision or the marketing of services, but their effect on the freedom to provide services 'was so remote, tenuous and indirect as hardly to constitute a restriction within the meaning of Article 59' (*Alpine Investments* (n 1); Opinion of AG Jacobs, para 58). A discussion of *Peralta* and its relations with *Alpine* can be found in OA Torgensen, 'The Limitations of the Free Movement of Goods and the Freedom to Provide Services—in Search of a Common Approach' (1999) *European Business Law Review* 371, 381. It is submitted there that 'the judgment in *Peralta* [...] confirmed a common approach to the Treaty provisions governing goods and services', therefore providing 'a striking contrast to that in *Alpine Investments*'. In Torgensen's opinion, *Alpine* 'was inconsistent with the Court's previous case-law concerning the free movement of services and [...] marked a deviation from the case-law concerning the free movement of goods'. I do not share that view.

[18] *Alpine Investments* (n 1); Opinion of AG Jacobs, para 51.

As follows from a well-established case-law,[19] Article 59 (now Article 49 EC) covers both discriminatory and non-discriminatory restrictions. The Court has indeed always interpreted ex Article 59 as requiring not only the elimination of all discrimination against a provider of services on the ground of its nationality but also the abolition of any restriction on the freedom to provide intra-Community services, even if it applies without distinction to national providers of services and to those of other Member States.

Second and more important, as the ECJ stated in paragraph 30 of *Alpine*:

> The first paragraph of Article 59 of the Treaty prohibits restrictions on the freedom to provide services within the Community in general. Consequently that provision covers not only restrictions laid down by the State of destination but also those laid down by the State of origin.[20]

The Court then concluded (paragraph 31):

> It follows that the prohibition of cold calling does not fall outside the scope of Article 59 of the Treaty simply because it is imposed by the State in which the provider of services is established.

In this context, the relevant fact to consider for the purpose of this analysis is that, as regards free provision of services in the common market, the Treaty makes no formal distinction between 'export trade' and 'import trade' in services.

In that field, a single provision of the Treaty, Article 49, plays the same role as played by Articles 30 and 34 together with regard to free movement of goods. Therefore, should an analogy be drawn between the application of Article 59 to rules such as the prohibition of cold calling and the case-law of the Court on free movement of goods, it would have to be with the case-law on Article 34 (restrictions on *exports* of goods), not on Article 30 (restrictions on *imports* of goods). In such circumstances, the *Keck* case-law was of no assistance in solving the case under scrutiny in *Alpine*; since said case-law does not concern the interpretation of Article 34 but of Article 30.

The question would, however, be different if the case pending before the national judge concerned the hypothetical application of the prohibition on cold calling to providers of services coming from another Member State.

[19] See, in this respect, Cases 279/80 *Criminal Proceedings Against Alfred John Webb* [1981] ECR 3305; 427/85 *Commission v Germany* [1988] ECR 1123; C-76/90 *Säger v Dennemeyer* [1991] ECR I-4221; C-288/89 *Collectieve Antennevorziening Gouda* [1991] ECR I-4007; C-275/92 *Schindler* [1994] ECR I-1039 and C-398/95 *SETTG v Ypourgos Engasias* (Greek Tourist Guides) [1997] ECR I-3091 para 16. As follows from that case-law, the Court has consistently adopted a broad interpretation of Article 59 in order to give the principle of free provision of services full effectiveness, even where it implied granting more favourable treatment to service providers from other Member States.

[20] The Court goes on to remind us that, as it has generally held, the right to freely provide services may be relied on by an undertaking as against the State in which it is established if the services are provided for persons established in another Member State. The Court referred to cases C-18/93 *Corsica Ferries Italia v Corpo dei Piloti del Porto di Genova* [1994] ECR I-1783 para 30, *Peralta* (n 17) para 40, and C-381/93 *Commission v France* [1994] ECR I-5145 para 14.

One final point should be made with regard to the parallel interpretation of the Treaty provisions on free movement of goods and free provision of services. The Court has given the notion of restrictions on exports of goods under Article 34 an interpretation which is narrower than that of the notion of restrictions on imports of goods under Article 30.

As a matter of fact, whereas Article 30 covers also non-discriminatory rules, the application of Article 34 requires the existence of a discrimination (a 'difference in treatment') between the domestic trade of the Member State concerned and its export trade, in such a way that it grants a particular advantage to national products or to the domestic market at the expense of the products or the trade of other Member States.[21]

In view of that, there was no need for a *Keck*-type judgment in the field of application of Article 34 of the Treaty. Nevertheless, it does not follow from the foregoing that the above-mentioned parallelism has been hampered by the *Alpine* ruling.

Indeed, as Advocate General Jacobs pointed out,[22] it is doubtful whether the case-law of the Court under Article 34 applies to rules of the exporting Member State concerning the marketing of goods. He stressed in that regard that

> a trader cannot be required by the exporting Member State to abstain from using in another Member State a form of advertising which is prohibited in the exporting State but is permitted in the other Member State in order to market his products in the latter, unless there is a good reason for the prohibition.

III. *DE AGOSTINI*

The situation in the *De Agostini* case was different from that examined in *Alpine*.

In *De Agostini*, the ECJ was called upon to rule on two questions referred by a Swedish court on the interpretation of Articles 30 and 59 of the Treaty and of Council Directive No 89/552/EEC of 3 October 1989 on the coordination of certain provisions laid down by law, regulation or administrative action in Member States concerning the pursuit of television broadcasting activities (Directive 'Television without Frontiers' or the 'TwF-Directive').[23]

The questions had been raised in connection with three applications made by the Swedish Consumer Ombudsman—the *Konsumentombudsman* (*KO*)—for injunctions to restrain De Agostini and TV-Shop from using certain marketing practices in television advertising concerning a children's magazine, skin-care products and a detergent.

[21] See, in this respect, cases 15/79 *Groenveld v Produktschap voor Vee en Vlees* [1979] ECR 3049 para 7, 155/80 *Oebel* [1981] ECR 1993 para 15, 172/82 *Fabricants Raffineurs d'Huile de Graissage v Inter-Huiles* [1983] ECR 555 para 12, and 47/90 *Delhaize et le Lion* [1992] *ECR* I-3669 para 12.

[22] *Alpine Investments* (n 1); Opinion of AG Jacobs, para 55.

[23] [1989] OJ L298/23.

De Agostini was a Swedish publisher belonging to an Italian group which advertised its children's magazine '*Everything about Dinosaurs*' on TV3 (broadcasting by satellite from the UK to Denmark, Sweden and Norway) and TV4 (a Swedish channel). The KO applied to the competent national court—the *Marknadsdomstol* (the Market Court)—to obtain an order prohibiting De Agostini from marketing the magazine in a way that attracted children below the age of 12, in contravention of the Swedish Marketing Practices Act.

TV-Shop was the Swedish subsidiary of TV-Shop Europe whose activity consisted in advertising products in television spots and subsequently arranging the telephone ordering and the postal delivery of the relevant goods. TV-Shop broadcasted 'infomercials' on TV3 and on the Swedish channel Homeshopping Channel for skin-care products and detergents. The KO took the view that such advertising contravened the prohibition of misleading statements laid down in the national legislation.

The defendants in the national proceedings argued that the Swedish legislation in question infringed the TwF-Directive, as well as Articles 30 and 59 of the EC Treaty.

As regards Article 30, the ECJ recalled its settled case-law since *Leclerc-Siplec*,[24] according to which legislation which prohibits television advertising in a particular sector concerns selling arrangements within the meaning of *Keck*, inasmuch as it prohibits a specific form of promoting a particular method of marketing products.

It then went on to hold that, in accordance with *Keck*, Article 30 will not oppose the Swedish legislation as long as it affects in the same way, in law and in fact, the marketing of domestic and imported products, and, if that condition is not met, insofar as the rules in question are necessary and proportionate to meet overriding requirements of general public interest or one of the objectives laid down in ex Article 36 of the Treaty and provided that such objectives or overriding requirements cannot be met by measures less restrictive of intra-Community trade.[25]

With respect to Article 59, the Court, after recalling its judgment in *Bond van Adverteerders*,[26] where it held that advertising broadcast for payment by a television broadcaster established in one Member State for an advertiser established in another Member State constitutes provision of a service within the meaning of the abovementioned provision,[27] proceeded to examine whether domestic rules such as those in question in the cases pending before the national court constituted restrictions on freedom to provide services prohibited by that Article of the EC Treaty.[28]

24 Case C-412/93 *Société d'Importation Édouard Leclerc-Siplec v TF1 Publicité SA and M6 Publicité SA* [1995] ECR I-179.

25 *De Agostini* (n 2) paras 40–47.

26 Case 352/85 *Bond van Adverteerders v The Netherlands State* [1988] ECR 2085.

27 *De Agostini* (n 2) para 48.

28 ibid, para 49.

The Court replied in the affirmative[29] since, as stated in *Gouda*,[30] where the rules applicable to services have not been harmonised, such restrictions may result from non-discriminatory application of national rules to persons established in the territory of another Member State who already have to satisfy the requirements of that State's legislation.[31]

In such circumstances, the Court considered that restrictions on cross-border television advertising could only be justified by the reasons set out in Article 56 of the EC Treaty, or by application of a rule of reason, and in compliance with a proportionality test, as admitted in *Cassis de Dijon*[32] for restrictions on free movement of goods. No reference whatsoever was made to the application of the *Keck* doctrine to the case under analysis.

That led some authors to conclude that in *De Agostini*, even if *Keck* was confirmed and refined with regard to Article 30, it appeared to be rejected in relation to Article 59. Such an assertion, even when formulated in a hypothetical way, deserves further reflection.

As Professor Stuyck noted in his commentary on *De Agostini*,[33] the approach taken by the Court in this case may be explained by the fact that, in interpreting ex Article 59, it did

> not examine the application of the Swedish advertising rules to the advertiser, as it did with respect to Article 30, but rather the application of those rules to the broadcaster, as a provider of services to the benefit of the advertiser.

In so doing, the Court took, as regards the advertiser, the same approach it has consistently taken when assessing the restrictive effects of advertising for goods, ie it examined them in the light of Article 30. Having carried out that test, the Court then applied Article 59 to a service provision (by the broadcaster to the advertiser), which has a more indirect link with trade in goods.

That does not necessarily mean that, in making the legality of the application of the national provisions to those services subject to the 'Cassis test',[34] the Court intended to rule out the relevance of the *Keck* doctrine in the field of services. Indeed, had the Court made explicit reference to the application of *Keck* in this case, the result would have been the same, as will be further elaborated in the section below. One can thus assume that the Court simply did not (yet) need to deal with such a delicate issue.

Nevertheless, the Court failed to explain why the service provided by the broadcaster to the advertiser should not be considered as a 'selling arrangement' involved in the marketing of goods. Neither did the Court address the question

[29] ibid, para 50.

[30] *Gouda* (n 19) para 12.

[31] ibid, para 51.

[32] Case 120/78 *Rewe-Zentral (Cassis de Dijon)* [1979] ECR 650.

[33] J Stuyck (1997) 34 *Common Market Law Review* 1446, 1467.

[34] The Court, in *De Agostini* (n 2) did not directly perform that test and rather preferred to refer it to the national court.

whether any different consideration should be given to a situation where other intermediaries intervene as providers of services between the broadcaster and the advertiser, or to a situation where the broadcaster is requested to advertise a service and not a good.

IV. IS *KECK* TRANSPOSABLE INTO THE FIELD OF SERVICES?

The fundamental change introduced in the Court's case-law by *Keck* stems from the distinction between, on the one hand, obstacles to free movement of goods which are the consequence of applying, to goods coming from other Member States where they are lawfully manufactured and marketed according to the legal requirements of those Member States, rules that lay down different requirements to be met by such goods (such as those relating to designation, form, size, weight, composition, presentation, labelling, packaging)—rules on the 'intrinsic characteristics' of goods—and, on the other hand, national provisions restricting or prohibiting certain 'selling arrangements'—measures regulating the 'manner in which trading activity is pursued'.[35]

Regarding the first type of rule, the test of proportionality, as laid down in *Cassis*, shall apply. In fact, the obstacles created by those rules constitute measures having equivalent effect to quantitative restrictions on imports[36] prohibited by Article 28 EC, even if those rules apply without distinction to products of different origins,[37] unless their application can be justified by an objective of public interest taking precedence over the free movement of goods.[38]

Concerning the second set of measures relating to 'selling arrangements', the Court takes the view, since *Keck*, that they fall outside the scope of Article 30,[39] as long as those provisions apply to all relevant traders operating within the national territory and as long as they affect in the same manner, in law and in fact, the marketing of domestic products and of those from other Member States.

[35] Those were the terms proposed by Advocate General Tesauro in his Opinion in Case C-292/92 *Hünermund v Landesapothekerkammer Baden-Württemberg* [1993] ECR I-6800 paras 20, 25 ('modalités d'exercice de l'activité commerciale', in the French version). The concept should cover, as the Advocate General put it, the questions relating to 'who sells what, and when, where and how sales can be effected'.

[36] Those measures are defined in *Dassonville* (Case 8/74 [1974] ECR 837 para 5) as consisting of 'all trading rules enacted by Member States which are capable of hindering, directly or indirectly, actually or potentially, intra-Community trade'.

[37] As regards prohibitions of or discriminatory restrictions on imports, those can only be justified by the reasons set out in Article 36 of the EC Treaty, insofar as they do not constitute a means of arbitrary discrimination or a disguised restriction on trade between Member States.

[38] The proportionality test under *Cassis* has to be carried out in three stages: first, the objective pursued by the national legislation has to be legitimate; second, the rules under scrutiny must be necessary and suitable for the attainment of that objective; third, there must be no other measures less restrictive to attain those objectives with an equivalent degree of effectiveness.

[39] Therefore, there is no ground to apply the test of proportionality.

According to Judge Joliet,[40] the Court's purpose in *Keck* was to make clear that it is not sufficient for Article 28 EC to apply that a national regulation concerns intra-Community trade in whatever way. For that to be the case, the marketing of imported goods must be affected more intensely than the marketing of national goods. The national measures must then be of a protective nature, therefore creating an advantage in favour of the domestic production.

The 'raison d'être' of the distinction operated by *Keck* lies, according to Joliet,[41] in the distinction between, on the one hand, rules that affect the inherent characteristics of the goods admitted to the market and thus condition the access to the latter—such rules cannot overburden the imported goods that already have to comply with the conditions laid down by the State of origin (the 'double hurdle' test)—and provisions that regulate the trading conditions of any product already on the market. Article 28 EC serves therefore as a tool for eliminating obstacles to intra-Community trade in order to establish a single integrated market, not an instrument of 'deregulation' of the economy intended to ensure the unhindered pursuit of trade in individual Member States.[42]

The judgment in *Keck* gave rise to a considerable flow of articles and commentaries in favour or against the solution adopted by the Court therein.[43] It is beyond the scope of this chapter to discuss all that literature. I shall only recall that criticism was directed, on the one hand, at the reasonableness or the necessity of the *Keck* solution and, on the other hand, at the lack of a clear definition in the judgment of the notions used to identify the different categories of rules.

Some authors would favour the test set out in Article 3 of Directive 70/50,[44] or prefer to follow the Opinion of Advocate General Jacobs in *Leclerc-Siplec*, where he proposed an alternative test based on the existence or not of a substantial restriction on access to the market[45] of the Member State concerned, in other words, a *de minimis* test.[46]

[40] R Joliet, *La libre circulation des marchandises: l'arrêt Keck et Mithouard et les nouvelles orientations de la jurisprudence*, Exposé présenté lors de la visite des Cours suprêmes à la Cour de justice le 6 juin 1994.

[41] ibid.

[42] ibid. See also Opinion of Advocate General Tesauro in *Hünermund* (n 35) paras 1, 28.

[43] A list of articles resorting to either of those categories can be found in P Oliver, *Free Movement of Goods in the European Community*, 3rd edn (London, Sweet & Maxwell, 1997) 100–13.

[44] Directive 70/50 EEC on the abolition of measures which have an effect equivalent to the quantitative restrictions on imports and are not covered by other provisions adopted in pursuance of the EEC Treaty (OJ, Special Edition) 1970 (I) 17. See A Mattera, 'De l'arrêt Dassonville à l'arrêt Keck' (1994) *Revue du Marché unique européen* 117.

[45] On the concept of market access and the role it played in some judgments of the Court in 1997, see P Eeckhout, 'Recent Case-law on Free Movement of Goods: Refining Keck and Mithouard' (1998) *European Business Law Review* 257–72.

[46] A *de minimis* rule was considered by Advocate General Tesauro (Opinion in *Hünermund* C (n 35) paras 21, 22) as being inconsistent with the current Court's case-law as well as very difficult, if not downright impossible, to apply in practice. Instead, Advocate General Tesauro highlighted the disparity between national laws as a factor that, by constraining the operators concerned to alter a sales plan lawfully put into practice in the Member State of origin, makes access to another national market more costly or less profitable for the operators in question and is thus liable to constitute an

Others criticized the ambiguity arising from the emphasis put on and the treatment reserved by the Court to the issue of discrimination ('in law and in fact');[47] some pointed to the lack of precision of notions such as 'selling arrangements' as a source of legal uncertainty. At all events, the fact is that *Keck* constitutes the actual state of the case-law as it stands regarding free movement of goods.

My question at this juncture is, as already indicated, whether the same rationale is suitable for application in the field of intra-Community provision of services. I submit that the issue of transposing *Keck* into the field of services will inevitably arise, at one time or another, in such a way that the Court will inevitably have to face the option between maintaining or striking down the parallel interpretation of Articles 28 and 49 EC and thus the coherence in the application of the Treaty provisions relating to the internal market.[48]

It is not disputed that the concept of 'selling arrangement' as laid down by the Court applies to measures concerning advertising or sales promotion, which relate to one of the most obvious conditions under which goods may be marketed. Advertising is indeed an excellent example to illustrate the point I would like to make with respect to the application of the *Keck* formula in the field of services, since it may be used to promote either goods or services, or even entities of another kind, such as persons,[49] images, names or places.

Moreover, as admitted by the Court,[50] advertising is also a service in itself.[51] As was held in *Bond van Adverteerders*,[52] advertising broadcast for payment by a television broadcaster established in one Member State for an advertiser established in another Member State constitutes provision of a service within the meaning of Article 49 EC. Like *De Agostini* some years later, this ruling emphasised the need for a clear identification of the services involved in each concrete case when assessing the application of different Treaty provisions (Article 28 or Article 49 EC).

indirect obstacle to the movement of goods within the Community (paras 22, 25). The fact is that mere selling arrangements within the meaning of *Keck* do not fall in principle within Article 28 EC because in general they do not have a substantial impact on intra-Community trade. If they have, then Article 28 EC applies and that is what the Court acknowledged by referring to a 'discrimination in law and in fact'. Nevertheless, some problems of interpretation arise, as examined by D Waelbroeck, 'L'arrêt *Keck and Mithouard*: les conséquences pratiques' (1994) 13 *Journal des Tribunaux—Droit européen* 165. Anyway, the Court itself used, in *Peralta* (n 17) para 24, as well as in further cases (C-96/94 *Centro Servizi Spediporto* [1995] ECR I-2883 para 41, and C-266/96 *Corsica Ferries* [1998] ECR I-3949, para 31), the expression 'legislation whose restrictive effects are too uncertain and indirect for the obligation which it imposes to be regarded as being capable of hindering trade between Member States'.

47 See, in this respect, D Waelbroeck ibid 164–65.

48 See J Stuyck (n 33) 1468. See also Opinion of Advocate General Gulmann in *Schindler* (n 19) para 56, and *Alpine Investments* (n 1); Opinion of AG Jacobs para 60.

49 Such as politicians, film stars, singers or top models.

50 See, eg Cases 155/73 *Sacchi* [1974] ECR 409 and 52/79 *Procureur du Roi v Marc Debauve and Others* [1980] ECR 833.

51 See also EC, 'Green Paper on Commercial Communications in the Internal Market' COM (96) 192 final, Brussels, 8.5.1996, 5.

52 *Bond van Adverteerders* (n 26). See also the reference made to this ruling in *De Agostini* (n 2) para 48.

Bond van Adverteerders concerned the distribution, by operators of cable networks established in a Member State, of television programmes supplied by broadcasters established in another Member State and containing commercials especially intended for the public in the recipient Member State. In that case, the Court identified at least two separate services within the meaning of Articles 49 and 50 EC: the first was provided by cable network operators to broadcasters; the second by broadcasters to advertisers.

More generally, if—as submitted by the Commission in its 'Green Paper' on Commercial Communications in the Internal Market[53]—one defines 'commercial communications' as 'all forms of communication seeking to promote either products, services or the image of a company or organisation[54] to final consumers and and/or distributors', this will include all forms of advertising, direct marketing, sponsorship, sales promotions and public relations. It will also cover the use of commercial communication services by all goods and service industries as well as public and semi-public bodies, charities and political organisations.

According to the Commission's Green Paper, within this service sector, two general types of service may be identified:

— The range of services offered by the commercial communications industry ('suppliers')—including advertising agencies, direct marketing companies, sales promotion designers, media buyers, sponsorship agents, public relation companies—or by 'specialised suppliers', such as market research companies, advertising film producers, mailing list brokers. The services of both kinds of supplier are provided to clients ('users') interested in making such communications to the public or to a part thereof.

— The range of delivery services offered by 'carriers' of commercial communications, which covers a wide range of organisations including the media (TV, radio and printed world), organisers of sports and cultural events, billboard site operators, postal and telecommunication services providers, who may work for both suppliers and users.

The economic importance of this sector in terms of both output and employment, and the role it plays for the information and the persuasion of the consumers or the public in general, make it an increasingly powerful factor of competition and of economic and technical progress, as well as of integration of national markets.[55] Advertising cannot therefore be relegated to the ancillary role of a mere 'selling arrangement', helping to boost the marketing of goods or other services. If necessary, it has to be appraised as a service in itself in light of Article 49 EC.[56]

[53] See n 51 above.

[54] Or any other entity, as stressed above.

[55] For an assessment of the role of advertising, see Opinion of Advocate General Jacobs in *Leclerc-Siplec* (n 24) paras 19–21.

[56] If, of course, all the necessary conditions are met, namely that advertising is provided for remuneration as a trans-frontier service within the meaning of Article 50 EC (see *Bond van Adverteerders* (n 26) para 12).

Of course, whenever a measure restricting or prohibiting a form of advertising or of sales promotion is liable to affect the trans-frontier sales of goods, Article 28 EC and the corresponding case-law[57] must be called upon to assess the legality of national legislation as regards EC law. That is what the Court did in *Clinique*,[58] *Mars*,[59] *Familiapress*[60] and *De Agostini*.[61]

[57] Including the *Keck* test in order to determine whether the measure in question falls within Article 28 or not. Indeed, the notion of 'selling arrangement' delimits the scope of that provision and thus forms part of its case-law. This consideration paves the way for an interesting discussion concerning the legal basis for harmonisation measures in the field of advertising. The case may be illustrated by the controversy about the legal basis of European Parliament and Council Directive 98/43/EC of 6 July 1998 on the approximation of the laws, regulations and administrative provisions of the Member States relating to the advertising and sponsorship of tobacco products [1998] OJ L213/). The validity of the said Directive was challenged before the Court of First Instance in Cases T-172/98, T-175/98 and T-177/98 *Salamander AG and Others v European Parliament and Council* [2000] ECR II-2487. By judgment of 27 June 2000 (not yet published in the ECR), the Court dismissed the applications as inadmissible. In the meantime, Germany had also brought an action for annulment of the Directive before the Court of Justice (Case C-376/98 *Germany v EP and Council*) and a number of companies initiated proceedings before a UK court which referred a question for preliminary ruling to the Court of Justice (Case C-74/99 *The Queen v Secretary of State for Health and Others, ex parte Imperial Tobacco Ltd and Others* [2000] ECR I-8599). As Advocate General Fennelly stated in his Opinion, delivered on 15 June 2000 (para 3), '[t]he issue of competence or legal basis is the most important issue in these cases'. From the stand point of free movement of goods, according to the *Keck* case-law, national rules on advertising shall be considered in principle as mere 'selling arrangements' since they are not designed to regulate trade in goods (see judgments in *Hünermund* (n 35) and *Leclerc-Siplec* (n 24)), provided that they comply with the conditions laid down in that case-law. One could then argue that, in a strict application of the *Keck* doctrine, insofar as such measures do not apply to the 'intrinsic characteristics' of the product and do not affect its content as was the case in C-368/95 *Vereinigte Familiapress Zeitungsverlags-und vertriebs GmbH and Heinrich Bauer Verlag* [1997] ECR I-3689, they do not constitute a 'measure of equivalent effect' caught by Article 28 EC and therefore are not liable to affect the functioning of the internal market. In such conditions, it could be argued that the existence of different national rules on advertising for tobacco products was not of such nature as to lawfully give rise to Community harmonisation measures based on Article 95 EC (ex Article 100a), at least insofar as they are of a general nature like a total or partial ban on advertising. It must be said that Advocate General Fennelly did not choose to include this approach in his Opinion.

[58] Case C-315/92 *Verband Sozialer Wettbewerb v Clinique Laboratories SNC and Estée Lauder Cosmetics GmbH* [1994] ECR I-317. The Court applied the *Cassis* test of proportionality to a German measure prohibiting the use of the name *Clinique* for a cosmetic product as being liable to mislead consumers and oblige the undertaking in question 'to bear additional packaging and advertising costs'.

[59] Case C-470/93 *Verein gegen Unwesen im Handel v Mars* [1995] ECR I-1936. The Court held a German measure prohibiting the importation and marketing of ice-cream bars presented—as part of a short publicity campaign covering the whole of Europe—in wrappers marked '+10%' as being against the Treaty (Article 30) on grounds that it 'may compel the importer to adjust the presentation of his products according to the place where they are to be marketed and consequently to incur additional packaging and advertising costs' and that the measure in question was neither proportionate to nor justified by the objective of consumer protection that it sought to attain.

[60] *Familiapress* (n 57). The judgment concerned the application to German magazines of an Austrian measure prohibiting periodicals to include games with prizes. The ECJ ruled that, although the national legislation in question referred to a method of sales promotion, it applied to the actual content of the product (a review) and did therefore not concern a mere selling arrangement. It further considered that, since the prohibition in question required publishers established in other Member States to alter the content of their papers, it jeopardised access of the product to the market of the importing Member State and, consequently, hindered the free movement of goods, thus constituting a measure of equivalent effect prohibited in principle by Article 30 of the EC Treaty. On *Familiapress* and other post-*Keck* judgments, see M Maduro (n 14).

[61] See section III above. The Court found that the Swedish legislation in question concerned selling arrangements, inasmuch as it prohibited a particular form of promotion of products. However, it

However, where the advertising is not linked with the sales promotion of goods but is used to promote services or persons, Article 28 EC is not applicable. The question then arises on whether, in a parallel application of Articles 28 and 49 EC, advertising can be considered as a selling arrangement for services. Furthermore, consideration should also be given, in this context, to the trans-frontier activity of operators such as advertising agencies consisting of the provision of services within the meaning of Articles 49 and 50 EC.

Let us suppose that it is the Member State of destination of the service (not the Member State of origin) that imposes the prohibition on cold calling examined by the Court in *Alpine Investments*. Let us also consider that cold calling services are not carried out by the provider of the services to be promoted (eg financial services, like in *Alpine*), but by a company specialised in cold calling which has among its clients both producers of goods and providers of services. Is it appropriate to give a different treatment to a national ban or a restriction on cold calling according to the object—goods or services—of that form of sales promotion? Should it be considered as a selling arrangement and examined in the light of paragraph 16 of *Keck* when goods are concerned and, conversely, be covered by the prohibition laid down in Article 49 EC if it involves trade in services?[62] Is there a reason for such different treatment?

In this context, one possibility, suggested by D Waelbroeck,[63] is to draw a distinction between rules on advertising which affect directly, as in *Clinique*, the designation of the products and rules of a more general nature not connected with the product itself (eg a general ban on advertising for alcohol). Such a line of reasoning could indeed be fruitful in terms of a possible transposition of the *Keck* case-law into the field of intra-Community provision of services. Still taking the domain of advertising services as an example, I hold that such transposition might rely on the distinction between two groups of measures:[64]

— Rules concerning the 'intrinsic' characteristics of the service (advertising), such as the content or the nature of the images used (eg prohibition of nudity or of violence in advertisements), the method or technique of

further held that an outright ban on a type of promotion for a product which is lawfully sold in the importing Member State might have a greater impact on imported products than on national ones and that, under such conditions, Article 30 might apply.

[62] According to the 'classic' case-law of the Court, the assessment to be made in order to examine whether a national regulation restricts or not, in an unlawful manner, the freedom to provide services, within the meaning of Article 49 EC, implies that discriminatory measures can only be justified by reasons of public policy, public security or public health (Article 46 EC), provided that they can be considered as proportionate, whereas non-discriminatory measures can be justified by overriding reasons of public interest (protection of workers or of consumers, protection of intellectual property, of fair trading or of pluralism, conservation of national and cultural heritage, linguistic policy, etc), if they are not already satisfied by the rules in the Member State of origin (principle of the country of origin legislation or of mutual recognition) and if they are not disproportionate (see *De Agostini* (n 2) para 52).

[63] ibid 163.

[64] Of course, this concerns only indistinctly applicable and non-discriminatory measures.

advertising or the way of presentation, which ought to be submitted to the proportionality test.

— Rules relating to the general or 'extrinsic' conditions in which advertising services can be provided (including a total or a partial ban, eg during certain hours) which ought to be considered as selling arrangements within the meaning of *Keck*.

The application of that test to cases such as *Alpine* (if 'reconstructed' as concerning measures taken by the Member State of destination) and *De Agostini* would probably lead to the same answers that have actually been given by the Court without recourse to the proposed distinction. Indeed, even if the prohibition imposed on 'cold calling' may be considered to relate to a selling arrangement as regards either trade of goods or of services, it could in fact more heavily affect the marketing of services from other Member States as compared to the domestic services, and thus particularly impede the access of the former to the market.

In *De Agostini*, it is clear that the prohibitions in question concerned the content of the advertisements, and not any general and extrinsic conditions in which the service could be provided.

The practical effects of such a change of perspective will thus probably be negligible; but it might be imposed for the sake of clarity and coherence of the case-law. Much will probably depend on the pressure litigants may put on the Court as a result of any new 'saga' in favour of the liberalisation of market access for services. Advertising might well be the privileged battle field.

17

*The Precautionary Principle in EC Law**

THE PRECAUTIONARY PRINCIPLE was first spelled out, at the EC level, in the field of environmental protection by the Maastricht Treaty. The European Court of Justice (hereinafter the 'ECJ' or the 'Court') dealt with some issues relating to a precautionary approach since 1994, in particular after the BSE cases.

It was nevertheless in the *Pfizer* case[1] that the CFI effected a remarkable systematisation of all the main constituents of the precautionary principle and of its conditions of application.

This article summarises the main findings of the Court in that judgment and compares it with further rulings. It emphasises the need to respect procedural requirements and the principle of proportionality before adopting preventive measures for the protection of human health in conditions of scientific uncertainty.

I. THE PRECAUTIONARY PRINCIPLE AS A GENERAL PRINCIPLE OF EC LAW

A. The Prehistory of Precaution

Even the most attentive reader revisiting the abundant literature on the general principles of EC law would not find a single reference to such a thing as a precautionary principle until the late 1990s. Indeed, distinguished authors like Pierre Pescatore,[2] TC Hartley,[3] J-V Louis[4] and others[5] do not even mention the precautionary principle among the general principles of Community law, in conjunction with the principle of good administration or otherwise.

* First published in (2004) 10 *European Public Law Review* 2, 369–406.

[1] T-13/99 *Pfizer Animal Health v Council of the European Union* [2002] ECR II-3305.

[2] See P Pescatore, 'Rapport communautaire—Les principes généraux du droit en tant que source du droit communautaire', in *Rapports 12e Congrès* (Paris, FIDE, 1986) 17–54.

[3] TC Hartley, *The Foundations of European Community Law*, 2nd edn (Oxford, Clarendon Press, 1988).

[4] J-V Louis, 'L'Ordre juridique communautaire', *Perspectives européennes*, 6th edn (Brussels, CCE, 1993).

[5] See, for instance, R-E Papadopoulou, *Principes généraux du droit et droit communautaire. Origines et concrétisation* (Athens/Brussels, Sakkoulas/Bruylant, 1996); T Tridimas, *The General Principles of EC Law* (Oxford, Oxford University Press, 1999).

François-Xavier de Dorlodot and Denis Waelbroeck[6] refer briefly to the 'principe de prudence, selon laquelle l'autorité doit agir raisonnablement et avec precaution',[7] as one of the general principles of Belgian administrative law. But no further elaboration was made and no definition of the precautionary principle was given, that could provide any basis for the building of an autonomous principle of EC law.

B. The Principle at International Level

The recognition of the precautionary principle started at the international level,[8] more precisely in the World Charter for Nature, adopted by the UN General Assembly in 1982. Several instruments of international law subsequently developed the concept in the field of environmental protection.[9]

Mention should be made, in this context, to the Ministerial Declaration at the Second International Conference on the Protection of the North Sea (1987) and to the new Ministerial Declaration at the Third International Conference on the Protection of the North Sea (1990).

In 1992, as a result of the UN Conference on Environment and Development (UNCED) in Rio de Janeiro, a reference to a precautionary approach was formally included in the Rio Declaration as Principle 15, as follows:

> In order to protect the environment, the precautionary approach should be widely applied by States according to their capabilities. Where there are threats of serious or irreversible damage, lack of full scientific certainty shall not be used as a reason for postponing cost-effective measures to prevent environmental degradation.

The same principle was subsequently taken up in similar words in the Preamble of the Convention of Biological Diversity (1992) and in Article 3 of the Convention of Climate Change (1992). It was further reasserted in the Paris Convention for the protection of the marine environment of the north-east Atlantic (September

[6] F.-X de Dorlodot et D Waelbroeck. 'Rapport belge—Les principes généraux du droit en tant que source du droit communautaire', in *Rapports 12e Congrès* (Paris, FIDE, 1986) 55–74.

[7] 'The principle of precaution, according to which the authority must act with reasonableness and caution' (my translation).

[8] The precautionary principle was discussed and analysed by important international organisations such as the UN Environment Program (UNEP), the International Law Commission (ILC), the World Trade Organisation (WTO), the Organisation of Economic Cooperation and Development (OECD), as well as the European Union. Moreover, the principle was raised in proceedings before international judicial bodies, such as the International Court of Justice, the International Tribunal for the Law of Sea and the Appellate Body of the WTO. See G Loibl, 'The Precautionary Principle in International Law' in E Freytag, T Jackl, G Loibl and M Wittmann (eds), *The Role of Precaution in Chemicals Policy* (Vienna, Diplomatische Akademie Wien, 2001) 13.

[9] The appearance of the precautionary principle at the international level in the field of environmental protection is attributed to a number of reasons. They are summarised by T Christoforou, 'The Origins, Content and Role of the Precautionary Principle in European Community Law' in (E Freytag, T Jackl, G Loibl and M Wittmann (eds), *The Role of Precaution in Chemicals Policy* (Vienna, Diplomatische Akademie Wien, 2001) 25.

1992) and in Article 10, paragraph 6, of the Protocol on Biosafety concerning the safe transfer, handling and use of living modified organisms resulting from modern biotechnology, adopted at the Conference of the Parties to the Convention on Biological Diversity (January 2000).

C. The Precautionary Principle in EC Law

At the EC level, the first explicit reference to the precautionary principle appears in the environment title of the EC Treaty, in Article 130r(2) [now Article 174(2)].

Nevertheless, in its original version, Article 130r, as added by the Single European Act (SEA), did not mention the precautionary principle as something different from the principles that preventive action should be taken, that environment damage should as a priority be rectified at source and that the polluter should pay.

It is indeed only since Maastricht that an explicit reference to the precautionary principle can be found in the Treaty. But from the outset, the commentators stressed the fact that the precautionary principle cannot be limited to the environmental field, as underlined by Article 6 of the Treaty, which provides that 'environmental protection requirements must be integrated into the definition and implementation of the Community policies and activities'.[10]

It is not surprising that the precautionary principle took no place in EC secondary legislation before it became a principle whose recognition in the Treaty made of it a general principle of statutory and judicial EU law.

As the ECJ stated in *Sandoz*:[11]

> In so far as there are uncertainties in the present state of scientific research with regard to the harmfulness of a certain additive, it is for the Member States, in the absence of full harmonisation, to decide what degree of protection of the health and life of humans they intend to assure, in light of the specific eating habits of their own population …

This ruling seems to represent the first manifestation, at the EC judicial level, of the perception of precaution as a criterion for public action.

But, even after its recognition in the Treaty, the precautionary principle did not find a clear resonance in the texts of regulations or directives.

[10] See, among others, LG Vaqué, L Ehring, C Jacquet, 'Le principe de précaution dans la législation communautaire et nationale relative à la protection de la santé' (1999) 1 *Revue du Marché unique européen* 79; A Alemanno, 'Le principe de précaution en droit communautaire—Stratégie de gestion des risques ou risque d'atteinte au Marché intérieur ?' (2001) 4 *Revue du Droit de l'Union européenne* 917; LG Vaqué, 'La definición del contenido y ámbito de aplicación del principio de precaución en el derecho comunitario' (2002) *Gaceta Jurídica de la Unión Europea y de la Competencia* 4. See also Council Resolution of 4 December 2000 on the use of the precautionary principle (Doc Council 14328/00).

[11] Case 174/82 *Sandoz BV* [1983] ECR I-2211 para 16.

However, even without being expressly mentioned, the principle started to 'impregnate' the legislation, laying behind the measures whose adoption is required from the Community institutions.[12]

General policy guidelines were set out, since 1997, by the Commission in the Green Paper on the General Principles of Food Safety[13] and in the Communication on Consumer Health and Food Safety;[14] by the European Parliament in its Resolution on the Commission Green Paper;[15] by the Council in its Resolution of 13 April 1999;[16] and by the Joint Parliamentary Committee of the EEA in its Resolution of 16 March 1999.[17]

In its Communication on the Precautionary Principle, of February 2000, the Commission finally considered 'that the precautionary principle is a general one which should in particular be taken into consideration in the fields of environmental protection and human, animal and plant health'.[18]

Further, in its Resolution of 4 December 2000 on the use of the precautionary principle,[19] the Council welcomed the Commission's initiative to present the communication on the precautionary principle and formally endorsed the broad lines of that communication.

[12] See P Icard, 'Le principe de précaution: exception à l'application du droit communautaire ?' (2002) 3 *Revue trimestrielle de Droit européen* 476/477. The author discusses the issue of whether the precautionary principle is to be considered a 'derogation' (when applied at the Community level) or as an 'exception' (if applied by national authorities) to general rules of Community law, notably under Article 30 EC. In any event, as the Council itself recalled (see Council Resolution of 4 December 2000, n 10), the precautionary principle applies to the policies and actions of both the Community and its Member States. This article will focus mainly on measures within the competence of Community institutions, even though many of the conclusions apply to measures that fall within the scope of intervention of national authorities. On this aspect, see L Krämer, 'Precaution, the Protection of Health and the Environment and the Free Circulation of Goods within the European Union' in E Freytag, T Jackl, G Loibl and M Wittmann (eds), *The Role of Precaution in Chemicals Policy* (Vienna, Diplomatische Akademie Wien, 2001) 42.

[13] Commission Green Paper on 'The General Principles of Food Law in the European Union'. Brussels 30 April 1997 COM (97) 176 final.

[14] Commission Communication on 'Consumer Health and Food Safety', Brussels 30 April 1997 COM (97) 183.

[15] European Parliament Resolution of 10 March 1998 on the Green Paper. Available in http://eur-lex.europa.eu/legal-content/EN/TXT/?qid=1399051902074&uri=CELEX:51998IP0009.

[16] 2171st Council meeting Consumer Affairs, Luxembourg, 13 April 1999. http://europa.eu/rapid/press-release_PRES-99-98_en.htm.

[17] Available in: http://www.efta.int/sites/default/files/documents/advisory-bodies/parliamentary-committee/jpc-resolutions/March-1999FoodSafety.pdf.

[18] On the 'legal authority' of the precautionary principle as a 'legal principle', see E Fisher, 'Precaution, Precaution Everywhere: Developing a 'Common Understanding' of the Precautionary Principle in the European Community' (2002) *Maastricht Journal of European Competition Law* 7–28, especially 15–18. See also Opinion of Advocate General Cosmas in *Fornasar* (n 40) para 34.

[19] See n 10 above.

D. The Earlier Case-Law of the Community Courts

The ECJ dealt with, in several of its judgments since 1994, some of the issues that were later, in more recent cases, expressly raised under the head of the 'precautionary principle'.

In *Angelopharm*,[20] the Court discussed, regarding the validity of Directive 90/121,[21] the extent of the obligation for the Commission to consult the competent scientific committee (in that case, the 'Scientific Committee on Cosmetology').

In *Pharos*[22, 23] the question at stake related specifically to the conditions under which the Commission was entitled to submit a scientific issue concerning public health for further advice to the competent scientific committee (the 'Committee for Veterinary Medicinal Products').

However, it was only in the judgments on the validity of the Commission Decision 96/239/EC of 27 March 1996 on emergency measures to protect against bovine spongiform encephalopathy (BSE) (hereinafter 'the BSE Decision' or 'the Decision'),[24] that the approach underlying the precautionary principle was first upheld by the Court.

These cases deserve further consideration not only in view of the importance of the issue as regards food safety and public health and its impact on public opinion, but also because the judgments laid the ground for the development of some fundamental notions by the CFI in *Pfizer*.

E. The BSE Cases

The BSE Decision imposed, on a temporary basis, a ban on exports of bovine animals, bovine meat and derived products from the territory of the United Kingdom to the other Member States and to third countries.[25]

The Decision was adopted by the Commission following the issue of two statements by the Spongiform Encephalopathy Advisory Committee (SEAC),[26] concerning the existence of a possible link between BSE and a variant of

[20] C-212/91 *Angelopharm v Hamburg* [1994] ECR I-171.

[21] Twelfth Commission Directive 90/121/EEC of 20 February 1990, adapting to technical progress Annexes II, III, IV, V and VI to Council Directive 76/768/CEE on the approximation of the laws of the Member States relating to cosmetic products [1990] OJ L71/40.

[22] T-105/96 *Pharos v Commission* [1998] ECR II-285.

[23] C-151/98 P *Pharos v Commission* [1999] ECR I-8157.

[24] [1996] OJ L78/47.

[25] Accordingly, the Decision suspended, on a provisional basis and in derogation of the general rules of Community law, application of the principle of free movement of goods. See Icard (n 12) 484.

[26] The SEAC is an independent scientific body that advises the UK Government.

Creuzfeldt-Jakob disease.[27] The Decision was based on the EC Treaty,[28] on Council Directive 90/425/EEC,[29] in particular Article 10(4) thereof, and on Council Directive 89/662/EEC,[30] in particular Article 9 thereof.

The Preamble to the Decision, after referring to the publication of new scientific information, the announcement of additional measures taken by the UK Government, the adoption by various Member States of measures banning imports of cattle or beef and veal from the United Kingdom and the opinion of the Scientific Veterinary Committee, stated that:

> ... under current circumstances, a definitive stance on the transmissibility of BSE to humans is not possible; ... a risk of transmission cannot be excluded; ... the resulting uncertainty has created serious concern among consumers; ... under the circumstances and as an emergency measure, the transport of all bovine animals and all beef and veal or derived products from the United Kingdom to the other Member States should be temporarily banned; ... the same prohibitions should also apply to exports to non-Member countries so as to prevent deflections of trade ... (fifth recital).

It was against this background that the Commission decided, in Article 1 of the Decision, to impose the abovementioned ban.

In its judgments in *National Farmers' Union*[31] and *United Kingdom v Commission*,[32] the Court upheld the Commission's position that, despite the fact that BSE previously existed, the new information provided by SEAC significantly altered the perception of the risk, which that disease represented for human health.[33]

The Court acknowledged that, under Directives 90/425 and 89/662, the Commission enjoyed a wide measure of discretion, particularly as to the nature and the extent of the measures that it could adopt[34] and that it did not clearly

[27] The BSE or 'mad cow disease', affecting both humans and various animal species through brain degeneration, was first detected in the United Kingdom in 1986. The probable origin of BSE is thought to have been a change in the method of preparing cattle feed containing proteins derived from carcasses of sheep affected by scrapie.

[28] Without mentioning any specific Treaty Articles.

[29] Council Directive 90/425/EEC of 26 June 1990 concerning veterinary and zootechnical checks applicable in intra-Community trade in certain live animals and products with a view to the completion of the internal market [1990] OJ L224/29, as amended by Council Directive 92/118/EEC of 17 December 1992 laying down animal health and public health requirements governing trade imports into the Community of products not subject to the said requirements laid down in specific Community rules referred to in Annex A (I) to Directive 89/662/EEC and, as regards pathogens, to Directive 90/425/EEC [1993] OJ L 62/49.

[30] Council Directive 89/662/EEC of 11 December 1989, concerning veterinary checks in intra-Community trade with a view to the completion of the internal market [1989] OJ L395/13), as amended by Directive 92/118.

[31] C-157/96 *National Farmers' Union* [1998] ECR I-2211 paras 30–32.

[32] C-180/96 *United Kingdom v Commission* [1998] ECR I-2265 paras 9, 10, 14.

[33] In the Commission's opinion, the SEAC announcements had reclassified the disease: it was no longer regarded merely as affecting cattle, but as a hazard to human health, which modified the risk assessment and justified the Commission's intervention.

[34] *National Farmers' Union* (n 31) para 39; *United Kingdom v Commission* (n 32) para 60.

exceed the bounds of its discretion by banning the exports of the animals and products concerned.[35]

The Court also examined the Decision at length in the light of the 'principle of proportionality'.

In its answers, the ECJ, after recalling the limits of judicial control in matters concerning the common agricultural policy, where the Community legislature has a discretionary power corresponding to its political responsibilities,[36] applied the following line of reasoning:[37]

- At the time when the contested decision was adopted, there was great uncertainty as to the *risks* posed by live animals, bovine meat and derived products;
- Where there is uncertainty as to the existence or extent of risks to human health, the institutions may take protective measures without having to wait until the reality and seriousness of those risks become fully apparent;[38]
- That approach is borne out by Article 130r(1)(2);[39]
- The decision was adopted as an emergency measure temporarily banning exports, subjected, moreover, to detailed scientific study and, consequently, to review after an overall examination of the situation;
- The Court upheld the concerns expressed by the Commission, the Scientific Veterinary Committee and one of its members regarding the scientific uncertainty concerning the risks of transmissibility of BSE and the lack of effectiveness of controls and other measures already taken;
- Consequently, the ban imposed by the Commission, amounting to a containment measure, designed to eradicate the disease, combined with market and other support measures, could not be regarded as a manifestly inappropriate measure;
- As regards the claim that alternative measures were possible, the Court considered that, in view of the seriousness of the risk and the urgency of the situation, the Commission did not react in a manifestly inappropriate manner by imposing, on a temporary basis and pending the production of more detailed scientific information, a general ban on exports of bovine animals, bovine meat and derived products.

Consequently, the Commission did not breach the principle of proportionality.

[35] *National Farmers' Union* (n 31) para 41; *United Kingdom v Commission* (n 32) para 62. See also, in this respect, paragraph 63 of the Order of 12 July 1996, C-180/96 R *United Kingdom v Commission* [1996] ECR I-3903.

[36] *National Farmers' Union* (n 31) paras 60–61; *United Kingdom v Commission* (n 32) paras 96–97.

[37] *National Farmers' Union* (n 31) paras 62–76; *United Kingdom v Commission* (n 32) paras 98–111.

[38] This passage contains all the basic elements of a general definition of the precautionary principle, which will be picked up again in subsequent judgments (see below).

[39] Quite surprisingly, when quoting Article 130r(2), the Court did not make reference to the precautionary principle, at the time already expressly enshrined in the EC Treaty by the Maastricht Treaty.

F. Other Cases before *Pfizer*

In neither judgment in the BSE cases did the Court make an explicit reference to the precautionary principle.[40]

Two months later, in *Bergaderm*,[41] the CFI expressly cited the two ECJ rulings, but still without identifying the principle by name.

However, in its judgment on appeal from the CFI decision in the *Bergaderm* case,[42] the ECJ was explicit in clarifying what was at stake in the formulations previously used: '... the appellants dispute the reference to the precautionary principle in paragraph 66 of the contested judgment'. This appears to be the first explicit reference to the principle in a Court ruling.

The Court explicitly mentioned the precautionary principle in its judgment in the *Lirussi and Bizzaro* cases,[43] together with the principle of preventive action, in relation to Article 4 of Directive 75/442/CEE of 15 July 1975, on waste,[44] in conjugation with Article 130r of the Treaty.

It was also invoked in *Greenpeace France*,[45] concerning the interpretation of Council Directive 90/220/EEC of 23 April 1990, on the deliberate release into the environment of genetically modified organisms (GMOs).[46]

According to that Directive, no product containing GMOs may be released into the environment before the competent authority of the Member State in which the product is to be placed on the market for the first time has given its written consent following a notification that must enable the national authority to carry out the required risk assessment.

The applicants in the main proceedings (Association Greenpeace France and Others) argued before the Court that an interpretation of the Directive to the effect that the Member States' powers are circumscribed would be contrary to the precautionary principle.

[40] Neither did Advocate General Tesauro in his Opinion of 30 September 1997, where only the principles of proportionality and of non-discrimination were discussed. Actually, the first reference to the precautionary principle in an Advocate General's Opinion appears in the Opinion of Advocate General Cosmas in C-343/95 *Diego Calì* [1997] ECR I-1547. But the Advocate General limits himself to quoting the new Article 130r(2) and the Rio Declaration, without mentioning principle 15. In further cases, the Advocates General, without providing a comprehensive analysis of the precautionary principle, nevertheless gave some contributions to understanding specific aspects involved in risk assessment, in the light of a 'precautionist' approach. See, in that context, Opinions of Advocates General Mischo (C-184/97 *Commission v Germany* [1999] ECR I-7837), La Pergola (C-94/98 *Rhône-Poulenc Rore et al v Licensing Authority* [1999] ECR I-8789), Cosmas (C-318/98 *Criminal proceedings against Giancarlo Fornasar et al* [2000] ECR I-4785) and Fennelly (C-352/98 P [2000] I-5291).

[41] T-199/96 *Laboratoires pharmaceutiques Bergaderm et al v Commission* [1998] ECR II-2805 para 66.

[42] C-352/98 P *Laboratoires pharmaceutiques Bergaderm et al v Commission* [2000] ECR I-5291 para 52.

[43] Joined Cases C-175/98 and C-177/98 *Paolo Lirussi and Francesca Bizzaro* [1999] ECR I-6881 paras 51–52.

[44] [1994] OJ L1/494.

[45] C-6/99 *Association Greenpeace France et al v Ministère de l'agriculture et de la pêche et al* [2000] ECR I-1651.

[46] [1990] OJ L117/15, as amended by Commission Directive 97/35/EC of 18 June 1997 adapting to technical progress for the second time Council Directive 90/220 [1997] OJ L169/72).

The ECJ pointed out that observance of the precautionary principle is reflected, first, in the notifier's obligation to immediately notify the competent authority of new information regarding the risks of the product to human health or the environment and the competent authority's obligation to immediately inform the Commission and the other Member States about this information and, secondly, in the right of any Member State provisionally to restrict or prohibit the use and/or sale on its territory of a product which has received consent where it has justifiable reasons to consider that it constitutes a risk to human health or the environment.[47]

Yet, one cannot say that the Court was effectively paving the way for a systematic application of the precautionary principle. Rather, it was giving a clear indication in favour of a 'prudential approach' as regards certain risks for human health or the environment.[48]

II. THE PRECAUTIONARY PRINCIPLE IN *PFIZER*

A. Scientific Uncertainty in the Commission Communication on the Precautionary Principle

As stated in the Communication from the Commission on the Precautionary Principle,[49] an analysis of that principle reveals two distinct aspects: (a) the political decision to act or not to act as such, which is linked to the factors triggering recourse to the precautionary principle; (b) in the affirmative, how to act, ie the measures resulting from application of the principle.

As regards the first aspect, the Commission rightly points out that:

> Whether or not to invoke the Precautionary Principle is a decision exercised where scientific information is insufficient, inconclusive or uncertain and where there are indications that the possible effects on the environment, or human, animal or plant health may be potentially dangerous and inconsistent with the chosen level of protection.

This formulation underlines the role and possible need of a precautionary principle as a legal tool intended to tackle the risks for public health or the environment in a context of scientific uncertainty.[50]

[47] See *Greenpeace France* (n 45) para 44 of the judgment. For an analysis of the *Greenpeace* judgment, see N de Sadeleer, 'Le statut juridique du principe de précaution en droit communautaire: du slogan à la règle' (2001) 1–2 *Cahiers de Droit européen* 116.

[48] The precautionary principle was also widely mentioned in C-1/2000 *Commission v France* [2001] ECR I-9989 (Opinion Mischo), but did not deserve an analysis by the Court.

[49] COM/2000/1 final, of 2 February 2000. On the Commission's Communication, see Guy Corcelle, 'La perspective communautaire du principe de précaution' (2001) *Revue du marché commun et de l'Union européenne* 447–54, at 450.

[50] In Icard's words (n 12) 471, 'le principe de précaution reformule le rapport du droit à la science en introduisant le doute' ('the precautionary principle modifies the relationship between law and science inasmuch as it introduces doubt in that relation'—my translation). For N de Sadeleer

B. Scientific Uncertainty in the *Pfizer* Judgment

The ruling of the CFI in *Pfizer*[51] is a landmark in the development of the notion of the precautionary principle, since it proceeds to a remarkable systematisation of all the main constituents of the principle and its conditions of application.

As recalled by the CFI,[52] it follows from the case-law[53] that, where there is scientific uncertainty as to the existence or extent of risks to human health, the Community institutions may, by reason of the precautionary principle, take protective measures, in spite of the fact that, in such a situation, a risk assessment cannot be required to provide the Community institutions with conclusive scientific evidence of the reality of the risk and the seriousness of the potential adverse effects were that risk to become a reality.[54]

Indeed, scientific uncertainty exists when there is no adequate theoretical or empirical basis for assigning possibilities to a defined set of outcomes.[55]

What is in each case the degree of scientific uncertainty that may trigger intervention of the competent authority on the basis of the precautionary principle is thus the first question to be answered.

C. The Risk to be Assessed

First of all, a 'danger' or a 'risk'[56] for the environment or for human health, namely the risk associated with the use of a given product, has to be present if a preventive measure is to be taken.

In *Pfizer*, the risk associated was the possibility that the use of an antibiotic called virginiamycin as an additive in feedingstuffs as a growth promoter for animals would give rise to adverse effects on human health, namely a transfer of

(n 47) 91, '[d]epuis l'avènement des temps modernes, le droit positif se conjugue avec la certitude scientifique. [...] Cette servilité du droit positif envers une science réputée infaillible fut pourtant dénoncée en raison de la montée en puissance de l'incertitude' ('since the coming of modern times, the law goes along with scientific certainty. [...] Such servility of positive law towards a science which was supposed to be infallible has been contradicted by the emergence of uncertainty'—my translation).

51 *Pfizer* (n 1).

52 ibid paras 139–40.

53 *United Kingdom v Commission* (n 32) para 99; *National Farmers' Union* (n 31) para 63; *Bergaderm* (n 42) para 66.

54 *Pfizer* (n 1) para 142. See also Council Resolution of 4 December 2000 (n 10).

55 This may be because of the novelty of the substance or activity concerned or because of complexity or variability in their context (Christophorou (n 9) 28). But 'uncertainty' should also be formally distinguished from 'ignorance', where some of the possible outcomes, at the time of assessing the activity or substance, are completely unknown or unknowable and, thus, fail entirely to be assessed. Uncertainty and ignorance may nevertheless coexist in a risk assessment thus further increasing the potential for error (Christophorou, ibid, 29).

56 'Danger' is the term used by the Community legislature in Directive 70/524 (n 59). In the Preamble of Regulation No 2821/98, the term 'risk' is preferred. It is doubtful whether both terms can be considered, in general, as equivalent (see below).

antimicrobial resistance from animals to humans, and, consequently, a reduction in the effectiveness of certain medicinal products in human medicine.

As follows from Article 11(1)(3) of Directive 70/524,[57] the Community institutions may withdraw authorisation of an additive in feedingstuffs where, as a result of new information or of a reassessment of existing information, there are 'detailed grounds' for establishing that the use of the additive 'constitutes a danger to animal or human health or the environment'.

In recital 5 to Regulation No 2821/98,[58] the Council found that there was a risk that it considered to be a 'serious reason'[59] for restricting the use of virginiamycin to medical use.

In the course of the process, the parties were opposed as to the reality and the seriousness of that risk and thus as to the need for the institutions to take the preventive measure.

D. The Apportionment of the Burden of Proof

Pfizer gives us a clear indication about how the burden of proof must be administered when applying the precautionary principle.

As held by the CFI,[60] it would be wrong to require scientific certainty before allowing action to be taken to protect health or the environment. There are limits to scientific knowledge at any moment in time. Moreover, there are risks that can be caused by multiple, confounding factors that sometimes take time to materialise.[61]

Rather, in the Court's view, in the process culminating in the adoption of any preventive measure, the Community institutions must comply with the requirements of a correct risk assessment. First, that the measure in question is adopted following as thorough a scientific risk assessment as possible, taking account of the particular circumstances of each case. Second, that the institutions had available, on the basis of that assessment, sufficient scientific indications to conclude, on an objective scientific basis, that the use of a given product or process constitutes a risk to human health.

[57] Council Directive 70/524/EEC of 23 November 1970 concerning additives in feedstuffs [OJ English Special Edition 1970 (III), 840], as amended in particular by Council Directive 84/587/EEC of 29 November 1984 [1984] OJ L319/13) and by Council Directive 96/51/EC of 23 July 1996 [1996] OJ L235/39, and supplemented by several Council and Commission decisions on the setting up of different Scientific and Standing Committees.

[58] Regulation (EC) No 2821/98 of 17 December 1998 amending, as regards withdrawal of the authorisation of certain antibiotics, Directive 70/524/EEC concerning additives in feedingstuffs [1998] OJ L 351/4, 29.12.1998 (http://eur-lex.europa.eu/LexUriServ/LexUriServ.do?uri).

[59] Within the meaning of Article 3a(e) of Directive 70/524 (n 56).

[60] See *Pfizer* (n 1) paras 164–65.

[61] Christoforou (n 9) 30.

It must be recognised that such apportionment of the burden of proof is consistent with the idea that the precautionary principle is a legal tool for dealing with risks, namely for human health, in a context of scientific uncertainty.[62]

In that context, as already pointed out, the Community institutions may, by reason of the precautionary principle, take protective measures without having to wait until the reality and seriousness of those risks become fully apparent. Otherwise, 'the precautionary principle [...] would be rendered devoid of purpose'.[63]

A fortiori, the Community institutions are not required, for the purpose of taking preventive action, to wait for the adverse effects of the use of a given product to materialise.[64]

But this does not allow for systematically reversing the burden of proof against the business community. This is clear where a prior approval procedure does not exist.[65] Only when a 'black list' of substances is drawn (after a careful risk assessment) or where prior approval is needed before the placing on the market of certain products ('positive list'), it is up to the business community to carry out the scientific work in order to demonstrate that a given substance is not potentially hazardous and should then be excluded from the list or deserves authorisation.[66]

In any case, as the Council pointed out,[67] the competent authorities should be able to decide case by case, on the basis of clear rules established at the appropriate level, who is responsible for providing the scientific data required for a fuller risk assessment, bearing in mind that a satisfactory balance should be struck 'between the public authorities, scientific bodies and economic operators, taking into account in particular the responsibility held by economic operators by virtue of their activities'.

E. The Rejection of a Purely Hypothetical Approach; Risk and Hazard

However, as the CFI rightly emphasised,[68] it is also clear from the case-law that a preventive measure cannot properly be based on a purely hypothetical approach to the risk, founded on mere conjecture that has not been scientifically verified.

Rather, as the CFI has held,[69] it follows from the Community Courts' interpretation of the precautionary principle, that a preventive measure may be taken only

[62] *Pfizer* (n 1) 139–40.
[63] ibid para 386.
[64] ibid para 141.
[65] Then, it is for the user, a private individual, a consumer association, citizens or the public authorities to demonstrate the nature of a danger and the level of risk posed by a product or process (Commission Communication on the Precautionary Principle (n 49) point 6.4).
[66] ibid. See also the references made below to the judgment of the CFI in *Artegodan*.
[67] See Council Resolution of 4 December 2000 (n 10).
[68] *Pfizer* (n 1) para 143.
[69] ibid para 144.

if the risk (or a 'serious threat'),[70] although the reality and extent thereof have not been fully demonstrated by conclusive scientific evidence, appears nevertheless to be adequately backed up by the scientific data available at the time when the measure is taken.

The use of a purely hypothetical risk as a basis for taking preventive measures is particularly inappropriate in those matters[71] where it is impossible to prove scientifically that there is no current or future risk associated with the use of a given product and therefore a 'zero risk' situation does not exist.

If one inverts the sentence the CFI used in paragraph 146 of *Pfizer*,[72] the conclusion would be that the precautionary principle can apply only in situations where there is a risk, notably to human health, which, although it has not yet been fully demonstrated, is not founded on mere hypothesis that have not been scientifically confirmed.

The latter considerations allowed the CFI to distinguish between 'risk', on the one hand, and 'hazard' or 'danger', on the other.

Whereas 'risk' constitutes a function of the probability that use of a product or a procedure will adversely affect the interest safeguarded by the legal order, 'hazard' or 'danger' is commonly used in a broader sense and describes any product or procedure capable of having an adverse effect on human health.[73]

As was argued by the applicant in *Pfizer* and further acknowledged by the Council, the mere fact that a 'hazard' existed would not have provided sufficient justification for withdrawing authorisation from a product on the basis of the precautionary principle, since any modern pharmaceutical product has some hazards.

F. Risk Assessment and Risk Management

As the Court has held in paragraph 148 of *Pfizer*, it is the purpose of a risk assessment to assess the 'degree of probability' of a certain product or procedure having adverse effects on human health and the seriousness of any such adverse effects.

The question arises, nevertheless, as to whether the precautionary principle, as a tool of risk analysis intended for risk control belongs under 'risk assessment' or under 'risk management'.

In its Communication on the Precautionary Principle, the Commission draws a distinction between recourse to a 'prudential approach' and application of the 'precautionary principle'. The Commission considers the former to be part of risk

[70] See ibid para 341.

[71] Such as the one at issue in *Pfizer* (n 1) (see para 145).

[72] Which, in my view, should not distort the Court's reasoning.

[73] See *Pfizer* (n 1) para 147. Since the purpose of the Court is to decide a concrete case, not surprisingly its reasoning is accompanied by the expressions: 'in such a situation' and 'in this context'. But the definitions given by the Court can easily be broadened, as we have done in the text.

assessment policy, which is determined before any risk assessment takes place, whereas application of the precautionary principle is part of 'risk management', when scientific uncertainty precludes a full assessment of the risk.

The question appears to be largely a taxonomic one and legally irrelevant, since application of the precautionary principle encompasses or, at least, presupposes a task of risk assessment.

Only in the light of such considerations can one understand why the Commission itself recognised that 'measures applying the precautionary principle belong in the general framework of risk analysis, and in particular risk management'.[74]

As regards risk assessment, the CFI analysed its two complementary components: ascertaining what level of risk is deemed unacceptable and conducting a scientific assessment of the risks.[75]

G. Defining the Political Objectives

As regards the first component, the Court observes that it is for the Community institutions to define the 'political objectives' which they intend to pursue and to determine the 'level of protection' which they deem appropriate for society.

As the Court also pointed out,[76] that finding can be justified on grounds of principle relating to the 'political responsibilities' and 'democratic legitimacy' of the Community institutions, either the Council or the Commission.

In the Court's view, it is by reference to the 'level of protection' which they deem appropriate that the competent Community institutions must determine the 'level of risk', which in their judgment is no longer acceptable for society and above which it is necessary, in the interests of protecting human health, to take preventive measures in spite of any existing scientific uncertainty.[77]

In some matters, the Treaty itself gives a clear indication as to the level of protection that must be pursued by Community institutions. This is what happens in the fields of public health, consumer protection and the environment. In all those fields, the Treaty[78] aims at a 'high level of protection'.

[74] As noted by E Fisher (n 18) 17, in the application of the precautionary principle, matters of process overlap with matters of procedure and substance. The principle operates in numerous different ways—as a principle of regulatory and institutional design, in the exercise of discretion with relation to a given issue, and as a principle that guides judicial review. E Fisher, ibid, 18, quotes P Schmitter as describing the principle as a 'generic principle of European governance arrangement'.

[75] See *Pfizer* (n 1) paras 149 ff.

[76] ibid para 201.

[77] Actually, in my view, this is only one possible way of presenting the sequence of decisions to be taken by the competent authorities. Indeed, it seems quite likely that in practice, in a number of cases, the authorities start by defining the acceptable level of risk, which then will serve as the reference to determine the appropriate level of protection.

[78] Articles 152(1), 153(1) and 174(2). The only difference is that, unlike the other two, Article 153 stipulates that consumer protection requirements shall only 'be taken into account'.

This approach is confirmed by the provision in Article 95(3), according to which when exercising their powers for the achievement of the internal market the Community institutions will take as a base a 'high level of protection' of health, safety, environmental protection and consumer protection.

By contrast, the Treaty is far less precise when dealing with other matters, such as social policy (Article 136 EC), education (Article 149(1)) industrial policy (Article 157(1)), economic and social cohesion (Article 158) or science and technology (Article 163(1)).

But, even if it is in the fields of health protection and the environment that the Treaty is particularly precise and stringent in giving the Community legislature the necessary indications as to the level of protection to be achieved, it is clear that the Community legislature enjoys, in any event, a broad discretion.

The function of the precautionary principle is to compel action when the risk assessment shows that the risk from authorising a substance, a process or an activity is likely to exceed the chosen level of acceptable risk.[79]

However, it is not always possible to determine in advance the level of protection appropriate to all situations.[80]

Indeed, how high is high enough remains to be seen according to the circumstances. As the ECJ held in *Peralta*[81] in the matter of environmental protection, Article 174 is confined to defining the general objectives of the Community in that matter. Responsibility for deciding, on proposal from the Commission, whether and what action is to be taken is conferred on the Council by Article 175.

Nevertheless, in exercising such a 'political discretion', it is clear that the Community institutions are bound by a number of legal constraints.

They must, first, act within the powers conferred upon them by the Treaty. For instance, pursuant to Article 152(5), Community action in the field of public health shall fully respect the responsibilities of the Member States for the organisation and delivery of health services and medical care and, in particular, shall not affect national provisions on the donation or medical use of organs and blood.

Second, Community institutions shall observe the rules laid down at the international level, namely by the United Nations, the World Health Organisation and the World Trade Organisation.[82]

[79] Christofouro (n 9) 35. In *Pfizer* (n 1) (see paras 335–38), the CFI ruled that, although there was no immediate risk, the Community institutions could properly adopt a 'cautious approach' and pursue the objective of preserving both the effectiveness of products used in human medicine and, given the ever-increasing difficulty of creating new antibiotics, the greatest possible number of antibiotics capable of being used in human medicine. The Court also ruled that the fact that an antibiotic can only be important in a treatment of a particular category of patients can on no account be a valid reason for not taking all the measures necessary to ensure that it continues to be effective (ibid para 340).

[80] Council Resolution of 4 December 2000 (n 10).

[81] C-379/92 *Peralta* [1994] ECR I-3453 para 57; see also C-284/95 *Safety Hi-Tech* [1998] ECR I-4301 para 43, and C-341/95 *G Bettati v Safety Hi-Tech* [1998] ECR I-4355 para 41.

[82] See C-61/94 *Commission v Germany* [1996] ECR I-3989 para 52, *Safety Hi-Tech* (n 81) para 22, and *G Bettati v Safety Hi-Tech* (n 81) para 20.

Third, as follows from Article 95(3) and Article 174(3), they must take account of every available scientific and technical data.

Fourth, the Community institutions, to comply with their obligation to ensure a high level of human health protection under Article 152(1), do not necessarily need to pursue the highest level of protection that is technically possible.[83] Article 174, in particular, authorises the Member States to maintain or introduce more stringent protective measures.

Finally, the Community institutions must act, already at the stage of defining the required level of protection, within the limits set forth by the general rules and principles of Community law.

As regards the former, we should stress the importance of the rules of the Treaty concerning the fundamental freedoms on which the single internal market is based. As both the Council[84] and the Commission[85] emphasised, the precautionary principle must not be used in order to introduce disguised trade restrictions or unjustifiable barriers to trade, in breach of Article 28 EC.

As to the latter, mention should be made, at this stage, to the 'principle of proportionality' and the 'principle of subsidiarity'. The first one will be addressed at greater length later in this chapter. As regards subsidiarity, the essential feature of Community action in the abovementioned fields is that it is intended to 'complement national policies' (Article 152(1), second subparagraph—public health) and to 'support, supplement and monitor the policy pursued by the Member States' (Article 153(3)(b)—consumer protection) and that it has to take into account 'the diversity of situations in the various regions of the Community' (Article 174(3)—environment).

In any case, it should also be borne in mind, as stressed in *Pfizer*,[86] that the level of risk deemed unacceptable will depend on the assessment made by the competent authority of the particular circumstances of each individual case. In that regard, the authority may take account, *inter alia*, of the severity of the impact on human health were the risk to occur, including the extent of possible adverse effects, the persistency or reversibility of those effects and the possibility of delayed effects as well as of the more or less concrete perception of the risk based on available scientific knowledge.

H. The Scientific Assessment of the Risks

As regards this second component of risk assessment, in matters such as the use of additives in feedingstuffs, the Community institutions are responsible for

[83] See *Safety Hi-Tech* (n 81) para 49, and *Pfizer* (n 1) para 152.

[84] Council Resolution of 4 December 2000 (n 10).

[85] Commission Communication on the Precautionary Principle (n 49) point 4.

[86] *Pfizer* (n 1) para 153.

carrying out complex technical and scientific assessment,[87] before any preventive measures are taken.

Following common definitions at both international and Community level, the CFI[88] defines scientific risk assessment as a scientific process consisting of the identification and characterisation of a hazard, the assessment of exposure to the hazard and the characterisation of the risk.

Scientific advice is crucial at all stages of the drawing up of new legislation and for the execution and management of existing legislation. Indeed, the duty imposed on the Community institutions by the first subparagraph of Article 129(1) of the Treaty to ensure a high level of human health protection means that they must ensure that their decisions are taken in the light of the best scientific information available and of the most recent results of international research.[89]

In order to fulfil its function, scientific advice must, in the CFI's strong words,[90] 'be based on the principles of excellence, independence and transparency'.

But what if, because of the inadequate nature of the available scientific data, it is impossible to carry out a full risk assessment, which may require long and detailed scientific research?

The answer of the Court[91] is, first, that in such situation the competent authority cannot be impeded from taking preventive measures,[92] when they appear necessary given the level of risk, which the authority deemed unacceptable for society.

Second, the CFI also observed[93] that in such situation the competent authority must weigh up its obligations and decide either to wait until the results of more detailed scientific research become available or to act on the basis of the scientific information available. The decision will be mostly influenced by the level of risk deemed unacceptable, account being taken of the particular circumstances of each case.

The decision about whether matters have gone beyond the acceptable level of risk must be based on as thorough a scientific risk assessment as possible. It is on that same basis that the competent authority must also decide, as part of its 'risk management' strategy, whether preventive measures are called for and which measures appear to be necessary and appropriate to prevent the risk from materialising.

In order to take its decisions in full knowledge of the facts, the competent public authority must be given sufficiently reliable and convincing information that enables it to understand the ramifications of the scientific questions that have

[87] See 14/78 *Denkavit v Commission* [1978] ECR 2497 para 20.

[88] *Pfizer* (n 1) para 156.

[89] See ibid para 158. See also Commission Communication on Consumer Health and Food Safety, (n 14).

[90] *Pfizer* (n 1) para 159.

[91] ibid para 160.

[92] At very short notice if necessary, the Court said.

[93] *Pfizer* (n 1) para 161.

been raised. This is the fundamental role of independent scientific experts, in particular that of the scientific committees set up at the national or the Community level to assist the national competent authorities or the Community institutions, as the case may be.[94]

As the CFI held,[95] only such way of proceeding can ensure that no arbitrary measures are taken.

When, as was the case in *Pfizer*, the competent Community institution must take action following a safeguard measure adopted by a Member State, as a result of new information or of a reassessment of existing information, based on detailed grounds for establishing that the use of a given product constitutes a danger to animal or human health or the environment, the necessary scientific assessment must be carried out both at the national level and the Community level.[96]

In particular, the Commission must examine whether the national measure is well founded, ie whether the Member State relied on detailed scientific grounds.

The Court also held that, once it decides to initiate the procedure laid down in the Community legislation for the adoption of measures at the Community level, it is for the Commission to carry out at Community level its own risk assessment in respect of the product concerned.[97] Such risk assessment is independent of that carried out by the national authorities; its lawfulness, which is subject to judicial review by the Community Courts, does not depend on the lawfulness of the safeguard measure taken by the national authorities, based on the national scientific assessment.

In any case, an assessment solely based on the situation in a single Member State is clearly not sufficient: a risk assessment at the Community level is required in order to justify the Community intervention.[98]

It is not clear whether the ECJ actually submitted the BSE Decision to this test. Had it been applied, the judgment rendered by the Court could have been somewhat different.[99]

[94] As stated in the Council Resolution of 4 December 2000 (n 10), 'in order to carry out the risk assessment, public authorities must have suitable research facilities and rely in particular on scientific committees and on relevant national and international scientific work'.

[95] *Pfizer* (n 1) paras 162 and 163.

[96] See ibid paras 177–84. In certain circumstances, divergent assessments of the risks to public health can legitimately be made by the Commission and by a Member State, without necessarily being based on new or scientific evidence. See C-3/00 *Denmark v Commission* [2003] ECR I-2643, 2690 para 63 (Opinion Tizzano), as regards application of Article 95(4).

[97] See also *Pfizer* (n 1) para 235.

[98] ibid para 329.

[99] But, as the Council held, 'owing to insufficient data and the nature or urgency of the risk, it may not always be possible to complete every stage systematically' (see Council Resolution of 4 December 2000 (n 10)).

I. The Role of Scientific Committees

As the Court stated in *Angelopharm*,[100] where it is the question of assessing whether or not a substance is injurious to human health, the drafting and adaptation of Community rules are founded on scientific and technical assessments which must themselves be based on the results of the latest international research which are frequently complex. The Commission is not in a position to carry out assessments of this kind itself.

The scientific committees then have the task of assisting the Community institutions on scientific and technical issues in order to enable them to determine, in full knowledge of the facts, which measures are necessary.[101]

The role of such committees was particularly detailed by the CFI in its *Pfizer* judgment insofar as the SCAN—Scientific Committee for Animal Nutrition is concerned.

SCAN carries out risk assessments and provides scientific advice at the request of the Commission. Like other similar committees set up within the framework of Community legislation, SCAN is, in view of the relevant provisions, an advisory body attached to the Commission.

That is why the Commission, when it requests an opinion from the committee, is not bound to accept the conclusions reached in that opinion.[102]

As the CFI also pointed out,[103] the role played by a committee of experts, such as SCAN, in a procedure designed to culminate in a decision or a legislative measure, is restricted to providing a reasoned analysis of the relevant facts of the case in the light of current knowledge about the subject, in order to enable the institution to take an informed decision.

For that to be possible, the competent Community institution must, first, prepare for the committee the factual questions that need to be answered before a decision is taken.

Then, the competent Community institution must assess the probative value of the opinion delivered by the committee. In that regard, it must ensure that the reasoning in the opinion is full, consistent and relevant.[104]

In light of a discrepant interpretation of the requirements resulting from the precautionary principle for a concrete case, the competent Community institutions can therefore depart from the committee's opinion and draw different conclusions from the available scientific data without distorting the committee's opinion.[105]

[100] See *Angelopharm* (n 20) paras 31–32.
[101] ibid para 34.
[102] *Pfizer* (n 1) para 196.
[103] ibid para 197.
[104] ibid para 198.
[105] ibid paras 204, 231.

But, as the Court pointed out:

> To the extent to which the Community institution opts to disregard the opinion, it must provide specific reasons for its findings by comparison with those made in the opinion. The statement of reasons by which it explains why it is disregarding the latter must be of a scientific level at least commensurate with that of the opinion.[106]

It must also be founded on the same purpose (eg the protection of human health) as the measure to be taken.[107]

Moreover, any time they take into consideration scientific material whose probative value was disregarded by the committee's opinion, the Community institutions are bound to be, as a minimum requirement, aware of its methodological limitations, following which such material is to be regarded only as purely indicative. Only under such conditions can the competent Community institution take into consideration such supplementary evidence without necessarily being obliged to request a formal opinion from the competent scientific committee.[108]

The Community institution may also disregard only part of the opinion. In that case, as the Court admits,[109] it may avail itself of those parts of the scientific reasoning, which it does not dispute, including minority opinions.

Nevertheless, one should be aware of the immanent risk of manipulation present in such possibility. The conduct of the Community institution has to rely strictly on objective grounds and no 'selective choice' of material can be accepted in that context.

No one could certainly think that the Court would uphold conduct of the Community institutions in contravention with such requirements. Indeed, the CFI only accepted that the Community institutions relied on certain aspects of the scientific analysis in the SCAN opinion because, at the same time, it took account, as supplementary material, of a number of international, Community and national bodies' reports and recommendations, which were drawn up on the basis of the best scientific data available at the time.[110]

As already pointed out, the Community institutions are entrusted with political responsibilities and democratic legitimacy, whereas the experts, members of a scientific committee such as SCAN, although they have scientific legitimacy, have neither democratic legitimacy nor political responsibilities. Subject to the legal constraints imposed on them and the competent judicial control, the Community institutions' views may thus prevail over experts' opinions since scientific legitimacy is not a sufficient basis for the exercise of public authority.[111]

[106] ibid para 199. In a recent judgment, the ECJ annulled a Commission decision because it failed duly to take into account the opinion of the competent scientific committee (see C-3/00, n 96 above, para 114).

[107] *Pfizer* (n 1) para 203.

[108] ibid para 298.

[109] ibid paras 199, 209.

[110] ibid paras 303–09.

[111] ibid para 201.

Nevertheless, it must be said that, if the Commission carries out its risk assessment on the basis, *inter alia*, of the committee's opinion, and the Council endorses the position adopted by the Commission, without asking for an alternative risk assessment, the Council is bound by the risk assessment carried out by the Commission.[112]

The question of whether the Commission is bound by an obligation to consult the competent scientific committee depends on the relevant provisions of Community law. As the Commission stated in its Communication on Consumer Health and Food Safety, consultation is not compulsory in all cases.[113]

In upholding such finding, the CFI might appear to retreat from a line of case-law followed in *Angelopharm*, *Pharos* and *Bergaderm*.[114]

Such is not the case. As the Court pointed out in *Pfizer*,[115] those precedents are not applicable to all cases, depending on the relevant provisions.

It is however particularly important to point out that, as the CFI also held in paragraphs 267 to 270 of the *Pfizer* judgment, since expert scientific advice is of the utmost importance in risk assessment to ensure that the regulatory measures adopted by the Community institutions have a proper scientific basis, it is only in exceptional circumstances and where there are adequate guarantees of scientific objectivity that the Community institutions may, when they are required to assess particularly complex facts of a technical or scientific nature, adopt preventive measures without obtaining an opinion from the scientific committee set up for that purpose at Community level.

J. The 'Political Committees'

The relevant legislation provides in some cases for the consultation of a committee of representatives from Member States. That is the case of the Standing Committee set up by Directive 70/524, which must be consulted by the Commission both at the stage of risk assessment and at the stage of risk management.

However, as the CFI pointed out,[116] the responsibilities conferred on such type of committee such as the Standing Committee must not be confused with those conferred on a Scientific Committee like SCAN, since they have a fundamentally different aim.

Indeed, as is apparent from the preamble to Decision 70/372, the Standing Committee was set up in order to ensure close cooperation between Member States and the Commission in the relevant sphere.

[112] ibid para 195.
[113] See ibid paras 257–65.
[114] *Angelopharm* (n 20), *Pharos* (nn 22 and 23) and *Bergaderm* (nn 41 and 42).
[115] See *Pfizer* (n 1) paras 262–63.
[116] ibid para 280.

The Committee, set up under Article 145 of the EC Treaty (now Article 202 EC) and made up of representatives from Member States and the Commission, is part of a mechanism for review by the representatives from Member States of the Commission's exercise of the powers delegated to it by the Council.

It is worth noting that the votes of the representatives from the Member States within the Standing Committee are weighted as provided for in Article 205(2) EC.

In such context, a committee of the same type as the Standing Committee must be regarded as a political body representative of the Member States and not as an independent scientific body.[117]

Against that background, even when the Standing Committee proceeds to analyse scientific material, the results of such analysis cannot be regarded as scientific advice based on the principles of excellence, transparency and independence, even though the members of the committee are assisted by experts appointed by the Member States who are capable of understanding and explaining the full significance of that scientific evidence.[118]

Furthermore, the results of the Standing Committee's analysis of scientific material are not published in a way that reveals a structured scientific analysis meeting the requirement that scientific advice should be transparent.[119]

Since the opinion of the Standing Committee cannot be regarded as a scientific opinion,[120] its work does not discharge the Community institutions from their duty to carry out a scientific risk assessment.[121]

K. The Importance of the Respect of Procedural Requirements

As stated in *Pfizer*,[122] whenever a specific procedure is provided for by the legislation or by internal regulations with the aim of obtaining an opinion from a scientific committee, that procedure is to be followed in each concrete case.

In the Court's view,[123] those formal requirements amount to significant procedural guarantees, which have to be respected in any circumstance.[124]

In particular, the obligation to state reasons is essential in order to enable the Community institutions to determine their position *vis-à-vis* the relevant problem in full knowledge of the facts.[125]

117 ibid para 283.
118 ibid para 285.
119 ibid para 287.
120 A comprehensive summary of the respective roles of the Standing Committee and of SCAN, as opposed to that of the Community institutions, can be found in paragraph 288 of *Pfizer*.
121 *Pfizer* (n 1) para 289.
122 ibid para 274.
123 ibid para 274.
124 This is confirmed by the judgment of the CFI in *Artegodan* (para 197), which is examined later in this chapter.
125 *Pfizer* (n 1) para 275.

In case of refusal of the scientific committee to deliver an opinion despite being consulted by the Commission, the latter can in general require the adoption of an opinion within a specified period, making use, when applicable, of the accelerated procedure provided for in the rules of procedure for urgent cases.[126, 127]

Furthermore, the Community institutions cannot properly rely on organisational difficulties within departments and committees set up by them to explain their failure to comply with a duty incumbent upon them, namely to carry out as thorough a scientific assessment of the risks as possible and, in that connection, to obtain if necessary an opinion from the relevant scientific committees before adopting preventive measures.[128]

The principle that the procedure must be *inter partes*, which applies in all administrative procedures initiated against a person which are liable to culminate in a measure adversely affecting that person is another fundamental principle of Community law,[129] but it does not apply in the context of the legislative process.[130]

However, by way of an exception and subject to express provisions, certain rights of the defence must be guaranteed during the adoption of a legislative act.[131]

According to settled case-law of the Community courts, where the Community institutions enjoy a broad discretion to adopt measures (namely preventive measures) that may seriously harm legally protected positions, the guarantees conferred by the Community legal order in administrative proceedings are of even more fundamental importance.[132]

As the ECJ held in *Technische Universität München*,[133] those guarantees include, in particular, the duty of the competent institution to examine carefully and impartially all the relevant aspects of the individual case.

Having that in mind, the CFI declared that a scientific risk assessment carried out as thoroughly as possible on the basis of scientific advice founded on the principles of excellence, transparency and independence is an important procedural guarantee whose purpose is to ensure the scientific objectivity of the measures adopted and preclude any arbitrary measures.[134]

In that context, the Council was also particularly clear in expressing the view that the risk assessment must 'ensure that all views are heard'. In the Council's view, to comply with the necessary requisites, 'an assessment of risk must also

[126] Eg Article 2(5) of Decision 97/579. See *Pfizer* (n 1) para 276.

[127] Conversely, the CFI considered, in T-120/96 *Lilly Industries* [1998] II-2571 paras 82–83, that the Commission was under an obligation to draw up a draft regulation including a given substance in a list of approved substances to be placed on the market where the competent scientific committee, having all the necessary information at its disposal, has given a favourable opinion.

[128] *Pfizer* (n 1) para 276.

[129] T-450/93 *Lisrestal and Others v Commission* [1994] ECR II-1177 para 42.

[130] T-521/93 *Atlanta and Others v European Community* [1996] ECR II-1707 para 70. See also *Bergaderm* (n 41) para 58.

[131] *Bergaderm* (n 41) para 59.

[132] See *Pfizer* (n 1) paras 170–71.

[133] C-269/90 *Technische Universität München* [1991] ECR I-5469 para 14.

[134] See *Pfizer* (n 1) para 172.

report any minority opinions. It must be possible to express such opinions and bring them to the knowledge of the parties involved, in particular if they draw attention to scientific uncertainty'.[135]

As a guarantee of objectivity and independence, the Council also considered[136] that 'those responsible for scientific assessment of risk must be functionally separate from those responsible for risk management, albeit with ongoing exchange between them'.

Finally, the existence of adequate consultation procedures should also be an indispensable concern of the public authorities. As the Council stated,[137] 'civil society must be involved and special attention must be paid to consulting all interested parties as early as possible'.

L. The Scope of Judicial Review

It is apparent from what has been held so far that the Community institutions enjoy a broad discretion in determining the level of protection that must be pursued in each case and the level of risk that they deem unacceptable for society. The same applies to the choice of the appropriate measures to be taken.

But, at the same time, it is also true that the precautionary principle provides the means to actually or potentially affected persons to control, if necessary by means of action before the courts, the way Community institutions take their normative decisions in evaluating scientific uncertainty, risks and costs and benefits of any protective action.

Nevertheless, as is clear from well-established case-law, when the Community institutions enjoy a broad discretion regarding the definition of the objectives to be pursued or the choice of the appropriate means of action, review by the Community judicature must be confined to examining whether the exercise of such discretion is vitiated by manifest error or a misuse of powers or whether the Community institutions clearly exceeded the bounds of their discretion.[138]

In circumstances such as those, the CFI took in *Pfizer*[139] a particularly strict approach in regards to its powers of review. Indeed, it follows from the Court's findings that, when the Community institutions are required to undertake a scientific risk assessment and to evaluate highly complex scientific and technical facts, judicial review must be limited. The Court is particularly assertive in holding that the Community judicature is not entitled to substitute its assessment of

[135] Council Resolution of 4 December 2000 (n 10).
[136] ibid.
[137] ibid.
[138] See *Pfizer* (n 1) para 166, and judgments cited in that paragraph.
[139] See ibid 169 and 323.

the facts for that of the Community institutions, on which the Treaty confers sole responsibility for that duty.[140]

It must also be borne in mind that the assessment made by the Community institutions can be challenged only if it appears incorrect in the light of the elements of fact and law that were available to them at the time when the contested measure was adopted.[141]

The Court may also control respect of the procedural requirements during the process leading to the adoption of a decision based upon the precautionary principle. This applies, as emphasised by the CFI in its recent judgment in *Artegodan*,[142] to review of the formal legality of any scientific committee's opinion.

As the Court stated,[143] it is only the proper functioning of the committee, the internal consistency of the opinion and the statement of reasons contained therein which are subject to judicial review.

As regards the latter aspect, the Court is empowered only to examine whether the opinion contains a statement of reasons from which it is possible to ascertain the considerations on which the opinion is based, and whether it establishes a comprehensible link between the medical and/or scientific findings and its conclusions. In that respect, in its opinion the scientific committee is obliged to refer to the main reports and scientific expert opinions on which it relies and to explain, in the event of a significant discrepancy, the reasons why it has departed from the conclusions of the reports or expert opinions supplied by the undertakings concerned. That obligation is particularly strict in cases of scientific uncertainty.

M. The Principle of Proportionality

As mentioned above, the principle of proportionality limits the discretion of the competent authorities when deciding what level of protection they deem necessary to pursue. Indeed, such level of protection should be proportionate to the perceived risk as defined under risk assessment.[144]

But it is at the level of risk management, in particular when they have to decide which concrete measures should be taken, that the institutions are typically bound to respect such principle.

[140] See also C-405/92 *Mondiet* [1993] ECR I-6133 para 32, *United Kingdom v Commission* (n 32) para 97, and C-120/97 *Upjohn* [1999] ECR I-223 para 34.

[141] *Pfizer* (n 1) para 324.

[142] Joined Cases T-74/00, T-76/00, T-83/00, T-84/00, T-85/00, T-132/00, T-137/00 and T-141/00 *Artegodan et al v Commission* [2002] ECR II-4945 (see para 199). This judgment is examined below.

[143] ibid para 200. See also T-27/98 *Nardone v Commission* [1999] ECR-SC I-A-267; ECR-SC II-1293 paras 30, 88.

[144] For instance, measures based on the precautionary principle should not aim at zero risk, something that rarely exists (Commission Communication on the Precautionary Principle (n 49) point 6.3).

As has been consistently held by the Community Courts, the principle of proportionality, which is one of the general principles of Community law, requires that measures adopted by Community institutions should not exceed the limits of what is appropriate and necessary in order to attain the legitimate objectives pursued by the relevant legislation, and where there is a choice between several appropriate measures, recourse must be had to the least onerous, and the disadvantages caused must not be disproportionate to the aims pursued.[145]

The principle of proportionality constitutes therefore an important limit to the discretionary power of the Community institutions when applying the precautionary principle.

In cases involving risk management, a 'cost/benefit analysis', in which the costs and benefits to society expected from the action envisaged are balanced against the costs and benefits that would apply if no action were taken, is a particular expression of the principle of proportionality.[146] In this context, the Council further stressed[147] that

> examination of the benefits and costs of action and inaction [...] must take account of social and environmental costs and of the public acceptability of the different options possible,[148] and include, where feasible, an economic analysis, it being understood that requirements linked to the protection of public health, including the effects of the environment on public health, must be given priority.

Once the competent authority has decided to take action on grounds of the precautionary principle, the principle of proportionality is called upon to ascertain the legality of the measures intended to pursue the defined objectives.

In such a context, a breach of the principle of proportionality will occur if the measure in question is manifestly inappropriate, regard being had to the legitimate objective which the competent institution is seeking to pursue[149] or in case it is shown that other, less onerous, measures exist and would have allowed the objective pursued by such measure.[150]

That is why, 'in selecting the risk management measures to be taken, consideration should be given to the whole range of measures enabling the desired level of protection to be achieved'.[151]

In some cases, a total ban may not be a proportional response to a potential risk; in other cases, it may be the sole possible response. Risk reduction measures should include less restrictive alternatives which make it possible to achieve

[145] See *Pfizer* (n 1) para 411; see also C-331/88 *Fedesa et al* [1990] ECR I-4023 para 13, and C-192/01 *Commission v Denmark* [2003] not yet reported, para 45.

[146] *Pfizer* (n 1) paras 408, 410.

[147] Council Resolution of 4 December 2000 (n 10).

[148] On the importance of 'legal culture' in shaping the precautionary principle and of the use of non-legislative forms of regulation, see E Fisher (n 13) 18–20. See also below.

[149] *Pfizer* (n 1) para 412; *Fedesa et al* (n 145) para 14.

[150] See *Pfizer* (n 1) para 451.

[151] Council Resolution of 4 December 2000 (n 10).

an equivalent level of protection, such as appropriate treatment, reduction of exposure, tightening of controls, adoption of provisional limits, etc.[152]

In general, it should be stressed that recourse to the precautionary principle does not necessarily mean adopting final instruments designed to produce legally binding effects. There is a whole range of actions available to decision makers that can be appropriate in attaining the protective goal, such as to fund a research programme, to issue recommendations for populations at risk or to inform the public about the possible adverse effects of a product or a procedure.[153]

Application of the principle of proportionality is of paramount importance whenever the respect of any of the fundamental freedoms enshrined in the Treaty is at stake. This is the case, in particular, of the free movement of goods and services[154] whose application can only be restricted, according to a well-established case-law of the ECJ, for the reasons set out, in particular, in Articles 30 and 46 EC[155] or for overriding requirements of general interest, provided that the measures in question are reasonable and do not constitute a means of arbitrary discrimination or a disguised restriction on trade between Member States.[156]

In either case, the said measure must be appropriate for securing the attainment of that objective and not go beyond what is necessary in order to attain it.[157]

As follows from the ECJ case-law,[158] these strict conditions for restricting the fundamental freedoms impend not only upon the Member States as regards measures they adopt in areas not subject to full harmonisation in EC law,[159] but also upon the Community institutions when acting within the limits of their competences.

There is no indication that this jurisprudence should not apply to the use of the precautionary principle.

Apart of the principle of proportionality, adequate consideration should also be given to the principles of 'equality' and 'non-discrimination'. As stated by

[152] Commission Communication on the Precautionary Principle (n 49) point 6.3.1.

[153] ibid point 5.2.2.

[154] See, on this point, LG Vaqué, L Ehring, C Jacquet (n 10) 103; N Sadeleer (n 47) 122; A Alemanno (n 10) 937.

[155] Among which the protection of public health.

[156] 8/74 *Procureur du roi v Dassonville* [1974] ECR 187; 120/78 *Rewe Zentral v Bundesmonopol verwaltung für Branntwein ('Cassis de Dijon')* [1979] ECR 249. According to the Council (Resolution of 4 December 2000 (n 10)), protective measures 'must not be applied in a way resulting in arbitrary or unwarranted discrimination; where there are a number of possible means of attaining the same level of health or environmental protection, the least trade-restrictive measures should be opted for'. See *Commission v Denmark* (n 145) paras 45–48, 53.

[157] See C-390/99 *Canal Satélite Digital* [2002] ECR I-607 para 33; Joined Cases C-388/00 and C-429/00 *Radiosistemi* [2002] ECR I-5845 paras 40–42; and C-14/02 *Atral* [2003] not yet published, paras 64 and 67.

[158] See, with regard to free movement of goods, eg 80-81/77 *Ramel v Receveur des Douanes* [1978] ECR 927; 179/78 *Rivoira* [1979] ECR 1147; 218/82 *Commission v Council* (rum quotas) [1983] ECR 4063.

[159] When a given area is fully harmonised, a Member State cannot avail itself of the provision in Article 30 to make exception to Article 28 (C-5/94 *Hedley Lomas* [1996] ECR I-2553 para 18; C-241/2001 *National Farmers' Union* [2002] ECR I-9079 para 48).

the Council, the measures adopted by the Community institutions 'should be consistent with measures already adopted in similar circumstances or following similar approaches, having due regard to the latest scientific developments and developments in the level of protection sought'.[160] The Community institutions should also give appropriate consideration to the protection of 'legitimate expectations',[161] as well as to the principle of 'sound administration' and the 'duty of care'.[162]

Although also limiting the discretion of the competent authorities when deciding what is the appropriate level of protection and whether to intervene (risk assessment), these principles are apparently more relevant at the level of risk management.

III. IS THERE LIFE AFTER *PFIZER*?

Only two months after the *Pfizer* ruling, the CFI had the opportunity to again disclose its views about certain aspects of the precautionary principle, in the judgment rendered in the *Artegodan* cases.[163] The judgment deserves commentary as regards some of its grounds.

Firstly, the Court interpreted the principle that protection of public health must take precedence over economic considerations[164] as requiring, in the context of the grant and management of marketing authorisations of medicinal products, the taking into account exclusively of considerations relating to the protection of public health.[165]

Even limited to the precise context of that case, the statement of the CFI is not exempt of criticism were it to be interpreted as meaning that a proportionality test is no longer necessary. This could, of course, not be the Court's intention but the form used to express its ruling seems to go too far.

Indeed, the 'primary purpose' of any rules concerning the production and distribution of medicinal products (to safeguard public health) must not be confounded with the 'sole' purpose. And the fact that, in the interest of public health and of the consumer of medicinal products, decisions on the authorisation to place medicinal products on the market must be exclusively based on the criteria

[160] Council Resolution of 4 December 2000 (n 10).

[161] Application of this principle in the context of health protection was discussed in T-210/2000 *Établissements Biret v Council* [2002] ECR II-47 paras 57–63.

[162] See, in this respect, C-248/199P *Monsanto* [2002] I-1 paras 92–93.

[163] *Artegodan* (n 142). See Sebastián Romero Melchor, 'La sentencia 'Artegodan' del Tribunal de Primera Instancia: el principio de precaución de nuevo en cuestión' (2003) *Gaceta Jurídica de la Unión Europea y de la Competencia* 42.

[164] See, in particular, Order in *United Kingdom v Commission* (n 35) para 93, and judgments in C-183/95 *Affish* [1997] ECR I-4315 para 43, and *Artegodan* (n 142) para 173.

[165] See *Artegodan* (n 142) para 174.

of quality, safety and efficacy[166] does not mean that only requirements related to the protection of public health must be taken into consideration.

Nevertheless, the Court confirmed, secondly, that a re-evaluation of the benefit/risk balance of a medicinal product must be carried out where new data give rise to doubts as to its efficacy or safety.[167] Moreover, in the Court's view, the requirement to carry out an evaluation of the benefit/risk balance of a medicinal product does not apply exclusively to the grant of a marketing authorisation, but applies in particular to the procedure for withdrawal of such an authorisation. Furthermore, after the marketing authorisation has been issued any new data or information must be submitted to the competent authorities in order to monitor the benefit/risk assessment.

The question is how limited might this benefit/risk evaluation be (expression of the principle of proportionality) by the (in the Court's opinion) exclusive consideration of public health requirements.

Thirdly, the CFI confirmed that, although the precautionary principle is mentioned in the Treaty only in connection with environmental policy, it is broader in scope. According to the Court, the principle is to be applied in order to ensure a high level of protection of health, consumer safety and the environment in all the Community's spheres of activity.[168] In view of that, the Court had no doubts in ruling that the precautionary principle can be regarded as an autonomous principle stemming from the Treaty provisions.

The Court then defined[169] the precautionary principle as a general principle of Community law requiring the competent authorities to take appropriate measures to prevent specific potential risks to public health, safety and the environment.

Such a statement seems to go beyond what had been held by the courts in *National Farmers' Union* and in *Pfizer*.[170]

On the one hand, in the former judgment, the ECJ held that where there is uncertainty as to the existence or extent of risks to human health, the institutions *may* take protective measures.[171]

On the other hand, it follows from *Pfizer*[172] that, although the competent authority *is not precluded* from taking preventive measures when it may prove impossible to carry out a full risk assessment, it must *weigh up its obligations* and decide either to wait until the results of more detailed scientific research become

166 See third recital in the preamble to Council Directive 93/39/EEC of 14 June 1993 [1993] OJ L214/22, amending, among others, Directive 65/65/EEC of 26 January 1965, on the approximation of provisions laid down by law, regulation or administrative action relating to medicinal products (OJ, English Special Edition 1965–1966, 20).

167 See *Artegodan* (n 142) para 178.

168 ibid para 183. Articles 152(1) and 153(1) EC refer more precisely to ensuring or taking into account a high level of protection 'in the definition and implementation of all Community policies and activities', and not in all 'spheres of activity'.

169 See *Artegodan* (n 142) para 184.

170 *National Farmers' Union* (n 31) and *Pfizer* (n 1).

171 See *National Farmers' Union* (n 31) para 63.

172 *Pfizer* (n 1) paras 160–62.

available or to act on the basis of the scientific information available. Moreover, the outcome of that balancing exercise will depend on the level of risk, which the authority deems unacceptable for society.[173]

A general obligation for the Community institutions to act in order 'to prevent specific potential risks', without reference to the conditions within which such obligation is to be fulfilled, had never been recognised before *Artegodan* as stemming from the precautionary principle.[174, 175]

It is true that such a general statement is mitigated by the reference further made, in paragraph 186 of the judgment, to 'the level of protection chosen by the competent authority'.

But one such reference is not sufficient to dissipate the impression that *Artegodan* expresses a more 'maximalistic' and less balanced approach than *Pfizer*.

It should nonetheless be said, in this respect, that the two judgments were delivered by two different chambers of the CFI and that the reason why *Pfizer*[176] is not even cited in *Artegodan*[177] is probably because *Artegodan* was already deliberated when *Pfizer* was made public.[178]

Under these conditions, I believe that no general change of approach can be inferred from the *Artegodan* judgment.[179]

Anyway, the judgment contains a number of other developments that deserve consideration. This is the case of the rules of evidence and the burden of proof.

At the outset, the CFI upholds the general approach taken by the Community institutions when an authorisation system is applied. In that system, it is for the undertaking seeking marketing authorisation of a product to prove, first, the efficacy of the medicinal product and, second, its safety.[180]

Subsequently, in case of an application for renewal of an authorisation, the validity of which is limited, the assessment of the product is to be carried out on the basis of the data and other information relevant to the monitoring of that type of product.[181]

Furthermore, it is only '[i]n exceptional circumstances, and following consultation with the applicant' that an authorisation may be made subject to certain

[173] ibid para 161.

[174] See also S Romero Melchor (n 163) 49.

[175] The fact that a general obligation is not imposed by the precautionary principle itself does not preclude the possibility that specific Community law provisions lay down such an obligation in concrete circumstances. But those are two different issues, which the CFI does not seem to have clearly distinguished. See, in this respect, *Giancarlo Fornasar* (n 40) paras 37–42, as regards obligations conferred upon Member States by Council Directive 91/689/EEC of 12 December 1991, on hazardous waste [1991] OJ L356/14.

[176] *Pfizer* (n 1). Judgment of 11 September 2002.

[177] *Artegodan* (n 142). Judgment of 26 November 2002.

[178] Such possibility calls into question the coordination between different chambers of the CFI.

[179] The CFI's judgment in *Artegodan* (n 142) was appealed by the Commission. The ECJ upheld the CFI's decision but the appeal did not discuss the conditions of application of the precautionary principle. See C-39/03 P *Commission v Artegodan and Others* [2003] ECR I-7885. See also C-39/03 P-R *Commission v Artegodan and Others* [2003] ECR I-4485.

[180] *Artegodan* (n 142) para 188.

[181] ibid para 189.

specific obligations, including, in particular, the carrying out of further studies following the granting of authorisation. Those exceptional decisions may be adopted only for objective and verifiable reasons, eg where in the present state of scientific knowledge the applicant cannot provide comprehensive information on the efficacy and safety of the product in question under normal conditions of use.[182]

In that system,[183] the holder of the marketing authorisation of a product is not required to provide evidence of the efficacy and/or safety of that product during the period of that authorisation's validity.[184] The onus is indisputably on the competent authority to provide[185] solid and convincing evidence, based on new, objective, scientific and/or medical data or information,[186] which, while not resolving the scientific uncertainty, may reasonably raise doubts as to the safety and/or efficacy of the product,[187] then justifying the suspension or withdrawal of a marketing authorisation.

Notwithstanding, as the Court pointed out,[188] the benefit/risk balance is to be assessed continuously on the basis of the progress of scientific knowledge leading to any new information or data submitted to the competent authorities.

For its part, the ECJ was called upon, at least in two or three different issues after *Pfizer*, to deal with questions related to the conditions of application of the precautionary principle.

In the first case,[189] the Court was asked, in substance, to rule whether Community law precludes application of provisions of national law that lay down zero tolerance for the presence of a certain kind of micro-organism[190] in fish products that are not chemically preserved.

[182] ibid para 190.

[183] And save in the special situation where authorisation is made subject to certain specific obligations.

[184] The system of prior authorisation allows the presumption that, during that period, in the absence of any solid evidence to the contrary, the product in question has a favourable benefit/risk balance, subject always to the possibility of suspending the authorisation in cases of emergency (n 142 para 195).

[185] Leaving aside the exceptional situation in which the competent authority makes a detailed acknowledgement that it had incorrectly assessed a product when taking the decision to grant or, as the case may be, maintain or renew the authorisation (ibid, para 194).

[186] Mere changes in a scientific criterion or, in more concrete terms, in good clinical practices—that is to say, therapeutic practices considered to be the most appropriate in the light of current scientific knowledge—even if based on a 'consensus' in the medical community, cannot on their own justify the withdrawal of a marketing authorisation of a medicinal product where those changes are not based on new scientific data or information (ibid, para 211). Where there is no such evidence, the need not to reduce the range of medicinal products available for the treatment of a particular disorder argues in favour of keeping the medicinal product on the market so that, in every case, the most appropriate medicinal product may be prescribed (ibid, para 195).

[187] As the CFI also pointed out (ibid, paras 191, 192, 194), acceptance that in cases of scientific uncertainty reasonable doubts as to the efficacy or safety of a product are capable of justifying a precautionary measure cannot be treated as equivalent to a reversal of the burden of proof.

[188] ibid, para 193.

[189] C-121/00 *Walter Hahn* [2002] ECR I-9193.

[190] More precisely *Listeria monocytogenes*.

In its response, the Court didn't mention the precautionary principle. After recalling that the national provisions in question constituted measures having equivalent effect to a quantitative restriction within the meaning of Article 28 EC,[191] the Court considered that, in the current state of scientific uncertainty in regards to the precise concentration of *Listeria monocytogenes*, it was for the Member States, in the absence of harmonisation, to decide what degree of protection of the health and life of humans they wished to assure, while taking account of the requirements for the free movement of goods.[192]

Against that background, the Court ruled that a national legislation laying down zero tolerance for *Listeria monocytogenes* was compatible with Community law.

The Court of Justice was later explicitly invited by the French Republic to apply the precautionary principle in *France v Commission*,[193] relating to the BSE problem.

However, having annulled the contested decision[194] for infringing Decision 2001/376/EC,[195] the Court ruled that there was no need to consider the plea alleging infringement of the precautionary principle as a result of poor risk management.[196]

It would of course be interesting to have a fresh reassessment by the Court of Justice of some of the questions dealt with in such a profound and extensive manner by the CFI.

We shall however have to wait for a new instance to contemplate such a fresh judicial application of the principles laid down by the CFI.

Such opportunity could occur, for instance, in relation to the future EU chemicals policy announced by the Commission in its White Paper of February 2001.[197]

[191] *Walter Hahn*, n 189 para 36.

[192] ibid, para 45.

[193] Case C-393/01 *France v Commission* [2003] ECR I-5405.

[194] Commission Decision 2001/577/EC of 25 July 2001 setting the date on which dispatch from Portugal of bovine products under the Date-Based Export Scheme may commence by virtue of Article 22(2) of Decision 2001/376/EC [2001] OJ L203/27.

[195] Commission Decision 2001/376/EC of 18 April 2001 concerning measures made necessary by the occurrence of bovine spongiform encephalopaty in Portugal and implementing a date-based export scheme [2001] OJ L132/17.

[196] The Court was also asked by the French Conseil d'État to rule on the validity of the Commission's decisions on BSE, 'having regard to the precautionary principle laid down in Article 174 EC' (*National Farmers' Union* (n 159)). However, the Court did not answer that question since France did not have standing to invoke the unlawfulness of said decisions before a national court after expiration of the time-limit to challenge their legality without raising an action for annulment before the ECJ. In his Opinion of 2 July 2002, Advocate General Mischo made some general comments on the precautionary principle. He argued namely that the fact that the precautionary principle has been enshrined in the Community legal order must not in any way mark the resurgence of unilateralism. Thus, Member States may not rely on it in order to obstruct at will the application of measures adopted in the context of the Community action. He also noted that the application of other fundamental principles such as proportionality and non-discrimination is inseparable from the precautionary principle.

[197] White Paper of the European Commission on Strategy for the Future Chemicals Policy COM (2001) 88 final, 16 February 2001.

The White Paper calls for a complete system of Registration, Evaluation and Authorisation of Chemicals (REACH), which could, according to industry estimations, render mandatory registration of about 30,000 chemicals and evaluation of about 5,000 of these chemicals.[198] For at least 850 chemicals, government authorisations would be required, and any chemical that is not authorised would not be allowed into the EU market.[199]

The big challenge facing the new chemicals policy, as explained by the White Paper, is how to 'ensure a high level of protection of human health and the environment [...] both for the present generation and the future generations while also ensuring the efficient functioning of the internal market and the competitiveness of the chemical industry'.

The Commission's proposals give rise to some important concerns regarding issues such as the resources needed to implement such a program, the protection of trade secrets or its effects on innovation and international trade, as compared to the objectives of public health and environment protection. There is no doubt that the principle of proportionality will certainly be called upon to scrutinise the legality of the Commission's proposals.

In the meantime, *Pfizer* will thus remain the seminal ruling on the precautionary principle that provides a solid basis for future developments of the case-law in this field.

IV. SUMMARY

The recognition of the precautionary principle in EC law appeared first in the field of environmental protection in Article 130r(2), as amended by the Maastricht Treaty. Its scope was subsequently widened so as to apply to other fields of EC law.

The ECJ has dealt with some issues relating to a precautionary approach since 1994. But it was only in the BSE cases that the approach underlying the precautionary principle was first upheld by both the ECJ and the CFI.

It was nevertheless in *Pfizer* that the CFI effected a remarkable systematisation of all the main constituents of the precautionary principle and of its conditions of application.

According to the Court, where there is scientific uncertainty as to the existence or extent of risks to human health, the Community institutions may, by reason of the precautionary principle, take protective measures, in spite of the fact that, in such a situation, a risk assessment cannot be required to provide the Community

[198] The REACH system applies to the so-called 'substances of very high concern' (SVHC), comprising carcinogens, mutagens and toxic substances for reproduction (CMRs) and persistent organic pollutants (POPs).

[199] On the future EU chemicals policy and the REACH system, see J-P Montfort, 'The EU Chemicals Policy Review from a Legal Perspective: For a Progressive, Coherent and Integrated Approach that Preserves the Internal Market' (2002) 11 (10) *European Environmental Law Review* 270. See also, Steffen Erler, *Chemical Risk Management under REACH: Regulatory Decision-Making* (Shawbury, Shrewsbury, Smithers Rapra, 2009).

institutions with conclusive scientific evidence of the reality of the risk and the seriousness of the potential adverse effects were that risk to become a reality.

A preventive measure cannot however properly be based on a purely hypothetical approach founded on mere conjecture that has not been scientifically verified and may be taken only if the risk, although the reality and extent thereof have not been fully demonstrated by conclusive scientific evidence, appears nevertheless to be adequately backed up by the scientific data available at the time when the measure is taken.

It is by reference to the level of protection, which they deem appropriate that the competent Community institutions must determine the level of risk, which in their judgment is no longer acceptable for society and above which it is necessary, in the interests of protecting human health, to take preventive measures in spite of any existing scientific uncertainty.

Scientific advice based on the principles of excellence, independence and transparency is crucial at all stages of the drawing up of new legislation and for the execution and management of existing legislation. Decisions of the Community institutions must be taken in light of the best scientific information available and of the most recent results of international research.

Community institutions also have to comply with procedural requirements and to abide by the limits of their powers, by the applicable rules of international law, by the Treaty provisions on the fundamental freedoms and by the general principles of Community law, mainly the principle of proportionality and the principle of subsidiarity.

As regards in particular the principle of proportionality, it limits the discretion of the competent authorities not only when deciding what is the level of protection they deem necessary to pursue (which must be proportionate to the perceived risk), but also when choosing the concrete measures to be taken.

Once the competent authority has decided to take action on grounds of the precautionary principle, the principle of proportionality is called upon to ascertain the legality of the measures intended to pursue the defined objectives.

A breach of the principle of proportionality will occur if the measure in question is manifestly inappropriate or in case it is shown that other, less onerous, measures exist and would have allowed the objective pursued by such measure. Application of the principle of proportionality is particularly important whenever the respect of any of the fundamental freedoms enshrined in the Treaty is at stake. This is the case, in particular, of the free movement of goods and services.

Judicial review by the Community courts is of paramount importance in order to control the way Community courts make their decisions in evaluating scientific uncertainty, risks and costs and benefits of any protective action.

In this context, the judgment of the CFI in *Pfizer* is the pivotal ruling on the precautionary principle, which provides the basis for future developments of the case-law in this field.

Index

www.ingramcontent.com/pod-product-compliance
Lightning Source LLC
LaVergne TN
LVHW052224200926
848481LV00001B/204

9781509909889